Praise for *Sea of Slaughter*

"In this masterpiece, Canada's most beloved naturalist-author is as angry about the assault on the living sea as Rachel Carson was about the land in *Silent Spring*." —Roger Tory Peterson

"His most ambitious work to date...Will prompt readers to reach for their checkbooks in support of animal conservation. This is a powerful indictment." —*Publishers Weekly*

"A hymn and a plea for life...A vast, articulate cri de coeur in which all the concerns of Mowat's lifetime come together." —*Globe and Mail*

"*Sea of Slaughter* deserves to stand with Rachel Carson's *Silent Spring* as an outstanding indictment of man's stupidity in alienating himself from nature." —*USA Today*

"Chilling...his most ambitious book...*Sea of Slaughter* should be enforced reading for anyone who pays lip service to environmental concerns." —*Toronto Star*

"When Farley Mowat writes, he bares his teeth...In *Sea of Slaughter*, he takes on the human race...Mowat writes about things we must never, never do again." —*Vancouver Sun*

"Buy this book, and buy a copy for those you love. In the end it's all of us who are threatened by the *Sea of Slaughter*." —*Edmonton Sun*

"Staggering...A keening, scholarly indictment of man's rapacious spirit." —*The Province* (Vancouver)

"A scathing indictment." —*Kingston Whig-Standard*

Sea
of
Slaughter

❖

FARLEY
MOWAT

STACKPOLE
BOOKS

Published by
STACKPOLE BOOKS
5067 Ritter Road
Mechanicsburg, PA 17055
www.stackpolebooks.com

Printed in the United States of America

10 9 8 7 6 5 4 3 2 1

First edition

Cover design by Peter Maher and Wendy A. Reynolds
Cover photograph by Peter Johnson/CORBIS/MAGMA

Library of Congress Cataloging-in-Publication Data

Mowat, Farley.
   Sea of slaughter / Farley Mowat.— 1st ed.
     p. cm.
   Originally published: Boston : Atlantic Monthly Press, c1984. With a new foreword and afterword.
   Includes bibliographical references and index.
   ISBN 0-8117-3169-3
  1. Extinction (Biology)—Atlantic Coast (North America)—History. 2. Extinction (Biology)—North Atlantic Region—History. 3. Nature—Effect of human beings on—Atlantic Coast (North America)—History. 4. Nature—Effect of human beings on—North Atlantic Region—History. 5. Endangered species—Atlantic Coast (North America)—History. 6. Endangered species—North Atlantic Region—History. 7. Extinct animals—Atlantic Coast (North America)—History. 8. Extinct animals—North Atlantic Region—History. I. Title.
QL88.15.N7M86 2004
333.95'4137'097—dc22

2004013833

Contents

Acknowledgments

This book has benefited greatly from the co-operation of the several scientists and specialists who have reviewed it. However, I have not always accepted their emendations or criticisms and must, in any case, remain solely responsible for any factual errors and for the interpretations I have placed upon events and circumstances.

My gratitude goes to: Dr. D.M. Lavigne, Associate Professor, College of Biological Science, University of Guelph, for his painstaking and illuminating comments on the chapters dealing with seals and walrus; Dr. D.N. Nettleship, Seabird Research Unit, Canadian Wildlife Service, for his considerable assistance with the chapters dealing with seabirds; Dr. Edward Mitchell, Arctic Biological Station, for his criticisms and suggestions regarding the chapters on whales and porpoises; Dr. Steve Wendt, Chief, Populations and Survey Divisions, Migratory Birds Branch, Canadian Wildlife Service, who provided material assistance for the chapters on birds other than seabirds; Dr. Nick Novakowski, formerly of the Canadian Wildlife Service, for his comments on the chapters dealing with land mammals; Dr. D.J. Scarratt, Department of Fisheries and Oceans, for his review of the fish chapters; Mr. Steve Best, consultant to the International Fund for Animal Welfare, for information on the animal welfare movement.

My heartfelt thanks for what must often have seemed like a hopeless task go to those who helped put the book together: to Alan Cooke, formerly of the Scott Polar Institute, who directed the historical research program; to Ramsey Derry, who took on the formidable task of editing the book; to Mary Elliott, who typed its many versions; to Harold Horwood, Jack McClelland, and Peter Davison, who encouraged and advised me as I struggled through the most difficult book I have ever tried to write.

Foreword

I was born in Vancouver, British Columbia, in 1936, and my earliest memories revolve around fishing. Dad and I would row around Stanley Park trolling for sea-run cutthroats. We'd jig for halibut off Spanish Banks and fish for sturgeon in the Fraser River and Dolly Varden and steelhead in the Veddar River. I can't relive my childhood experiences with my grandchildren because the fish are gone.

My family owns a cottage on an island in the Pacific Ocean, six hours from our home in Vancouver. On the last ferry we must take to get there, we rejoice at the sight of eagles, salmon, schools of herring and, if we're lucky, a porpoise or killer whale. It seems that despite pressures of population and development, there are areas where the natural world is still intact. Then our neighbour, Dan, who has lived all of his eighty-four years in this area, recounts how, as a boy, he could hear the salmon slapping the water miles before their arrival, fill a punt with herring in a few minutes by raking them off the kelp and easily catch abalone, red snapper and ling cod. Today, most of the spawning creeks have lost their salmon runs to logging, development or commercial fishing, herring have been devastated by a fishery to send roe to Japan, and abalone, red snapper and ling cod are virtually extinct around the island.

So why do we rejoice on returning to our cottage? Because we live in a big city, a biological desert filled primarily with human beings and a few domesticated species and pests. The city is our baseline reference and is so diminished in biodiversity that even a groomed public park can seem rich, while our island environment seems abundant and unsullied.

These days, society seems hooked on rapid change and novelty, and the knowledge of elders is marginalized as irrelevant. Thus we no longer remember what once was. I, like most people on our island, only acquired the land recently. Many of us are "part-timers" who live in a city and visit the island whenever possible. In other words, we don't make a living there, witness changes through the year or observe the seasonal succession of plants or animal migration. Nature becomes a shallow holiday experience, a titillation like the movies or video games.

More and more, that's how it is around the world. When I was born, the global population was a third what it is now, most of today's technology from television to plastics, computers and satellites was still to be developed, consumers expected and demanded less, and economies were still primarily community and nationally focused. These four factors—population, technology, consumption and global economics—have wreaked havoc with the planet.

Humans possess large brains, which enable us, uniquely among species, to look ahead and make deliberate choices to maximize our future survival. But we will only succeed when we learn from the past and recognize that our long-term health and well-being are intimately tied to the state of all Earth's other species.

The kind of degradation in species abundance and diversity I have witnessed in the Pacific was long foreshadowed in the Atlantic. When Farley Mowat first published his urgent cry from the heart, *Sea of Slaughter*, there was still much that could be saved. The tragedy of our time is that we have failed to act on the alarms and, instead, have continued the massacre. Since *Sea of Slaughter* first appeared, the northern cod fishery has collapsed, ending five centuries of Newfoundland culture built on cod. The collapse could have been avoided had we heeded Mowat's prescient warning.

Like Rachel Carson's classic, *Silent Spring*, Farley Mowat's book is a warning to humanity and a lament for the rest of life on Earth. And like that of *Silent Spring*, the message of *Sea of Slaughter* is even more relevant and urgent today: the appalling exploitation of Earth's resources must stop.

David T. Suzuki
February 2003

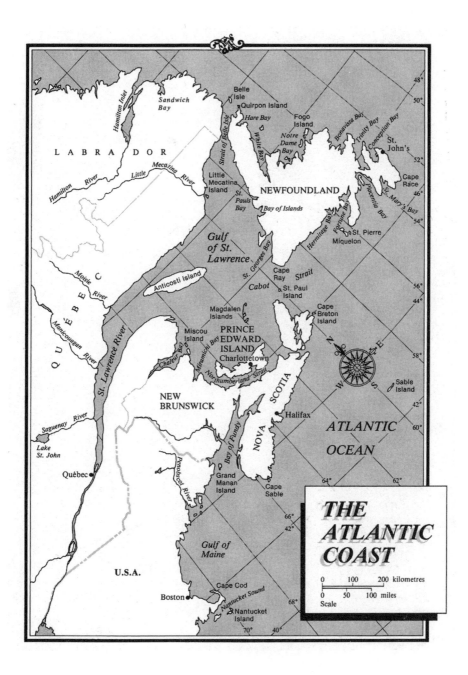

THE
ATLANTIC
COAST

| 0 | 100 | 200 kilometres |
| 0 | 50 | 100 miles |

Scale

The Why and the Wherefore

The *S.S. Blommersdyk* was a Liberty ship built of slabs of rusty steel welded into a vaguely nautical shape in a wartime yard. In mid-September, 1945, she sailed from Antwerp, laden with souvenirs of the late cataclysm destined for a war museum in Canada. I was nominally in charge of this grim cargo. A veteran at twenty-four, I was on my way home, determined to put the years of anti-life in the war behind me, desperate to find my way back to the solace of a living world where birds still sang; where creatures large and small rustled through the forests; where great ones swam in the silence of the sea.

It was a slow passage over an autumnal ocean. As the only passenger on board, I spent much of my time on the bridge at the invitation of the elderly Master. He was keenly interested in the animals inhabiting the world of waters, and, finding that I shared his pleasure in them, Captain DeWitt devised a game. Posted one on either wing of the bridge, we would peer through binoculars for hours, seeking to identify a whale or porpoise or bird before the other spotted it. Often enough the sharp-eyed old skipper made a fool of his youthful guest.

On our fourth day out of the English Channel he abruptly ordered the helmsman to haul hard a-port, then called to me, "There she blows! Old Cachalot himself!"

I watched, enthralled, as we bore slowly down on a scattering of sperm whales. They were cruising on the surface, signalling their presences along a broad arc of the horizon with watery jets. We held position in their midst for an hour and it was with reluctance that the Captain brought his ship back on her westward course.

A day or two later a pod of blue whales crossed our bows, sleek behemoths that have no equal for size or majesty on the lands or in the seas. Another day we were overtaken and entertained by a school of porpoises doing aquabatics in our bow wave. As we approached the edge of the Grand Banks I was the first to spot a thicket of smoky plumes to the northward; the skipper again altered course to intercept, and we steamed into the company of half-a-hundred bottlenose whales. Far from seeking to avoid us, they altered to collision course and came so close alongside that one big bull misted us with his steamy, fishy breath.

Time slipped quickly by on that passage. Not far from the drowned Virgin Rocks we tallied eleven kinds of seabirds in a single day, estimating their combined numbers at several hundreds of thousands. Entering the Strait of Belle Isle we passed a stately procession of fin whales outward bound; and Captain DeWitt delightedly saluted them with our hoarse steam whistle. Clearing the eastern end of Anticosti Island in the Gulf of St. Lawrence, we steamed in fog and dead calm weather through seemingly endless rafts of birds, mostly eider and scoter ducks, interspersed with faery flights of phalaropes, that rose under our bows and skittered away into the mists.

By the time we docked in Montreal, the Captain and I had logged thirty-two kinds of seabirds and ten species of sea mammals, together with such bizarre creatures as swordfish, giant jellyfish, and an enormous basking shark. For me it had been a voyage out of a long darkness...into the light of life.

The eastern seaboard inexorably drew me back to it. In the spring of 1953, my father and I sailed his portly old ketch, *Scotch Bonnet*, down the St. Lawrence River toward the Gulf. Just past Quebec City we had the illusion that winter had returned, for the grassy islets and the broad sweep of cattail marshes below Cap Tourmente were whitened by thousands of snow geese gathering strength for the long flight to their Arctic breeding grounds. Passing Gaspé we sailed close under the towering ledges of Bonaventure Island and were umbrella'd by a living cloud of gannets. We stayed a while with a lobster fisherman at West Point on Prince Edward Island and were astounded to watch him boat more than 300 of the green-shelled creatures from one haul of his traps.

We met many whales on this voyage, too. During the graveyard watch on a black night in mid-Gulf we were visited by a pod of grampuses—so-called killer whales. My father was dozing at the wheel when one of them leapt sky-ward, close alongside. The concussion when its seven- or eight-ton body smacked into the water was like the crack of doom. I think my father never slept on watch again.

Entering the Atlantic through Canso Strait, we were caught in the tail of a hurricane and blown out to Sable Island where we became the cynosure of the lustrous eyes of scores of curious seals. As *Scotch Bonnet* made her way back to the coast of Nova Scotia, crossed the Gulf of Maine, and sailed on to Long Island Sound we were in almost constant contact with the dwellers of the seas.

Through the subsequent three decades I lived much of my time in the Gulf of St. Lawrence and along the Atlantic seaboard, my commitment to the region growing with the years. I spent almost two years sailing in grey storm seas with the men of the North Atlantic salvage tugs in order to write about them. Several of my other books have been about this area, including ones on the days of sail, early Norse explorations, the human side of the sealing story, and the way of life of the outport fishing villages.

My wife and I settled in Newfoundland for several years, exploring the coasts and surrounding seas in our small schooner, voyaging to St. Pierre, and visiting Labrador. I spent many days on the fishing grounds in everything from a four-oared dory to a 600-ton stern dragger, watching the glitter and gleam of countless multitudes of fishes being brought aboard—fishes ranging from pencil-sized capelin to barn-door halibut weighing 400 pounds.

In 1967, we sailed our vessel up the great river to Ontario, but I found that the inland could not hold us. So we returned, to make a home on the sandy scimitar of the Magdalen Islands in mid-Gulf. Here I became so familiar with the massive grey seals that they would permit me to sunbathe with them on the same patch of beach. And from here I extended my explorations to Anticosti Island, the Gaspé coast, and the shores of Prince Edward Island. Here, also, I came to know the legions of harp seals that once whelped in countless thousands on the pack ice of the Gulf and off the northeast coast of Newfoundland. I visited the seal nurseries at both locations...and witnessed the red slaughter that ensued when the sealers came amongst them.

In 1975 my wife and I moved to Cape Breton to another home beside the sounding sea. Now, however, the sea was sounding a sombre and warning note. For some years past I had been bothered by the uneasy impression that the once familiar richness and diversity of animate life I had known in the oceanic world and on its landward verges were diminishing. There was a perceptible reduction in the numbers of seals, seabirds, lobsters, whales, porpoises, foxes, otters, salmon, and many other such whose presence I had come to take for granted. For a time I tried to persuade myself that this was a transient and perhaps cyclic phenomenon. But when I consulted my own notes made in these maritimes over a span of three decades, I found grim confirmation for my intimation of unease. During those thirty years the apparent numbers of almost all the larger kinds of animals, and many of the smaller ones, had radically decreased.

Deeply perturbed, I canvassed the memories of fishermen and woodsmen neighbours, some of whom had lived as many as ninety years. Even if their recollections were gilded by the mists of memory and by the age-old duty to tell a good yarn, their accounts convinced me that there had been a mass decline in both the volume and diversity of non-human life, and that it was still going on.

Questing further afield for understanding, I found that the Atlantic seaboard was not alone in suffering an intolerable depletion of animate life. Alarmed naturalists and scientists the world over were reporting an almost universal diminution of non-human life at what many of them suspected was an accelerating rate. The secretary of the Smithsonian Institution was said to have remarked that if the current trend continued, there would be few wild creatures "bigger than a breadbox" left alive by the middle of the twenty-first century except those maintained by us for our own selfish purposes.

As the 1980s approached, three questions loomed ever larger in my mind. If the natural life in the eastern seaboard had lost so much ground during a single human generation, how much might it have lost since European men began their conquest of this continent? And, if that loss had been on a scale comparable to what was happening now, what did it portend for the ongoing existence of all life on this planet—human and non-human—since, in the last analysis, life is indivisible? Finally, if animate creation was indeed being done to death by man, what could we do to halt the slaughter before it was too late?

Our understanding of the present and our ability to plan with wisdom for the future rest on possession of sure knowledge of the past. So, in order to find my way toward answers to these questions, I needed a history of natural life on this continent since Western man first put his mark upon it. I made a thorough search for one. I found books on the extinction of individual species, such as the passenger pigeon and the Plains buffalo, and there were works that listed animals for whom extinction threatens. But there was no chronicle of the overall diminution of natural life.

In 1979, I reluctantly found myself undertaking such a history myself. I had barely begun what turned into five years of work before I realized that I would have to accept some limitations. One book (or one lifetime) would not suffice for even a superficial description of the destruction that has taken place throughout North America since the arrival on the scene of Western man (by which I mean the bearers of Western culture, as distinct from the aboriginal inhabitants).

In the main, I restricted my study to the region with which I was most familiar, the northeastern Atlantic seaboard. This is a comparatively small portion of the earth's surface, but it had an incredibly rich natural history, and the destruction of its creature life reflects in miniature the history of the exploitation of such life throughout the entire domain of modern man, a domain that has now come to encompass almost the entire surface of this planet. What happened in my chosen region is happening on every continent and in every ocean.

This region includes the coasts, islands, adjacent hinterlands, and adjoining seas of eastern North America from about mid-Labrador south to the vicinity of Cape Cod, and westward to embrace the Gulf of St. Lawrence and the lower reaches of the St. Lawrence River. It was to this quarter that the first European voyagers—Norsemen from Greenland and Iceland—came during the final decades of the tenth century. They lit the way for others, and, by the middle of the fifteenth century, adventurers from Europe proper were feeling their ways into New World waters. By 1500, Portuguese, English, French, and Basques had probed most of the coasts and were settling into the first stages of the still-ongoing exploitation of the New Founde Lands. So the time frame of this book is from about 1500 until the present.

The human history of this period was, and remains, essentially a history of exploitation. This is, therefore, a central theme; but I have dealt with it from the standpoint of the victims. We human beings have spokesmen enough to argue and justify our cause. The other creatures have pitifully few. If, in making myself their advocate, I appear somewhat misanthropic, I offer no apologies except to say that it is not my business to offer even token exculpation or justification for the biocidal course that modern man has steered...is steering still.

I have restricted the book to mammals, birds, and fishes, with the major emphasis on sea mammals. I give much of the available space to these mainly because if we *should* change our attitude toward "the other beasts," the sea mammals seem to have the best chance for recovery and survival in a world where many terrestrial mammals are being physically squeezed out of existence by our destruction of their habitats and by our burgeoning appetites.

This is not a book about animal extinctions. It is about a massive diminution of the entire body corporate of animate creation. Although a number of the chapters tell the stories of animals that have indeed been extirpated, the greater part of the book is concerned with those species that still survive as distinct life forms but have suffered horrendous diminishment. Many have been reduced to little more than relic populations that continue to exist by whatever grace and favour mankind sees fit to extend to them.

Some who read this book in manuscript found the stories it tells so appalling that they wondered why I had committed myself to five years in such a pit of horrors. What did I hope to accomplish? It is true that this book describes a bloody piece of our past—it records what we have accomplished in one special region during 500 years of tenure as the most lethal animal ever to have appeared upon this wasting planet. But perhaps, with luck, this record of our outrageous behaviour in and around the Sea of Slaughter will help us comprehend the consequences of unbridled greed unleashed against animate creation. Perhaps it will help to change our attitudes and modify our future activities so that we do not become the ultimate destroyers of the living world...of which we are a part.

PART I

The Fowles of Sea and Air

When I was still a child, but already enamoured of the mysteries of the natural world, a relative gave me a portfolio of reproductions of Audubon's birds, painted more than a century earlier. All the plates were fascinating, but the one that stood out then, and still does in memory, depicted a strange, penguin-like creature standing on a forbidding ledge of rock. The caption (added since Audubon's time) told me little more than the bird's name; that it was flightless—and that it was extinct.

"Extinct" meant little to me then, other than that this was a creature I would never meet. Over the years, as the dread import of the word burned into my consciousness, it came to be indissolubly linked to the austere image of Audubon's great auk.

Because the flightless auk, or spearbill as it was called by those who knew it in life, was one of the first of man's victims in the Sea of Slaughter, I tell its story first before examining what has happened to the other seabirds, with whom the spearbill shared the oceanic world.

By way of contrast, the story then moves on to a family of birds whose members bestrode the borders where oceans meet the land. One of these, the Eskimo curlew, was annihilated a century after the great auk had vanished out of time. These two stories together span the full five centuries since European man began his assault on avian life in North America. The curlew's surviving relatives are the subject of the fourth chapter. The final chapter in this section describes the varied fates inflicted on some of the many other birds that once abounded in the northeastern regions of the New World.

1
Spearbill

"The 12th day of April, having then been 27 days from Poole, we came on soundings and knew it to be the Bank of Newfoundland. We would have understood this well enough from other indications for it seemed as if all the Fowles of Air were gathered thereunto. They so bemused the eye with their perpetual comings and goings that their numbers quite defied description. There can be but few places on Earth where is to be seen such a manifestation of the fecundity of His Creation."

This eighteenth-century commentary reflects the astonishment of early European visitors on their first encounter with the astronomical congregations of seabirds on the northeastern approaches to America. It was truly a world of wings. Elfin dovekies, swallow-like storm petrels, deep-diving murres, puffins, and auks, soaring kittiwakes, aerobatic shearwaters, fulmars, and skuas, and great-winged gannets all contributed to the multitudes. In storm and calm, by day and night, in winter and summer, the oceanic birds formed islands of life upon the surface of the sea while others of their kinds filled the air above with seemingly endless skeins and clouds of flickering pinions.

All were able fishermen, spending the greater part of their lives on, over, and under salt water, going ashore only briefly to "propagate their kind." All were at home with Ocean; but there was one amongst them which was uniquely so, for it had entirely abandoned the world of air.

A large and elegant creature, boldly patterned in glossy black above and gleaming white below, it was totally flightless, its wings having metamorphosed into stubby, powerful, feathered fins more suitable to a fish than to a bird. In truth, it could cleave a passage through the deeps with speed and manoeuvrability surpassing that of most fishes. A sleek undersea projectile torpedoing into the dark depths to 300 feet and more, it could remain submerged a quarter of an hour. On the surface, it floated high and proud, flamboyantly visible, having no need to hide itself since it had no airborne enemies.

Paired couples lived dispersed over the endless reaches of the North Atlantic but, on occasion, thousands would congregate to form vast flotillas in especially food-rich regions. Once a year the couples came to land on some isolated rock or desolate islet to rear their single chicks. Ashore, they were impressive figures, standing so tall that their heads reached as high as a man's midriff. They walked bolt upright with shambling little steps and the rolling gait of all true sailors. Intensely social during the breeding season, they crowded into rookeries that held hundreds of thousands of rudimentary nests so closely packed that it was difficult for the adult birds to move about.

Through the long course of time this exceptional creature bore many names. The ancient Norse called it *geirfugel*—spearbird, while the even more ancient Basques knew it as *arponaz*—spearbill. Both names paid tribute to the great bird's massive, fluted mandibles. Spanish and Portuguese voyagers called it *pinguin*—the fat one—a reference to the thick layer of blubber that encased it. By the beginning of the sixteenth century most deep-water men of whatever nation had adopted some version of this later name, as *pennegouin* in French, and *pingwen* in English. Indeed, it was the first, and the true, penguin. But before the nineteenth century ended, all of its original names had been stripped from it and it passed out of time carrying a tag attached to dusty museum specimens by modern science...great auk. I shall refer to it by the names bestowed on it by those who knew it in life.

During the aeons when scattered bands of prehistoric human beings flourished along the European coasts, the spearbill flourished, too. Its likeness is found in Spanish cave paintings and carved in stone in Norway, and its bones have been excavated from neolithic kitchen middens as far to the south as the Mediterranean coast of France. Clearly the spearbill was contributing to human survival 10,000 and more years ago; yet the predation of our ancestors had no evident effect upon its range or abundance. It was not until the human hunter began his transition into industrial man that the toll began to grow exorbitant.

By A.D. 900, the spearbill was no longer being killed primarily for food; it was being slaughtered for its oil and for its soft, elastic feathers, both of which had become valuable trading commodities throughout much of Europe. So avidly was it hunted on the European coasts thereafter that, by the mid-1500s, only a scattering of its eastern Atlantic breeding colonies had escaped destruction. By a century later only one remained, on the bleak and forbidding island of St. Kilda in the Outer Hebrides. In 1697, St. Kilda was visited by a certain Mr. Martin who left us this succinct account.

"The gairfowl is the stateliest as well as the largest sort [of seabird], of a black colour, red about the eyes, a large spot under each eye; a long broad bill; it stands stately, its whole body erected, its wings short, flies not at all; lays its egg upon the bare rock which if taken away she lays no more for that year...it appears the first of May and goes away the middle of June."

Sometime before 1800 it went away from St. Kilda for the last time . . . never to return.

Look now at a time before Europe began to cast its engulfing shadow over the New World.

A little cluster of men gather in darkness beside two bark canoes drawn up on a stony beach in what will one day be known as Newfoundland. They peer earnestly into the pre-dawn sky. Slowly the light strengthens, revealing a few tendrils of high cloud in the western dome. There is no threat of wind. The men smile their satisfaction at one another and at the tall, tawny one who leads them on this June day.

As they wade into the landwash, carefully holding their fragile craft clear of the kelp-slimed rocks, the sun explodes over the hills behind them. On the sea horizon, a string of looming shadows begins to take on the contours of a low-lying archipelago. Aimless catspaws riffle the water as the canoes drive out from land toward the distant islands, leaving the scattered tents of the People to dwindle into insignificance against a sombre wall of forest.

In the full glare of morning, the islands become haloed with a glittering haze of flashing wings as their inhabitants depart the land to begin the day's fishing. Phalanx after phalanx of arrow-swift murres and puffins fill the air with their rush and rustle. Above them, massed echelons of snowy gannets row steadily on black-tipped wings. Terns, kittiwakes, and larger gulls fly arabesques betwixt and between until the sky seems everywhere alive with flight.

The sea through which the canoes ease swiftly is living, too. Endless flotillas of the big black-and-white divers, that fly in water instead of air, stream outward from the low-lying islands. The first flock comes porpoising past the canoes. The men cease paddling and their leader touches a bone amulet hanging around his neck, upon which is carved an image of the spear-billed bird.

The morning is half-spent before the paddlers close with the island of their choice, and now the multitudes that have remained ashore to incubate their eggs or brood their young begin to take alarm. Soon they are rising in such numbers that the sky is obscured as by a blizzard. So vast is this air-borne armada that the sun's light is dimmed and the surface of the sea hisses from the rain of droppings falling into it.

As the canoes approach the island, winged masses descend on them like the funnel of a tornado. The rush of air through stiffened pinions and the harsh clangour of bird cries make it hard for the men to hear each other's shouts as they leap overside and carry the canoes to safety on the sloping rocks of the foreshore.

They move with hunched shoulders, as if cringing under the weight of furious life above them...and ahead. Not twenty feet from the landing place, rank after serried rank of spearbills stand, so closely packed that they seem almost shoulder to shoulder. Here stands an army of occupation hundreds of thousands strong. It covers almost the entire surface of the mile-long island. Each individual bird is incubating a single enormous egg in a shallow depression in the stinking mass of guano that everywhere overlies the ancient rock. The birds nearest the intruders turn as one to face the threat, bodies erect and fearsome beaks thrust out.

The men move warily, each holding his long, pointed paddle before him like a lance. The leader pauses, fingers his amulet again, and, in a voice hardly audible above the shrieking hubbub, makes his apology for what he and his companions are about to do.

Abruptly the paddles become flails. At the first thud of wood on bone and flesh, the foremost ranks of spearbills begin to break and fall back, each bird stumbling clumsily into those behind. Confused by the crush, those in the rear strike angrily at neighbours who are being pushed across the invisible boundaries of each one's tiny territory. Defence of territory becomes more pressing an issue than defence against the human intruders, and chaos ripples through the massed battalions.

While some of the men continue flailing at the nearest birds until they have killed three or four dozen of them, the rest hurriedly fill sealskin shoulder bags with eggs. Not ten minutes after landing they begin their retreat, dragging the slain birds by their necks and humping the heavy bags of eggs to the beached canoes. Loading and launching are done with the urgency of thieves. Each man seizes his paddle and, half-deafened by the noise, half-choked by the almost palpable stench, they flee as if pursued by devils. None looks back at the pandemonium still sweeping the Island of the Birds.

This vignette is set at the Port au Choix Peninsula, which juts out from the west coast of Newfoundland into the Gulf of St. Lawrence. Here archaeologists have been sifting through the rich remains of a series of aboriginal cultures that drew heavily upon the sea for sustenance.

Reliance on the spearbill in particular is revealed by the great quantities of bones uncovered in middens, living sites, and even in graves. One grave alone yielded more than 200 spearbill mandibles while another contained the image of a spearbill incised on bone.

The Port au Choix people were by no means unique in their relationship with the spearbill. Kitchen middens all the way from Disco in northwest Greenland south as far as Florida yield spearbill bones. The big birds provided the littoral dwellers of the western Atlantic seaboard with eggs and meat in and out of season. Greenland Inuit (like seventeenth-century Scots on the Hebrides) rendered spearbill fat and stored it against winter needs in sacks made from the birds' own inflated gullets. Indians from Labrador to Cape Cod smoked or dried the meat, which would then keep for months. The Beothuks, the last native inhabitants of Newfoundland, even ground the dried contents of spearbill eggs into a kind of flour from which they made winter puddings.

Yet with all of this, the thousands of years during which the bird provided a vital source of sustenance to generations of human beings seem to have had no appreciable effect on the spearbill population. Those early peoples were never in danger of eating themselves out of house and home by levying too heavy a toll. They took no more than they needed with the result that, when Europeans arrived on the scene, they found spearbill rookeries scattered along the coasts all the way from Labrador to Cape Cod. And the great divers were so abundant on some of the offshore fishing banks that early chroniclers could only describe them as uncountable.

One April day in 1534, two Breton smacks of the sort usually employed in the cod fisheries at *Terre Neuve* put to sea from the port of Saint Malo. They were not, however, going fishing. They were under charter to a hawk-visaged, forty-two-year-old entrepreneur named Jacques Cartier for a commercial reconnaissance of the inland sea the French called *La Grande Baie*, now the Gulf of St. Lawrence.

The two little sixty-tonners crossed the Western Ocean successfully to make landfall at Cape Bonavista in northeastern Newfoundland. Here they encountered a tongue of Arctic pack ice driving south with the Labrador Current and were forced to seek shelter in the fishermen's harbour at Santa Catalina. While they waited for the ice to release them, the seamen assembled and rigged two *barques*, thirty-foot fishing cutters brought across the ocean broken down in sections. Eventually, as Cartier's chronicler recorded, the wind veered offshore, blowing the ice seaward and opening a passage along the Newfoundland coast to the northward.

"On the 21st of the month of May we set forth from harbour...and sailed as far as the Isle of Birds, which island was completely surrounded and encompassed by a barrier of ice, broken and split into cakes. In spite of this our two barcques were sent off to the island to procure some of the birds, whose numbers were so great as to be incredible, unless one has seen them for himself, for although the island is scarcely a league in circumference it is so exceeding full of birds that one would think they had been stowed there [as one would stow the hold of a ship].

"In the air and round about on the water are a hundred times as many as on the island itself. Some of these birds are as large as geese, being black and white with a beak like a raven. These stay always in the water, not being able to fly in the air because they have only small wings, about half the size of a man's hand, with which, however, they move as quickly through the water as the other birds fly through the air. And these birds are so fat it is a marvel to behold. We call them *Apponatz*, and in less than half an hour our two barques were laden with them as if laden with stones. Of these birds each of our ships salted four or five casks, not counting those we were able to eat fresh."

In the spring of the following year Cartier took a second expedition into the Gulf and again stopped at the Isle of Birds where a new, but equally astonished chronicler had this to add:

"This island is so exceedingly full of birds that all the ships of France might load a cargo of them without anyone noticing that any had been removed. We took away two barque loads to add to our stores."

So reads the earliest surviving record of an encounter between Europeans and spearbills in North America; but it was assuredly not the first. The course Cartier's Bretons steered into the Gulf had been established before 1505, and his Isle of Birds was already a well-known sea-mark on the route. Now called Funk Island, it is a thirty-five-foot-high slab of granite, half-a-mile long by a quarter wide, lying some thirty miles off the Newfoundland coast. Its name is an archaic English word meaning an atrocious stench. Funk Island not only lay on the usual route into the Grand Bay via Belle Isle Strait, it also lay well clear of the dangerous reefs that fringe the adjacent mainland coast and inshore islands. For these reasons it was the preferred rookery at which inbound ships could call to fill their casks with salted spearbill carcasses; but it was by no means the only such rookery in the region. Forty miles to the east, in the mouth of Bonavista Bay, are two islands each of which also once bore the name Funk, but are now called Stinking Islands.[1] At about the same distance southwest lie twin Penguin Islands. There are also several bird islands in the nearby Wadham group, on

---

[1] The Funk Island of today is often referred to in the plural. This is a survival of a much earlier usage when "The Funks" was a generic name applied to many bird islands, especially those used by spearbills along the northeastern coasts of Newfoundland.

one of which local fishermen found a veritable charnel house of partly burned bones they identified as the remains of "pinwins" slaughtered and boiled to make oil. Other northeastern Newfoundland sites include the North and South Penguin Islands off Musgrave Harbour and Penguin Island near Baccalieu.

Spearbill rookeries probably flourished along most of the 5,000-mile coast of Newfoundland. In 1536, an English expedition visited the south coast. What follows is an abridged account taken from Richard Hakluyt's *Principal Navigations...of the English Nation.*

"One, Master Hore of London, encouraged divers gentlemen to accompany him on a voyage of discovery upon the Northeast parts of America: wherein his persuasions took such effect that many gentlemen very willingly entered into the action with him.

"From the time of their setting out they were at sea above two months until they came to [the region] about Cape Breton. Shaping their course from thence Northeastward they came to the Island of Penguin, whereon they went and found it full of great fowls, white and gray and as big as geese, and they saw infinite number of their eggs. They drove a great number of the fowls into their boats and took many of their eggs. They dressed [the birds] and eat them and found them to be very good and nourishing meat."

Hore's island is to be identified with one lying fifteen miles off Cape La Hune in the middle of Newfoundland's south coast. The first Europeans to discover it were Portuguese who gave it the name it still bears. As was the case with Funk on the northwest coast, this Penguin Island provided a convenient place for vessels inbound from Europe to the Gulf via the southern route to fill their salt-meat casks with spearbill carcasses.

A third famous rookery existed well within the Gulf itself, and also was visited by Cartier in 1534.

"We came to...two islands...as steep as a wall so that it was impossible to climb to the tops. These islands were as completely covered with birds, which nest there, as a field is covered with grass...we landed on the lower part of the smaller island and killed more than a thousand murres and *apponatz*, of which we took away as many as we wished in our barque. One might have loaded, in an hour, thirty such barques."

These two rocky pinnacles with flat and almost inaccessible tops jut out of the Gulf some ten miles northeast of the main Magdalen Island archipelago. In Cartier's time, they were called Isles de Margaulx because of the immense flocks of gannets nesting on the high plateaux. The smaller island was surrounded by broad ledges just above storm tide level, and it was here that spearbills nested.

As well as providing an important sea-mark, Isles de Margaulx (now the Bird Rocks) served as a convenient "sea-poultry market" where passing vessels could take on stores of meat and eggs. However, it was only one of many such rookeries in the vicinity. The then-uninhabited Magdalen group seems to have had several spearbill colonies. The density of their populations may be judged by the fact that even the one on Bird Rocks, which was physically much restricted and very exposed, managed to survive annual raids by ships' crews for more than a century. When Samuel de Champlain visited the Rocks in 1620, he found the birds "in such abundance that they may be killed with sticks"; and as late as the end of the 1600s, Charlevoix noted that the islets still harboured "a number of fowl that cannot fly."

The problem of locating and identifying spearbill colonies in other parts of the northeastern seaboard is difficult, but is assisted by the salient fact that the big birds never came ashore and seldom approached it except for the four to six weeks in the spring and early summer when they were egg-laying, brooding, and rearing their young. Consequently, when we find an otherwise suitable island that has at one time borne the name Penguin, or some variant thereof, there is a strong presumption that it once held a spearbill breeding colony.

Additional criteria include the following.

The site must have been free of large resident predators such as wolves, bears, and men, although occasional raids by any of these (and we know that both Indians and polar bears raided Funk Island) would presumably have had little effect on colonies numbering in the hundreds of thousands. Smaller mammals such as foxes and mink would have posed a much lesser threat to birds the size of geese armed with such formidable bills.

The rookeries must, of course, have been usable by flightless birds; but this does not necessarily require a gently sloped transition between land and water. Antarctic penguins making a landing can shoot out of the sea with enough momentum to carry themselves ten feet up the sheer face of an ice-foot and land comfortably on the high lip. The site itself need only have been reasonably level and free of heavy vegetation and tree growth. Because they were flightless birds, which had to swim to wherever they were going, preferred rookeries needed to be located within a comparatively short distance of good fishing grounds so that adults could forage for their young without excessive expenditure of time and energy.

A final point is that great auks were only vulnerable to native peoples *when* they were on their rookeries; thus, the presence of their bones in any quantity in human sites can be taken as clear indication of a colony reasonably near at hand.

The Atlantic coast of Labrador was probably not favoured as a spearbill breeding ground, being too much encumbered with pack ice during the summer season. However, the northern bays of Newfoundland provided ideal conditions and may have supported as many as twenty rookeries, some of them extremely large.

Newfoundland's west coast seems to have had rookeries on Lark Island, the Stearing Islands off Cow Head, Gregory Island in Bay of Islands (where a headland and a deep bay bear the Penguin name), Green Island off Flowers Cove, and Shag Island at the entrance to Port au Port Bay, and in St. John's Bay.

The south coast of Newfoundland was evidently well-endowed with spearbill colonies, including Virgin Rock in Placentia Bay (from which seventeenth-century French fishermen and soldiers are reported to have provided themselves with spearbill meat and eggs); Green Island near St. Pierre et Miquelon, which, according to local tradition, may still have harboured a few *pengouins* until the beginning of the eighteenth century; Bird Island at the mouth of Fortune Bay; Penguin Island, which we have already discussed; and the Ramea group where, so I was told by an old man of mixed European and Indian blood from nearby Burgeo, the last *penwins* were killed on Offer Rock soon after his Micmac ancestors emigrated to Newfoundland from Cape Breton, which would have been about 1750.

The north shore of the Gulf of St. Lawrence was exceptionally good seabird territory, at one time harbouring scores of colonies and rookeries on its innumerable islands. There is no way of knowing now how many were occupied by spearbills, but the big, flightless birds were probably hunted from most of them by sixteenth-century Basque whalers for whom this would have been a minor act of slaughter.

There are few suitable sites for seabird rookeries in the southern Gulf, except Bonaventure Island. However, in 1593, the English vessel *Marigold* found *pengwyns* at Cape Breton Island during the breeding season, and the birds were still being reported from there in 1750 as *peringouins*. The Cape Breton Micmacs have a tradition that their ancestors took spearbills and eggs on St. Paul Island in Cabot Strait, from an unidentified island in Chedabucto Bay, and from Sea Wolf Island.

Rookeries along the Atlantic coast of Nova Scotia may have been comparatively few in number due to a shortage of suitable sites, but that they did exist seems evident from the fact that, as late as 1758, local Indians were bringing *pengwins* into Halifax to supply the colonists.

The southern tip of Nova Scotia and the opposite shores of New Brunswick across the mouth of the Bay of Fundy offered a number of excellent spearbill sites. When Champlain visited the Tusket Island group in the early summer of 1604, he found quantities of nesting seabirds which he called *tangeaux* and which his men killed with sticks. Some ornithologists contend that "tangeaux" means gannets, but on the very next page of his own account, Champlain describes what is undoubtedly a gannet colony on a high island now called Gannet Rock, eleven miles north of the Tuskets, and identifies the bird as *margos* (margeaux), which *is* the French name for gannet. Noddy Island and Devil's Limb, south of the Tuskets, may also have been home to spearbill colonies, along with Machias Seal Island and at least some of the islands in the Grand Manan assemblage.

Farther south, along the coast of the Gulf of Maine, early accounts testify to the one-time presence of spearbills in considerable numbers. Some modern authorities insist these reports must all refer to migratory birds that bred at some far northern rookery such as Funk Island. The fact that many were seen and killed during the breeding season is explained on the supposition that these were immature or non-breeding birds.

However, in 1603, Captain George Weymouth landed on a small island in the mouth of Maine's Muscongus Bay and was much impressed to find "very great egg shells, bigger than goose eggs." It is certainly within the realm of probability that these were the shells of spearbill eggs (amongst the largest eggs laid by any North American bird), which had been collected by Indians at rookeries on Monhegan or Manana Island some ten miles offshore, in the manner of the Newfoundland Beothuks at Funk Island.

David Ingram, an English sailor who was marooned on the shores of the Gulf of Mexico in 1568 and walked north to Nova Scotia, described a bird of "the shape and bigness of a goose, but their wings are covered with small, callow feathers and cannot fly: You may drive them like sheep." Which is a good description of spearbills and their behaviour at a rookery. Josselyn, visiting New England circa 1670, described "the *Wobble*, an ill-shaped fowl having no long Feathers in their Pinions, which is the reason they cannot fly." The spearbill was the *only* flightless bird Josselyn could have encountered and, since "Wobble" seems an apt description of the way it must have walked on land, and spearbills never *came* to land except to breed, I accept this as a strong indication of colonies on the New England coast. Audubon remembered an old hunter from the Boston area who told him that great auks were still present about Nahant and other islands when he was young.

The finding of spearbill bones in Indian middens along the New

England coast, and even as far south as Florida, establishes the fact that they were once found far to the south of the range currently ascribed to them by many biologists.

The importance of seabird rookeries to transatlantic seamen was enormous. These men were expected to survive and work like dogs on a diet consisting principally of salt meat and hard bread. The meat was mainly lean and stringy beef or horse, and the bread was a biscuit baked to the consistency of concrete and usually shot through with weevils. Even these almost inedible staples were frequently in short supply due to the miserliness of ship-owners who seemed to believe that "wind and water" were enough to feed a sailor. Indeed, it was usual to supply the ships with only enough salt meat for the outward voyage, leaving the hard-driven, half-starved men to forage for themselves upon arrival. Apart from fish (most kinds of which if eaten as a steady diet in cold latitudes can result in chronic malnutrition because of a low fat content), the most convenient single source of food in season was what could be had from the bird rookeries.

Initially, seabirds of a dozen or more species crowded the offshore islands and islets. Most were good fliers who could, and often did, nest on ledges and cliff faces where they were difficult to reach. Furthermore, adults tended to take wing at the approach of an intruder and so could seldom be killed in quantity except with a profligate expenditure of shot and powder. Consequently, the main weight of European predation fell on the most readily accessible species—of which the spearbill was especially attractive because of its large, fat, and well-muscled carcass. Its eggs, too, were preferred above all others, not only because of their great size (as long and broad as a human hand), but because they were so easily collected. There was no question about it: so long as it lasted, the spearbill was the best buy in the shop.

Analysis of Cartier's and other contemporary accounts gives some conception of the magnitude of the destruction visited on the spearbill colonies. Cartier's thirty-foot fishing barques were built to carry about four tons and, since the weight of an adult spearbill was twelve to fifteen pounds, a fully-loaded barcque could transport up to 650 birds. Two such barque-loads might have strained the storage capacity of a sixty-ton vessel—but that is the amount, so we are told, that each vessel laded. However, some Basque ships sailing those waters displaced as much as 600 tons and could have comfortably stowed away several thousand spearbill carcasses—sufficient to last the summer season through and probably enough to feed the sailors on the homeward voyage.

In the 1570s, Captain Anthony Parkhurst wrote: "at an Island named Pengwin we may drive them on a plank into our ship, as many as will lade her...There is more meat on one of them than on a goose. The Frenchmen that fish near the grand bay do bring but small store of meat with them, but victual themselves always with these birds."

A few years later, Edward Hayes, master of one of Sir Humphrey Gilbert's ships, described "an island named Penguin [because] of a fowle there breeding in incredible abundance, which cannot fly...which the Frenchmen take without difficulty...to barrel up with salt."

Around 1600, Richard Whitbourne noted: "These Penguins are as big as geese and...they multiply so infinitely upon a certain flat island that men drive them from hence upon a board, into their boats by the hundreds at a time, as if God had made the innocency of so poor a creature to become such an admirable instrument for the sustenation of man."

The idea that God created all living creatures to serve man's needs was not, of course, unique with Whitbourne. It is deeply ingrained in Judeo-Christian philosophy and continues to provide one of the major rationalizations with which we justify the wholesale destruction of other animals.

Justifiable or not, the mass destruction of seabird rookeries in the New World proceeded apace. The birds were a staple of fishermen and settlers alike. Writing of the French presence in the region around 1615, Lescarbot tells us that "The greatest abundance [the people have] comes from certain islands where are such quantity of ducks, gannets, puffins, seagulls, cormorants and others that it is a wonderful thing to see [and] will seem to some almost incredible...we passed some of those islands [near Canso] where in a quarter of an hour we loaded our longboat with them. We had only to strike them down with staves until we were weary of striking." Courtemanche, writing in 1705 about the north shore of the Gulf, describes the rookeries there and adds: "for a whole month they slaughter them with iron-tipped clubs in such quantity that it is an incredible thing."

As guns and powder became cheaper and more available in the early eighteenth century, the seabird slaughter took on a new dimension, as this note from Cape Breton, circa 1750, attests. "The birds fly by in swarms to go to their laying in spring on the bird islands...At this time there is such prodigious carnage that we shot up to 1000 gunshots every day."

The carnage resulting from the "gunning" of adult birds in passage to, from, and at the rookeries grew with the passing centuries. As late as 1900, punt-gunners on the north shore of the Gulf were shooting, in a single day, "half-a-boat load, which would be about four or five hundred eiders, scoters, puffins, murres, gulls etc."

As if the destruction of adults and partly grown young was not horrendous enough, the seabirds had also to endure a mounting wastage of their eggs. Egging began in a relatively small way with casual raids on rookeries by ships' crews and fishermen seeking food for themselves. As John Mason, writing about life in Newfoundland around 1620, put it: "The sea fowles are Gulls white and gray, Penguins, Sea Pigeons, Ice Birds, Bottlenoses and other sorts...[and] all are bountiful to us with their eggs, as good as our Turkie or Hens, with which the Islands are well replenished."

This began to change after the beginning of the eighteenth century, by which time the rapid growth of population along the Atlantic seaboard was creating a commercial market for many "products" of land and sea... amongst them seabird eggs. Egging now became a profitable business and professional eggers began to scout the coasts, denuding every rookery they could find. By about 1780, American eggers had so savaged the bird islands along the eastern coasts of the United States that they could no longer supply the burgeoning demand from cities such as Boston and New York. Consequently, the export of seabird eggs became a profitable business for the British colonies to the north.

As was to be expected, the spearbill was a foremost victim in early times when it was still abundant. Aaron Thomas wrote this succinct description of penguin egging in Newfoundland.

"If you go to the Funks for eggs, to be certain of getting them fresh you pursue the following rule:—you drive, knock and Shove the poor Penguins in heaps. You then scrape all their Eggs in Tumps in the same manner you would a heap of Apples in an Orchard...these Eggs, from being dropped some time, are stale and useless, but you having cleared a space of ground... retire for a day or two...at the end of which time you will find plenty of Eggs—fresh for certain!"

If, as the St. Kildans claimed, the spearbill laid only a single egg, and did not lay again that year once the egg was destroyed, the result of such wholesale destruction can easily be foreseen.

A British naval captain investigating commercial egging in Newfoundland reported: "Parties repair [to the Funk Islands] to collect eggs and feathers. At one time a very considerable profit could be gained but lately, owing to the war of extermination, it has greatly diminished. One vessel nevertheless is said to have cleared 200 Pounds currency in a single trip."

William Palmer, who visited Funk in 1887, added this postscript: "What must have been the multitudes of birds in former years on this lonely island. Great auks, murres, razorbills, puffins, Arctic terns, gannets undoubtedly swarmed, and were never molested except by an occasional visit from the now-extinct Newfoundland red man; but now since the white fisherman began to plunder it, how changed. Today but for the Arctic terns and the puffins the island may be said to be deserted. [Although] sixteen barrels of murres and razorbill eggs have been known to be gathered at a time and taken to St. John's, we did not see a dozen eggs."

It is to John James Audubon that we owe the most graphic account of what the egging business was like. In June of 1833, Audubon visited Nova Scotia where he met a party of eggers who, having taken some 40,000 seabird eggs, were selling them to an exporter in Halifax for twenty-five cents a dozen. A few days later, while visiting a bird island, he encountered two eggers "who had collected 800 dozen murres' eggs and expected to get 2000 dozen...the number of broken eggs on the island created a fetid smell scarcely to be borne." However, it was not until 1840, when he spent some weeks on the north shore of the Gulf of St. Lawrence, that Audubon experienced the full horror of the ugly business. What follows is a condensed version of his account.

"The Eggers great object is to plunder every nest, no matter where, and at whatever risk. They are the pest of the feathered tribes, and their brutal propensity to destroy the poor creatures after they have robbed them is abundantly gratified. But I could not entirely credit all their cruelties until I had actually witnessed their proceedings.

"Their vessel is a shabby thing. Her hold sends forth an odour pestilential as a charnel house. Her crew, eight in number, throw their boat overboard and seat themselves, each with a rusty gun. One of them sculls the skiff toward an island for centuries past the breeding place of myriads. At the approach of the vile thieves, clouds of birds rise from the rock and fill the air around, wheeling and screaming over their enemies.

"The reports of several muskets loaded with heavy shot are now heard, while dead and wounded birds fall heavily on the rock or into the water. The remaining birds hover in dismay over their assailants who land and walk forward exultingly. Look at them! See how they crush the chick within its shell, how they trample on every egg in their way. Onward they go, and when they leave the isle not an egg that they can find is left entire.

"They regain their filthy shallop and sail to another island a few miles distant. Arrived there they re-act the same scene, crushing every egg they can find. For a week they travel until they have reached the last breeding place on the coast. Then they return, touching at every isle in succession, and collect the fresh eggs which have been laid since their previous visit.

"With their bark half filled with fresh eggs they proceed to the principal rock where they first landed. But what is their surprise to find others there helping themselves. In boiling rage they run up to these other Eggers. The first question is a discharge of muskets, the answer is another. One man is carried to his boat with a fractured skull, another limps with a shot in his leg, and a third feels how many teeth have been driven through the hole in his cheek. At last, however, the quarrel is settled—the booty is to be divided.

"These people also gather all the eider down they can find; yet so inconsiderate are they that they kill every bird that comes in their way. The eggs of Gulls, Guillemots and Ducks are searched for with care; and they massacre the Puffins and some other birds in vast numbers for their feathers. So constant and persevering are their depredations that these species have [largely] abandoned their ancient breeding places. This war of extermination cannot last many years more."

The wholesale destruction continued unabated until there were few if any accessible seabird rookeries from Labrador to Florida still worth robbing. In 1919, Dr. Arthur Bent summed up the results of this ruthless despoliation of the seabirds in his monumental *Life Histories* of North American birds.

"Their worst enemies are, of course, human beings, who have for generations killed them in enormous numbers and robbed them of their eggs unmercifully, until they have been practically extirpated."

Not content to slaughter adult spearbills at a fearsome rate and to destroy uncounted numbers of their eggs for "the sustenation of man," European invaders of the New World were quick to find more ways to exploit the birds.

By the latter part of the sixteenth century, the demand for oil had become insatiable and train oil was fetching premium prices.[2] Unfortunately for the spearbills, the blanket of fat that served to insulate them from the frigid North Atlantic could be rendered into an excellent grade of oil. The Basques were probably the first to exploit this opportunity as an adjunct to their

---

[2] Mineral oil was as yet effectively unknown, and vegetable oils were scarce and unduly expensive. In consequence most commercial oil was made from animal fats. One of the chief sources of this was the sea, and oil derived from sea animals was generically known as trayne, or train oil. As we shall see, train was one of the most important and lucrative products produced from New World waters.

massive whaling enterprises in New World waters; but it soon became a profitable sideline to the fisheries pursued by other nations.

Crude tryworks were commonplace in most fishing harbours by 1600. They were fired up whenever the fishermen had the time and opportunity to make an incidental haul of some local form of life which would make train. Thus seals, walrus, whales, porpoises...and seabirds all served their turn. Because of its great size, high fat content, and availability, the spearbill was, and remained, the prime target amongst the seabird tribes for as long as it lasted. Round about 1630, so Nicolas Denys tells us, French ships fishing for cod often loaded ten to twelve puncheons of penguin oil as well. Since thousands of spearbill carcasses were needed to produce such a quantity of train, it is apparent that this was no petty enterprise. Nor was it limited to the French. English, Spanish, and Portuguese cod fishers were butchering the birds for oil on a similar scale, and some were even making special voyages to isolated rookeries where they would set up portable tryworks during the spearbill breeding season. They were able to boil oil on even the most barren rocks by feeding the fires with skins and carcasses after the layer of fat had been removed. Some of the more profligate and ruthless of the oilers used the entire bird, as Aaron Thomas, writing about Funk Island as it was near the end of the eighteenth century, confirms.

"While you abide on this Island you are in the constant practize of horrid crueltys, for you not only Skin [the Penguins] *Alive*, but you burn them *Alive* also...You take a Kettle with you and kindle the fire under it, and this fire is absolutely made from the unfortunate Penguins themselves."

Boiling the corpses for train did not exhaust the opportunities for Europeans to profit from the destruction of seabird populations. Although immense summer runs of small school-fish such as herring, capelin, mackerel, and squid normally provided fishermen with bait in any required quantity, there was sometimes a hiatus between the runs, or before the school-fish "struck in" to the coast. Shore-based fishermen soon found a solution to such temporary bait shortages—particularly during June and July. Raiding parties would sweep the seabird islands, massacring adults and young alike. The corpses would then be torn into fragments with which to bait the hand lines that were the principal form of cod-fishing gear.

In the days of their abundance, penguins made up a major part of the seabird bait and this destruction, added to the kill for food and oil, had its inevitable result. No single species, no matter how numerous in the beginning, could have withstood such carnage indefinitely. By the mid-1700s, only a handful of shrunken and beleaguered rookeries still existed. Then a new scourge was visited upon them.

During the latter part of that century, wide-awake entrepreneurs, mostly from New England, began exploiting a growing demand for feathers and down used in bedding and for upholstery both in America and in Europe. Each spring, droves of schooners from as far south as Chesapeake Bay appeared on the coasts of Newfoundland and the Gulf, intent on ransacking the islands where colonial seabirds nested. At first they concentrated on eider ducks, taking not only the down with which the nests were lined, but also shooting and netting countless thousands of adults. So ruthless were they that the once seemingly inexhaustible eider flocks were soon diminished to "worthless remnants." The pillagers then turned on the seabird rookeries, including the last remaining spearbill colonies.

In 1775, Newfoundland authorities petitioned Britain to stop the massacre. "Contiguous to the North part of the Island are a great many islands where birds breed in abundance and which were of great service to the inhabitants for food in winter and for bait for catching fish during summer...[these inhabitants are] now almost deprived, as a great part of the birds have been destroyed within a few years by crews of men who kill them in their breeding season for feathers, of which they make a traffic...we pray an entire stop except for food or bait."

A decade later, colonist and diarist George Cartwright made this prophetic journal entry: "A boat came in from Funk Island laden with birds, chiefly penguins...Innumerable flocks of sea fowl breed [there] every summer, which are of great service to the poor inhabitants who make voyages there to load with birds and eggs...but it has been customary in late years for several crews of men to live all summer on that island for the sole purpose of killing the birds for the sake of their feathers; the destruction they have made is incredible. If a stop is not soon put to that practise, the whole breed will be diminished to nothing, particularly the penguins, *for this is now the only island they have left to breed upon*; all other lying so near the shores of Newfoundland, they are continually robbed." (Italics mine.)

The indignation of the merchant aristocracy of Newfoundland was not exactly selfless, as these comments by the Reverend Philip Tocque reveal. Before 1800, Tocque wrote, the penguin "was plentiful on Funk Island [where] incredible numbers were killed...Heaps of them were burnt as fuel...there being no fuel on the island. [Before the destruction wrought by the feather trade] the merchants of Bonavista used to sell these birds to the poor people by the hundred-weight, instead of salt pork."

The most grimly graphic description of what was taking place comes from Aaron Thomas.

"At some Leagues distant from the Northern Shore are the islands of Fogo, Stinking Island and Funk Island. They are generally called the Funks from the stinking Smell which salutes your Nose on landing on them. I shall be particular on Funk Island. My observations on that place will apply to other Islands.

"Funk Island is a barren spot inhabited only by Penguins and other Birds. The astonishing quantity which resort to this Island is beyond...beliefe. As soon as you put your foot on shore you meet with such Thousands of them that you cannot find a place for your feet and they are so lazy that they will not attempt to move out of your way.

"If you come for their Feather you do not give yourself the trouble of killing them, but lay hold of one and pluck off the best of the Feathers. You then turn the poor Penguin adrift, with his Skin half naked and torn off, to perish at his leasure. This is not a very humane method, but it is the common Practize.

"I had the following information from a person in St. John's...'About twenty years ago when this kind of Traffick was Lawfull, I made two Trips to the Funks. In these Trips I gathered, with one person with me, half a Ton of Feathers and as many Eggs as sold in St. John's for Thirty Pounds!'

"This skinning and taking the Eggs from the Funks is now prohibited and they are allowed to take the Birds only for Bait to catch Fish with. [But] about three years ago some fellows were detected in this kind of Plunder. They were brought to St. John's and flogged at a Cart's Tail. But I am told there is a quantity of Feathers [still] purloined from these Islands every year."

Complaints about the destruction of the penguins were now being heard from another quarter as well. Through almost three centuries the strikingly patterned birds had served inbound seamen as infallible indicators that they had arrived over the Grand Banks and so were approaching a land whose dangerous coasts were often hidden by impenetrable fogs. From earliest times, rutters and pilots (books of sailing directions) used by the west-faring nations contained some variant of the following excerpt from the 1774 edition of *The English Pilot*.

"You may know you are on the Bank by the great quantities of fowles but none are to be minded so much as the Pengwin, for these never go without the Bank as the others do, for they are always on it." By 1792, Sir Richard Bonnycastle was reporting to the English authorities that "this sure sea-mark on the Grand Banks has now totally disappeared, from the ruthless trade in eggs and skins." Two years later the Colonial Secretary in London finally forbade the destruction of penguins for the feather trade because "they afford a supply of food and bait, and are useful in warning vessels that they are nearing land."

This prohibition not only came too late, it was virtually ignored in Newfoundland where some merchants had decided that if they could not make the Yankees desist from a good thing, then they had best join them. The consequence was that, by 1802, the last penguin rookery in North America, on that lonely rock called Funk, had been destroyed.

Whereas it had taken our forebears a thousand and more years to extirpate the spearbill from European waters, it took modern man a mere three centuries to exterminate it in the New World. Although this was an undoubted victory in our ongoing war against the rest of animate creation, the perpetrators of it, and we their inheritors, have been reluctant to claim the credit.

Hardly had the last North American spearbills been sent to join their European cousins in oblivion when their disappearance was being explained away with the nostrum that, because they were naturally such timid birds, they had "chosen to withdraw to" regions where men seldom went. Some apologists even maintained that the domain of the birds had always been the High Arctic. According to an American ornithologist, writing in 1824:

"The great auk or northern penguin inhabits only the highest latitudes of the globe, dwelling by choice and instinct amidst the horrors of a region covered with eternal ice. Here it is still commonly found upon the floating masses of the gelid ocean."

When a succession of Arctic explorers failed to report the slightest trace of a spearbill, living or dead, in the "gelid ocean," an even more remarkable attempt to bury the memory of the bird appeared. The suggestion was made that "in all probability, the so-called great auk of history was a mythical creature invented by unlettered sailors and fisherfolk." Evidence as to the bird's non-existence was adduced from the discovery of a number of counterfeit eggs made of plaster and some stuffed specimens found to be patched together from the skins of several kinds of seabirds, all for sale to gullible collectors.

This instinct to erase the spearbill from history, and so from conscience, was confounded by a late nineteenth-century discovery on Funk Island of huge quantities of recent penguin beaks, bones, and even a few carcasses partly preserved in guano. When these arrived in Europe they created a sensation in the scientific community, whose members avidly bid against one another to purchase them. As a contemporary publication put it: "The large quantity of remains obtained on Funk Island by Professor Milne have been bought by many museums and private collectors and have proved useful in filling a much felt want."

The "want" was the acquisitive passion that motivated so many wealthy nineteenth-century men, for whom natural history rarities were what Monets and Gaugins are to modern art collectors. Fortunes were spent scouring the world in pursuit of scarce specimens. It was a fiercely competitive business, conducted in the name of science and enlightenment; and it was the ultimate cause of extinction for scores or hundreds of species already in jeopardy. It is still being conducted by unscrupulous zoos and natural history museums, with similar results.

Indisputable recognition that the great auk was no myth, but had once—and not long since—been a creature of flesh and blood, reopened the question of how and why it had disappeared. Most authorities still insisted that man could not possibly have been to blame, but there were a few dissenters. One was a distinguished Danish scientist, Professor J. Steenstrup who, in 1855, gave it as his opinion that: "The Geirfugl's disappearance must not be regarded as a migration, much less a natural dying out, but as an extirpation [that] has its chief cause in the devastations wrought by men."

This was a refreshingly forthright statement of the truth, even though the good professor tried to ease his own species off the hook by adding: "Yet the bird, while disappearing, has helped to the attainment of a higher object; as it has been for a long space of time one of the means that have essentially facilitated the prosecution of fishing on the Banks of Newfoundland." Than which, there could hardly have been a more worthwhile cause! Certainly this sentiment still commands the support of those who believe that the death of any animal, or species, which contributes thereby to the satisfaction of human desires is not only justifiable but somehow tinged with a kind of nobility.

Although by shortly after 1800 the spearbill had apparently vanished from human ken, *it was not yet extinct*. Unknown to the world at large, one rookery remained. One remnant colony, probably numbering no more than a hundred individuals, had managed to avoid contributing to a "higher object." It owed its survival, first, to its isolation, clinging precariously to a sea-girt, storm-and-tide-battered rock called Eldey, which lay outermost in a chain of volcanic islets stretching southwest into the Atlantic from Cape Reykjaness in Iceland and, second, to the fact it harboured so few geirfugel that even the local people no longer considered it worth raiding.

But no place in the world is safe from the truly dedicated collector, and somehow word of this lost, last colony reached avid ears in Europe. About 1830, some Reykjavik export merchants began receiving letters inquiring about geirfugels and their eggs and offering princely prices for any that could be found. At least one merchant was quick to grasp the golden opportunity. His name was Siemson—let it be long remembered.

Siemson made an arrangement with the fishermen of the villages of Stadur and Hafnir at the tip of the Reykjaness Peninsula and each spring thereafter, weather permitting, the local men raided Eldey. By 1843, between fifty and seventy-five geirfugels and an unknown number of their eggs had passed through Siemson's hands, to end up as jealously guarded treasures in collectors' cabinets throughout western Europe. There most remained sequestered until changing times brought about the sale of a number of these private collections of natural curiosa. On March 4, 1971, the director of Iceland's Natural History Museum attended an auction at Sotheby's famous rooms' and bid and paid $33,000 for one stuffed geirfugel, which presumably had been killed on Eldey. The money had been raised by public subscription and, as the director said, he could have raised twice that sum, so eager were Icelanders to restore this dusty fragment of a lost heritage to the island republic.

Others, whose nations had also contributed to the destruction of the spearbill, were less interested in refurbishing its memory. During the 1960s, Newfoundland biologist Dr. Leslie Tuck, a world authority on the Alcidae (the family to which science has assigned the spearbill), produced a new explanation for its descent into extinction...and a new exculpation for mankind. According to Dr. Tuck, the great auk was already a relic species when Europeans discovered it off the shores of North America. Having run its evolutionary course it had reached, literally, a dead end. Its degeneration had proceeded so far, Tuck claimed, that as long ago as 3000 B.C. the only rookery still in existence in the New World was the one on Funk Island... and it was already in the final stages of natural decline when modern man arrived upon the scene. If nothing else, this is a truly elegant alibi, with the onus so effortlessly shifted from the culprits to the victims.

Another Canadian point of view was expressed by a functionary in the federal Department of Fisheries and Oceans. It throws light upon the current attitudes of that department toward the remaining seabirds in Canadian waters. "No matter how many there may have been, the Great Auk had to go. They must have consumed thousands of tons of marine life that commercial fish stocks depend on. There wasn't room for them in any properly managed fishery. Personally, I think we ought to be grateful to the old timers for handling that problem for us."

This adherence to an outmoded theory justifying the destruction of "worthless" species for the presumed good of others, which we value commercially, was an attitude I encountered time and time again.

The 3rd of June, 1844, dawned clear and windless, and the heavy swell that had been thundering against the coast for days had died away. Three fishermen of Stadur—Ketil Ketilsson, Jon Brandsson, and Sigurdur Islefsson—made their way down to the shore where their open boat lay beached, looked searchingly at sky and sea, exchanged a few laconic comments, and concluded that this might be a fit day to try for Eldey.

The lack of wind was a mixed blessing for it meant they would have to row the heavy boat some fifteen miles offshore, but its absence offered some assurance that they would be able to land on Eldey's steep cone when they eventually arrived. The calm weather held and, shortly before midday, they scrambled ashore on Eldey's sea-worn lava cliffs under a haze of screaming murres and gulls. An account of what ensued was obtained from the fishermen by a fellow Icelander some years later.

"As they clambered up they saw two Geirfugel sitting among numberless other sea-birds, and at once gave chase. The Geirfugel showed not the slightest disposition to repel the invaders, but immediately ran along the high cliff, their heads erect, their little wings extended. They uttered no cry of alarm and moved, with their short steps, about as quickly as a man could walk. Jon, with outstretched arms, drove one into a corner, where he soon had it fast. Sigurdur and Ketil pursued the second and seized it close to the edge of the rock. Ketil then returned to the sloping shelf whence the birds had started and saw an egg lying on the lava slab, which he knew to be a Geirfugel's. He took it up, but finding it was broken, dropped it again. All this took place in much less time than it took to tell."

A broken egg upon a barren rock. The period that marked the end.

2

Sea Fowle

Mass destruction of seabirds was not, of course, limited to the spearbill. That unfortunate was simply a terminal example. Many other species suffered as severely, yet escaped annihilation because of their astronomical original numbers, widespread distribution, or their ability to breed in remote or otherwise inaccessible places. This chapter briefly recounts the histories of these oceanic birds under assault by modern man upon the northeastern approaches to North America.

The use of seabirds for bait seems to have begun almost as soon as European fishermen began exploiting New World waters. By the late 1500s, according to Whitbourne:

"The sea fowles do not only feed those who trade [to Newfoundland] but also they are a great furthering of divers ships voyages, because the abundance of them is such that the fishermen do bait their hooks with the quarters of Seafowle on them: and therewith some ships do yearly take a great part of their fishing voyages, with such bait."

It was easy enough to do.

Nicolas Denys, making a raid on the rookeries at Sambro Island near Halifax, found "so great an abundance of all kinds [of sea-birds] that all my crew and myself, having cut clubs for ourselves, killed so great a number... that we were unable to carry them away. And aside from these the number of those which were spared and which rose into the air, made a cloud so thick that the rays of the sun could scarcely penetrate it."

Pressure on the bird colonies to furnish bait mounted inexorably. In 1580, more than 300 European ships were already fishing the northeastern approaches, and that number quadrupled before 1700. In 1784, there were 540 deep-sea vessels alone, most of them using birds for bait during at least part of the fishing season. By 1830, an additional fleet of several hundred New England schooners was fishing the Labrador coast and the Gulf of St. Lawrence, making extensive use of birds.

Apart from the shipborne fishery, growing numbers of planters and by-boat (transient) shoremen fished from innumerable coves and harbours, and all of these regularly used seabirds for bait. Some continued to do so, particularly in Newfoundland and Labrador, well into modern times.

Dr. Arthur Bent visited the Magdalen Island Bird Rocks in 1904 and found that they were being regularly raided by bait-seeking fishermen who would scale the cliffs with ladders and ropes and slaughter as many as 500 gannets in an hour. Bent noted that forty vessels were supplying themselves from the Bird Rocks, the gannets "being roughly skinned and the flesh cut off in chunks." Another method, still in use in the twentieth century at Cape St. Mary's, where the sheer cliffs guarding a gannet colony cannot be scaled, was to set water-logged planks or logs adrift nearby, with a herring tied to each. The gannets, diving in their spectacular way from great heights, would not detect the fraud in time and so would break their necks in scores and hundreds. Gannets, murres, razorbills, and other deep divers were taken in quantity with small-mesh nets into which the birds swam, and drowned.

Even cormorants were used for bait. Although initially their colonies were to be found everywhere along the coasts at least as far south as Georgia, by 1922 they had been so reduced that the great cormorant was for a time thought to have been "extirpated as a breeding bird in North America."

Until late in the nineteenth century, American and Canadian bankers used to make an early voyage that depended for bait on adult oceanic birds. Called the "shack fishery," it mainly used the flesh of the graceful shearwaters and fulmars. The birds were killed by dorymen using five- or six-fathom lines to each of which a multitude of small mackerel hooks baited with cod livers was affixed. The procedure they followed is described in an 1884 report to the United States Fish Commission.

"The fishermen derive much gratification from the sport, not only from the excitement it affords but on account of the prospective profits in obtaining a good supply of birds for bait. When a victim has been hooked it struggles most energetically to rise in the air, or by spreading its feet it holds itself back as it is dragged through the water. At times a bird may disengage the hook but usually the barbed point is well fastened and the bird is landed in the boat. The fisherman crushes its skull with his teeth or strikes it with his 'gob stick'. This may continue until perhaps two hundred birds are captured."

Sometimes shearwaters were taken to the ship alive.

"Perhaps a dozen or so of them are put in a hogshead on the deck of the vessel then the fishermen bring about an internecine war by stirring them up with a stick. The birds evidently imagine their comrades are avowed enemies and, pitching into their neighbours, a general fight and terrible commotion ensues while the feathers fly in all directions, much to the amusement of the men. The fishermen also sometimes tie two together by the legs which enables the birds to swim, but keeps them in unpleasant contact, the consequence being that they fight until one or both succumb."

Shearwaters and fulmars were still being slaughtered for bait by Newfoundland fishermen as late as 1949.

Not even the small, robin-sized petrels (also called Mother Carey's chickens) were immune. "The most common and effective way of killing them was with a whip which was made by tying several parts of codline to a staff five or six feet in length. The petrels were tolled by throwing out a large piece of codfish liver and when they had gathered in a dense mass, swish went the thongs of the whip cutting their way through the crowded flock and killing or maiming a score or more at a single sweep. The cruel work went on until maybe 400 or 500 were killed."

Although adult seabirds were preferred because their flesh held together better on the hook, the available supply seldom came close to meeting the demand. So the young were butchered too. On some rookeries, in some seasons, hardly a young bird reached maturity. A fisherman from Bonavista Bay in Newfoundland once described to me a bait raid in which he took part.

"'Twas late in June-month and the young turrs [murres] was well growed. We was seven men and a half-a-dozen youngsters in two trap boats, and we had gob sticks with iron heads onto them. We come up to the rock just after sunrise and went right off to work. Everywhere you walked the young turrs was thick as hair on a dog. Ticklasses [kittiwakes] and old turrs was overhead in thousands and thousands and the stink when the sun come up was like to choke a shark. Well, we set to, and it was whack-whack-whack until me arms got that tired I could hardly swing me stick. I was nigh covered-up with blood and gurry and the slime they hove up when they was hit. Fast as we knocked 'em over, the young lads hauled them off to the boats in brin bags. She was only a little bit of an island, so it didn't take we all day to clean her up. And I don't say as how what we left behind was enough to make a good scoff for a fox. Them boats was built to carry fifty quintal [about two-and-a-half tons] and they was well loaded. Enough bait so as every boat in the cove could fish free and easy for a fortnight afterwards."

Here now is a look at the status of some of the major threatened seabird species of the northeastern seaboard of America.

Often called Mother Carey's chicks, or sea swallows, the little storm petrels are the disembodied wraiths of ocean, riding the vortex of wind and water far at sea except for the brief interval when they come ashore to reproduce. They breed in shallow burrows they excavate in sod or soil and in crevices amongst the rocks, flying to and from their rookeries only in darkness. So secretive are they that one can walk across a turf-clad clifftop honeycombed with their burrows and be unaware that hundreds and thousands of them lie quiet underneath one's feet. Leach's storm petrel once bred in enormous numbers on islands and headlands south at least to Cape Cod, but the encroachments of modern man and his associated animals have deprived them of most of their one-time rookeries, except in Newfoundland. According to Dr. David Nettleship of the Canadian Wildlife Service, the population status is uncertain in Newfoundland and Labrador but still declining elsewhere in eastern Canada and New England.

The magnificent northern gannet, with its white plumage and black-tipped wings spanning nearly six feet, was once one of the most spectacular seabirds of the eastern seaboard. In 1833, even after the species had already endured more than three centuries of unrelenting slaughter, Audubon could still write of a summer visit to the Bird Rocks in the Gulf of St. Lawrence in this wise: "At length we discovered at a distance a white speck which the pilot assured us was the celebrated rock of our wishes. We thought it was still covered with snow several feet deep. As we approached I imagined that the atmosphere around us was filled with [snow] flakes but . . . I was assured there was nothing in sight but the gannets and their island home. I rubbed my eyes, took out my glasses, and saw the strange dimness in the air was caused by the innumerable birds . . . When we advanced the magnificent veil of floating gannets was easily seen, now shooting upward as if intent on reaching the sky, then descending as if to join the feathered masses below, and again diverging to either side and sweeping over the surface of the ocean."

In Audubon's time, the gannet colony on Bird Rocks is believed to have numbered over 100,000 individuals. When Europeans first appeared on this continent there were scores of such rookeries, many harbouring at least this many breeding birds. By the middle of the nineteenth century, only *nine* rookeries still survived in all of North America. By 1973, the six remaining colonies mustered a grand total of 32,700 pairs of adult gannets—a decrease of about 20 per cent since as recently as 1966. By 1983, there had been a further decrease in the Gulf population of as much as 10 per cent, the result chiefly of toxic chemical poisoning in the fish that sustained the Bonaventure Island colony.

The small size and restricted distribution of the remaining North American gannet populations make the bird highly vulnerable to further, and perhaps fatal, decline due to toxic pollution, increased human fishing efforts, and accidental spills that must inevitably occur with the development of an offshore oil industry.

Two species of cormorant, the great and the double-crested, formerly bred not only along sea coasts from mid-Labrador southward but beside freshwater lakes and rivers, too. They were exceedingly abundant and remained so into the seventeenth century, probably because Europeans considered their rank and oily flesh unfit for food. However, once birds became staple bait for the cod fisheries, both species began to suffer colossal wastage. Crowded together in great colonies on bare rocks or in dense stands of trees, their young could be easily killed in enormous quantities and, because of their stringy musculature, the meat "hung together" well on the cod hooks.

When bird bait ceased to be of much importance, there was no slackening in the devastation of the cormorants. By the beginning of the twentieth century many fish stocks had visibly declined, and fishermen concluded that cormorants were among the principal villains. This led to a deliberate attempt to wipe them out, chiefly by raids on their rookeries during which all eggs and chicks would be ground under foot and as many adults as possible shot down. A latter-day refinement is to spray the eggs with kerosene as they lie in the nests. This seals the microscopic pores in the shells and results in the asphyxiation of the embryos within. Since the adults are not aware that the eggs will never hatch, they often continue to brood them until too late in the season to attempt a second laying.

The campaign against the cormorants has been so successful that, by 1940, fewer than 3,000 great cormorants existed in Canadian waters. Having been granted a modicum of protection after World War II, the species might have been expected to recover, but such has not been the case, mainly because malevolent persecution by commercial and sport fishermen continues. In 1972, I investigated a raid on a major breeding colony of double-crested cormorants on the Magdalen Islands. Five men armed with .22 rifles had spent a morning shooting adults off their nests in a spruce grove, leaving the ground littered with parental corpses. What seemed far worse was the multitude of dead and dying young, both in the nests and on the ground—victims of starvation consequent upon the deaths of their parents.

As fish stocks continue to diminish, the vendetta against cormorants, and other fish-eating animals, can be expected to intensify, with the connivance of some game and fisheries officials who still cling to the discredited belief that cormorants are indeed a menace to the fisheries.

Four species of the marvellously accomplished, black-capped fliers called terns once bred in uncounted colonies on islands, beaches, and sandbars in both fresh and salt water throughout the Atlantic seaboard. They do not seem to have been deliberately attacked by man until the middle of the nineteenth century, when their colonies were devastated by feather hunters supplying the millinery trade. Tern wings, tails, and sometimes the entire skins were used to embellish women's hats, and such was the intensity of the ensuing carnage that all terns became comparatively rare. A large share of the blame for their ongoing diminishment must, however, be laid to the loss of nesting sites through human occupation, degradation of the beaches where the birds once bred, and toxic chemical poisoning. All four species are in trouble, with the roseate and Caspian terns reduced to vestigial remnants and the once superlatively abundant Arctic and common terns suffering the most serious current rate of decline.

With one exception, the gulls seem to have benefited from recent human activities. The small, black-headed laughing gull, once common on the Atlantic seaboard from the Gulf of St. Lawrence south, is now a rarity. However, herring, ring-billed, and black-backed gulls and kittiwakes have staged a quite remarkable comeback from a centuries-long decline during which they and their eggs were taken in enormous quantities for human food. Paradoxically, their success is largely due to the massive and wasteful destruction of sea life by modern fisheries, and to the consequent surfeit of offal and carrion available to them. They have also benefited hugely from the enormous outpouring of gull-edible garbage excreted by our society.

Auks, guillemots, murres, and puffins form the family called Alcidae. Its members are sea animals *par excellence*, spending the great bulk of their lives on and under the waters and as little time as possible in the air or on the land. Most are intensely colonial on their breeding grounds, and many also tend to live in great congregations when at sea. Of all seabirds, this is the family that has suffered most at the hands of modern man, and suffers still.

The razorbill looks very much like a great auk but is only about a third as large. Although it has so far escaped its cousin's fate, principally because of its retained ability to fly, it is now one of the two least numerous members of its family—an unfortunate distinction it shares with the black guillemot.

Generally living in mixed colonies with its relative, the murre, the razorbill was formerly found from about Cape Cod northward but is now restricted to Atlantic Canada and the west coast of Greenland. The fifty-seven existing Canadian sites contain only about 15,000 pairs—an insignificant remnant of a species that probably numbered well over a hundred times that many at first European contact.

The two species of murres, common and thick-billed, taken together were, in all likelihood, the most numerous seabirds in North American waters when Europeans first arrived. The thick-billed murre bred from the northern Gulf and eastern Newfoundland to Baffin Bay. It was secure from modern man in its Arctic habitat until fairly recently and still musters a population in excess of three million individuals, although its numbers are declining. By contrast, its surviving breeding population in the ten remaining rookeries on the eastern Atlantic seaboard amounts to 2,500 pairs at most.

Nettleship says the thick-bill has suffered "major declines in numbers throughout most of the North Atlantic during the last 30–40 years (probably a 30–40% reduction in the eastern Canadian arctic)." The chief causes for this will be looked into a little later, but the salient fact that emerges from these figures is that even animals well insulated from the rapacity of modern man, as were the Arctic thick-billed murres, can have no guarantee of a future in the world we are moulding.

It has recently been revealed that hunters in power boats using modern shotguns still kill as many as 400,000 murres, most of them migrant thick-billed murres, in the waters off Newfoundland and Labrador every winter; at least another 200,000 are reportedly killed by Greenlanders. In the case of this species, the kill today is probably *greater* than it has ever been in the past.

The common murre once occupied much the same range as the razorbill. Its colonies were to be found on as many as 200 rookeries in the Gulfs of Maine and St. Lawrence and along the coasts of the Canadian Maritime Provinces. It is now found at only twenty-six sites, restricted to the northern part of the Gulf of St. Lawrence, Newfoundland, and southern Labrador and to one tiny colony of fifty pairs in the Bay of Fundy.

The gnomish Atlantic puffin, long a figure of fun for cartoonists and storytellers, is in perilous condition. Its breeding distribution in the western Atlantic is today restricted to the region from mid-Labrador south to the northern part of the Gulf of Maine, with a scattering of small colonies on the west Greenland coast. Nearly 70 per cent of the total extant North American population, amounting to about 700,000 breeding birds, is concentrated on three islands in Witless Bay in southeastern Newfoundland. Here, in what is now a provincial seabird sanctuary, the last effectives of a species that once numbered in the several millions are making their final stand.

Like the storm petrels, puffins are intensely colonial and generally nest in burrows, which gave them some protection from natural predators and, later, from eggers and bait hunters, although they still suffered heavily from such assailants. If this had been all they had to suffer at our hands, they might have managed to sustain themselves; but along with the storm petrels, the majority of their colonies were destroyed by the plague of alien animals we unleashed upon them. These included feral cats and dogs that dug out the burrows; sheep, goats, and cattle that trampled them in; and hogs released on bird islands to root out and fatten on young and old alike.

They also included another marauder Europeans brought to North America in their train. In the early summer of 1959, I visited the bold islet called Columbier that rises almost sheer from the sea near St. Pierre. The steep and spongy slopes and the flat centre of the island were so honey-combed with puffin burrows that it was difficult to move without stepping into one. The air was filled with feathered bullets, as hard-flying parent puffins exploded underfoot or drove in from seaward to protest my intrusion. Below me, I could see flotilla after flotilla of them on the water waiting for me to leave. Although I could only guess at their numbers, I am sure there must have been at least 10,000 on Columbier.

That winter, an old and rat-infested Newfoundland schooner drove ashore on the islet. The crew took to the boats and rowed to St. Pierre, but the rats landed on Columbier. In 1964, an ornithologist visited the islet and found no more than a few dozen puffins trying to rear their young. The rest had been driven away or had been eaten by the rats, which had multiplied into a Pied Piper's legion.

Although the slaughter of seabirds by early Europeans was on a mind-bog-gling scale, it was no worse—if more direct—than the destruction being visited on them now.

Some of the most disastrous damage being done to seabird populations is the result of a technological breakthrough in the fishing industry—the intro-duction of gill nets made of synthetic monofilament. This material is virtually invisible under water, and diving birds become enmeshed in it, without ever knowing it is there, and drown.

Since the establishment of a drift-net fishery for Atlantic salmon off the west coast of Greenland in the late 1960s, an average of a 250,000 murres have been drowned annually, and, in one year alone, 500,000 to 750,000 of them perished in the nets. Along the coasts of Newfoundland, professional fishermen have been compelled to move these new nets away from the vicinity of seabird colonies because removing dead birds from the mesh consumes too much fishing time. On the other hand, some "part-time" fishermen deliberately set nets close to colonies, "fishing" for birds instead of cod. The casualties include all species of diving birds, but none suffer more catastrophically than puffins and murres. There appears to be no end in view to this senseless destruction; "nothing can be done about it," according to Fisheries officials I consulted.

Innumerable seabirds are also being destroyed by oil spills and oil slicks. When the tanker *Kurdistan* broke up off southwest Newfoundland during the winter of 1978, much of her cargo of bunker oil floated back and forth for months at the mercy of wind and tide. From what I saw and was told by observers who checked the beaches in Cape Breton and southern Newfoundland, I conclude that not less than 150,000 and perhaps as many as 300,000 seabirds, including ducks, perished as a result of this single spill. Marine insurers anticipate that at least one such major "accident" will occur in northwestern Atlantic waters every four or five years and at least one minor spill every six months. Even a minor one can kill 100,000 seabirds.

In the Arctic, the last remaining great colonies of northwest Atlantic seabirds will be at deadly risk if the projected northern oil-tanker traffic becomes a reality. Ecologists have calculated that a single major spill near the ice-ridden entrance to Lancaster South could, and probably would, effectively destroy the largest single concentration of breeding seabirds still extant in North America. And it is admitted by all who are involved that, sooner or later, such a disaster is statistically inevitable.

The story is not yet fully told.

Oceanic pollution, particularly in restricted waters, by poisonous chemical wastes, including pesticides, has been increasing through the past several decades. Many bird specialists are convinced that the rapid decline in fish-eating seabird populations in the Gulf of St. Lawrence (the sewer outlet for the entire Great Lakes drainage system) is primarily due to ever-rising concentrations of toxic chemicals in the birds' tissues and, in particular, in their reproductive organs, making them (or their eggs, if they manage to lay any) infertile. Irrefutable evidence as to the existence of this sort of biotic damage has been available since the DDT investigations of the 1960s, but such evidence is generally overlooked. The reason seems obvious enough. If it be publicly admitted that fish are being poisoned, and in turn are poisoning their consumers—bird or human—who amongst us will continue to buy fish?

There is more.

Surveys of coastal headlands, beaches, reefs, islands, and islets from mid-Labrador south to Florida indicate that only about three out of every 100 suitable sites for seabird colonies are still occupied, even by vestigial populations. The numbers continue to decline as existing colonies are displaced and sites pre-empted or rendered useless to the birds by our intrusions, including such uniquely human ones as military installations and naval and air force target ranges.

Finally, we come to the most primal threat of all: starvation.

As far back as the late 1960s, a ghastly phenomenon was beginning to exhibit itself at one of the world's largest surviving puffin colonies, on the island of Røst off the northwest coast of Norway. Although 500,000 chicks were being hatched there every spring, fewer and fewer were living to reach the age of flight. Year by year, the mysterious mortality grew worse until, by 1977, it was estimated that only one chick in 1,000 was surviving. Then a study by Norwegian ornithologists found the solution to the mystery. It was horribly simple. Gross commercial overfishing of herring and other small school-fishes in the northeastern Atlantic had brought about a collapse in their populations, and all the animals that depended on them for sustenance—including larger fish, and seabirds such as the puffin—were being starved. In 1980, almost the entire hatch of puffins on Røst perished of starvation. According to a report written at the time, "They were replaced by millions of [carrion] beetles. Tens of thousands of dried-out puffin chicks littered the colonies like little mummies...the stomachs of the dead chicks were crammed with gravel and earth, a sign of acute starvation." The tragedy was repeated in the summer of 1981, and most of the puffin chicks hatched that year never found their wings but remained upon the island to rot or mummify.

The Røst shambles is being repeated in the northwestern Atlantic as a result of the destruction of capelin by the commercial fishing industry.[1] By 1979, the offshore capelin stocks—once the staff of life for countless other animals inhabiting the approaches to the continent—had been fished into commercial extinction, and the same process of destruction was being applied to the inshore stocks. With the disappearance of the capelin, starvation stalked the seabird colonies, especially those of the Alcidae. The last great puffinry in North America, in Witless Bay, began to suffer savagely. In 1981, fewer than 45 per cent of the chicks hatched there lived to become

---

[1] For further details of this massacre, see the discussion of baitfishes in Chapter 11.

fledglings, and those that did were so undernourished as to have been unlikely to have survived the rigours of their first winter at sea. This massive starvation probably dates back to 1978 although no one was on the islands then to witness it. There is little doubt that, unless the exploitation of capelin by man is radically curtailed, the puffins, razorbills, murres, and other species of seabirds will be pushed even closer to extinction. Many other kinds of sea animals that are less visible to the human eye, including a score or more of fish species, will also be forced into severe and dangerous decline.

Unfortunately, those in positions of power in industry and government seem quite content to let the seabirds disappear. Their rationale is simplicity itself. If, and when, the capelin recover from the disastrous destruction of the 1970s and 1980s, few seabirds will remain alive. Therefore there ought to be more capelin available to enhance corporate fishing profits.

For some decades past, an internecine war has been in progress between the Canadian Wildlife Service and the Department of Fisheries and Oceans over the fate of all animals that can be seen to compete in any way with man for a share of the "harvest of the sea."

It is a battle between David and Goliath, but in this case David has neither a lethal sling at his disposal nor the support of the mercenary god of modern times. The CWS does what it can; and Fisheries and Oceans undoes it. If the ultimate decision rests with Fisheries and Oceans, then the once-mighty colonial seabird population of the northeastern seaboard has but small prospects of survival.

3
Swiftwings

It was known to the Nascopie Indians of Ungava as *swiftwings*, in recognition of its superlative powers of flight. Other native peoples knew it by a variety of names, none more appropriate than the one given it by aboriginal Patagonians. They called it by a word best translated as *cloud of wonder* because of its autumnal appearance in flocks of such overwhelming magnitude that they darkened the Patagonian skies.

Poles distant from Patagonia, the Inuit of the tundra plains bordering the Arctic Ocean from Bathurst Inlet west to Alaska's Kotzebue Sound knew it, too. They called it *pi-pi-piuk* in imitation of its soft and vibrant whistle, which was their certain harbinger of spring. As late as 1966, an old Inuk living on the shores of Franklin Bay could still tell me what it had been like when pi-pi-piuk returned from whatever distant and unknown world had claimed it during the long winter months.

"They came suddenly, and fell upon us like a heavy snow. In my father's time it was told they were so many on the tundra it was like clouds of mosquitoes rising in front of a walking man. Their nests and eggs were in every tussock of grass. At the end of the hatching moon there were so many of their young scurrying about it was as if the moss itself was moving. Truly, they were many! But when I was still a child, they were few. And one spring they did not come.

It was in that same year, he told me, that his people first heard about the incomprehensible slaughter in which we, the *Kablunait*, had immured ourselves—the First World War. When the pi-pi-piuk failed to reappear in subsequent years, the Inuit speculated that perhaps they had been destroyed by us in one of our inexplicable outbursts of carnage.

"One need not look too far to find the cause which led to the destruction of the Eskimo Curlew. On its breeding grounds in the far north it was undisturbed. And I cannot believe that during its migrations it was overwhelmed by any great catastrophy at sea which could annihilate it...several other birds make similar, long ocean flights without disaster. There is no evidence of disease, or failure of food supply. No, there is only one cause: slaughter by human beings; slaughter in Labrador and New England in late summer and fall; slaughter in South America in winter and slaughter, worst of all, from Texas to Canada in spring."

So wrote Dr. A.C. Bent, dean of American ornithologists in the 1920s. His was a verdict that must have taken some courage to express since the good doctor had himself killed tens of thousands of birds, including Eskimo curlews, both in pursuit of sport and in the name of science.

Curlews are of the sandpiper and plover kind, collectively known as wading birds or shorebirds because most of them haunt shorelines and shallows. However, the erect, long-legged, and long-necked curlews with their gracefully down-curving beaks are as much at home in upland meadows, pampas, prairies, and tundra plains as they are by the sea.

The Eskimo curlew, which I shall hereafter call by its Nascopie name, was the smallest of the three North American curlews. It stood only about a foot high and weighed no more than a pound, but it was by all odds the most successful of the three. Although it seems to have mated for life, it was nevertheless intensely social, living in close company with millions of its fellows in what was, in effect, a single close-knit nation.

Because no one region could feed its multitudes for long, it was a nomadic nation possessed of flying and navigational skills that enabled its members to avail themselves of the resources of two continents in the course of an annual migration of phenomenal length and complexity.

This journey began on the tundra breeding grounds where the perpetual daylight of the brief summer season resulted in an explosive reproduction of insect and other small forms of life. The eggs of the swiftwings were timed to hatch just as this outburst reached its peak so that the young birds, which were able to run about and forage for themselves within minutes of their hatching, had ample food available. Nevertheless, there was not enough to feed both them and their millions of parents. The adults mostly subsisted through the weeks of nest-building, egg-laying, and brooding on reserves of fat acquired during their northbound migration; but by the time the eggs hatched, these inner resources were running low and could not be replenished locally without endangering the survival of the young.

The swiftwings had evolved the answer to this problem. Before the young were even out of their natal down, the adults drew together in enormous flocks and flew away. To us this might seem heartless, even brutal, but it was not. Although flightless, the young were fully capable of caring for themselves—so long as food was plentiful. The departure of their parents helped ensure that this would be the case.

As early as mid-July, horizon-filling flights of hungry adults departed on their search for sustenance. Because of their enormous and concentrated numbers they needed equally immense and concentrated food supplies, not only to satisfy their urgent current needs, but also to build new reserves of body fat with which to fuel their ongoing odyssey.

The munificent larder they required did not lie close at hand. To reach it, they had to cross the continent from west to east, flying roughly 3,000 miles. Their objective was Labrador and Newfoundland, where extensive stretches of open heathland nurtured (and still does) a low-growing species of bush that quite literally carpeted hundreds of thousands of square miles—a bush with juicy, pea-sized berries that begin to ripen as early as the middle of July. This fecund plant is known to science as *Empetrum nigram*, but to the residents of Newfoundland and Labrador it was, and remains, the curlew berry. It was the principal support of the swiftwings in late summer. They fed upon it with such gusto that their bills, legs, heads, breasts—even their wing feathers—became royally stained with rich purple juice.

The arrival of the feeding flocks left an indelible impression on human observers. In 1833, Audubon witnessed their arrival on the south coast of Labrador. "They came...in such dense flocks as to remind me of the passenger pigeon...flock after flock passed close around our vessel and directed their course toward the mountainous tracts in the neighbourhood." In 1864, a Dr. Packard watched the arrival of a single flock, "which may have been a mile long and as broad...[the cries of the birds] sounded at times like the wind whistling through the ropes of a thousand-ton vessel; at others like the jingling of a multitude of sleigh-bells." And in 1884, Lucien Turner observed them in northern Labrador with an artist's eye. "Each flock flew in a wedge shape, the sides of which were constantly swaying back and forth like a cloud of smoke...or in long dangling lines which rise or twist spirally...At other times the leader plunges downward followed by the remainder of the flock in graceful undulations, becoming a dense mass, then separating into a thin sheet spread wide again...reforming into such a variety of shapes that no description would suffice...[the flocks] alight on level tracts from Davis Inlet to the Gulf of St. Lawrence, each day adding to their number until the ground seems alive with them. They feed on the ripening berries, becoming wonderfully fat in a few days."

"Wonderfully fat" expressed it perfectly. After only a week on the berry grounds the birds had become so plump that, if shot in flight, the corpses often split like over-ripe peaches when they struck the ground. And they *were* shot, everywhere that men lived along the coasts of Labrador and Newfoundland.

In the 1770s, so Captain Cartwright noted in his journal, a hunter could count on killing 150 curlews in a single day with only the crude muzzleloader of those times. A century later, Labrador hunters with improved firearms were routinely killing thirty curlews at a shot. Most fishermen kept loaded guns in their boats and on their fishing stages, "and shot indiscriminately into the great flocks as they wheeled by."

These "liveyers," as the local people called themselves, were not the only curlew hunters. During the latter part of the nineteenth century, many foreigners visited Labrador to enjoy the curlew hunt. In 1874, ornithologist Dr. Eliot Coues described a typical entertainment of this sort. "Although six or eight gunners were stationed at the spot and kept up a continual round of firing upon the poor birds, they continued to fly distractedly about our heads, notwithstanding the numbers that every moment fell."

If local residents found powder too expensive or in short supply, they stalked the swiftwings at night on their roosting grounds, dazzling them into immobility with bull's-eye lanterns, then striking them down "in enormous numbers" with clubs and flails. Hardly an outport family in Newfoundland and Labrador failed to begin the winter with several casks of curlews preserved in salt or in the birds' own rendered fat.

There was commercial slaughter, too. Employees of the Hudson's Bay Company at Sandwich Bay annually put up tens of thousands of curlews in hermetically sealed tins, which were shipped to London and Montreal to be consumed as a gourmet specialty. A government official who visited Sandwich Bay in the late 1800s reported seeing 2,000 curlews hung up like bunches of enormous grapes in the company warehouse—the result of one day's shooting.

Meantime, what of the young that had been left behind? As soon as their flight feathers and wing muscles were sufficiently developed, they, too, took to the high skies and performed the seemingly miraculous feat of rejoining their parents on the berry barrens of Labrador and Newfoundland.

Toward the end of July, the united flocks began to leave the berry grounds, drifting restlessly southward, some pausing briefly on the Magdalen Islands where they were once reported in millions and on Prince Edward Island before moving down the Nova Scotia peninsula.

Gunners waited for them everywhere. In the 1760s, hunters on Lunenburg common frequently killed a bushel-basket-full with a single musket shot. They killed for the pot or for the market. A century later a new breed of gunner, the self-styled sportsman, joined in the fusillade. One English visitor to Prince Edward Island did not think curlews "offered a very high order of sport." Nevertheless, they provided an opportunity to enjoy oneself: "The weather at this season is so charming, the labour so light, and the birds such delightful eating that the pursuit is worth it. And sometimes they do give very pretty sport as they wheel over the decoys. I once shot one on a marsh; its companion took a short flight then re-alighted beside the dead bird, quietly waiting there until I had reloaded my gun and was ready for him. This simple pair had probably just arrived from the remote north where that cruel, devouring monster, man, had never set foot. A short stay in Prince Edward Island teaches these birds a lesson." There were many such lessons to be learned, and the cost of learning was appallingly high.

Early in August the southward trickle swelled to a mighty torrent and now there was no hesitation. Except for brief interruptions due to bad weather, the winged river maintained an almost unbroken flow until early September saw the last of the young birds leave Newfoundland and Labrador.

The massed millions of swiftwings did not usually follow the New England coast southward but streamed off the coasts of Newfoundland and Nova Scotia heading over the open Atlantic directly for that portion of South America lying between the mouths of the Amazon and the Orinoco Rivers— a sea passage of nearly 3,000 miles. Superb fliers that they were, they appear to have made this journey non-stop; but supposing they did encounter heavy weather, it would have been no tragedy, for they were able to land on water and take off again when conditions improved. Severe easterly gales sometimes deflected part of the high-flying stream over the New England coast, with the result that hundreds of thousands of swiftwings unexpectedly alighted on shores, marshes, even on farmers' meadows.

New Englanders looked upon such visitations as manna from the skies. They called the visitors dough-birds because they were so plump. According to a nineteenth-century account, "their arrival was the signal for every sportsman and market hunter to get to work, and nearly all that reached our shores were shot." Such enormous numbers landed on Nantucket Island one autumn in the 1840s that the supply of shot and powder was exhausted and, to the disappointment of the residents, the butchery had to be "interrupted." A Cape Cod sportsman, irritated by the activities of the market hunters, complained: "Those birds which may come, can not, if they would, remain any longer than is absolutely necessary for they are so harrassed immediately after landing that the moment there occurs a change in weather favourable to migration they at once depart." Dr. Bent remembered "hearing my father tell of the great shooting they used to have when I was a small boy, about

1870. As he has now gone to the happy hunting ground I cannot give the exact figures, but he once saw a wagon loaded full of 'dough birds' shot in one day."

Sportsmen of those times differed little from those of today except that they had more living targets available to them. They believed, as they still do, that hunting for sport was not only beyond reproach, but was almost a duty if one was to qualify as a proper man.

A number of them published books describing their successes and extolling the virtues of those who dedicated themselves to "this natural and healthy outdoor pursuit." Nevertheless, they wrote with some equivocation. The verb "to kill" was almost never used. Instead, their prey was "captured," "collected," or even "brought to hand." Blood did not flow upon the pages of these books. The emphasis was on the skill, sense of fair play, and gentlemanly conduct of the author, and on his honest affection for and admiration of the God-given beauties of nature, which were the real reasons he enjoyed the sport.

Sportsmen of those days kept careful account of their shooting scores, either in their own "game books" or in the record books of the sporting clubs to which many of them belonged. Most such clubs owned or leased their own hunting hotels and controlled great stretches of beach and marshland exclusively reserved for the guns of their members. One such was the Chatham Hotel on Long Island, patronized by New York sportsmen. It provided almost unlimited opportunities to practise gunners' skills and sportsmanship on the vast flocks of shorebirds, including curlews, that frequented the eastern seaboard beaches during migrations. The Chatham prided itself on enabling its well-heeled members to establish and maintain reputations as "number one, first class, sportsmen." One such member was a Mr. James Symington, who chalked up the following score in the Club's record book in just three autumnal days in 1897.

beattle-heads (black-bellied plover)	393
jack curlews	55
golden plover	18
mud snipe (dowitcher)	674
jack snipe	37
calico bird (turnstone)	7
redbreast (knot)	149
peeps (small sandpipers and plover)	382
Total	1,715

Not all sportsmen shot wading birds for the same lofty reasons. Some did so—if one can credit this—as *practice* for shooting at clay pigeons. According to one of them: "It was my habit to indulge myself in a few hours gunning on the beaches before engaging in friendly competition at the [trap shooting] Club. Nothing so exercises one's abilities in this regard as to meet the challenges of those swift, elusive birds, particularly those of the plover family."

When the mighty river of southbound swiftwings eventually reached the South American coast, it vanished. Nothing is known about its subsequent movements until it reappeared over Paraguay and Uruguay, winging steadfastly southward toward its wintering grounds on the rolling pampas stretching from central Argentina south to Patagonia. Here the swiftwings at last came to rest after a journey from their Arctic breeding grounds of nearly 10,000 miles.

By the nineteenth century it had become a broken rest. From the Falkland Islands north to Buenos Aires, the great flocks were harried from place to place by ranchers, settlers, and sportsmen who slaughtered them not alone for food and fun, but even to provide cheap food for pigs.

With the coming of the northern spring, the survivors reformed and the shimmering pampas air again filled with the flash of wings. We know little about the northward journey after the departure from Argentina in late February until the flocks darkened the dawn skies of the Gulf coast of Texas a few weeks later. I suspect that both spring and autumn migrations flew through the centre of the southern continent, taking advantage of the food to be found on the vast plateau prairies of the interior such as the campos of Brazil, where they would have encountered few people of European origin, and few guns.

After their return to our continent the flocks drifted slowly northward, pacing the march of spring across the greening immensity of the Great Plains. Here was food in plenty to restore them after the long flight from the Argentine and to build the reserves that would be vital to a successful breeding season on the High Arctic nesting grounds. The preferred food at this season was insects, especially grasshoppers. The curlews were remarkably adept at harvesting these, as a report written in 1915 attests.

"The Eskimo Curlew was a bird of such food habits that it is a distinct loss to our agriculture that it should have disappeared. During the invasion of the Rocky Mountain grasshopper [in the 1870s] it did splendid work in the destruction of grasshoppers and their eggs. Mr. Wheeler states that in the later seventies these birds would congregate on land which had not yet been plowed and where the grasshoppers' eggs were laid, reach down into the soil with their long bills and drag out the egg capsules which they would then devour with their contents of eggs and young hoppers, until the land had been cleared of the pests...A specimen examined in 1874 had 31 grasshoppers in its stomach...the bird also often alighted on plowed ground to feed on the white grubs and cutworms."

Some idea of the effect the curlews' appetites must have had on insect pests is suggested by Professor Lawrence Bruner's description of the size of the flights that visited Nebraska during the late 1860s. "Usually the heaviest flights occurred coincident with the beginning of the corn-planting time, and enormous flocks would settle on the newly plowed fields and on the prairies where they searched industriously for insects. The flocks reminded the settlers of the flights of passenger pigeons [which they had seen in the East] and thus the curlews were given the name of 'prairie pigeons'. The flocks contained thousands of individuals and would form dense masses of birds extending for a quarter to half a mile in length and a hundred yards or more in width. When such a flock would alight the birds would cover 40 or 50 acres of ground."

The vital service rendered by the curlews to settlers trying to farm the plains, particularly in Oklahoma, Kansas, and Nebraska, was, to say the least, ill-requited. Along with Texas, these three states became one enormous slaughterhouse for the swiftwings. Here, where they had been and would have continued to be of enormous assistance to the agricultural efforts of the human invaders, their race was ultimately destroyed.

Professor Myron Swenk described how their annihilation was brought about: "During the [spring] flights the slaughter of these poor birds was appalling and almost unbelievable. Hunters would drive out from Omaha and shoot the birds without mercy until they had literally slaughtered a wagonload of them, the wagon being actually *filled*, and with the sideboards on at that. Sometimes when the flights were unusually heavy and the hunters well supplied with ammunition, their wagons were too quickly and easily filled, so whole loads of the birds would be dumped on the prairie, their bodies forming piles as large as a couple of tons of coal, where they would be allowed to rot while the hunters proceeded to refill their wagons with fresh victims and thus further gratify their lust for killing. The compact flocks and tameness of the birds made this slaughter possible, and at each shot usually dozens of the birds would fall. In one specific instance a single shot from an old muzzle-loader into a flock of these curlews brought down 28 birds while for the next half mile every now and then a fatally wounded bird would drop to the ground...So dense were the flocks when the birds were turning in their flight one could scarcely throw a brick or missile into it without hitting a bird.

"There was no difficulty getting close to the sitting birds, perhaps within 25 or 35 yards, and at this distance the hunters would wait for them to rise on their feet, which was the signal for the first volley of shots. The startled birds would rise and circle a few times, affording ample opportunity for further murderous discharges of the guns, and sometimes would re-alight in the same field, when the attack would be repeated. Mr. Wheeler has killed as many as 37 birds with a pump gun at one rise. Sometimes the bunch would be seen alighting on a field 2 or 3 miles away, when the hunters would at once drive to that field with a horse and buggy, relocate the birds, and resume the fusillade and slaughter."

This kind of butchery, be it noted, was done solely in the name of sport! However, by the 1870s, commercial gunners in the East had so savaged the passenger pigeon (which had been the staple of the wild bird market, and whose numbers had been thought to be infinite) that the public appetite for edible wild birds could no longer be sated by it.

The penetration of the railroads through the prairie states at about this same time stimulated "some smart fellows" in Wichita, Kansas, into filling the gap with the corpses of "prairie pigeons." The first carload-lots of spring-killed curlews, preserved on ice, reached New York in 1872 and were snapped up at such high prices that the fate of the remaining swiftwings was sealed forthwith.

During the spring of 1873, the butchery of curlews on the Great Plains mushroomed to a massacre of such proportions that, by 1875, no large curlew flocks were to be seen crossing Texas. In the spring of 1879, the last great flights were seen in Kansas; and by 1886, puzzled gunners in Labrador, Newfoundland, Nova Scotia, and New England were wondering where the great flocks had gone.

One of the most widely accepted explanations for the rapid disappearance of what had been one of North America's most abundant birds was that it had been exterminated by western farmers using poisoned bait to protect their seed corn from "the depredations of these insatiable pests." As an exculpation, this one was typical of our attempts to vindicate the mass destruction visited by us on other forms of life. And in this case, as in most, it was a blatant lie. Far from eating the farmers' seed, the curlews had been of great assistance in helping the crop to grow at all.

The annihilation of the swiftwings for short-term gain, together with the reduction to relict levels of the millions of associated insect-eating birds that once checked insect plagues on the western plains of Canada and the United States, has cost grain farmers an estimated $10-$15 billion since 1920 in losses suffered directly from such insect infestations and as the price paid in attempts to curb such visitations through the use of chemical poisons and other means.

That cost is ongoing. It must continue to be paid, presumably in perpetuity, not just by Great Plains farmers and those of the campos and pampas of South America, but by all of us. The wanton destruction of the Eskimo curlew provides a classic example, not only of the ruthlessness of modern man, but also of his imperishable stupidity.

During the final years of the nineteenth century, only a very few flocks remained to run the gamut of the guns as they made their way north through the Dakotas and the Canadian prairies to the relative security of the Mackenzie Valley corridor. Along the Arctic coast the Inuit waited, and they, too, wondered what had happened to the pi-pi-piuk that had once come spiralling down upon the tundra as thick as falling snow.

At the turn of the century, Nascopie Indians walking across the caribou barrens, ankle-deep in a carpet of ripe curlew berries, wondered what had happened to the multitudes of swiftwings that had once gorged themselves on those high plains.

The last curlews to be seen in the Halifax market were sold there in the fall of 1897; by 1900, Newfoundland and Labrador fishermen were complaining that "you can't get a taste of a curlew anywhere." In 1905, a sportsman named Green, who for decades past had shot over Miscou Island in Bay Chaleur, expressed "a pang of regret shared by all naturalists, sportsmen and epicures, for the curlew is rapidly disappearing."

On the pampas of Patagonia, gauchos hefted their *bolas* as they searched in vain for the flocks that did not come—flocks that had once descended in such masses that a single throw of the leaden balls might kill a dozen birds.

The swiftwings were failing fast but, as Dr. Bent noted, "No one lifted a finger to protect them until it was too late." In fact, Dr. Bent's ornithological peers did just the opposite. As the curlews became rare in life, so did their "specimen" value soar. Scientists began to compete fiercely with each other to acquire the skins of those few that still remained. According to the well-known American naturalist, Dr. Charles Townsend, a flock of eight swiftwings appeared at Sandwich Bay in the fall of 1912. Seven were promptly killed and the skins of five were gratefully received in the name of science at Harvard by yet another famous American ornithologist, William Brewster, who added them to the enormous collection of "study skins" in the university's collection. To quote again from Dr. Bent: "The last kills in Nebraska were made in 1911 and 1915. On March 11, 1911...two birds were shot by Mr. Fred Gieger...they are at present in the collection of Mr. August Eiche...No Eskimo Curlews were noted in 1914 but a single bird was killed south of Norfolk, Nebraska on the morning of April 17, 1915. It came into the possession of Mr. Hoagland, who had it mounted."

By 1919, the skin of a swiftwing was worth $300, and with such a price on their heads the few remaining survivors had little chance. In 1924 and 1925, the last two individuals ever to be seen in the province of Buenos Aires were both collected for Argentina's Museo Naçional de Historia Natural.

By then, Dr. Bent had already epitomized the "natural history" of the swiftwings. "The story of the Eskimo Curlew is just one more pitiful tale of the slaughter of the innocents. It is a sad fact that the countless swarms of this fine bird...which once swept across our land are gone forever, sacrificed to the insatiable greed of man."

Gone forever? Not quite...not yet. In 1932, a single bird was killed at Battle Harbour on the Labrador coast for the University of Michigan's collection. Another was collected on Barbados in 1963. In addition, there have been several sight records, mostly in the Northwest Territories and in Texas, where one was photographed in 1962.

There remains at least the possibility that a handful still survive—some authorities think as many as twenty—but they are little more than spectral beings, no more able to fill the wind with their swift wings than the dead can rise again.

❖ 4

The Sporting Life

Although the elimination of the Eskimo curlew was perhaps the most spectacular and barbaric tragedy to strike the great family of shorebirds and waders, it does not stand alone. Some forty species, ranging from the minute least sandpiper to the imposing long-billed curlew, frequented the eastern seaboard at the time of first European contact, either as birds of passage or as breeding summer residents. All, without exception, were shot, netted, or otherwise slaughtered on a fearful scale.

Most abundant of the three curlews found in eastern North America was the Eskimo, but the most individually impressive was the sicklebird, now known as the long-billed curlew. Although its major breeding grounds were on the western prairies, it migrated along the Atlantic coastal flyway in considerable numbers.

Standing two feet tall on pipe-stem legs, it swung a curving bill six inches in length. Its great size and piercing cries gave it pride of place among the shorebird kind. Unfortunately, these very characteristics, plus the fact that it was excellent eating, made it a prime target as a pot bird. Although in the sixteenth and seventeenth centuries it seems still to have been an abundant migrant from the Gulf of St. Lawrence region south along the coast to Florida, by the eighteenth century it had become scarce and by the latter part of the nineteenth century it had been virtually eliminated from eastern North America.

Those that survived into the heyday of the sport hunter were eagerly sought as spectacular trophies. "The sickle-bird was a fine game bird," wrote Dr. A.C. Bent. "Its large size made it a tempting target. It decoyed readily and could be easily whistled down by imitating its notes. And the cries of a wounded bird would attract others which would circle again and again until they too were killed."

This instinctive rallying to a stricken comrade is characteristic of the shorebird family. It served them well before our coming since the confusing, noisy flight of an aroused flock tended to distract predators, affording the intended victim a chance to escape. When used as a defence against a man with a gun, however, it simply invited mayhem. As a Toronto sportsman wrote in 1906, "The strong desire of shorebirds to succour any one of their kind which has been wounded is a fortunate thing indeed since it enables even a tyro hunter to kill as big a bag as he might wish."

By the 1920s, Dr. Bent had become apprehensive that the sicklebird might be doomed to follow the Eskimo curlew into extinction. His fears may yet be justified in our time for, although the great curlews still exist in parts of the western plains (where I used to marvel at them in my youth), their breeding range has been so reduced by our agricultural practices, and their numbers so thinned by illegal hunting, that the outlook for their continuing survival remains deeply shadowed.

The third of the curlews, the Hudsonian, or jack curlew as gunners called it (it is now known as the whimbrel), was similar to the slightly smaller Eskimo but had a much more diffuse distribution. It bred right across the Arctic and migrated along both Pacific and Atlantic coasts and through the interior as well. Consequently, it was somewhat less vulnerable to mass destruction than its cousins.

I first encountered it at Churchill, on the west coast of Hudson Bay, where it was so uncommon that only after days of squelching through sodden muskeg did I finally flush a female from her nest in a moss tussock. Later I met a veteran Hudson's Bay Company trader who had come out to Churchill from the Orkneys in 1870 as a teen-age apprentice. He recalled that, in his early years, Hudsonian curlews had been so numerous he and other apprentices had collected barrels of their eggs, which they preserved in isinglass for winter use. He told me that in early August he had seen the birds gathered in such multitudes on the mud flats that he and a Cree helper once killed more than a thousand in a morning shoot. He even showed me a daybook in which he had recorded his hunting scores while stationed at Moose Factory. His spidery handwriting listed daily curlew kills in 1873 of from 200 to 300. "Mostly for sport," he told me. "Even the [sled] dogs couldna eat all they puir birds."

The destruction wrought by white men in the Arctic, horrendous as it may have been, was as nothing to the slaughter that took place in the south. Much of what I have written about the butchery of the Eskimo curlew applies equally to the Hudsonian, but with the significant difference that the jack curlew was generally found in smaller, widely separated flocks scattered over a much greater range and so escaped the concentrated fury visited on its cousin. It suffered fearfully, but not mortally.

It is possible that the surviving population is now holding its own. In any event, the Hudsonian was a familiar visitor to Newfoundland when I lived there during the 1960s. Every autumn, the wild whistle of the birds would echo and re-echo from the berry barrens as small flocks—never more than forty or fifty—pitched in, to stuff themselves with curlew berries. They were a poignant reminder of earlier times when the skies of Newfoundland and Labrador were darkened by massed flights of swiftwings and jacks.

In Newfoundland, and in the Magdalens, I was occasionally lucky enough to see small flocks—never containing more than four or five—of another of the "big waders"—the Hudsonian godwit. Two species of godwits were found in eastern North America by early Europeans, who noted that they looked and acted very much like curlews, except that their bills curved down instead of up.

Not much smaller than the sicklebird, the largest of the two—the marbled godwit—occurred and may even have bred from the southern Gulf of St. Lawrence south to Florida; but it was so eagerly sought after for the pot and, later, as a game bird that by 1900 it had virtually disappeared from the eastern reaches of the continent. A remnant population still exists on the Great Plains.

The Hudsonian godwit is about the size of the swiftwing and its way of life is strikingly similar. Both bred in the High Arctic and both followed much the same elliptical migration route. Both, needless to say, were exposed to similar devastation. However, the Hudsonian godwit is a somewhat warier bird than the Eskimo curlew, flies in smaller flocks, and part of its population evidently winters in regions uninhabited by man. Although officially pronounced extinct in the mid-1920s (at about the same time that the Eskimo curlew was thought to have been exterminated), the godwit had, in fact, survived. It is now much esteemed as a rarity by birdwatchers anxious to add it to their life-lists. Unfortunately, it is still being shot by illegal gunners, particularly in the Mississippi Valley during spring migration. Furthermore, it is legally hunted on parts of its winter range in South America where sportsmen continue to take advantage of its habit of rallying to the aid of wounded comrades. "On more than one occasion several birds have dropped to my gun," wrote a visiting Englishman in Argentina. "The flock would then sweep round and hover over the [wounded] individuals in the water, uttering loud cries of distress, regardless of my presence in the open, and renewed gunfire . . . the birds were so closely packed together that the shots went 'into the brown' and caused innumerable cripples."

Some ornithologists hold out hope that the species may yet stage a come-back. But the Hudsonian godwit remains perilously close to the point of no return, represented by no more than a few thousand surviving individuals.

One of the large waders that summered in the northeastern maritime region was the willet, a bird the size of an Eskimo curlew but with a flashy black-and-white wing pattern that gave it the name flagbird. As late as the 1830s, it summered regularly along most of the Atlantic seaboard from Newfoundland south, despite the fact that for at least 200 years settlers had systematically collected its eggs for food and had shot adults throughout the breeding season. Market and sport hunting in the nineteenth century finally tipped the scales against it and by 1900, thought Dr. Bent, "it seemed as if this large, showy wader was destined to disappear from at least the northern part of its range. It had entirely ceased to breed in many former haunts and was nearly extirpated in others."

Fortunately for the flagbird, persecution stopped short of annihilation, and it is now returning from the brink. In recent years small breeding colonies have appeared as far north as Cape Breton Island and, while there is little likelihood it will ever again be abundant, it is at least no longer threatened with extinction.

Most spectacular of all the big waders is the oystercatcher. Almost as large as the sicklebird, of striking white and dark plumage, it appears to wear a black hood from which projects a long and heavy orange-coloured bill. Big, gaudy, and gifted with a piercing whistle that can be heard half a mile away, it once nested in large colonies on sandy beaches from Labrador to the Gulf of Mexico. The dominant shorebird wherever it was found, its meat was much prized, as were its hen-sized eggs, both by transient fishermen and by latter-day settlers. Sport hunters and casual gunners made a target of it simply because it was so conspicuous.

Audubon reported it on the north shore of the Gulf of St. Lawrence as late as the 1830s but, because it is now so rare and restricted to the southern part of its one-time range, most modern ornithologists contend that he must have been mistaken. Not so. As early as the 1620s, Champlain casually noted the presence of the *pye de mer* (the name by which the similar European oystercatcher is still known in France) in the Gulf of St. Lawrence; in the 1770s, Cartwright listed the sea pie as resident in south Labrador, not far from where Audubon later reported it.

One of its major strongholds was Cobb Island in Virginia, from which it had been almost extirpated by 1900. H.H. Bailey tells how this came about. "This large, showy bird fell an easy mark to the spring gunners, breeding as it did during the height of the spring migration of [the other shorebirds]... Nesting amongst the dunes back from the ocean, over which the spring gunners tramped daily, these birds were right in their line of travel and were either killed or their nests broken up."

As the oystercatcher became increasingly rare, scientific collectors moved in on the few remaining colonies and, not content with collecting eggs for their "cabinets," collected the adults as well; and to such effect that, although the bird is now rare in life, it is very well represented in the collections of "study skins" in North American museums.

Isolated pairs and even a few small colonies survive and breed from Virginia south, but except in nature preserves they are having a hard time hanging on due to the ever-increasing encroachment of modern man on their ancestral beaches. Dune buggies, hovercraft, and other recreational vehicles, together with hordes of holiday makers, have usurped most of their former breeding grounds. Thus there is little prospect of their ever again becoming more than exotic rarities on the Atlantic coast of North America.

Prior to about 1800, the lesser shorebirds ("beach birds" as they were usually called) were not heavily persecuted. Their small size did not warrant the expenditure of shot and powder as long as their larger relatives could be killed in any desired quantity. By the end of the eighteenth century, this situation was changing fast. The large waders were already becoming scarce; the human population (and therefore the market for game birds) was growing apace; and the cost of guns, shot, and shell was falling.

As the new century got under way, still another element was added to the hell's brew that was about to engulf the beach birds. North Americans were growing increasingly wealthy; and wealth produces both the leisure and the means to indulge in sport. For many if not most Americans raised in the tradition of guns and gunning, sport translated into the killing of animals.

So began the "recreational" bloodletting that continues into our day; but it was applied to the beach birds in the nineteenth century on a scale never seen before, and which can never again be equalled simply because most of the targets have been blown away.

A settler at Cape Cod in the seventeenth century would, twice a year, have seen the phenomenon of the beach birds in its full magnitude. Beginning in early April, the sands of the Cape's seemingly endless beaches would begin to disappear under a feathered carpet growing and spreading in kaleidoscopic patterns with each passing day. Overhead, the pale skies would have been threaded, skeined, then shadowed by newly arriving flocks forming such enormous masses that one of the early Nantucket colonists described them as being like smoke rising from forest fires burning from horizon to horizon.

The beach birds were coming north, and they would continue to sweep the sands with an unbroken storm of wings for a month or more. Even in summer the beaches remained under the sway of those several species that stayed to nest. By comparison with those that had passed through, these stay-behinds were the few. Yet they were numerous enough to provide a staple supply of eggs and meat to human residents along the shores of Massachusetts Bay for generation after generation.

And in the autumn! Beginning in mid-August, the visitation would repeat itself, this time swollen by the addition of young-of-the-year and of adults of several species that did not pass that way in spring. As late as 1780, it was said that on a September day when the wind was easterly the sound of wings and the blended voices of those drifting millions could drown out the beat of the breaking seas themselves.

The enormity of this visitation was not confined to Cape Cod. Sandbars in the St. Lawrence River at Tadoussac are not now and never have been an important stop for beach birds. Nevertheless, the migrant flights were mightily impressive when Samuel de Champlain saw them there in the early 1600s.

"Here are such great numbers of plovers, curlews, snipes, woodcock and other kinds that there have been days when three or four sportsmen would kill more than three hundred dozen, all very fat and delicate to eat...I and a few others passed the time...in hunting...principally of snipes, plovers, curlews and sandpipers, of which more than twenty thousand were killed." To which the Jesuit, Father Sagard, added, "One kills a great number by a single harquebus shot; for when it is fired at the level of the ground the sand kills more than the powder and shot; this is vouched for by a man who with a single shot killed three hundred and more."

The feathered cape woven by the beach birds rippled over *all* the beaches of eastern North America until the European invaders tore it to bloody shreds. What follows is a mere synoptic record, restricted to only a few of the species involved in one of the great atrocities of our times. Much is quoted directly from Dr. Bent's monumental record, *Life Histories of North American Shorebirds*.

We begin with the starling-size red-backed sandpiper (now called dunlin), an Arctic nesting species which, like so many shorebirds, winters in South America.

"These birds, in conjunction with several others sometimes collect in such flocks as to seem, at a distance, a large cloud of thick smoke...it forms a very grand and interesting appearance. At such times, the gunners make prodigious slaughter among them; while, as the showers of their companions fall, the whole body [of the flocks] often alight, or descend to the surface with them, till the sportsman is completely satiated with destruction.

"During their aerial excursions, while whirling about, they crowd so close together that many are killed at a single shot...Mr. Brasher informed me that he killed 52 by discharging both barrels...and I have known one instance where an officer of the Army bagged 96 birds from one discharge.

"In former years extensive flights took place [on the south shore of Lake Erie] upon which bushels of them are said to have fallen to a single gun... ...On October 29, 1897, I killed 53 of these birds out of two flocks...and this is the nearest approach to a flight that has occurred of late years."

Most sportsmen refused to believe that the disappearance of the beach birds had anything to do with shooting them. In typical fashion, Toronto sportsmen explained the disappearance of the former enormous flocks as a result of their having "been scared away by the greater numbers of railroad engines."

The knot, called beach robin or red-breast by hunters, was a very abundant migrant all along the Atlantic coast of North America during the nineteenth century. Before 1850, wrote George Mackay, "at Chatham, Nauset, Wellfleet, Cape Cod...Tuckernuck, Muskeget Islands they would collect in exceedingly large numbers, estimates of which were useless. Often when riding on the stage coach on Cape Cod, immense numbers of these birds could be seen as they rose up in clouds. It was at this time that the vicious practice of 'fire-lighting' then prevailed and a very great number were thus killed on the flats at night...The procedure was for two men to start after dark at half tide, one carrying a lighted lantern [to dazzle them], the other to seize the birds, bite their necks, and put them in a bag...they approached the birds on their hands and knees...I have it from an excellent authority that he has seen, in the spring, six barrels of these birds taken in this manner, at one time on the deck of the Cape Cod packet for Boston. He has also seen barrels of them which had spoiled during the voyage, thrown overboard in Boston harbour. The price of the birds at that time was 10 cents per dozen. Mixed with them were turnstones and plover. Not one of these birds had been shot, all having been taken by 'fire-light'."

The dowitcher, a snipe-like bird called brown-back by market hunters and the sporting fraternity, was equally persecuted, as described by Dr. Bent: "Immense numbers were shot in the past...They are the least shy of shore-birds...easily decoyed...and keep close together. They alight in a compact bunch and many are killed by a first discharge, and those that remain fly a short distance away when hearing what they think to be the call of a deserted comrade [a decoy call] they wheel about and come skimming bravely back to the murderous spot...again and again they are shot at...the remainder loath to leave their dead and dying companions [until only] one or two may escape.

"They have decreased very fast...and we now see them [only] singly or in bunches not exceeding 10 or 12."

Wilson's snipe, or jack snipe, is one of the few shorebirds still listed as a "game bird" and so it can be legally shot: "Exceedingly abundant [in the latter half of the 1800s] as the oft-quoted achievement of James A. Pringle will illustrate. He was not a market hunter but a gentleman sportsman who shot for the fun of it and gave the birds away to his friends. His excuses for excessive slaughter and his apologies for not killing more are interesting; he writes: *The birds being only in the country for a short time I had no mercy on them and killed all I could, for a snipe once missed might never be seen again.* Between 1867 and 1887 he shot, on his favourite hunting grounds in Louisiana, 69,087 snipe but his scores fell off during the next ten years for he increased his grand total of snipe only to 78,602. His best day, undoubtedly a world record, was December 11, 1877 when he shot in six hours 366 snipe."

The lesser yellowlegs is a rather small, long-legged wader that Dr. Bent felt should not "be in the gamebird class, though I must confess it has some gamey qualities. It is, at times, absurdly tame; it decoys very easily, returns again and again to the slaughter and its little body is so small that many lives must be sacrificed to make a decent bag. However it is interesting sport to sit in a well-made blind on a marsh, with decoys skilfully arranged, and show one's skill in whistling up these lively and responsive little birds. After all, [sport] gunning is not so much a means of filling up the larder as an excuse for getting out to enjoy the beauties of nature and the ways of its wild creatures." He adds that one noted sportsman "killed 106 yellow-shanks by discharging both barrels of his gun into a flock while they were sitting along the beach."

The destruction of the yellowlegs did not take place in the North alone. As late as 1925, Stuart Danforth observed them migrating through Puerto Rico, where they were "surprisingly tame, and it is slaughter, not sport to shoot them...hunters kill as many as twenty with one shot." And Dr. Alexander Wetmore, visiting Argentina in 1926, noted "migrant flocks, many of whose members offered sad evidence of inhospitable treatment at the hands of Argentine gunners, in the shape of broken or missing legs."

The yellowlegs will serve as well as any other shorebird to underline the singularly unpleasant fact that mass shooting "into the flock" of any of the beach birds could result in crippling as many birds as were killed or fatally wounded. The majority of the flying wounded were fated to die within a matter of days, though some would linger on. Even a single pellet lodged in muscle tissue would sooner or later kill its host from lead poisoning.

The greater yellowlegs is a larger cousin of the lesser but, according to Dr. Bent, a more legitimate target: "The greater yellow-legs is a fine game bird. Large numbers have been shot in past years...a hunter near Newport, Rhode Island, shot 1,362 in eight seasons...Dr. Townsend reports that 463 greater yellow-legs were sent from Newburyport to a single stall in Boston market on one day. I know an old gunner who celebrated his eightieth birthday a few years ago by shooting 40 yellow-legs.

"It is a pity that the delightful days of bay-bird shooting which were such a pleasant feature of our earlier shooting days, had to be restricted. Those were glorious days we used to spend on Cape Cod...in the good old days when there were shorebirds to shoot, and we were allowed to shoot them, blinds were scattered all along the marshes and flats...wooden or tin decoys painted to imitate yellow-legs or plover were set up in the sand or mud within easy range. Here in a comfortable blind the hunter could lounge at ease, bask in the genial sun of early autumn, smoke his pipe and meditate, or watch the many interesting things about him...Suddenly he is wakened from his reveries by the note of the winter yellow-legs...he whistles an imitation of its note; the bird answers, and, looking for companionship circles nearer...scales down to the decoys, where it meets its fate. Perhaps a whole flock may slip in...There is an ever changing panorama of bird life in the marshes, full of surprises and delights for the nature lover."

One of those "surprises and delights" was the group of beach birds collectively known as peeps because of the chick-like call notes of their foraging flocks. Peeps include all the "small fry"—such species as least, semipalmated, and white-rumped sandpipers, semipalmated and piping plovers, and the sanderling—most of which tend to associate with one another, forming flocks that were formerly of such magnitude, according to an early nineteenth-century observer, that "One hardly dares to estimate their numbers for fear of being taken for a mere prevaricator."

Their flocks were huge, but individually the peeps were insignificant in size, weighing only an ounce or two. One might have expected such inconsequential little puffs of feathers to escape the massacre visited on their larger relatives, but as the bigger beach birds were progressively destroyed the guns of sportsmen, pot, and market hunters alike turned equally savagely upon the peeps.

"In the absence of larger birds, the gunners used to shoot these tiny birds in large numbers, and it must be admitted they were delicious eating. At his blind [the hunter] would call down with his tin whistle any passing flock. A projecting spit of mud...afforded a convenient alighting place for the Peeps, and was their death trap, for here they could be raked with gunfire. The terrified and bewildered survivors spring into the air and, circling over their dead and dying companions, afford several more effective shots which shower the victims down into the mud and water. Only a remnant of the flock escapes.

"The fact that so many of these birds could be easily killed with one shot and they were so fat and palatable, broiled or cooked in a pie, made them much sought after by the pot hunter. As large shore birds grew scarcer and it became more and more difficult for the gunner to fill his bag, 'Peep' shooting, even by sportsmen, was in vogue...

"To bring down a score of birds from a close-packed flock required but little skill...I have gone out to shoot these birds for the table and with five discharges I secured on one occasion 82 birds."

The surprises and delights must have seemed endless in those days; but perhaps none surpassed those offered by the resplendent golden plover. This pigeon-sized bird, close companion and almost alter ego to the Eskimo curlew, came within a feather of sharing the curlew's fate. In Dr. Bent's words, its story "furnished a striking picture of the ruthless slaughter that has squandered our previous wealth of wild life."

The golden plover's original abundance, like that of the Eskimo curlew, was almost inconceivable. And so was the slaughter. Audubon described a typical massacre that took place near New Orleans in the spring of 1821: "The gunners had assembled in parties of from 20 to 50 at places where they knew from experience that the plovers would pass...When a flock approached, every individual stationed at nearly equal distances from each other whistled in imitation of the plover's call note, on which the birds descended, wheeled and ran the gauntlet, as it were. Every gun went off in succession, and with such effect that I several times saw a flock of a hundred or more reduced to a miserable remnant of five or six...This sport was continued all day and at sunset when I left one of these lines of gunners they were as intent on killing more as they were when I arrived [before dawn]. A man near where I was seated had killed 63 dozens. I calculated the number [of hunters] in the field at 200, and supposing each to have shot only 20 dozens, 48,000 golden plovers would have fallen there that day."

Edward Forbush described what it was like at Nantucket where, in the 1840s, "Two men killed enough to fill a tip-car two-thirds full [about 1,000 birds] in one day." Twenty years later, in August of 1863, "Golden plover and Eskimo curlew landed on the island in such numbers as to darken the sun. Between seven and eight thousand were killed." By 1890, golden plover had been so depleted in the East as to be of only negligible interest, but in that year, two Boston wholesalers of wild game received from the West forty barrels closely packed with curlews and plover—mostly plover.

Robert Roosevelt wrote of the flocks he hunted on Long Island in the 1860s: "Before us several acres were literally covered with the ranks of the much-desired, the matchless golden plover...not less than 3,000 closely packed...They rise with 'a sounding roar' to which the united reports of our four barrels savagely respond, and we hasten to secure our spoils."

Famed naturalist W.H. Hudson knew the golden plover in Argentina (where it was called chorlo) during the latter part of the nineteenth century. "After its arrival in September, the plains in the neighbourhood of my home were peopled with immense flocks of this bird...there was a marshy ground [nearby, to which] the golden plover would resort every day at noon. They would appear in flocks from all quarters, flying like starlings in England coming to some great roosting centre. I would then mount my pony and gallop off joyfully to witness the spectacle. Long before coming in sight of them the noise of their voices would be audible. Coming to the marshy grounds I would pull up my horse and sit gazing with astonishment and delight at that immense multitude of birds...looking less like a vast flock than a floor of birds, in colour a rich, deep brown...a living, moving floor and a sounding one as well...it was like the sea [or] more like the wind on, let us say, thousands of tight-drawn wires...vibrating them to shrill sound...but it is indescribable, and unimaginable...[however] as population increases on the pampas these stupendous gatherings are becoming more and more rare. [In my boyhood] it was an exceptional thing for a man to possess a gun and if Chorlos were wanted a gaucho boy with a string a yard long with a ball of lead attached to each end could knock down as many as he liked."

Hudson saw the golden bird in its golden age. However, by the last decades of that century, its destruction by Argentine gunners was second only to the butchery it was subjected to on the Great Plains of North America during its spring migration to the Arctic. By 1910, some American ornithologists were beginning to harbour the suspicion that the plover was in danger of extinction. Luckily that fate was averted when, in 1916, the spring hunt for shorebirds was prohibited in the United States and Canada and, still later, most were given full protection throughout the year.

Golden plover, peeps, and other beach birds survive. Of the smaller shorebirds, only one, the piping plover, once a common breeding species all along the eastern seaboard from the Gulf of St. Lawrence to Virginia, seems in immediate danger. Although reduced to a tiny remnant population during the days of uncontrolled hunting, it was making a successful comeback until, in recent years, man so encroached upon the beaches where it breeds that it is now officially listed as a threatened species. At most, no more than 300 pairs can still be found in Atlantic Canada.

We may take some encouragement from the survival of the other species but, considering the nature of the beast that lurks within our own, it should be qualified by an ever-present awareness that the carnage committed on the shorebirds in the recent past can all too readily break out again directed at some other form of animate creation.

5

And Other Birds of Air

When Europeans arrived on the northeastern seaboard they encountered an infinity of ducks, geese, and swans amongst myriad other birds. Nicolas Denys gives some idea of their profusion in the 1620s. "All my people are so surfeited with game...they wish no more, whether Wild Geese, Ducks, Teal, Plover, Snipe...[even] our dogs lie beside this meat [without touching it] so much are they satiated with it...So great an abundance of Wild Geese, Ducks and Brant is seen that it is not believable, and they all make so great a noise at night that one has trouble to sleep."

Two kinds of swans were amongst the multitudes. The trumpeter bred across the continent, perhaps as far south as Nova Scotia and east to Newfoundland. Today it is no longer to be seen east of Manitoba and its entire existing population has been reduced to about 2,000 pairs, mostly concealed in remote lake valleys in Alaska and British Columbia. The smaller, whistling swan once migrated along the Atlantic coasts in enormous flocks, but now is seldom if ever seen on the eastern seaboard.

The swans were slaughtered not for meat alone, but especially for their densely feathered breasts, known and much valued in the millinery and clothing trades as "swan skin." There are records of over a thousand whistling swans being butchered on a single occasion, stripped of their breast skin and feathers, and left to rot.

Canada, snow, and brant geese abounded along the northeastern coasts, especially in migration. The snow goose is now never seen there; the brant is fast vanishing due partly to a mysterious die-off of eel grass, which is its main winter food, perhaps a result of our pollution of the sea. Old Honker, the Canada goose, still remains in evidence, but in sadly diminished numbers.

Some two dozen kinds of ducks originally lived in or migrated through the northeastern region and, as all early records attest, were found in astounding numbers. They were so abundant initially that most species remained relatively numerous until the beginning of the nineteenth century. Thereafter they were subjected to such prodigious carnage at the hands of market and sport hunters that many species were devastated to the point of near annihilation; and one was exterminated.

Sportsmen and commercial hunters alike shot them over live decoys, frequently from hunting boxes sunk in marshes or floating at surface level. In the 1800s, one such typical "hide" built by a market hunter yielded forty-four brant to a single shot and between 1,000 and 1,500 during one winter.

Batteries of 8-gauge shotguns were mounted in shoreside "blinds," and smooth-bore guns with a calibre not much less than that of a small cannon were carried on swivels in low-slung punts that could be concealed in reeds and rushes. Some of these punt guns fired a quarter-pound powder charge and could kill or wound hundreds of swimming waterfowl with a single discharge.

Dr. Bent describes a favourite method used by New England sportsmen, the "duck stand": "This consists of a small house or shanty equipped with sleeping bunks for several men...Along the shore is built a fence or stockade...there are portholes cut in the fence so that several men can shoot through it without being seen. The house and the fence are completely covered with branches of freshly cut pine and oak...which renders the whole structure practically invisible...The stand is built where there is a beach or a point in front of it...Sets of wooden decoys...are anchored at some distance out...A large supply of live decoys, semidomesticated black ducks, mallards and Canada geese, are kept in pens...behind the enclosure, and a few are tethered on the beach...or allowed to roam about...With all this elaborate equipment ready for action the gunners, I can hardly call them sportsmen, spend their time inside the house, smoking, talking, playing cards, or perhaps drinking, while one man remains outside on the watch...Should a flock... alight in the pond, he calls the others and they all take their places at the portholes, with heavy guns, ready for the slaughter. The quacking of the decoys gradually tolls the wild birds in toward the beach...Each gunner knows which section of the flock he is to shoot at and waits in anticipation until the birds are near enough and properly bunched, when the signal is given to fire. If the affair has been well managed most of the flock have been killed or disabled on the water, but, as the frightened survivors rise in hurried confusion, a second volley is poured into them and only a few escape."

Dr. Bent's description of what happened to the wood duck is representative of the fate of many of its inland dwelling relatives: "The wood duck has always been able to hold its own against its natural enemies, but it has yielded to the causes of destruction brought about by the hand of man and by the encroachments of civilization. The wholesale cutting down of forests and draining of swampy woodlands has destroyed its nesting sites and made its favorite haunts untenable. Its beautiful plumage has always made it an attractive mark for gunners, collectors, and taxidermists, and its feathers have been in demand for making artificial trout flies. Almost anyone who has found a wood duck's nest has been tempted to take the eggs home to hatch them, as the ducks are easily domesticated and make attractive pets. It is so tame and unsuspicious that it is easily shot in large numbers and it has been extensively caught in traps. From the great abundance, noted by all the earlier writers, its numbers have been reduced to a small fraction of what they were; in many places, where it was once abundant, it is now unknown or very rare; and it has everywhere been verging towards extinction. Fortunately our attention was called to these facts...before it was too late, and now that suitable laws have been enacted for its protection...it has been saved from extinction."

Even the smallest of eastern seaboard ducks, the diminutive teal, received no quarter, as Audubon tells us: "Nothing can be more pleasing to an American sportsman than the arrival of this beautiful little duck...He sees advancing from afar...a flock of green-winged teals...Hark! two shots in rapid succession! Here and there lies a teal, with its legs quivering; there, one is whirling round in the agonies of death; some, which are only winged, quickly and in silence make their way toward a hiding place, while one, with a single pellet in his head, rises perpendicularly with uncertain beats, and falls with a splash on the water. The gunner has charged his tubes...and the frightened teals have dressed their ranks, and flying, now high, now low, seem curious to see the place where their companions have been left. Again they fly over the dangerous spot, and again receive the double shower of shot. Were it not that darkness has now set in, the carnage might continue until the sportsmen should no longer consider the thinned flock worthy of his notice. In this manner...I have seen upwards of six dozen shot by a single gunner in the course of one day."

Nineteenth- and early twentieth-century sport hunting amounted to nothing less than unbridled massacre. During one autumnal weekend in 1884, my own paternal grandfather and three companions armed with double-barrelled 10-gauge shotguns, shot 140 canvasbacks, 227 redheads, about 200 scaups, 84 blacks, about five dozen teal, and enough additional assorted kinds to quite literally fill the four-wheeled farm wagon that brought them and their trophies home. I have some old sepia-toned photographs of the results of that particular foray, which was by no means unique.

Although sport hunting was bad enough, it was as nothing to the slaughter conducted by market hunters. During the 1880s, millions of wild ducks, geese, and swans were sold in public markets and private butcher shops in towns and cities of Canada and the United States, to which must be added millions more that spoiled because of lack of refrigeration or were wounded or killed but not recovered. This was big business, employing thousands of commercial hunters, wholesalers, and other middlemen. Incidentally, the manufacturers of guns, shot, and shell earned enormous profits.

At the peak of this industrial destruction it is believed that eight million waterfowl were being slaughtered annually. By the beginning of World War I, this massacre—both spring and fall—had so reduced waterfowl populations that the extirpation of a dozen or more species seemed assured. It was at this crucial juncture that Canada and the United States collaborated in framing the Migratory Birds Convention Act, which became law in 1917 and, for the first time, provided a mechanism for protecting waterfowl and many other migratory birds. After the war, prohibition of the spring hunt and the imposition of bag limits began to allow most ducks and geese to recover somewhat.

One species, the flamboyant harlequin duck, has not managed to do so, and its continuing survival remains in doubt. For the piebald Labrador duck, protection came too late. This large and strikingly patterned black-and-white bird was originally known as the pie duck. It was unique in that it was found *only* on the northeastern seaboard of America, breeding on islands in the Gulf of St. Lawrence, on the Labrador coast, and, probably, on the Newfoundland coast; wintering along the shores of New England perhaps as far south as Cape Hatteras. Closely related to the eider family, it resembled them in many of its habits and suffered in the same way from New England and Canadian eggers and feather pirates who raided the island colonies of both, stealing the eggs, then ripping up the nests and shooting females to obtain the valuable down.

Eiders initially abounded in the waters of the northeastern seaboard. Yet here is what naturalist Charles Townsend had to say about them at the beginning of the twentieth century. "If this senseless slaughter [egg hunting and the feather trade] is not stayed the eider will continue to diminish until it is extinct. On the Maine coast—the bird's most southern [existing] breeding station—there were less than a dozen pair breeding in 1905...Farther north...on the Nova Scotia coast not more than two or three [pairs] remain to breed, while on the coast of Newfoundland and of the Labrador Peninsula...where they formerly bred in immense numbers, but a remnant is left...Before the arrival of the white man—nature's worst enemy—the Indian, the Esquimaux, the fox and the polar bear helped themselves from the abundant feast...Little or no harm was done...this natural pruning had little effect upon the birds as a whole. During the nineteenth century, however, the drain on those wonderful nurseries of bird-life was fearful and now but a pittance of the mighty host remains."

Robbed of their eggs, their nesting colonies ravaged to provide down, shot on the breeding islands *and* in both spring and fall migration by commercial and sport hunters along the southward coasts, the western Atlantic population of eiders and pie ducks both seemed doomed.

Fortunately for the eider it had sister populations in the Canadian Arctic, Greenland, and the northeastern Atlantic, from which, after the Migratory Birds Convention Act came into force, colonists began repopulating the North American seaboard. Unfortunately for the pie duck, it had no sister population anywhere in the world.

The last Labrador duck reported from the United States was shot in New York in 1875, and there are no later records in the scientific literature. There are some residents' reports of it having been seen on the Labrador in the 1880s; but after that—nothing. Today all that remains of the pie duck are some forty-four stuffed skins scattered in museums and private collections, mostly in the United States.

Commercial egging and the feather trade are now things of the past, but the future of the surviving sea ducks is clouded by the same threats that hang over all seabirds: loss of breeding sites, reduction of available food, pollution poisoning, illegal egging, and unregulated hunting in remote regions such as the Arctic and parts of South America.

There is also the annual legal slaughter. In 1982 the bag by sportsmen in Newfoundland, Nova Scotia, New Brunswick, and Quebec alone included 800,000 ducks and 100,000 geese. To this we must add an additional 20 to 30 per cent to cover the death of wounded birds and of those that died of poisoning after ingesting spent lead shot picked up from the bottoms of ponds, lakes, and swamps.

As late as the mid-nineteenth century at least one pair of loons nested on almost every lake and moderate-sized pond throughout the whole of the northeastern portion of the continent, from as far south as Kentucky and Virginia north to and including the High Arctic. The several species of great divers made their presence felt not only by their size and splendour, but especially through their voices, which conveyed the very essence of wilderness.

In autumn, the adults led their young out to sea where their aggregate numbers became apparent as they gathered to spend the winter along the coasts from Newfoundland to Florida. There they came to grief. During the latter half of the nineteenth century, when gunning became not just a sport but a fanatical passion, loons were popular as flying targets, even though they were generally considered to be inedible. So quick in diving that they were believed to be able to submerge between the flash of a gun being fired and the arrival of the shot; so strong and swift in flight that they were seen as an irresistible challenge to the skill of every gunner; and so imbued with life that only the heaviest charge could kill them outright, they were the sportsman's target *par excellence*. If a rationale was required to legitimize their slaughter, it could be said—and was, quite wrongly—that, as fish eaters, they were a menace to salmon fry and trout and ought to be exterminated. The gunners did their best; and so did sport fishermen, who made a practice of searching out the nests and smashing the eggs therein.

Surviving common loons today represent only a small fraction of those that, 100 years ago, filled the summer evenings with their haunting cries. Innumerable lakes and ponds know them no more, and each passing year sees fewer of them. During the past two winters, thousands have been found dead on Atlantic beaches, victims of poisoning by chlorinated hydrocarbons, heavy metals, and other toxins picked up in plankton eaten by small fish and concentrated in the loons' tissues until the dose proved lethal. There is reason to fear that the cry of the loon may soon become as rare as the cry of the wolf over the greater portion of this continent.

Some of the most spectacular of all birds were the large, long-legged egrets, ibises, and herons, many of which were cursed with striking plumage that made them irresistible to sport and trophy gunners and for industrial exploitation by the infamous bird-plume trade. They were slaughtered in uncounted millions for the adornment of women's hats and other such fashionable purposes during the nineteenth and early twentieth centuries. Although most species lived to the southward of the region with which we are concerned, several kinds were once found on the northeastern seaboard.

The magnificent heron-like white ibis, clad in snowy plumage except for black wing tips and brilliant red legs and bill, has not been known to breed north of the Carolinas in recent times. Early references, however, suggest this was not always so. In 1536, Hore's expedition to southern Newfoundland and Cape Breton "saw also certaine great foules with red bills and red legs, somewhat bigger than herons," which could only have been this species. And in the account of the voyage of the *Marigold* to Cape Breton in 1593, we are told that "as they viewed the countrey they saw... great foule with red legs." An indubitable white ibis was killed in Nova Scotia as late as 1959. It was listed as "accidental."

The showy roseate spoonbill, which is not even mentioned in the scientific literature as ever having been found in Canada, is another of the big waders that was at least a visitor to the Gulf of St. Lawrence region in early times. Nicolas Denys described and correctly named it in the mid-1600s as "the *Palonne* [Spoonbill] which has the beak about a foot long and round at the end like an oven shovel."

The statuesque great blue heron is still one of the most highly visible birds of the eastern seaboard, yet what we see today is no more than a shadow of its past abundance. Until well into the nineteenth century its tree-top colonies, often containing hundreds of nests, were to be found beside most rivers and lakes, and on many sea-girt islands, from the Gulf of St. Lawrence southward. As late as the 1870s it was not unusual to find congregations of herons numbering in the thousands gathered in stately phalanxes on the mud flats of the Bay of Fundy. Tidal marshes and wetlands everywhere along the coasts of New England abounded with the birds, both in migration and as breeding residents.

They appear not to have been seriously molested until after mid-century, when sport fishing developed its enormous vogue. As sportsmen depleted available stocks of game fishes, the fraternity reacted as they have always done, by savaging those animals that could be thought of as competitors. Because the great blue heron ate small fishes (though almost exclusively of non-game species) and because it was so visible, a merciless campaign was mounted against it. Sport hunters assisted their fishermen compeers by shooting it whenever they had a chance. Breeding colonies were regularly ravaged and eggs, young, and adults massacred. On one occasion, a well-forested island in Penobscot Bay was put to the torch simply to destroy a heron rookery. Although now officially forbidden, harassment of the remaining colonies continues.

Two species of cranes once migrated through and probably bred on the northeastern seaboard. The largest, the whooping crane, may well have been the most remarkable bird in North America. Standing nearly five feet high, it was a long-legged, long-necked, pure white creature, except for black wing tips and a crimson-coloured face. It is famous today because of the attention that last-ditch efforts to save it from extinction have evoked.

That the whooper and the smaller sandhill crane were common in the northeastern region is confirmed by many references dating back to the mid-1500s. Both species were still abundant enough to constitute important staples in sixteenth- and seventeenth-century table fare. Even as late as the early 1700s, Charlevoix could remark: "We have two cranes of two colours; some quite white, and others of a light grey. They all make excellent soup."

Such huge and prepossessing birds could not hope to escape the rapacity of European man. Sport and market hunters slaughtered them mercilessly.

By the mid-1800s, the whooping crane was gone and the sandhill reduced to extreme rarity in the eastern portion of the continent.

After thirty years of dedicated effort, conservationists in the U.S. and Canada have been able to nurse the whooping crane back from a population of only thirty-one in 1955 to perhaps three times that number in 1984. These survivors mostly breed on the trackless muskegs of Wood Buffalo National Park in northwestern Canada and winter on the Aransas Refuge in Texas. Despite the care and protection given them, the long-term survival of the species remains in jeopardy.

Birds that could be exploited for food, fun, profit, or all three were as abundant on dry land as in the marshes and over the seas. The best-known example of a land bird of apparently limitless profusion was the passenger pigeon, about which so much has been written that I need add little more. However, one aspect of its story has been overlooked. At first European contact the pigeons were abundant throughout the eastern seaboard region, as well as in the interior.

Cartier noted them on Prince Edward Island in 1534. In 1605, Champlain visited some islands in the Gulf of Maine, "Upon [which] grow so many red currants that one can see nothing else in most places, and there are countless numbers of pigeons, whereof we took a goodly quantity." Josselyn, in New England in the early 1600s, wrote of: "The Pidgeon, of which there are millions of millions. I have seen a flight of Pidgeons in the spring, and at Michaelmas when they return back to the Southward [stretching] for four or five miles, that to my way of thinking had neither beginning nor ending, length nor breadth, and so thick that I could see no Sun; they joyne Nest to Nest, and Tree to Tree by their Nests, many miles together in Pine-Trees. But of late they are much diminished, the English taking them with Nets. I have bought at Boston a dozen of Pidgeons, ready pull'd and garbidgd for three pence."

In 1663, James Yonge found them "innumerable" on the Avalon Peninsula of Newfoundland. Lahontan, about 1680, wrote: "We resolv'd to declare War against the Turtle-Doves, which are so numerous in Canada that the Bishop has been forc'd to excommunicate 'em oftner than once, upon the account of Damage they do to the Products of the Earth."

Terribly vulnerable on their densely colonial nesting grounds, they were shot, gassed, blown up with black powder, seared with torches, netted, clubbed, and butchered in any and every way that could suggest itself to the fertile minds of the European invaders until, by about 1780, they had been effectively exterminated from the northeast. The story of their final destruction in the mideastern United States during the nineteenth century is so revolting that I am happy not to have to repeat it. The last recorded wild specimen seems to have been shot at Penetanguishene, Ontario, in 1902. The last passenger pigeon on earth, sole survivor of the billions that had greeted European man as he began his pillage of a continent, died captive in the Cincinnati Zoological Gardens in September, 1914.

The wild turkey, ancestor of our domestic turkey, was initially abundant throughout eastern North America, at least as far north as southeastern New Brunswick. Essentially woodland birds, they could hold their own against bows and arrows but were helpless against guns. As settlement spread westward, the newcomers exterminated each successive turkey population for food, feathers, and the market. By the mid-1800s, the species was effectively extinct in northeastern North America. Attempts have been made to reintroduce it here and there, but these are usually only successful when the bird is semi-domesticated on so-called game farms and preserves.

Early Europeans encountered two kinds of game birds that were at once strange, yet vaguely familiar. One kind, in two forms, the English called "grous," referring to what we now know as ruffed grouse and spruce grouse; the other they called "heath-cocke" or "pheysant."

The heath hen, as it later came to be known, was as large as the female European or ring-necked pheasant, which it superficially resembled. It was found from Cape Breton southward at least to Virginia, wherever open heathland or savannah existed. In aboriginal days, there were great stretches of such country, particularly near the coasts. In the 1670s, these big, meaty birds, whose barely surviving western cousins are called prairie chickens, were so numerous on "the ancient, brushy site of Boston, that labouring people or servants stipulated with their employers not to have Heath Hen brought to table oftener than a few times a week." However, there was no stopping the wholesale slaughter of the birds through such mild restraints, and by the latter part of the eighteenth century they were already scarce. By 1830, the heath hen was extinct on the North American mainland, although a few hundred still survived on the island of Martha's Vineyard in Massachusetts. Despite attempts to protect them there, a disastrous grass and forest fire in 1916, coupled with steady poaching, eventually diminished the stock beyond recovery. By 1930, only a single representative of the once vast heath hen population remained alive. It attracted much attention from tourists and scientists, who came in such crowds to see it that it several times narrowly avoided being run over by cars. Sometime during the winter of 1932 it disappeared. The suspicion remains that it ended up in the "scientific" collection of some avid "naturalist."

Rock and willow ptarmigan were once enormously common in Newfoundland, Labrador, and along the north shore of the Gulf of St. Lawrence. In winter, they formed gigantic flocks that drifted across the frozen barrens and blew through the spruce forests. In 1626, a planter at Renews on Newfoundland's east coast killed 700 in one day. As late as 1863, one family living at the Strait of Belle Isle shot and snared 1,100 ptarmigan during a two-month period. In 1885, Napoleon Comeau reported a flock "over a half-a-mile long and from 60–100 yards wide, a continuous mass" on the north shore of the St. Lawrence estuary and, during that winter, the scattered residents of the district killed about 60,000. Another 30,000 were killed between Mingan and Godbout during the winter of 1895.

They were shot in stupendous quantities in Newfoundland by local and market gunners, who were reinforced by visiting sport hunters from Canada and the United States who camped along the trans-island railway line. Individual bags of 300-400 birds were not uncommon in the late 1800s.

Both species still exist in Newfoundland but are now comparatively rare, and the rock ptarmigan seems to be restricted to only a handful of localities in the western mountains of the province. Ptarmigan are probably still common in the interior of Labrador, but the great winter flocks that used to come out to the Gulf coast are no longer seen.

Birds of prey have been treated as enemies ever since European settlement began. Eagles were and by many still are regarded as "wolves of the air" and accused of killing anything from human babies to small calves. All but the smallest hawks are still generically called "chicken hawks," and every missing hen is laid to their door. Owls are believed to be inveterate killers of roosting fowl, up to and including domestic turkeys. Added to the catalogue of sins attributed to them by farmers come the even harsher accusations of sportsmen, who would eliminate all hawks and owls because of their supposed appetite for water fowl and upland game birds and, in the case of the osprey, of game fish. Shot, trapped, and poisoned as vermin, all large species of owls and hawks, and all eagles, have been devastated throughout North America, not least in the eastern Maritimes.

The magnificent golden eagle, which once bred and ranged throughout the region, has long been practically extinct in the East and is barely surviving elsewhere in North America.

Because its livelihood was gained mostly from fish carrion, which commercial fishermen produce on a grand scale, the bald eagle did better. It still inhabited the Atlantic coast in fair numbers until the end of World War II. Thereafter the great birds rapidly began to disappear. Ornithologists noted that, although nests were built and eggs laid, the eggs seldom hatched or, if they did, the young were sickly and often died. It was not until Rachel Carson's revolutionary book, *Silent Spring*, revealed the damage being done by pesticides and related poisons released into the environment by industrial man that anyone drew the right conclusion. Bald eagles were being rendered infertile by pesticides, particularly DDT. Nor were they alone. Almost every major avian predator was also suffering severely, some—such as the peregrine falcon—to the verge of extinction. In fact, the lordly peregrine now *is* extinct in eastern North America, except for a few pairs artificially raised and released in the faint hope of re-establishing a vanishing species in an environment that is constantly being flooded with new and even more virulent pesticides, herbicides, and other lethal chemicals.

The bald eagle, be it said, is making a comeback in parts of southern Newfoundland and on Cape Breton Island. In the summer of 1984, Nova Scotia presented the government of the United States with six young eagles from Cape Breton, "to help bolster the numbers of the U.S. national symbol." Today, only an estimated 1,600 pairs of bald eagles still survive in the lower forty-eight United States, out of an aboriginal population in the hundreds of thousands.

Pesticide poisoning and illegal hunting, especially by sport fishermen, almost brought an end to the fish eagle called the osprey and, in fact, have succeeded in exterminating it from about 80 per cent of its former range in eastern North America. The species is now showing signs of a resurgence, but any gains stand to be temporary if we continue to saturate the land and seas with new pollutants.

The broad-winged hawks called buteos, which used to soar everywhere over forests and clearings, have been substantially reduced. They are still being persecuted by ignorant men who will not understand that these hawks have always been the farmer's friends, depending, as they do, mainly on rodents for their daily bread. The swift-winged Cooper's hawk is now so rare as to be endangered, and the largest of North American owls, the great grey, seems to be no better off.

Some few bird species have profited by the European invasion, particularly seed-eaters that thrive in open fields and clearings but are small enough to avoid becoming targets for sportsmen's guns. However, most of the smaller species of the northeastern region whose diets consist mainly of insects have suffered appalling losses in recent years from insecticide and herbicide spraying. Many of the chemicals kill small birds on contact but, if not directly lethal, kill indirectly when the birds eat contaminated insects. Predators and carrion-eating animals in turn are poisoned when they eat the poisoned birds.

I walked through a mixed forest in south-central New Brunswick one fine spring day in 1973 and, quite literally, could find no living creature. No bees buzzed amongst the blossoms, no squirrels chattered. During several searching hours, I heard not one syllable of birdsong. Later, I learned why that forest had become a silent sepulchre. The New Brunswick forest service had subjected it to aerial spraying two days earlier to control a suspected outbreak of spruce budworm. The insecticide had killed most insects and had either killed or driven away every bird.

Such spraying is routinely conducted over huge areas of New Brunswick, Newfoundland, and Nova Scotia every year, despite the overwhelming preponderance of evidence testifying to the fact that it is destroying life on an enormous scale (including, probably, some human life) and is self-defeating in that it kills the natural enemies of the very pests it is intended to control. After thirty years of annual spraying, New Brunswick still has a severe spruce budworm problem. And few birds sing.

The record of our dealings with the birds is black indeed. But there are some shafts of light in view. During the latter half of this century more and more people have become enamoured of the living bird, in its own living world. A spring weekend on the Atlantic seaboard now brings many thousands of men, women, and children to the woods, the marshes, and the shores—not to kill, but to watch with wonder and delight the urgent ebb and flow of the migrating flocks.

Belatedly we seem to be learning to like these creatures for themselves, not for their feathers or their flesh. Perhaps we are beginning to narrow the abyss our recent forebears opened between our species and the avian kind. If so, perhaps there are grounds for hope that we may be able to find our way back into that lost world, where all life was one.

PART II

Meat, Hides, and Fur

Birds take to the air to escape from man. Fish retreat to the depths of ocean. Terrestrial mammals have no such avenues of escape from one of their own number who has become the most ruthless and intractable destroyer of all time. Therefore, it is no surprise to find that the roster of the vanished and the vanishing should contain so many mammalian species.

They have suffered so heavily as to prompt a contemporary biologist to write, "No large mammal species has survived in the eastern part of North America without man's help." Rephrased to avoid the circuitous thinking that encourages us to evade recognition of the consequences of our actions, this translates as: Every large mammalian species in the eastern part of America has been destroyed by modern man—except those he has chosen to protect for his own selfish purposes. These, as we shall see, are few enough.

Nor have our depredations been limited to the bigger beasts. Large or small, all suffered crushing devastation if any profit was to be gained thereby; or if they seemed to pose even the threat of competition with our rapacious appetites. Meat, hides, and fur were the initial rewards attendant on the slaughter of most of the animals whose stories follow. Today a new motivation overrides those older ones: the slaughter keeps its bloody pace, largely in the name of recreation for mankind.

6
White Ghost

As a neophyte naturalist of fourteen years of age it was my good luck to go on a field trip to the northern Manitoba coast of Hudson Bay with my great-uncle, Frank Farley, who was a noted ornithologist. In those days, ornithologists spent most of their time amassing collections of specimens, and Uncle Frank was no exception. His collection of birds' eggs was famous and, as his acolyte, I was expected to add to it.

Early one June morning he sent me off to reconnoitre the Bay shore in search of hawk nesting sites. These proved few and far between, and it was not until mid-afternoon that I came to a massive snout of rock that seemed superbly suited to a hawk's aerie. Sure enough, in a cleft some fifty feet above the beach was the uncouth stick-and-seaweed construction of a pair of rough-legged hawks. While the great birds wheeled disconsolately over-head I stole their eggs, wrapped them in cotton wool, and stowed them in my haversack. That done, I looked around.

Below me the icy waters sucked and seethed, but to the eastward a rust-red object emerged from the grey sea. My field glasses revealed the shattered remnant of a stranded ship. Hawks and eggs were instantly forgotten, for few things will fire a boy's imagination so hotly as a wreck. This one consisted of the forward half of a small coastal freighter. I climbed through a maze of twisted plates until I was standing high on the angled rise of the bow. Then I discovered I was not alone.

No more than a hundred yards away, three ivory-white bears were ambling toward me. The leader of the trio seemed unbelievably huge though its followers were not much bigger than a pair of spaniels. It did not need a naturalist to realize that here was a female and her cubs. Comprehension terrified me. "Always stay clear of a sow bear with cubs!" was a maxim that had been dinned into me by all the trappers and backwoodsmen I had ever met. Though they had been referring to the relatively small black bear of the northern forests, I felt the warning must apply in spades to the monstrous apparition padding toward me with such fluid ease.

I thought of fleeing, but to move would have been to reveal myself and I had no stomach for a race. The light breeze was in my favour and so I had some hopes the trio would pass by without ever realizing I was crouching in abject fear in the eyes of a dead ship.

They were within ten yards of the wreck when, for no apparent reason, the female stopped abruptly, reared back on her ample haunches, and extended her forelegs for balance so that her immense paws hung down before her, revealing their long, curved claws. Perhaps I moved. She looked up and for a moment our glances locked. Her black nose wrinkled. She sniffed explosively, then, with a lithesomeness that was astonishing in so huge a beast, she slewed around on her haunches and was off at a gallop in the direction she had come, closely followed by the pair of awkward, bouncing cubs.

My own departure was almost equally swift. I retreated so precipitately that the eggs in my pack had become an omelet by the time I reported back to Uncle Frank. He was annoyed about the eggs and incredulous about my reported encounter. However, when I prevailed upon him to return with me to the wreck (armed this time), footprints on the beach the size of dinner plates convinced him of the truth of my story. He had never, so he told me, heard of a polar bear accompanied by cubs being seen so far to the south, and he intended to report the occurrence to some esoteric scientific journal.

For him, my encounter was only an unusual record. For me, it was the forever memorable first meeting with one of the most magnificent, least understood, and most persecuted animals on earth.

At a weight of 1,200 pounds or more and a length of up to eleven feet, the white bear is one of the largest terrestrial carnivores extant. It is unmatched in agility and strength. Ernest Thompson Seton describes one capturing a 100-pound seal in the water, then leaping up onto the edge of an ice floe "with his prey in his teeth, like a Mink landing a trout." It has been seen to kill a beluga, weighing about two tons, in the whale's own element, then drag the carcass above tide line.

A long-lived animal, it can attain an age of forty years. It is equally at home on solid land or floating ice where its flowing, loose-limbed gait can carry it along at thirty miles an hour. It can leap ten-foot crevasses and scale nearly sheer cliff faces and ice pinnacles. Its performance is equally astounding in the water. Layered with fat that not only provides it with insulation and flotation but can also sustain it for weeks during a time of food shortage, it is equipped with a thick coat of water-repellent hair enabling it to withstand prolonged immersion in icy seas that would kill other members of the bear family. Its enormous paddle paws, up to a foot in diameter, can propel its sleekly streamlined body through the water at six knots. Ships have encountered white bears swimming strongly 300 miles from the nearest land and showing no signs of distress.

Most of us are familiar with the creature through that hoary media cliché, the photograph of a white bear lolling disconsolately in the concrete pool of a city zoo during a heat wave. That image is perhaps intended to ease the discomfort of sweating humanity by suggesting that what we endure is as nothing compared to the misery of an animal that is only comfortable in perpetually frozen realms of ice and snow. For this, as the caption tells us, is the *polar* bear.

The name is an historic misnomer, adopted as recently as the 1800s. Prior to that, the animal was almost universally known as the white bear.[1] First-century Romans were familiar with it by that name, which was used in simple contradistinction to the brown bear found throughout Eurasia. From well before the Christian era, captive white bears ranked amongst the proudest possessions of kings and tribal chieftains. In mediaeval times, even Christian bishops kept them in their elegant palaces. Indeed, white bears seem to have been revered as touchstones of superhuman power throughout the north temperate zone of Eurasia since time immemorial. According to Imperial Japanese records dating to A.D. 658, they were kept at court both in Japan and Manchuria where they were venerated as agents of the supernatural. Lesser luminaries would settle for a pelt, for teeth, or even for one of the great, curved claws. All three were believed to be talismans of extraordinary worth.

Where did these captive white bears come from? Certainly not from the polar regions to which the species is now restricted, for this was *terra incognita* in those distant times. All the evidence suggests that the European ones were trapped as youngsters along the Norwegian coast as far south as Bergen, or on the shores of the Gulf of Bothnia in the Baltic Sea. Eastern bears seem to have come from Japan's (now Russia's) Kuril Islands, where a remnant wild population survived until as late as the 1690s. The Norwegian and Baltic bear clans were not so lucky. Both had been exterminated before the tenth century began. Thereafter, captive animals and pelts came first from Iceland and later from Greenland. In 1253, King Henry III had a live white bear from Greenland in the Tower of London and considered it one of his greatest treasures.

---

[1] Some maritime peoples also called it sea bear or water bear. When science first recognized its existence, in 1774, the Latin tag chosen for it was *Ursus maritimus*, not *Ursus polaris*.

It is clear that, in times past, the white bear was not restricted to polar regions either in Europe or in Asia. Nor was it in America. In fact, the animal most often singled out for notice by early voyagers to the northeastern coasts of the New World was the white bear. As the historic record clearly shows, this was not due to its novelty but to the fact that it was one of the commonest large mammals to be seen.

The sagas of Norse adventurers who sailed the Labrador and Newfoundland coasts around A.D. 1000 all mention the white bear, and only that species. Thorfinn Karlsefni even named an island off southeastern Labrador in honour of it.

Although almost everything else relevant to John Cabot's 1497 voyage has been lost, a map from that period showing Cabot's *Prima Terra Vista* still exists. It carries this legend: "[Here] *there are many white bears.*" Another reference comes from the results of a later voyage by Cabot's son, Sebastian. "He [Sebastian] says there are great numbers of bears there, which eat codfishes...the bears plunge into the midst of a shoal of these codfishes and... draw them to shore...this is thought to be the reason why such large numbers of bears do not trouble the people of the country [because they had so much fish to eat]."

Many discoveries made by early Portuguese explorers are also preserved only on ancient charts. Such a one is the so-called Munich-Portuguese map that bears the following legend inscribed to the westward of Newfoundland: *"This land Gaspar Corte Real...first discovered* [in 1501] *and brought home men of the woods and white bears."*

The earliest account of encounters with white bears is in Jacques Cartier's voyage of 1534. A white bear was found on Funk Island, where it had presumably been living the life of Riley on a diet of great auks. The following day, Cartier's ship overtook a white bear swimming in the open sea and his men killed it. While reconnoitring the Gulf of St. Lawrence a short time later, Cartier found bears on Brion Island in the isolated Magdalen archipelago. These, too, were almost certainly of the white kind, enjoying the abundance of seals, walrus, and seabirds then inhabiting the Magdalens.

Two years after Cartier's first voyage, the English expedition of Master Hore was wrecked in a fiord on the south coast of Newfoundland. Richard Hakluyt, who interviewed some of the survivors, tells us that they saw "Stores of bears, both black and white, of whom they killed some and took them for no bad food." It is notable that this is the first mention in the early annals of black bears, which, being forest animals, were only occasionally to be encountered on the coasts. Hore's people, however, seem to have penetrated rather deeply into the country, up a fiord that may well have been the one that to this day is called White Bear Bay.

Its name is by no means unique. At least twenty White Bear Bays, Lakes, Rivers, Coves, and Islands still dot the map of Newfoundland. Together with a good many more in Labrador, they testify to the one-time presence and abundance of their majestic namesake throughout this region.

That the north shore of the Gulf of St. Lawrence was also white bear country is attested to by the misadventure of Marguerite de La Roche. This young French noblewoman accompanied her relative, La Rocque de Roberval, in 1542 on a voyage of intended settlement bound to Quebec. However, Marguerite and her lover behaved "immorally" during the long Atlantic crossing, which so incensed Roberval that he had the guilty pair cast away, together with a maidservant, on Ile des Démons, which is one of the Mecatina group. Two years later Marguerite was discovered there by some French fishermen, her lover, maid, and a child born to her on the island having died. We are told that one of the several problems she had to contend with was "bears, white as an egg."

Île des Démons was not the western extremity of the white bear's range. This extended at least as far as the estuary of the St. Lawrence River. Indeed, as late as the 1930s, an old female white bear was reportedly killed near Lac St-Jean at the head of the Saguenay River.

Some light on how far south white bears ranged may be shed by the story of David Ingram. Although he was apparently never north of Nova Scotia, he spoke of "beares, both blacke and white." Even in early colonial times white bears are reputed to have ranged south to Delaware Bay, and one was killed in the Gulf of Maine in the eighteenth century.

The white bear may only have been an accidental visitor to the land of the Delawares, but it was uncomfortably common in the countries of some of the more northern tribes. Writing of the Gulf of St. Lawrence region about 1575, André Thevet reported that white bears so "infest their houses that the [native] inhabitants make pits which they cover with leaves and branches"— presumably in an effort to conceal and protect their food supplies.

Nor were the aborigines the only ones to be so plagued. Mid-sixteenth-century Basque whalers fishing the Gulf found them a nuisance as they prowled about the tryworks where the oil was rendered helping themselves to whale meat and blubber as if it was theirs by right. But, as Anthony Parkhurst reported from Newfoundland in 1574–78, the plethora of white bears was not without its advantages. There was, he said, such a "plentie of bears everywhere . . . that you may kill them as oft as you list: their flesh is as good as young beef." However, he added, "the Beares also be as bold [as the local foxes and] will not spare at midday to take your fish before your face, and I believe would not hurt anybody unless they be forced." That Parkhurst was referring to the white bear is evident not only from his description of their behaviour, but also from the testimony of Stephen Parmenius, who briefly visited eastern Newfoundland in 1583 and noted: "Beares also appear about the fishers stages of the Country, and are sometimes killed, but they seem to be white as I conjectured from their skins."

This boldness has always been one of the white bear's most notable and, as far as Europeans are concerned, disturbing characteristics. Yet its audacity seems to be based not on brute arrogance so much as on the calm belief that it has no enemies and therefore can go where it pleases with impunity. In the days when contact with it was restricted to native peoples, this confidence was usually well placed. Although primitive man could and did kill white bears, he usually chose to avoid conflict, partly because discretion was the better part of valour and partly due to an admiration for the animal that amounted to something close to veneration. For their part, the bears reciprocated by adopting a live-and-let-live attitude toward mankind. This lack of aggressiveness seems to have surprised early explorers but, on the whole, they did not reciprocate it.

It was, of course, *de rigeur* in Judeo-Christian-dominated cultures to believe that all large carnivores were inherently savage and ferocious animals that should be treated as inimical and destroyed whenever possible. The white bear was no exception. From as early as the sixteenth century it bore a horrid reputation as a man-eater that much preferred crunching human skulls to seal skulls. Such canards were legion, although the stark truth is that only a handful of authentic records attest to unprovoked attacks by white bears on human beings—and some of these are suspect.

Although the bears had co-existed successfully with aboriginal mankind, they were unable to do so with the new human interlopers. Fed up (quite literally) with eating fish, whether salt or fresh, European fishermen summering on New World coasts lusted after red meat; and one of the most readily accessible sources of such was the white or water bear, as they sometimes called it. Abundant on the fishing coasts from Nova Scotia "down" the Labrador and west to the estuary of the St. Lawrence, it flaunted its presence, not just by reason of its colour but because it had so little fear of man that it would neither hide nor flee when he appeared. To the contrary, it deliberately sought out fishermen's shore establishments, which its perceptive nose could detect from many miles away, where it felt free to help itself from flakes and drying racks, thereby infuriating the human owners. For these several reasons, together with the fact that its shaggy pelt was a valuable curiosity in Europe, it early became a target for destruction.

The wonder is that it lasted as long as it did. Nevertheless, toward the end of the seventeenth century its numbers had been so sadly reduced that it was a rarity in southern Newfoundland, where it had by then acquired a mythical reputation. Baron Lahontan wrote of it in 1680: "The White Bears are monstrous Animals . . . they are so fierce that they will come and attack a Sloop in the Sea with seven or eight men in it . . . I never saw but one of them . . . which had certainly tore me to pieces if I had not spy'd it at a distance and so had time to run back to shelter to Fort Louis at Placentia [on Newfoundland's southeast coast]."

Paradoxically, the European impact that resulted in the destruction of water bears in the southern and eastern regions of the Gulf of St. Lawrence had the opposite effect along the northern coast. From Belle Isle Strait westward was white bear country *par excellence*, providing them with enormous and accessible herds of harp and hood seals during the winter and early spring; grey and harbour seals, together with young walrus, throughout the year; seabird eggs and young on the numberless fringing islands in late spring; swarming summer and autumn schools of salmon in the many rivers; cod and flatfish in the estuaries; and berries and other vegetation on the land. In aboriginal times it had also provided occasional gargantuan feasts in the form of stranded whale carcasses.

In the sixteenth century Basque whalers began to work the northern coast of the Gulf. Thereafter, the number of whale carcasses increased at such a rate that not all the water bears in eastern North America could have consumed this bounty. Such a glut of food became available as a result of the Basque slaughter of the great whales that the white bear population seems to have exploded. So numerous did they become that the entire region began to acquire a singularly menacing reputation.

If this reputation was not actually invented by the canny Basques as a means of keeping competitors away from their immensely lucrative whale fishery, it was certainly enhanced by them. Anticosti Island, in the centre of the Basque whaling ground, became particularly notorious for its bears. In the first quarter of the seventeenth century, so Champlain tells us, not even the natives would go near the place because "they say that a number of very dangerous white bears are to be found there." Another Frenchman, Father Sagard, sailed past the island in the 1630s and noted that "on the Island of Anticosti it is said there are white bears of enormous size, which eat men."

However, the century-long free lunch supplied by the whalers turned out to be a mixed blessing for the bears. When the supply of whale carcasses dwindled away during the early 1600s, the swollen bear population had to hustle for a living. Furthermore, their huge numbers were now attracting the mercenary interest of the French, who had by then suborned the north-shore Indians into becoming furriers and had equipped them with guns. With firearms in their hands, the natives outmatched the bears. They also ceased to regard them with traditional reverence, once it was understood that bear pelts could be translated into trinkets and brandy at French trading posts. By the beginning of the eighteenth century the resident white bears, not only of Anticosti but of the whole north shore of the Gulf, were being hurried after their Newfoundland brethren—into oblivion.

They held out somewhat longer in and about Belle Isle Strait where, as late as 1707, the French trader Courtemanche found them still common. But by 1766, when famed English naturalist Joseph Banks visited the Belle Isle region, the only trace of white bears he could find was the report of a female with two cubs seen earlier on the Newfoundland side of the Strait.

The bears were still holding their own on the Atlantic coast of Labrador, which had not yet been infested by Europeans. In 1775, the Moravian missionary Jens Munk coasted north along that shore as far as Davis Inlet and recorded that "This land abounds with Deer, Foxes, White and Black Bears." However, it was Captain George Cartwright, first European to establish a "plantation" (a trading post-cum-seal-fishery-cum-anything-else that could be turned to make a pound) in southeastern Labrador, who left us one of the best accounts of the life and times of the great white bear on the Atlantic seaboard of America.

Cartwright operated several salmon fisheries, one of which was in Sandwich Bay on White Bear River—so called by him because it was also fished, and heavily so, by white bears. What follows is condensed from his account of a visit to nearby Eagle River on July 22, 1778.

"About half a mile upriver, I came to a very strong shoot of water, from thence I saw several white-bears fishing in the stream above. I waited for them, and in a short time, a bitch with a small cub swam close to the other shore, and landed a little below. The bitch immediately went into the woods, but the cub sat down upon a rock, when I sent a ball through it, at the distance of a hundred and twenty yards at the least, and knocked it over; but getting up again it crawled into the woods, where I heard it crying mournfully, and concluded that it could not long survive.

"The report of my gun brought some others down, and another she bear, with a cub of eighteen months old came swimming close under me. I shot the bitch through the head and killed her dead. The cub perceiving this and getting sight of me made at me with great ferocity; but just as the creature was about to revenge the death of his dam, I saluted him with a load of large shot in his right eye, which not only knocked that out, but also made him close the other. He no sooner was able to keep his left eye open, than he made at me again, quite mad with rage and pain; but when he came to the foot of the bank, I gave him another salute with the other barrel, and blinded him most completely; his whole head, was then entirely covered with blood. He blundered into the woods; knocking his head against every rock and tree that he met with.

"I now perceived that two others had just landed about sixty yards above me, and were fiercely looking round them. The bears advanced a few yards to the edge of the woods, and the old one was looking sternly at me. The danger of firing at her I knew was great, as she was seconded by a cub of eighteen months; but I could not resist the temptation. I fortunately sent my ball through her heart, and dropped her; but getting up again, she ran some yards into the woods; where I soon found her dead, without her cub.

"The captain and Jack coming up, I was informed that Jack had shot one of those white ones which first passed me; that the beast had gone up on a small barren hill, some little distance within the woods, and there died.

"Leaving them to skin this bear, I advanced higher up the river, until I came opposite a beautiful cataract. There I sat down upon some bare rocks, to contemplate the scene before me, and to observe the manoeuvres of the bears; numbers of which were then in sight.

"I had not sat there long, ere my attention was diverted to an enormous, old, dog bear, which came out of some alder bushes on my right and was walking slowly towards me, with his eyes fixed on the ground, and his nose not far from it. I rested my elbows, and in that position suffered him to come within five yards of me before I drew the trigger; when I placed my ball in the centre of his scull, and killed him dead: but as the shore was a flat reclining rock, he rolled round until he fell into the river.

"On casting my eyes around, I perceived another beast of equal size, raised half out of the water. He no sooner discovered me, than he made towards me as fast as he could swim. As I was not then prepared to receive him, I ran into the wood to make ready my unerring rifle. Whilst I was employed in that operation, he dived and brought up a salmon; which he repeatedly tossed up a yard or two in the air, and letting fall into the water, would dive and bring it up again. Being now ready, I advanced to the attack, and presently perceived him, standing in the water with his fore paws upon a rock, devouring the salmon. I crept through the bushes until I came opposite to him, and interrupted his repast, by sending a ball through his head; it entered a little above his left eye, went out at the root of his right ear, and knocked him over, he then appeared to be in the agonies of death for some time; but at last recovered sufficiently to land on my side of the river, and to stagger into the woods.

"Never in my life did I regret the want of ammunition so much as on this day; as I was by the failure interrupted in the finest sport that man ever had. I am certain, that I could with great ease have killed four or five brace more. They were in such plenty, that I counted thirty-two white-bears but there were certainly many more, as they generally retire into the woods to sleep after making a hearty meal.

"Having now only two balls left beside that in my rifle, I thought it was most prudent to return to the boat and wait the return of the other people. It was not long before they came down; for they were not able to skin the second bear. Although his body was afloat in the water and nothing but his head rested upon a flat rock, yet they could not lift even that up. We judged him to be as much as twelve hundred pounds weight; nor could he well be less than that, as he stood six feet high, as his carcass was as big as the largest ox I ever saw. Thus ended in disappointment, the noblest day's sport I ever saw: for we got only one skin, although we had killed six bears."

Cartwright encountered white bears at all seasons. In late April of 1776, one of his men "saw the tracks of near a hundred white-bears which had lately crossed Sandwich Bay." He also recorded the species as still to be found in Newfoundland. It clearly whelped in south Labrador since he not only correctly gives the whelping time but refers to females with young cubs. In discussing the farming possibilities of Labrador, he concluded it would be too difficult and expensive "to fence against the white-bears and wolves," which were clearly *the* major predators of the region. It is also of interest that in Cartwright's time not only were a great many white bears living on the Labrador, they were co-existing with at least 600 Inuit and an even larger number of Nascopie Indians. But, as elsewhere, co-existence with Europeans proved to be a different proposition.

In the opinion of orthodox biologists, all occurrences of white bears along the Atlantic coast south of Hudson Strait refer, by definition as it were, to *polar* bears, which is to say to polar-*dwelling* bears. Conventional wisdom has it that these bears go adrift on the Arctic pack while hunting seals far from land and are then carried south, willy-nilly, until the ice melts under them and they are forced to swim to the nearest shore. Having regained solid ground, so the scenario runs, they dutifully set out to trek back to their Arctic homes, an overland journey which, in the case of those unfortunate enough to have landed in Nova Scotia, spans at least 1,000 miles, measured as the goose flies.

The peripatetic polar bear hypothesis carries some appearance of plausibility because, in our own times, the only white bears to be found along the Atlantic seaboard *are* almost certainly strays from Arctic or sub-Arctic regions—for the very good reason that the endemic population has long since been exterminated.

The possibility that these "ice drift" bears are in fact recapitulating an ancient pattern of involuntary colonization, just as their ancestors must have done aeons ago, and that they are failing now because they are being destroyed as fast as they arrive, is decisively rejected. Yet the orthodox explanation is even less acceptable since it would have required an enormous circulation of bears drifting aimlessly southward on the ice for many months of every year, then toiling laboriously northwards along the rock-ribbed coasts for as many months again, in order to account for the known abundance of white bears in the south in earlier times. Although appropriate to birds, an annual roundelay of such proportions would exhaust even as powerful an animal as the white bear, let alone allow him and her sufficient time and opportunity to propagate their kind.

The crux of the argument against a southern population lies, first, in the contention that the polar bear is specifically and exclusively adapted to far northern regions and therefore could not establish itself elsewhere; and second, in the belief that, because it is only found in polar regions now, this must always have been the case. But what about those special Arctic adaptations? Take colour, for example. White does have an obvious advantage for animals that spend a major part of their lives surrounded by ice and snow. And the polar bear *is* white during the winter; but then so are the varying hare and the ermine weasel, whose ranges extend south to Nova Scotia. In summer, hare and weasel acquire new brown coats; and in summer the hair of the white bear takes on a muddy, yellowish cast that provides good camouflage from a hunter working the landwash at the edge of the sea, whether in the north, which is also snow-free in the summer, or as far southward as one might care to go.

Another supposedly limiting adaptation is that polar bears can only exist where ice seals are abundant—the implication being that such conditions obtain only in the Arctic and sub-Arctic. The truth is that ice seals were found in near astronomical numbers off Newfoundland, south Labrador, and in the Gulf of St. Lawrence from December through to April. Furthermore, white bears will happily eat any species of seal and, in aboriginal times, both grey and harbour seals existed in enormous quantities not only in all the waters just mentioned, but south to Cape Cod and beyond. What is even more to the point, the white bear is in no way limited to a seal diet. He is, in fact, one of the most opportunistic feeders in the animal kingdom.

There is also the argument that pregnant white bears must be able to find deep snowdrifts in which to den, and therefore reproduction is quite impossible except in Arctic regions. As we shall shortly see, this contention is as fallacious as the rest. The fact of the matter is that the white bear was never any more a prisoner of the Arctic than were the bowhead whale, walrus, beluga, white wolf, white fox, or any of a dozen species whose survivors in our time are now restricted to the frigid zone simply because they have been destroyed by us elsewhere.

During the spring of 1969, ornithologists from the Canadian Wildlife Service making an aerial search for goose nesting grounds about forty miles south of Churchill, Manitoba (and close to where I saw my first white bear), were startled to find "polar bears in such numbers the entire region seemed infested with them." A follow-up investigation that winter revealed fifty *earth-dug* dens occupied by female white bears with their cubs.

This was just the beginning of one of the most extraordinary mammalian discoveries of recent times. Continuing surveys revealed the existence of a polar bear "zone" extending nearly 500 miles southward from Churchill almost to the bottom of James Bay, inhabited on a permanent basis by at least 1,500 white bears, including 600 breeding females. The mere existence of such a massive assemblage was astonishing enough; what made it even more so was the fact that they were living as far to the south as the latitude of southern Labrador on the one hand and the prairie city of Calgary on the other.

Almost equally surprising was that a population of this size—it represented about a tenth of the known world population of white bears—could have remained undetected for so long. The explanation for that lay partly in the fact that nobody expected *polar* bears to be found so far south, but it was mainly due to the nature of the drowned morass known as the Hudson Bay Lowlands, where they lived. These lowlands consist of a soggy strip of coastal tundra bordering the west coast of James Bay and running north almost to Churchill. Inland lies a tangle of black spruce bog where the sole vertical relief is provided by occasional eskers, ancient raised beaches, and permafrost hummocks, in which the white bears excavate their dens. Virtually impenetrable in summer because of its saturated nature, the region is rendered most difficult of approach from seaward by a fringing barrier of mud and rock tidal flats that, in places, extends eight miles out from "shore." In past times, even the natives treated the Lowlands much as the Bedouin treat the Empty Quarter of Arabia, and European traders and trappers bypassed it, considering it to be a worthless wasteland.

From July through December, when James Bay and Hudson Bay are ice-free, the bears remain ashore, where they lead an indolent life, sleeping, playing, denning, and feeding on berries, grass, kelp, small mammals, flightless ducks and geese, fishes, and marine life gleaned on the vast tidal flats. Although the population is densest near the coast, individuals range as much as 100 miles inland where they present helicopter-borne observers with the odd spectacle of polar bears trying to conceal their vast bulks behind clumps of scraggly spruce.

In November almost all the adults except pregnant females move to the shore and congregate while waiting for the sea ice to thicken so they can go seal hunting. In November of 1969, an aerial survey counted about 300 of them assembled near Cape Churchill, while hundreds more crowded the coastline to the south—more white bears than had ever been seen in one region of the world in human memory.

Pregnant females begin the winter in the security of maternity dens, some of which have been in use for centuries. These earth-dug homes often boast several rooms, with ventilation shafts. Here, during late December or early January, the young—usually twins—are born as naked, unformed little things about the size of guinea pigs, which are not mature enough to leave the dens until late March.

The winter seal hunt, mostly for bearded and ring seals, is the nomadic time; but studies using radio collars have shown that these bears are nomadic only in a very limited sense. Their winter range seems to be generally restricted to the ice of southern Hudson Bay, and the tagged animals seldom wander more than a few hundred miles from home. In other words, they go no farther afield than is necessary to find food. Since food is evidently in good supply, these southern bears are generally healthier, larger, and live in much greater density than their cousins in polar regions.

Some mammalogists who have participated in studies of the lowland bears now privately concede that the white bear may also have once flourished as a permanent resident in the Sea of Okhotsk in the western Pacific (it is known to have bred on the Kurils, Sakhalin, and Kamchatka), the Aleutian Islands, and southeast Alaska...and even along the northeastern Atlantic seaboard, including the Gulf of St. Lawrence. In view of the accumulated evidence, such a conclusion is difficult to avoid.

During the first decade of the seventeenth century, Europeans began pushing northward from their own continent in an avid search for train oil—the black gold of their times. The Spitzbergen archipelago was soon discovered and, by mid-century, scores of whaling ships were working its waters. These were the precursors of a burgeoning fleet that bloodied the northern oceans during succeeding centuries with an unparalleled massacre of marine mammals, something we will be looking at in ensuing chapters.

Chief amongst the victims were whales, walrus, and seals, but whalers and sealers early learned that as much as twelve gallons of good train could be rendered from the carcass of a big water bear. Moreover, the vast, shaggy pelts commanded high prices from aristocratic Europeans who coveted them as rugs for their chilly, stone-floored mansions and castles. Thus, from the start of northern voyaging, white bears were killed whenever opportunity offered; but until near the end of the eighteenth century they had not been systematically hunted, partly because firearms were not yet effective enough to inspire confidence to face the great white bear. But, by the early 1800s, the availability of new and much deadlier guns helped give the white bear prime-target status.

As the other marine mammals were hunted to scarcity, bears became increasingly sought after. Some skippers visited places especially favoured by them, systematically slaughtering all that could be found. An effective ploy was to place well-armed men in ambush near the carcass of a whale. On one occasion the crew of a Norwegian sealer in the East Greenland ice killed thirty ice bears, as they called them, using a dead whale as bait.

The magnitude of the slaughter mounted with the passing years. New England whalers working the Labrador coast during the 1790s killed every white bear they could find and traded for bear pelts with the Labrador Inuit, whom they provided with guns and turned into year-round bear hunters. By the early 1800s this had had a dual effect: the Inuit were reduced to about half their former numbers through disease acquired from the whalers; and *Nanuk*, as the Inuit called the white bear, became a vanishing species along the whole of the Labrador coast where, only half a century earlier, Cartwright had found it in abundance.

The Inuit were not alone to blame. Increasing numbers of fishermen, fur trappers, traders, and even missionaries were now invading the Labrador and most of them killed white bears on sight. By 1850, few were to be seen, and those few were usually sighted along the barrel of a rifle. There is one reference to a pair of young cubs captured alive at Square Island in south Labrador, which suggests that a handful may still have been breeding there as late as 1850. But soon thereafter, there were none.

The once vigorous and abundant white bear population that had occupied the coasts of the northeastern approaches to America had been annihilated. By then, mass destruction was being visited on the white bear almost everywhere it lived. With the virtual extinction of the bowhead whale, Arctic oilers turned upon the bear with terrible effect. In 1906, the crew of a Norwegian vessel in Greenland waters killed 296 ice bears during a single summer. During the 1909 and 1910 "fishing seasons" British whalers in Canada's eastern Arctic waters butchered 476 and rendered their fat into train oil. Meanwhile, Yankee whalers in the North Pacific were wreaking equal havoc on white bears there.

The end of Arctic whaling brought no great relief to the remaining bears. Norwegian, Scottish, and Newfoundland sealers working the harp and hood seal herds off Newfoundland, Labrador, and Greenland killed every ice bear they encountered. Nor were they the only scourge. As early as 1820, a mania for Arctic exploration gripped Europe and America as expedition after expedition went north: some to seek the legendary Northwest and Northeast Passages; some to try to reach the Pole; some in the name of science; and some for sport. All took it for granted that any living creatures they might encounter were theirs to do with as they saw fit.

In 1909 Ernest Thompson Seton had this to say about their treatment of the white bear: "It has been the custom of Arctic travellers to kill all the Polar Bears they could. It did not matter whether the travellers needed the carcasses or not. In recent years this senseless slaughter increased, since more travellers went north and deadlier weapons were carried. One Arctic explorer told me that he personally had killed 200 Polar Bears and had secured but few of them."

The behaviour of Robert Peary, one of the two American claimants to the discovery of the North Pole, is typical. He used such larger animals as caribou, walrus, musk ox, and bear as the principal source of food, fuel, and clothing for an exploration machine that, in its final stages, included platoons of Inuit dragooned into his service, together with hundreds of sled dogs. Furthermore, he compelled both his own men and the Inuit to trap or shoot any and all furbearers whose pelts were salable in the United States, including especially white bears.

The destruction brought about by Arctic expeditions of the never-abundant mammalian life of northwestern Greenland and Ellesmere Island was on such a grand scale that entire regions were denuded of large animals; in consequence, some bands of Inuit starved to death. The treatment meted out to the bears by Peary's expeditions alone resulted in the destruction of at least 2,000 of them. Indeed, racking up a big score of polar bear kills became an attainment in itself for many self-styled explorers. In private yachts and chartered vessels, rich gunmen from Europe and the United States found their ways to most of the known retreats of the white bear, shooting all that they could find.

Some of them wrote heroic accounts of derring-do against the "ferocious white killer of the North." This helped father a new fashion. As the twentieth century unfolded, polar bear rugs, complete with the stuffed heads gaping in long-toothed snarls, became status symbols for people of pretension and kindled a new kind of commercial hunt. It still continues and may even be gaining in intensity because of its extreme profitability. In 1964, a good polar bear pelt, untanned, fetched $1,000. Today, such a pelt commands a good deal more. By 1964 the combined commercial and trophy hunt employing ski-equipped aircraft and snowmobiles had become so destructive that even some of the dullard minds in government bureaucracies began to feel faint stirrings of alarm about the future of the bear that had, by then, become a *polar* bear in fact as well as name. With the exception of the Hudson Bay Lowlands, the polar region was the only area where it still endured.

The following year, the First International Scientific Meeting on the Polar Bear was convened by those nations with white bear populations—Canada, the U.S., the Soviet Union, Denmark (for Greenland), and Norway (for Spitzbergen)—to see if there really were grounds for concern. Among the weighty conclusions reached by the experts was that "Intensive polar bear hunting by whalers and sealers since the 17th century has probably resulted in a reduced population." There was no agreement as to how great that reduction might have been and, more to the point, none on how many white bears might remain alive. American scientists offered a figure of 19,000; the Soviets countered with an estimate of 8,000.

Statistics on the annual kill were even less precise. Canada's delegates thought it might "approach 600" within their territory. The figure for the U.S. kill, which was mostly made from aircraft by sportsmen and commercial hide hunters on the ice packs off Alaska, was thought to be about 1,000. Norwegian experts professed to have no idea how many were killed by their nationals.

With a single exception, none of the polar bear countries thought the creature's survival was threatened. The exception was the Soviet Union, which a decade earlier had become convinced the bear was endangered and, as of 1957, had placed it under full protection.

The decade following the congress saw the slaughter continue unabated in Alaska, Greenland, Canada, and Spitzbergen as well as, and particularly, on the ice in international waters. By 1968, it had reached an admitted total of 1,500 white bears a year with a real kill probably well in excess of 2,000. Such depletion of a species whose females only give birth every third year, and whose total world population was no more than 20,000, threatened eventual extinction. Nevertheless, most of the polar bear nations remained unconcerned.

As late as 1976, a Canadian government publicity release insisted that polar bears were still "abundant and adequate...Despite international controversy concerning the decline in populations there is a harvestable surplus in Canada." Nevertheless, the statement continued peevishly, "it has been increasingly difficult for Canadians to export the valuable polar bear hides because of restrictions by other nations"—a reference to embargoes on the import of the skins of endangered species, which many western nations now considered the white bear to be. "Canada's position," the release concluded, "emphasizes sound management principles rather than a rigid form of protection."

The head of the Canadian Wildlife Service's Polar Bear Project added his opinion that a ban on the killing of white bears would be "protectionist overreaction." Adopting such a course, he explained, would make it difficult for scientists to carry on useful research and adequate management, by preventing the collection of biological specimens (read: dead bears). As things stood, he emphasized, Canada was leading the way in determining the future of the polar bear.

The nature of that future was spelled out in another government publication of the same period. Raw polar bear hides, it jubilantly reported, were fetching from $500 to $3,000 each on the international market. Consequently, the annual permissible harvest of 630 Canadian bears, as recommended by management scientists, was worth over a million dollars in pelts alone, plus at least half that much again in fees and services charged to hunters from the United States, Europe, Japan, and the Middle East. Good economic sense together with good science dictated that the harvest should continue.

It has continued. Although in 1972 the U.S. banned polar bear killing in Alaska except for subsistence hunting by native people and, a year later,

Norway followed the Soviet Union's lead by banning *all* polar bear hunting in its territory, Canada continues "harvesting" the bears, as does Greenland. Since 1973 the commercial killing of white bears has been effectively a monopoly held by these two countries. It is a very lucrative one. In 1984 Canadian quotas will allow the killing of about 700, and Greenland will kill about 300. The Japanese, who now buy up to 95 per cent of these "novelty" furs, will pay as much as $5,000 for an especially good one, and South Koreans will pay up to $3,000 for a dried polar bear gallbladder, which they use for medicinal purposes. Furthermore, sport hunters will each pay an average of $15,000 for the privilege of killing a bear.[2]

There is some good news. Ontario, which controls much of the Hudson Bay Lowlands, has established the Polar Bear Wilderness Park on the west side of James Bay, and the resident bears are fully protected there. Manitoba, which is now reaping a good return from tourists travelling to Churchill to see wild white bears, has forbidden the killing of them except by native people. In the Soviet Union, the bear population has increased so dramatically that, in some places such as Wrangell Island, it may be approaching aboriginal levels. The image of the great white bear has become a symbol of enlightened conservation in the Soviet Union where, as else-where, those who believe that non-human forms of life deserve the right to exist are frequently at odds with those who believe they were placed on earth to be used or, as it may be, abused by man as he sees fit.

Along the northeastern seaboard of America the white bear is now little more than a fast-fading wraith. Since 1960 perhaps two dozen have come south on the pack ice, but at least fifteen of these have been intercepted by Norwegian sealers off Newfoundland and killed "in self defence." In the spring of 1962, one that escaped the sealers walked into the outport village of Rose Blanche on Newfoundland's southwest coast. First seen emerging from the village cemetery, its appearance caused such panic that all hands fled for the safety of their houses. The bear paid them no heed. Making its way to the water, it swam off toward the harbour entrance where it encountered two men in a dory. They deflected it with yells and by banging their oars against the gunwales. The bear thereupon changed course toward the opposite shore of the harbour. By dint of frantic rowing, the men reached

---

[2] To Canada's publicly expressed indignation, the United States has now declared the polar bear an endangered species and has forbidden the import of its hides, which may discourage American trophy hunters from killing it.

their fishing store, snatched up their guns, and were in time to shoot it dead as it stood, perplexed, in the landwash, unsure of which way to go.

A more recent visitation took place in eastern Newfoundland on May 9, 1973, when a young bear, already wounded, walked into the outskirts of the village of New Chelsea, near Heart's Content. It threatened no one and no thing but, like all of its kind over the long years, it was met with gunfire.

"Comin' down the road there, he looked like a bloody big ghost!" remembers one of those who saw it die.

Indeed. A great White Ghost.

❖ 7

The Brown and the Black

Once upon a time there were three bears. There was a white bear, a brown bear, and a black bear...

We have seen what happened to the white one. Here is what has happened and is happening to the others.

If the one-time presence of the white bear on the Atlantic seaboard has been largely ignored by history, another ursine giant who was the white bear's peer has been totally forgotten. When Europeans began arriving in the New World, an enormous brown bear roamed the continent from Mexico to Alaska; eastward over the whole of the Great Plains to the Mississippi and Manitoba; and across the entire Arctic mainland from Pacific to Atlantic. Since it was absent from the eastern forest regions, it was not encountered by the invaders of the lower continental mainland until they reached the Mississippi country about 1800; but, at least a century earlier, traders into Hudson Bay had met the great creature and named it the "grizzled bear." It has since borne many names, such as silver-tip, roach-back, and grey bear, but grizzly is the enduring one.

Grizzlies were so named because a mantle of light grey or "grizzled" fur composed of silver-tipped hairs covers their huge, squat heads and massively humped shoulders. Ranking with the white bear as the largest carnivore on the continent, an adult male grizzly may weigh 1,000 pounds and can be a fearsome spectacle as it rears back on its haunches to peer down upon mere man from a height of seven or eight feet.

Usually tolerant of human beings, unless wounded, cornered, or protecting cubs, the big bears were nevertheless treated circumspectly by most aboriginal peoples who, before the coming of firearms, took care to avoid provoking them. However, European settlers regarded all bears as inherently treacherous and dangerous beasts that ought to be killed on sight, and the grizzly seems to have especially inflamed their animosity.

It was remorselessly pursued, shot, trapped, or poisoned by ranchers who accused it of being a sheep and cattle killer. The charge was, and is, grossly exaggerated. When such accusations have been investigated, it has often been shown that the grizzly was simply scavenging the carcass of an animal that had died of natural causes or had been killed by some other predator. However, even had this truth been accepted, the settlers would probably not have altered their attitude. The great bear drew upon itself to a singular degree modern man's malevolent hatred of any other creature that seems capable of challenging our dominion.

Within less than a hundred years of its discovery in the West, the grizzly had been exterminated wherever agriculturalists settled. Today it continues to exist—precariously—mainly in national parks and a few remote wilderness areas. It is one of the most sought-after prizes of trophy hunters—that peculiar breed whose chief pleasure seems to lie in slaughtering large animals in order to hang their stuffed heads on rec-room walls as macabre testimony to machismo.

Another major element in the destruction of the great bears was the killing of enormous numbers for "scientific purposes." As an example of the atrocities committed in the name of science, the fate of the grizzly can hardly be bettered.

During the latter part of the nineteenth century and well into the twentieth, an American mammalogist, Dr. C. Hart Merriam, was the acknowledged "supreme authority" on North American bears. He earned this eminence by spending a professional lifetime in the employ of the U.S. Biological Survey, collecting and examining the skins and skulls of grizzlies with a view to subdividing them into a complicated system of species and subspecies. In 1918, he published his findings.

"In my Preliminary Synopsis of the American Bears [I recognized] eight grizzlies and big brown bears of which five [were new to science. I did] not suspect that the number remaining to be discovered was anything like so great as has since proved to be the case. The steady influx of specimens resulting from the labors of the Biological Survey, supplemented by the personal efforts of a number of hunter-naturalists, brought to light many surprises...and beginning in the spring of 1910, a fund placed at my disposal made it possible to offer hunters and trappers sufficient enducement to tempt them to exert themselves in securing needed specimens. As a result, the [U.S.] national collection of grizzly bears has steadily grown until...it now far excels all other collections in the world together.

"Nevertheless...knowledge of the big bears is by no means complete... Many bears now roaming the wild will have to be killed and their skulls and skins sent to museums before their characters and variations will be fully understood and before it will be possible to construct accurate maps of their ranges. Persons having the means and ambition to hunt big game may be assured that...much additional material is absolutely required to settle questions [of race and species] still in doubt."

What the good Dr. Merriam succeeded in doing was to separate the grizzly into a total of seven species and seventy-seven subspecies, to fifty-eight of which his name was attached as the discoverer. Alas for ambition. Modern scientists have invalidated most of his discoveries, and the maps of the grizzly's range, which Merriam felt could only be drawn accurately if a lot more "specimens" were killed, became mere cemetery charts where the bones of the bulk of the grizzly population of North America rot unremarked.

However, more than 9,000 "study specimens" of the grizzly, carefully garnered by science assisted by "hunter-naturalists," are held in storage in the great museums of America against the day when, perhaps another Dr. Merriam will undertake a new revision of the species and subspecies of a vanished animal.

Through several centuries, stories trickled out of the vast Labrador/Ungava wilderness about a creature that, from the descriptions, could hardly have been anything except a grizzly. Added to these were matter-of-fact records from fur traders who bought skins of "grey," "grisly," or "grizzly bears" from the Inuit of the coast and the Indians of the interior. However, because none of these skins fell into the hands of scientists or ended up in museum collections, the accumulating evidence that grizzly bears existed in the region was ignored.

In 1954, C.S. Elton, an Oxford-based expert on animal population dynamics, published a paper setting out the evidence that a grizzly not only *had* inhabited much of Labrador/Ungava but might still exist. Unfortunately, as Elton pointed out, "No white man has ever certainly seen alive the barren-ground grizzly to which the natives refer... [scientists therefore] have mostly shelved the question of its existence and identity."

The definitive rejection had been made in 1948 by Dr. R.M. Anderson, chief mammalogist to Canada's National Museum. "Admittedly," said Anderson, "some kind of Grizzly or 'big Brown Bear' is legendary in northern Quebec or Ungava, but no...specimen...has ever been examined, and so I shall not have much confidence [in its existence] until a skin with skull, and feet with claws, has been produced, and the specimen should have a pedigree or abstract of title to show where it came from."

In 1974, Anderson's sarcastic dictate was still being defended by a successor to his post, Dr. A.W.F. Banfield, who gave it as his considered opinion that no race of grizzly bear had been native to Labrador/Ungava in historic times. "Hearsay accounts of grizzlies," he opined, in an oblique reference to Elton, "have misled scientists more often than not, perhaps more in the case of the rumoured presence of the bears in the Ungava peninsula of Northern Quebec and Labrador." Here is a synopsis of the evidence Anderson and Banfield so cavalierly rejected.

Although nothing exists in print to tell us what early Europeans knew about the great brown bear, the Descelier World Map, dating to about 1550, shows two well-drawn bears on the shore-ice off Labrador, accompanied by the legend *ours sur les glaces*. Both bears are of equal size, but one is white and the other brown. A third bear, also brown, is depicted standing on the Labrador land mass. Barren ground grizzlies in the central Arctic are known to frequent sea ice where, although white bears are quite at home, black bears seldom if ever venture.

One of the first English settlers in Labrador, Captain George Cartwright, recorded the presence there of a species of bear different from the white and black bears. Cartwright never penetrated into the interior and so did not see the strange bear himself, but on the basis of what his interpreter could gather from the natives, he described it as "a kind of bear very ferocious, having a white ring around its neck." This agrees with accounts offered by present-day Indians of the region when referring to the Great Bear of the Montagnais and the *Mehtashuee* of the Nascopie—both of which were very large brown bears that were fierce and dangerous if aroused. Cartwright's white ring about the neck is probably a half-understood reference to the grizzly's silvery-grey mantle.

References to the big bears became more numerous and more specific in the nineteenth century. The Hudson's Bay Company was then operating trading posts on the Ungava Coasts and occasionally in the interior as well, while Moravian missions had posts along the Atlantic coast of Labrador. One of the early HBC factors, John Maclean, spent six years trading at Fort Chimo near the bottom of Ungava Bay after four years serving the Company in what is now British Columbia, where he had become familiar with the western grizzly. In a report on the Ungava District for 1837–38, he lists black, grissle, and Arctic (viz. white) bears as being among the local fur resources. In a book about his trading experiences in Ungava, he added that "The black bear shuns the presence of man and is by no means a dangerous animal; the grisly bear, on the contrary, commands considerable respect from the 'lord of creation'...When we consider the great extent of country that intervenes between Ungava and the 'far west' it seems inexplicable that the grisly bear should be found in so insulated a situation...the fact of their being here, however, does not admit of a doubt, for I have traded and sent to England several of their skins."

HBC fur returns for Ungava District for the seasons 1838–39 and 1839–40 still survive. In 1838, one black bear skin was traded and, in the following year, one black and four "grey bears"—grey bear being the HBC trade term for grizzly. Reports by other HBC employees substantiate Maclean's observations. Captain William Kennedy, who served in Ungava District during the 1860s, stated that many bear skins were received at Fort Chimo, Fort Nascapie, and the George River post and sold in the trade as a variety of the (western) grizzly. And a Mr. Mittleberger, a retired HBC factor living in the U.S., is quoted in 1884 to the effect that the grizzly was still found in Labrador in his time, which seems to have been the 1870s.

The trading records of the six Moravian missions strung along 300 miles of the Labrador coast, from Makkovik in the south to Nachvak in the north, show that the Moravians had regularly traded for skins of "grey" or "grizzly" bears through more than a century, buying the last one in 1914.

During the latter part of the nineteenth century, interior Labrador and Ungava began attracting scientific travellers. One of these, the ethnologist L.M. Turner, was at Fort Chimo from 1882 to 1884. Turner had no doubts about the existence of the grizzly in that region. "The brown or barren-ground bear appears to be [now] restricted to a narrow area and is not plentiful, yet it is common enough to keep the Indian in wholesome dread of its vicious disposition when enraged."

That the bears had indeed become rare by that time was confirmed by A.P. Lowe, a government geologist who made extensive explorations of north-central Labrador and Ungava between 1892 and 1895. He reported that "specimens of the barren-ground bear are [now] obtained only at infre-quent intervals...[but] there is no doubt that this species is found in the barrens of Labrador...skins are brought at intervals to Fort Chimo when the Indians have a favourable chance to kill it. On other occasions they leave it alone, having a great respect for, and fear of its ferocity and size."

By 1894, there were probably few left alive. The Hudson's Bay Company seems not to have traded any skins after that year, and the Moravians only one. But around 1900, an independent trader named Martin Hunter, who had a post on Anticosti Island, bought some large brown bear pelts. According to Hunter, the animals that produced these skins were of "immense size and very savage. One skin I got measured seven feet broad by nine feet long and showed no fewer than eleven bullet holes in his hide."

These skins may have come from southern Labrador. Newfoundland writer and naturalist Harold Horwood tells me that "Labrador natives, both white and Indian, state positively that the [grizzly] bears were once found as far to the south and east as the Mealy Mountains, a barren, broken range between Goose Bay and Cartwright."

Dillon Wallace, an American traveller who spent part of the winter of 1905–06 at Fort Chimo before making his way overland to Hamilton Inlet, reported "a very large and ferocious brown bear that tradition says inhabits the barrens to the eastward of George River. Mr. Peter McKenzie told me that, many years ago, when he was stationed at Fort Chimo, the Indians brought him one of the skins of the animal, and Ford, [the trader] at George River [Post] said that, some twenty years since, he saw a piece of one of the skins. Both agreed that the hair was very long, light brown in colour, silver tipped and of a very different species from either the polar or black bear... The Indians speak of it with dread, and insist that it is still to be found though none of them can say positively that he has seen one in a decade."

Elton believes that, after 1900, a remnant of the original population lingered on in the almost impenetrable triangle of mountain tundra lying west of the Torngat range in northern Labrador. This region could well have been the provenance of the bear that yielded up its skin to the Moravians during the winter of 1913–14. The skin was traded by Inuit who hunted caribou in the tundra triangle.

One last glimpse of the great bear of the barrens may have been permitted us as late as 1946, when the crew of a Royal Canadian Air Force survey plane flying low over the open tundra about a hundred miles northwest of Chimo spotted three bears. The trio consisted of "one largish brown bear followed by two smaller ones." Both the pilot and the navigator-observer were familiar with northern fauna and were certain that these were neither black nor polar bears.

Despite all of this evidence, and more, the scientific establishment continued to deny the existence, past or present, of a resident population of grizzly bears east of Hudson Bay. However, since 1975, the denials have been muted. In that year, while excavating a late eighteenth-century Inuit midden at Okak Bay on the Labrador (not far from the site of a Moravian mission and trading post), Harvard anthropologist Steven Cox uncovered the well-preserved skull of a grizzly bear.

The Okak skull is that of a young female. It possesses certain unusual characteristics that have led some specialists to speculate that a Labrador/Ungava grizzly, long-separated from its cousins to the west of

Hudson Bay, had evolved into a distinct race. Probably we shall never know for certain whether the demise of the Nascopies' *Mehtashuee* marked the extermination of a distinct life form. What we do know is that the great grizzled bear of Ungava and Labrador is gone forever.

According to the late Dr. Francis Harper, an American zoologist who travelled extensively in Labrador, the northeastern grizzly, which he believed to have been a distinct species, perished as a direct result of the introduction of firearms to the Labrador/Ungava peninsula. On the one hand, Indians and Inuit then had the means (the incentive was provided by the traders) to attack the great bears that, until then, had been virtually invulnerable. On the other hand, firearms resulted in such massive destruction of barren ground caribou that the remaining bears, which depended on caribou carrion for a large part of their sustenance, were fatally reduced by starvation and attendant disease.

As we have been, so we remain.

Grizzly bears still survive in significant numbers in national parks and other such preserves. However, the species is not safe even there in the face of growing pressure to "ban the bears" from vast areas of many parks on the grounds that they pose a threat to the increasing hordes of human beings who go there purportedly for contact with the natural world.

Sterilized contact, apparently, is what such people want. There is very little doubt but that they will get it. Scores or even hundreds of grizzlies are being "disposed of" in national parks in the United States and in western Canada. Sometimes they are shot outright. Sometimes they are live-trapped and transported to peripheral regions where there is insufficient food to support more than the existing bear population. Sometimes they are dumped over the boundaries of the parks where they are quickly dealt with by commercial hunters, some of whom take only the gallbladders, which, as in the case of the polar bear, they sell for huge prices to Oriental buyers.

Wherever wild grizzly populations still exist they are being killed, not only by sport and commercial hunters but as a result of government programs designed to placate the human hunters of caribou, moose, elk, deer, mountain goats, and sheep. Having over-hunted these animals, the hunters are now blaming the grizzly and the wolf for a consequent shortage of game and are demanding their destruction.

Even the remnant of the barren ground clan living west of Hudson Bay is not exempt. Although nominally protected in Canada's Northwest Territories, they may still be killed "in self-defence." Considering the reputation with which we have saddled the grizzly, any gunner, white or native, who chooses to kill one can rest assured of immunity from the law. During a tour of the western Canadian Arctic in 1967, I heard of eight grizzlies and a number of polar bears having supposedly been shot "in self-defence." Not one of these cases was investigated by the authorities.

The surviving barren ground bears probably do not number more than 300. They cannot or, at least, will not live in proximity to human activities, and so are further threatened by the escalation of massive "resource development" across their one-time domain. Through the past several decades, there seems to have been a migration by some of them from the Arctic prairies into the rocky, lunar-looking wilderness north of Chesterfield Inlet. Here they may be temporarily secure from molestation, but in a brutally inhospitable corner of the world where only a handful of bears can hope to sustain themselves.

One wonders whether, at some future time, learned experts will not contend that the barren ground grizzly of whatever provenance was no more than a legendary creature.

In his gleaming ebony coat, the bulky but agile black bear plays a dual role in the wilderness scenario contrived by modern man. He is viewed on the one hand as a somewhat comic and rather endearing creature who nevertheless can bring a delicious shiver of apprehension to the camera-adorned tourist; on the other as a savage potential killer seen through the telescope of a high-powered rifle by a sportsman acting out his fantasy of being Daniel Boone.

Paradoxically, the black bear is thus one of the mainstays of wilderness tourism, and at the same time he is a prime ingredient in the bloody potpourri of "harvestable" big game animals.

When Europeans first arrived, black bears abounded from Atlantic to Pacific, from sub-Arctic timberline south into Mexico. They occupied the whole of the Atlantic seaboard with the exception of a few islands such as Sable and the Magdalens, which were too far offshore for such essentially terrestrial animals to reach. Moreover, they occupied this territory in such numbers that early settlers sometimes referred to them as "that Plague of Beares."

In 1750, one Thomas Wright spent several months on then uninhabited Anticosti Island, and he later wrote a little book about his experiences, which includes this passage: "The Bears, who are the principal inhabitants of this island, are so numerous that in the space of six weeks we killed fifty-three and might have destroyed twice that number had we thought fit... These animals have been so little molested by mankind, that we have frequently passed near them without their discovering the least fear; nor did they ever show any inclination to attack us, except only the females in defence of their young."

Wright's observations give us a glimpse of the black bear as it must have been at the time of first European contact—one of the commonest large mammals; inoffensive toward man yet relatively fearless of him. Confirmation of its abundance is commonplace in early records from New England, from the region that became the Atlantic Provinces of Canada, and from the domain of New France. As late as 1802, new settlers on the St. John River in New Brunswick complained that bears were so numerous ("the woods are infested with them") that, in irrational panic, they drove their cattle onto islands in the river, and women and children refused to leave the shelter of their cabins unless accompanied by a man armed with gun or axe.

The initial size of the black bear population can be estimated. Around the year 1500, between 100,000 and 120,000 lived to the eastward of a north-south line that would pass through the present cities of Boston and Quebec. Because they were mainly forest dwellers they seem to have held their own rather well during the early period of coastal exploration and maritime exploitation; but after settlement began in earnest, their numbers quickly waned.

Settlers and colonists slaughtered bears not simply for meat, fat, and fur, but because they saw the animals as a threat to agriculture. Whereas native people viewed bears with respect shading into reverence, the newcomers reserved *their* respect for the bear killers. Successful bear hunters enjoyed great prestige. They were viewed as saviours of the settlements in the same sense that hunters of Indians were. They are epitomized by the likes of Daniel Boone, that insatiable butcher who massacred as many as 2,000 black bears, thereby earning himself an heroic niche in American mythology.

As with so many other animals, the black bear has been consistently maligned. Yet reports of wanton attacks on human beings are statistically very rare. As for the threat they pose to farming, confirmed losses inflicted on farmers by bears in the Peace River district of Alberta, which has one of the few remaining significant bear populations in contact with agriculture, annually average something like a tenth of a cent on the dollar. This loss is mostly accounted for in beehives destroyed by a few bears unable to control their lust for honey. The vast majority of reports of bears of *any* species killing livestock reveal themselves, on investigation, to be reports of bears scavenging animals already dead.

In Cape Breton the once abundant black bears were systematically reduced to a mere handful restricted to the confines of a national park, because they were regarded as inveterate sheep-killers. The bears were destroyed, yet sheep losses continued and have now reached such proportions that sheep farming has generally become uneconomical in Cape Breton. The culprits, it now appears, are, and probably always were, uncontrolled domestic dogs.

In fine, it is not now possible, nor has it ever been, to establish a valid case against the black bear as a species seriously inimical to human enterprise. Despite this, the persecution has never slackened. In Quebec, in 1956, government bounty of $10 a head was paid on 4,424 black bears. In addition, *prizes* to a value of $9,000 were presented to the bounty hunters with the biggest scores. Most of these bears were killed in remote areas of the Gaspé and southern Ungava where there was no possibility of their having been in conflict with human interests. The prizes served, however, to attract a goodly number of foreign sportsmen, mainly from the United States.

According to the generous estimates of government wildlife officials, the black bear population of the entire eastern Canadian maritime region, including much of eastern Quebec and all of Ungava, does not now number more than 10,000. The species is totally extinct on Prince Edward Island and virtually so in most other settled regions.

What of the black bear's future? I quote from a recent Canadian government pamphlet: "Management should be directed toward the maintenance of populations in remote areas for hunting, and limiting the numbers in more settled areas where problems of predation arise. Once considered an undesirable predator and a nuisance, black bears are rapidly gaining popularity as a prized game animal... A spring hunt is especially appealing to the many sportsmen who prefer large game, since it provides them with the opportunity to hunt big game at a time when other animals are protected... Undoubtedly the status of black bears as game animals will be enhanced in future as human populations expand and the demand for game species increases."

A small but illuminating example of how the policy works was reported by a Toronto newspaper in August, 1981: "In central and northern Ontario more than 36 black bears had to be killed by conservation officers because [the lateness of the wild] berry crops had forced the bears out of the woods and closer to populated areas." The image of these "conservation" officers diligently practising current wildlife management is one that tends to stick in the mind, if not the throat.

"More settled areas" evidently include national parks. Between 1950 and 1979, park wardens in Canada's Jasper and Banff parks killed 523 black bears and deported 547. The black bear population in these two enormous parks is now "thought to be" only about 300. Current policy dictates that people are to have precedence in these "nature preserves" and too many bears, whether blacks or grizzlies, apparently have an inhibiting effect upon the "recreational activities of park guests." Clearly man's inhibiting effect on wildlife is not the point at issue.

With a current Canadian "potential sportsmen's harvest" of about 30,000 black bears a year, as recommended by Canadian provincial and federal experts, it is to be expected that the gunners will be able to shed enough blood to satisfy them...for the nonce. But when the last black bears have gone the route of their white and brown cousins, what will the sportsmen turn to then, poor things?

8
The Musk Bearers

The decline of the fur-bearing animals of northeastern America embraces almost every species of any monetary worth but is best epitomized by what happened to the musk bearers (so called because most of them have musk-producing scent glands), including marten, fisher, ermine (weasel), otter, wolverine, and mink. Most of these were especially valued for their dense, short-haired fur, which was of a quality greatly esteemed for dress and decoration by wealthy Europeans. In consequence, they provided the sustaining basis for the early trade in peltry from the New World.

Initially the most sought-after member of the family was the marten. About the size of a small cat, it was clothed in a soft, rich fur that usually ranged from buff to reddish-brown but could be almost black. All marten pelts were of great worth, but the rather rare black colour phase, known as sable, was so costly that its use was mainly restricted to royalty.

Martens were found everywhere coniferous forests grew, from the edge of the tundra south through most of the New England states. For a predator, the species was extraordinarily abundant, which, of course, it could only have been so long as its prey—chiefly squirrels, rabbits, and other small mammals—were equally abundant. In mid-seventeenth century, Josselyn reported the marten as being "innumerable" in New England and, as late as 1749, two Canadiens and two Indians caught 400 on Labrador's Northwest River in a single winter. Even as late as 1902, a single trapper working a previously unhunted part of Anticosti Island killed 300 in a year.

By the mid-1700s, the French in Canada were annually exporting 30,000–40,000 martens, mostly trapped by Indians in Nova Scotia and New Brunswick. At the same time, large quantities were also being exported from Newfoundland and the New England colonies. In 1768, Captain Cartwright wrote of the marten in Newfoundland: "A creature with which the whole country abounds, and is of all others most easily entrapped by the furrier... it follows every track made by man, is allured by the smell of provisions, haunts buildings [and so is] easily turned to its own destruction."

As the nineteenth century began, what must originally have seemed an inexhaustible supply of martens began to fail as human predation mounted.

Toward the end of the 1800s, they had become rarities throughout the eastern part of North America—even in the interior of Labrador. John Rowan gives us a sorry glimpse of what was happening to the last of the agile little animals in the 1870s. "Martens have of late years been destroyed by trappers by means of poison laid in little pellets of grease [which] preserve the poison from the weather. Sometimes a crow flies off with one of these ... and drops dead. A fox in turn picks up the crow, so that many more animals are destroyed than are found by the poisoner." In the same period, Tocque, in Newfoundland, wrote: "[although] formerly great numbers were taken by the [Micmac] Indians, they are now but seldom met with."

By the early decades of the twentieth century, the marten was believed to be extinct on Anticosti and was definitely so on Prince Edward Island. By the 1950s, it had disappeared from Cape Breton, had almost vanished from the rest of Nova Scotia, was verging on extinction in Newfoundland, where the distinct local race had been internationally listed as an endangered species, was gone from most of New England, and was rare in eastern Quebec and Labrador.

Since then, some action has been taken to prevent its complete extinction. Martens are now officially protected in Newfoundland and Nova Scotia where relict populations of a few score, or possibly hundreds, may still survive. The species has been re-introduced into some other regions, including New Brunswick, where it had been extirpated. However, if only because of its loss of habitat, it is unlikely that it will ever recover more than a fraction of its original numbers.

The lithe and graceful otter is one of the most attractive of our native mammals. It is now rare although at first contact it was so abundant, and so tame, that it was used as a staple food by summer cod fishers and early settlers. Science does not officially recognize the fact, but there seem to be two distinct races in the eastern seaboard region. The smaller of the two, generally brown in colour, inhabits fresh water and is seldom more than four feet long. The other, which may grow to as much as five feet in length, is sometimes so dark as to appear black and lives in and by salt water. Countrymen from Newfoundland and Labrador make a clear distinction between the two kinds, which they claim not only look unlike but have a different quality of fur and behave in different ways.

At least one large salt-water otter has lived for several years on and near my peninsular property in Cape Breton. I see it rarely but, in winter, it makes use of my snowshoe trails through the woods—perhaps hunting rabbits—

and its tracks are nearly twice the size of a "normal" otter. One summer day in 1977, it emerged from the forest onto an open beach a hundred yards in front of me as I was walking my three dogs. They spurted after the animal, which paused, drew itself up on its hind legs, and awaited their approach. Nonplussed, the dogs skidded to a halt a few feet distant, and only then did the otter, which seemed nearly as big as a dog itself, nonchalantly lower itself to the beach, amble into the sea, and swim leisurely away. This individual, or one like it, dives for mussels and bay scallops in several fathoms of water well offshore, then cracks and eats them under an isolated spruce at the tip of a windswept gravel bar where it and, doubtless, its ancestors have amassed a veritable kitchen midden of empty shells. This is behaviour of a kind I have never seen mirrored by a freshwater otter.

It seems to have been the "maritime" form that suffered first at the hands of invading Europeans. Anthony Parkhurst, circa 1578, tells us that "Of Otters we [the fishermen] may take like store [with the bears, which were so numerous] everywhere, so you may kill them as oft as you list." Denys, in the early part of the next century, wrote, "The taste is very much the same [as the French otter] but they differ from those in France in this, that they are... longer and blacker." Almost without exception, early commentators refer to the animal in terms such as "very common," "plentiful," or "abundant," and it is usually clear from the context that they are referring to the marine form. Cartwright, in 1768, wrote that the islands in northern Newfoundland were occupied by otters and, at the turn of that century, furriers in Exploits Bay depended heavily on trapping otters from salt water.

The freshwater form early came to the attention of the French as they worked their way into the interior via the St. Lawrence system. It must have been at least as abundant as its marine counterpart. Lahontan, around 1680, described a month spent with a band of Indians in the Saguenay country, during which "the Savages took about two hundred and fifty Canada Otters; the best of which... are sold in France for four or five [crowns]."

Fur returns for the nineteenth century show that a great number of river otters were still being killed, but the supply of marine otters had dwindled to the point where the few pelts that appeared at European fur sales were simply regarded as being especially large and dark Canada otters. By the time the twentieth century opened, both kinds had become scarce.

There seems little likelihood of any marked improvement in their status. Not only do they still have to contend with deliberate destruction for the fur business, but they have lost and continue to lose more and more of their original habitat. There are now few places left where they can find security.

As one Canadian mammalogist noted in 1975, "Many otters are killed each year in lakes and coastal areas by hunters cruising in boats or waiting for the moose or game bird on shore. This senseless plinking at Otters combined with heavy trapping of the species could cause great depletion, even extermination in some regions."

This is an understatement. By 1975, the otter was extinct in Prince Edward Island and so rare in Nova Scotia and New Brunswick that the annual "harvest" from these two provinces had shrunk from several thousands at the beginning of the century to a mere 560. In 1976, the total kill of otters from the whole of Canada was only 16,000 and the federal Wildlife Service considered that the species was being "harvested to its full potential"—whatever that may be.

Anyone who sees an otter in the wild these days can count him or herself lucky. As for our descendants, they may never know the otter at all, except in company with so many other once but no longer abundant animals—as dull denizens of zoos.

The fox-size fisher (so-called) is a scaled-up version of the marten. It is as swift and agile as its cousin and just as much at home in the upper branches of the forest. More elusive than its smaller relative, the fisher seldom permits itself to be seen by man. Nevertheless, it is very curious and, therefore, as easy to trap as the marten. It depends heavily on porcupines and varying hares for its food but, strange to say, does not fish for a living; in fact, it displays a cat-like aversion for water.

The name "fisher" is obviously a misnomer, a fact that has long mystified naturalists. I think the explanation is one of transposed identity. As we shall see, two similar-looking species of musk bearers originally inhabited the northeastern seaboard. One was indeed a fisherman and came to the attention of Europeans early on. The other was a denizen of dense forests, whose existence was not widely known until the age of settlement was well advanced. When the first animal, the *true* fisher, was driven into extinction, I believe its name was insensibly transferred to the look-alike animal that bears it today. The original name by which the woodland animal we now call fisher was known to Indians and early French and English traders was *pékan* or pekan.

Always elusive in life, the pekan is a vague presence in the historic annals except as a statistic in fur returns which, incidentally, show that the pelt of the female commanded a premium price, thus exerting extra pressure on the species in its struggle to survive intensive hunting. The fur returns also show that it was trapped relentlessly, and in such numbers that, by the end of the nineteenth century, it had been effectively destroyed throughout most of its northeastern range.

Its natural history is so scantily recorded that there is no clear-cut evidence that it inhabited Newfoundland before the arrival of Europeans. If it did, it is now totally extinct there. It had also become extinct on Anticosti and Prince Edward Island before 1900 and was exterminated in Nova Scotia before the 1930s. It is now all but extinct in the northeastern United States and so rare in Gaspé and in New Brunswick that, as long ago as 1935, some biologists were expressing the fear that it might already have been extirpated throughout the whole northeastern portion of its former range.

Such might well have been the pekan's fate had it not been for an astonishing reversal in our perception of its value. The years immediately after World War II saw an explosive growth in the pulp and paper industry throughout the northeastern seaboard region, with a consequent massive over-harvesting of the forests. By the late 1950s, it had already become apparent that trees were being consumed faster than natural growth could replace them. But since a reduction or even stabilization of paper and pulp production was unthinkable (to the contrary, it had to be increased), more raw materials had to be made available through other expedients.

It was therefore decided that there must be less waste and "greater utilization." The way chosen to achieve these ideal industrial objectives was to attempt to destroy other living things which might be taking toll, no matter how natural a one, of the chosen trees. So began the crusade against "forest pests."

Pests are those life forms that are seen to compete with us in our quest for profits through the exploitation of natural resources. Consequently, insects such as the spruce budworm, which have existed as part of a balanced forest community since time immemorial, are pests. So are hardwoods such as maple and birch trees that have the temerity to grow amongst stands of spruce and pine we covet for the pulp machines. They all must go.

The war to exterminate the perceived competitors of the pulp industry in Atlantic Canada and the New England states has now been raging for more than thirty years. The principal weapons used have been, and remain, noxious aerial sprays. Thousands of tons of such poisons as DDT and organo-phosphate insecticides have drenched forests, fields, rivers, and lakes; and their baleful effects have recently been reinforced by the spraying of hardwood defoliants containing ingredients used in the infamous Agent Orange that devastated plant, animal, and human life alike in Vietnam.

As to the results achieved by this ongoing chemical warfare, it is worthy of note that in New Brunswick, for example, the spruce budworm remains persistently alive and vigorous despite having been under intensive aerial attack through three decades; the general devastation wrought by the rain of poison on vertebrate life has been incalculable.

Insects and hardwoods are not the only life forms accused of reducing the amount of pulp available to the mills. Porcupines and varying hares are also considered pests since both eat tree bark, especially in winter when other food is hard to get. However, they in turn are eaten by the pekan, and the discovery of this fact led the pulp and paper industry to require of the governments of Nova Scotia, New Brunswick, and Quebec that the pekan, or fisher, be protected in all stands of "marketable" timber, and be re-introduced where it had already been exterminated.

The behest was obeyed with the happy result that the pekan reappeared on Anticosti Island and in parts of Nova Scotia and New Brunswick. Unfortunately, the big martens did not justify their existence by waging the hoped-for war of extermination against porcupines and hares and, in consequence, the pulp and paper industry lost interest in them. The interests of others, though, had been aroused by the modest comeback of the fisher, and provincial Fish and Game authorities responded by opening a trapping season on the animals. Thus, in 1976, sixty-four pekans were legally trapped in Nova Scotia and 172 in New Brunswick. This is thought to have represented as much as 80 per cent of the number born that year.

It would appear that unless the pekan finds another champion as powerful as the pulp and paper industry, the likelihood of its continuing survival is tenuous at best.

If the pekan has had some quondam friends amongst modern men, the wolverine has not. As large as a medium-sized dog, the chunky wolverine looks somewhat bear-like. It is equipped with stout claws, sharp teeth, remarkably tough skin, and a steely musculature that, in combination, protect it from most potential enemies.

Early man was no threat to its survival. Native peoples regarded the powerful "little bear" with exasperated respect, seeing in it the personification of a puckish spirit who liked to play sharp tricks on humankind. The wolverine has a remarkable faculty for locating and successfully raiding food caches, human or otherwise. Indians met this challenge, not by attempting to eliminate the raiders, but by constructing ingenious tree-caches the animal could not reach.

Europeans were not so passive. When wolverines raided storage depots built by early colonists, making light of massive barriers of logs, earth, and even stones, the owners were infuriated. They became even angrier when they began commercial furring and discovered their traplines being patrolled by wolverines, who not only ate the corpses of captured animals but, with what seemed like deliberate contempt, sprang traps set for them, then defecated on the traps.

The wolverine had no redeeming features in European eyes. Its tough and musky flesh was almost inedible, and its comparatively coarse fur of little commercial value. So the newcomers personified it as Indian Devil and characterized it as a truly wicked beast endowed with satanic cunning. Reputedly driven by a savage blood lust and possessed of an insatiable appetite (glutton was another of the names bestowed on it), it became the object of a remorseless vendetta. Because of the wolverine's sagacity and its ability to avoid traps and guns, victory over it remained elusive until the invaders stumbled on a fatal weakness in its defences. Being much attracted to carrion—the riper the better—the wolverine proved peculiarly vulnerable to the use of poison.

It is important to realize that the word "trapper" is often a misnomer. From the earliest days of the European fur trade in North America, the name "poisoner" would have been equally appropriate. Although traps and snares were an essential part of the trappers' death-dealing equipment, these men also relied heavily on arsenic and strychnine and whatever other poisons they could acquire. They continue to do so in our time. Despite laws prohibiting it, some modern "trappers" have graduated to the use of sophisticated and fearsome new chemical killers such as those routinely used by Canadian and U.S. government agencies against "pests and vermin."

By about 1700, poison had come to be considered the only sure way to destroy wolverines, and it has remained in favour ever since. During the winter of 1948–49, I stayed for a time with a white trapper in northern Manitoba. One day he found what might have been a blurred wolverine trail crossing his trapline. He reacted by hurriedly making several wolverine "sets." These consisted of piles of rotten caribou guts liberally laced with cyanide. During the succeeding few days, as I accompanied him around his trapline, I noted three foxes, a lynx, some forty or fifty ravens and Canada jays, and two sled dogs from a nearby Indian encampment, all lying dead near the baits. They were some of the usual by-products of the poisoner's trade. We did not, however, find a wolverine; probably because there had not been one in the vicinity in the first place. That winter, only five were traded from the whole of Manitoba north of Reindeer Lake, a region embracing about 200,000 square miles of what had once been prime wolverine territory.

Originally, the wolverine ranged over most of the northern half of the continent from Pacific to Atlantic and from the shores of the Arctic Ocean south at least to Oregon and Pennsylvania. Not only was it one of the most widespread of predators, it was also one of the most successful. Today it is extinct throughout more than two-thirds of its former range. It has been extirpated from Prince Edward Island, Nova Scotia, New Brunswick, and the northeastern United States. It is so rare as to be virtually extinct in much of the rest of its original habitat, including Labrador and most of Quebec and Ontario. During the trapping season of 1976–77, not one was reported as having been trapped to the eastward of Quebec City, and this despite the fact that wolverine fur had by then become a valuable article of trade.

Wolverine hair possesses the unique property of inhibiting the formation on it of frost crystals. Inuit and Indians took advantage of this quality by using wolverine fur to trim their parka hoods. The expanding popularity of fur-trimmed parkas, which began as a fashion fad in the 1960s and has now become an essential part of outdoor winter recreation, particularly by snow-mobilers and others such, resulted in a great demand for previously almost worthless wolverine pelts. By 1980, a good pelt was fetching $200. Today, a top-quality untanned wolverine skin can fetch as much as $500. Tomorrow...who can tell?

One thing is certain. As the wolverine edges closer to extinction, and its skin becomes ever rarer, it will also become more and more valuable. So the spiral of death will tighten, if we permit it, to its inexorable end.

As I have hypothesized, the name "fisher," now carried by the pekan, probably originated with a related but quite separate species now vanished from this earth. It might well have vanished from memory, too, had it not been for a twentieth-century discovery in a Maine Indian kitchen midden of bone fragments from an animal unknown to science. Although considerably larger, the bones were mink-like in character and so zoologists christened the unknown creature "giant mink." What follows is an attempt to unmuddle the true nature and re-establish at least something of the history of a lost species.

Early European venturers found a good many familiar animals in the New World, and of those that were new to them, one seemed to combine the elements of several known kinds. In body shape and gait it was reminiscent of a greyhound, while in its agility and some of its habits, it seemed rather more feline. Although generally fox-red in colour, its short, dense fur seemed more akin to that of a marten. Its head was otter-like and it lived an aquatic sort of life, fishing for its dinner along rocky, exposed sea coasts and from remote, outer islands.

Being a coastal creature it was probably one of the earliest fur-bearers to come to the attention of Europeans. Its pelt would have commanded a goodly price since it combined some of the admired qualities of otter and marten with a unique reddish hue. We have no way of knowing what its European discoverers called this unusual creature; indeed, some of the early voyagers seem to have been in doubt about what to call it themselves.

The earliest mention of it may be a reference in Sir Humphrey Gilbert's late sixteenth-century proposal for establishing a colony in the New World. As noted earlier, in his advertising brochure for the project, he lists some of the exploitable resources of the western seas, such as seals, whales, and horse-fyshe (by which he meant the grey seals). He also includes a species described only as a *fyshe like a greyhound*. Unable to find any species of fish that even remotely answers to this description, and forgetting that to a man of the sixteenth century anything, including mammals, that lived in salt water was a "fish," historians have dismissed the mysterious creature as a flight of fancy. Yet no less an authority than the renowned English naturalist Joseph Banks, who voyaged to Newfoundland in 1766 to study the local fauna, made the following observation while in Belle Isle Strait.

"About the middle of [September] an Extraordinary animal was seen by Mr. Phipps...bigger than a Fox, tho not much, in make and shape nearest compared to an Italian Greyhound, legs long, tail long and tapering...[it] Came up from the Sea."

Neither Phipps nor Banks could identify this animal although both were accomplished zoologists familiar with the fauna of the north temperate zone. The similarity to Gilbert's *fyshe like a greyhound* seems too striking to be mere coincidence.

Early in the seventeenth century, the creature may have been known in New England as the water marten. William Wood, writing about the fauna there, gives a list of "Beasts living in the water." It includes otter, beaver, muskrat, and a kind of "martins," which Wood describes as "being good fur for their bigness," by which he evidently meant valuable fur because of being larger than the ordinary marten. What was this animal? It cannot have been the marten we know today—besides being small, it detests water of any kind. It seems unlikely that it was the mink, which is even smaller than any marten, weighing at best a mere two pounds.[1]

---

[1] Because of their small size, inconspicuousness, and wide distribution, the two smallest musk bearers, the weasel and the mink, have managed to survive the European invasion more successfully than their larger brethren. Nevertheless, the populations of both are probably only fractionally as abundant as they were at first contact.

The early French also seem to have been familiar with the creature but have lumped it in with the otter family. In his description of the fur-bearers of Acadia, New France, and Newfoundland, Lahontan describes the "Winter and Brown Otters," worth "4 Livres 10 sous," and the "Red and Smooth Otters," worth "2 Livres." From other sources, we know that the blackish marine otter was sometimes listed as a winter otter, so it would seem that Lahontan is here bracketing marine and freshwater otters together under the description "Winter and Brown." What then are the "Red and Smooth" ones that are only worth half as much, presumably because of their smaller size? Are they the original fisher?

The creature seems to have retained the identity of fisher, or fisher cat in New England, until the main focus of the fur trade shifted west away from the depleted coasts and into the still abundantly stocked interior of the continent. Perhaps as early as 1800, trapper-traders transferred the fisher's name to the pekan of the interior because it bore a resemblance to the coastal creature now left behind in physical fact, and soon to be left behind in memory as well. Certain it is that at about this juncture the original fisher, reduced to a remnant of its original numbers, began to be known as sea mink, the name by which it would be called until the end of its existence.

A fish like a greyhound, water marten, red otter, fisher cat, sea mink— this multiplicity of names has so confused the identity of the animal that perhaps it is not surprising that science failed to recognize its existence until the discovery of its bones left no alternative. Still, it is hard to understand how it could have been so neglected for so long by both natural and social historians. It is surprisingly easy to establish its one-time presence along the more than 10,000 miles of coastline fringing the Atlantic approaches from Cape Cod to mid-Labrador. Its abundance can be inferred from the fact that, although it was heavily exploited from the onset of the European invasion, a remnant population managed to exist until well into the nineteenth century.

During the late 1700s, we have records of Nova Scotian whites and Micmac Indians regularly hunting sea mink on islands from La Have north to Halifax, to which town the pelts were taken to be sold. On one occasion, a Micmac woman was relieved there of several sea mink skins, plus the pelt of a bear, in exchange for a quart of wine.

Less is known about its presence in the northern part of its range, but in 1766 French settlers at the northern tip of Newfoundland told Joseph Banks that "they every now and then See these animals in Hare Bay, and an old Furrier we spoke with told us he remembered a skin sold for five Guineas."

The Maine coast seems to have been a preferred habitat. Periodically, men with specially trained dogs would visit islands frequented by sea mink. They went in daylight because, perhaps as a consequence of their long persecution, the animal was largely nocturnal, feeding by night and lying up in caves, rock crevices, and other such shelters by day. The dogs were quick to pick up what was described as the strong but not unpleasant musky scent of the quarry and would lead the hunters to its hiding place. If this could not be broken open with pick, shovel, and crowbar, the hunters might smoke the creature out with burning sulphur or pitch. If the crevice was shallow, they might fire black pepper into it from muzzleloading guns. If all else failed, they did not hesitate to insert powder charges and blow the refuge open, though odds were the animal would be so mutilated that its pelt would be worth little.

Up to 1860, a few sea mink skins were still being offered for sale in Boston every year, but after that date it was seldom seen, alive or dead. The last Maine record is of one killed on an island near Jonesport in 1880. The last known survivor of the species anywhere was killed on Campobello Island, New Brunswick, in 1894.

So perished a unique and, as Joseph Banks noted, extraordinary animal. Its like will not be seen again. Yet, for a time, something of it will remain. Scattered along the rock-bound coasts from Maine to Newfoundland are a number of small islands that once provided welcome haven to sea mammals and birds alike.

Each bears the self-same name...now meaningless.

Mink Island.

9

The Passing of the Buff

The first great source of wealth to be exploited by Europeans in the northeastern reaches of the New World was oil. Next came fish. The third was not, as we have been taught to believe, fur. It was a more mundane commerce in the skins of those large mammals that lent themselves to the making of leather.

Encapsuled in our plastic age, we have already forgotten the universal and overwhelming importance of leather in the lives of our ancestors. Early seamen used it for cordage on their vessels and, in some cases, sheathed their boats with it. In one form or another it has shod mankind since dim antiquity. Through the millennia it clothed aristocrats and peasants alike. It was essential to a thousand artisan and agricultural trades and was invaluable in domestic life, where it appeared in forms ranging from the bellows that revived the hearth fires to tooled morocco binding on rare books. However, nowhere was it used in greater quantity than in warfare.

Prior to the fifteenth century, armies not only marched on leather or rode chargers saddled and reined with it, individual soldiers carried leather shields or wore heavy leather clothing as a form of armour. Because of its toughness and durability it remained in favour with the military even after firearms largely negated its protective role. Well into the nineteenth century, leather was still being used in huge quantities for military software.

Before the discovery of the Americas, leather for military clothing had long been a specialty product known variously throughout western Europe as *bufle*, *buffle*, or simply *buff*. This was a particularly stout though supple leather of a whitish-yellow colour. The name was derived from the Greek word for wild ox, reflecting an ancient preference for skins of the aurochs, the archetypal wild cattle of mythology.

By mid-fifteenth century, both the aurochs and Europe's only other wild cattle, the wisent (later, bison), had been mostly hunted to death and, for want of anything better, buff was being made out of the greatly inferior hides of domestic cattle. This was true everywhere except in Portugal where a product as good as the original was still being produced from the imported skins of a mysterious creature the Portuguese called *bufalo* and whose identity and native heath was a closely guarded trade secret.

120

The Portuguese had discovered it during their explorations of the west African coast, which began about 1415. The mystery animal was in reality the African wild ox, which to this day bears the name Cape buffalo. The Portuguese carried its hides home, where they were turned into splendid buff that sold at premium prices all over Europe.

That first buffalo had to share the name with a second species after Vasco da Gama rounded Cape of Good Hope in 1498, then sailed eastward to a landfall on the Malabar coast of India. Here, he encountered an Asian wild ox whose hide had the desirable qualities of the African variety. It was distinguished from the first by the name water buffalo, and its hides, too, went to strengthen the Portuguese buff monopoly.

The third wild ox to bear the name was also discovered by the Portuguese, probably at about the same time as the second—but on the western shores of the Atlantic Ocean.

This was the North American buffalo. An enormous creature—a big bull could weigh over a ton, measure twelve feet in length, and stand seven feet high at the shoulders—it roamed most of the continent and was at home from the Arctic Circle to the shores of the Gulf of Mexico.

Immensely adaptive, it dominated a bewildering variety of habitats ranging through sub-Arctic spruce bogs, alpine meadows, the Great Plains, the massive hardwood forests of the east, and the sub-tropical forests of the south. At least four distinct races had evolved: the Plains buffalo; the wood buffalo, a larger, darker animal inhabiting the forests of the northwest; the Oregon buffalo, a mountain-dwelling cousin of the Plains variety; and finally the eastern buffalo, largest and darkest of all, which claimed the forested eastern half of the continent as its homeland.

By any standards these animals were all extraordinarily successful. Having outlasted the only predators that were ever their physical equals—prehistoric beasts such as the sabre-toothed cats and the enormous dire wolves—they had had no difficulty holding their own against aboriginal man through the twenty to forty millennia of his occupancy of North America. At about the year 1500 they are believed to have numbered more than 70 million individuals and were perhaps the most numerous large mammalian species on the planet.

Although the bloody history of the Plains buffalo is relatively well known, that of the eastern buffalo has been consigned to oblivion. Neither historians nor biologists seem even to be aware of the magnitude of its aboriginal herds, or of the fact that it was the dominant large herbivore of the Atlantic seaboard when the European invasion began.

The black-robed, forest-dwelling eastern buffalo was not only the largest of its kind, it also bore the greatest sweep of horns and its extraordinarily tough hide was proof against penetration by any except the sharpest of weapons. For native bowmen or spearmen on foot (and it will be remembered that there were no domesticated horses in the Americas until the Spaniards introduced them), it made exceedingly formidable prey. In consequence, and also because the woodland Indians had a plethora of easier prey at their disposal, buffalo seem to have seldom been hunted by them. However, northeastern tribesmen sometimes took the risk to obtain the huge, woolly hides because there were no better winter sleeping robes. It may well have been some of these robes, stolen or traded from east-coast Indians by the first Portuguese, that alerted them to a bonanza in buff in this New World.

During the first third of the sixteenth century the Portuguese maintained a monopoly on North American buff, but then the French got wind of it. After his 1542 excursion up the St. Lawrence River, the Sieur de Roberval noted that the natives "feed also on stagges, wild boares, *bufles*, porsepines…" Before another decade had passed, the French were themselves busily trading for buffalo skins. By mid-century, they had virtually supplanted the Portuguese. In the Gulf of St. Lawrence, two nephews of Jacques Cartier "continued from year to year to traffic there with the said savages, in the skins of bufles, [and] bufle calves." The French also expanded the trade to the south. Pedro Menendez wrote angrily to his master, King Philip II of Spain, to complain about French inroads on the coast. "In 1565," he reported, "and for some years previous, buffalo-skins were brought by the Indians down the Potomac River and there carried along shore in canoes to the French about the Gulf of St. Lawrence. During two years 6000 skins were thus obtained."

Before very long, buff manufactured in France had become particularly renowned. As Charlevoix wrote: "There is none better [than this hide] in the known world; it is easily dressed, and though exceeding strong, becomes as supple and soft as the best chamois." According to the Bristol merchant Thomas James, it was equivalent in toughness to walrus leather, and a great deal was imported from France into England, where entire regiments were outfitted with it. At least one, the famous Buffs, even took its name from the leather worn by its soldiers.

The English were initially behind in getting their share of this new wealth. Nevertheless, by 1554 they at least knew what a buffalo was, as is evidenced by John Lok's comment that an elephant was "bigger than three wilde Oxen or Buffes." By the 1570s, they knew what it looked like. "These Beasts are of the bigness of a Cowe, their flesh being very good foode, their hides good lether, their fleeces very useful, being a kind of wolle...it is tenne yeares since first the relation of these things came to the eares of the English."

Anthony Parkhurst, who fished Newfoundland waters from 1574 to 1578, befriended some Portuguese seafarers who promised to pilot him to Cape Breton and into "the River of Canada"—the St. Lawrence. To his annoyance they reneged, but he seems to have learned from them of the existence of "buffes...in the countries adjacent [to Newfoundland] which [buffes] were very many in the firm land [mainland]."

It was at about this time that another English sailor, John Walker, made what was probably a buccaneering visit to Norumbega—the Maine coast/Bay of Fundy region—which was then coming under French influence. Walker explored the lower reaches of the St. John River where he and his men "founde...in an Indian house...300 drye hides, whereof the most parte of them were eighteen feet by the squire." We are told these hides came from "a kinde of Beaste much bigger than an [domestic] Oxe," and that Walker carried his stolen hides to France where he sold them for forty shillings each—a large sum in those times. The report concludes by adding: "With this agreeth David Ingram, and [he] describeth that beast as large, supposing it to be a certain kind of Buffe."

David Ingram was the English seaman marooned on the coast of the Gulf of Mexico in 1568 by John Hawkins. Ingram spent the next two years walking north, mostly along the Atlantic seaboard, in search of fellow Europeans, meantime being succoured by the native people. He eventually met a French trader in what is now central Nova Scotia and got passage to France with him, thence making his way back to England. Here, in 1582, he was interviewed by agents of Sir Humphrey Gilbert and told them: "There is a very great store of these Buffes [in the coastal regions he travelled through] which are beasts as big as two oxen...having long ears like a bloodhound with long hairs about their ears, their horns be crooked like rams horns, their eyes black, their hairs long, black and rough and shagged as a goat. The hides of these beasts are sold very dear." In another context, Ingram is quoted as speaking of "[Norum]Bega, a country or town of that name...wherein are good store of [wild] Oxe Hides."

Historians contend that the skins Walker stole (and which the Norumbega Indians had probably amassed to trade to the French) were moose hides, but such a conclusion is not warranted in view of their size—

"eighteen feet by the squire." By the squire, or square, means the measurements of two adjacent sides multiplied to give the square footage, which is how such hides were sold. Even when stretched, hides of the biggest moose do not exceed fifteen feet on the square, while those of the wood buffalo—the largest surviving race—though nevertheless smaller than the eastern buffalo, *do* measure up to eighteen feet.[1]

Sir Humphrey Gilbert was especially interested in Ingram's story and Walker's voyage because, during the 1570s, he was trying to mount a colonizing venture with the intention of establishing English suzerainty over Newfoundland, Norumbega, and Nova Scotia. He had to persuade potential backers that the venture would show a profit, and he concluded that buffs would help to do just that. In 1580, he dispatched a Portuguese named Simon Ferdinando on a voyage to the Norumbega coast, from which Ferdinando brought back "many great hides" that are elsewhere identified as buffalo hides.

By this time the French were becoming alarmed at the prospects of an English encroachment on their buff monopoly. In 1583, Etienne Bélanger took a party of Frenchmen from Cape Breton as far south as Cape Cod in what was perhaps an attempt to forestall the English who, in the following year, according to Hakluyt, traded with the Indians of the Virginia coast for buff hides. These are probably but two of many ventures seeking a fortune in hides such as the one John Walker reaped in Norumbega.

It is unlikely that they met with such good luck. By 1590, after about a century of increasingly intense exploitation, it appears that most of the buffalo that had once lived between the Hudson River/Lake Champlain valley and the sea had already perished. As the century ended, so did the days of the species' abundance anywhere east of the Appalachian Mountains. To sixteenth-century natives of the eastern seaboard region, buffalo hides had been what beaver skins later became for tribes farther to the west—the currency with which to purchase guns, metalware, trinkets, and booze. The magnificent black wild oxen of the eastern forests, which had taken small harm at the hands of men armed with stone-tipped weapons, fell in windrows before the same men now armed with guns. The stink of their rotting carcasses was the first whiff of a stench that would sweep across an entire continent.

---

[1] Confusion has crept in because, after buffalo had been exterminated on the eastern seaboard, the French hide trade switched to moose, while retaining the name "buff" to identify the product.

During the first few decades of the new century, numbers of eastern buffalo still existed, but only well inland from the coast. In 1612, Sir Samuel Argoll sailed about 200 miles up the Potomac River to the vicinity of what is now southern Pennsylvania where, "Marching into the Countrie, I found great stores of Cattle as big as Kine, of which the Indians who were my guides killed a couple, which we found to be very good and wholesome meat, and are very easy to be killed, in regard they are heavy, slow and not so wild as other Beasts of the wilderness." "Easy to be killed *with firearms*" is how this passage should be read.

Too easy. Buffalo were not again recorded on the Potomac after 1624 and, far to the northward in the Huron region of New France, the story was the same. By 1632, according to the Jesuit priest, Father Sagard, although "some of our Brothers have seen skins of them" none had been seen in life for some years past. Even Samuel de Champlain, who as early as 1620 had listed *bufles*, together with moose and elk, as valuable resources of New France, seems to have come on the scene too late to encounter the living animal. About 1650, Pierre Boucher reported: "As for the animals called buffaloes, they are [now] to be found only.........about four or five hundred leagues from Quebec toward the west and north."

Remnants of the eastern buffalo still held on in the central and southern portions of their range. Thus the Sieur de La Salle recorded their presence as late as 1680 in what are now New York, Pennsylvania, some western portions of New England, and south to Georgia. Courtemanche, in about 1705, reported that *boeufs* were still innumerable in the valley of the Illinois River.

West of the Appalachian mountain barrier they continued to survive until the last years of the seventeenth century, when a surge of Europeans came pouring over the passes following deep-cut trails made by the buffalo themselves. Daniel Boone was in the forefront of this invasion and he and his contemporaries spoke of places like Blue Licks, a salt lick where buffalo paths converging from all directions "were cut deep into the earth like the streets of a great city."

These "hardy pioneers," as they are so often referred to in history books, were not so much settlers as wandering ravagers whose sights were set on peltry rather than on land. They spread rapidly westward bringing such destruction to all the larger forms of life that, by 1720, the only survivors of the eastern buffalo consisted of a few small herds that had been bypassed and overlooked in the dark defiles and recesses of the Cumberland and Allegheny ranges. By 1790, according to a New York Zoological Society report, those hidden in the Alleghenies had "been reduced to one herd numbering 300–400 animals which had sought refuge in the wilds of the Seven Mountains where, surrounded on all sides by settlements, they survived for a short time by hiding in the almost-inaccessible parts of the mountains."

It was indeed a short time. During the bitter winter of 1799–1800, the herd, by then shrunken to fewer than fifty, was surrounded by gunners on snowshoes. Immobilized in belly-deep drifts, the animals were slaughtered where they stood. The following spring, a bull, a cow, and her calf were found in the same region. The cow and calf were promptly shot. The bull escaped, only to be killed a little later at Buffalo Crossroads near Lewistown.

Now the end was near. In 1815, a solitary bull is said to have been killed near Charleston, West Virginia. No more were reported until 1825, when a cow and her calf were found deep in the fastnesses of the Alleghenies. To find them was to kill them. So perished the last known relicts, not only of the eastern buffalo but of all the wild ox east of the Mississippi River.

The passing of the eastern buff went unremarked, and probably unnoticed. The latter-day conquistadors who were then busily "conquering the West" were already engaged in a new slaughter—one that would soon become an all-engulfing tornado of destruction.

By around 1800, according to the assessment of naturalist-writer Ernest Thompson Seton, some 40 million buffalo remained alive in North America, almost all of them west of the Mississippi Valley. It had taken European man and his weapons three centuries to dispose of the first several million. It would require rather less than 100 years to obliterate the rest in one of the most wanton exhibitions of unbridled ferocity in the long list of atrocities man has committed against animate creation.

The Plains, Oregon, and wood buffalo were systematically slaughtered because of three interlinked motives. First, as part of a genocidal design on the part of the Americans to destroy the western Indian nations (which depended for their very existence on the buffalo); second, because of the profits to be obtained therefrom; and third, because of an untrammelled lust for killing.

The first motive is laid bare in a statement by General Philip Henry Sheridan, which epitomizes the prevailing policy of the U.S. government and military: "The Buffalo Hunters have done more in the past two years to settle the vexed Indian Question than the entire regular army in the last 30 years. They are destroying the Indians' commissary. Send them powder and lead if you will, and let them kill, skin and sell until they have exterminated the buffalo!" Sheridan later told Congress it should strike a medal honouring the hide hunters, with a dead buffalo on one side—and a dead Indian on the other.

By about 1800, most of the large land mammals of eastern North America whose hides were suitable for the manufacture of leather, including the eastern buffalo, eastern elk, woodland caribou, and, in most regions, even the moose, were either commercially extinct or verging on it.[2] Yet the demand for leather of all kinds had never been greater and was growing by leaps and bounds. The exploitation of the western buffalo herds opened up a magnificent opportunity for profit. This was reinforced by the growth of a vigorous demand for buffalo robes—tanned hides with the thick, woolly hair still attached. These had a great vogue in Europe but especially in eastern North America, where they inspired a positive rage of fashionable acquisition. Everyone, it seemed, simply had to have one or more buffalo carriage robes.

Mass slaughter on the western plains combined with mass production in eastern factories between them were soon producing a flood of buffalo-hide products ranging from machinery belting to policemen's coats. During the 1840s, 90,000 buffalo robes alone were annually being sold in eastern Canada and the United States. However, these represented only the tip of a deadly iceberg of annihilation.

Seton estimated that only one out of every three Plains buffalo killed was ever even skinned. Furthermore, many of the skins that *were* taken were used locally in their raw state for such things as tarpaulins to protect haystacks against the weather, for fencing materials to confine the sod-busting pioneers' small livestock, or as easily replaceable roofing and wall sheathing.

The potential for profit was not limited to robes and leather, either. Many hundreds of thousands of animals were shot solely for their fat, which, rendered into tallow, was used in great quantities by eastern industries. Uncounted other thousands were killed for their tongues alone, these being considered a great delicacy. But the greatest slaughter, apart from that for hides, was the meat hunt, which provided the staple food for construction

---

[2] The eastern elk, which was common and widespread throughout the Atlantic seaboard region, is now extinct. The woodland caribou, once almost equally widely distributed and abundant, is virtually extinct throughout its eastern range. Having suffered such persecution by hide hunters and, later, from sportsmen that it was extirpated from much of the seaboard region, the moose remains moderately common in a few places, such as Newfoundland, but has vanished from about three-quarters of its original eastern range.

crews then crawling like ant armies across the plains, leaving behind them the glittering steel paths of new railroads reaching out to span the continent.

By 1842, again according to Seton, the combined kill had reached 2.5 million buffalo a year and the great western herds were melting like their own tallow in an incandescent fury of destruction. In 1858, James McKay, a Red River trader and trapper, travelled for twenty days on horseback with a pony train through what was to all intents and purposes one continuous herd of buffalo—"on all sides, as far as the eye could see, the prairie was black with them." Five years later, buffalo were a "thing of the past" throughout the whole of the region McKay had traversed.

Farther to the south, the Union Pacific Railway reached Cheyenne in 1867, penetrating to the heart of the remaining buffalo country. The iron horse brought with it innumerable white hunters and, at the same time, split the remaining buffalo into a south herd and a north herd.

"In 1871," Seton tells us, "the Santa Fe Railway crossed Kansas, the summer ground of the southern herd, now reduced to 4,000,000." There followed a sanguinary slaughter by hide hunters, and by sportsmen who were now beginning to come west to take a hand in the massacre just for the fun of it. Between 1872 and 1874, these two agents of destruction between them *recorded* a kill of 3,158,730! One sportsman, a Dr. Carver, boasted of having killed forty buffalo in a "twenty minute run" on horseback and of having slaughtered 5,000 during a single summer.

To paraphrase Seton's account: that was practically the end of the southern herd. A few scattered bands lingered on in out-of-the way places, but they, too, were relentlessly hunted down. The very last, a group of four individuals, were found in 1889 by a party hunting mustangs. The buffalo took alarm and fled westward. They were chased for several miles and a man named Allen fired four shots into a cow. She ran another two miles to a lake and, wading into the deepest water, stood at bay until death overcame her. A photographer then took a picture of the triumphant party with her skin and meat. The other three buffalo were killed a little later on.

The northern herd did no better. Although until 1876 severe winters coupled with the presence of hostile Indians discouraged white hunters, in that year U.S. troops "pacified" the Indians and encouraged an onslaught by hide and meat hunters. Then, in 1880, the Northern Pacific Railway opened a way into the central region, and that was the end of the last great buffalo herd on earth.

By 1885 none were known to remain alive in a state of freedom, yet their presence still endured. In 1887, William Greeb, an English naturalist, travelled through the West on the Canadian Pacific Railway. "Crossing and recrossing in all directions," he wrote, "were the tracks of the buffalo and the skulls and bones of these fine animals bleaching in the sun. At some of the water tanks where we stopped, heaps of bones and skulls have been collected for export to sugar refineries and to the manure-works of civilisation." As far as profits were concerned, the buffalo were good to the last bone.

Between 1850 and 1885, more than 75 million buffalo hides had been handled by American dealers. Most were shipped east on the railroads, which had contributed heavily to the extinction both directly and indirectly. William Frederick Cody, "Buffalo Bill," who was hired as a meat hunter by the Kansas Pacific Railway to feed its work gangs, gained much of his fame from having butchered 4,280 buffalo in a single eighteen-month period.

The railway companies also used buffalo to entertain their passengers. When a train came within rifle range of a herd it would be slowed or halted, the windows would be rolled down, and the passengers would be invited to have some sport, using guns and ammunition thoughtfully provided by the company. Men *and* women took advantage of this opportunity to enjoy themselves. No attempt was made to make use of the resultant carcasses, except that a trainman would sometimes cut out a few tongues to be served to the ladies and gentlemen at their next meal in tribute to their marksmanship.

Apologists for the destruction of the buffalo admit that their end was unfortunate, but they insist it was inevitable. The buffalo had to go, they say, to make room for more effective use of the land. That is another example of the dubious rationale used by modern man to justify the destruction of other species. Specialists studying the question of the meat-producing capacity of various ranges and grazing animals have recently concluded that the ability of the western plains to produce beef under human management has never exceeded, or even equalled, the ability of the same range to produce buffalo meat *without* human husbandry. All that was achieved by exterminating the buffalo and replacing them with cattle was to substitute a less successful and less valuable domestic animal for a more valuable and more successful wild one.

In any case, the buffalo were not butchered to make room for farmers. That excuse had not yet been invented at the time of their massacre. The brutal truth is that one of the most magnificent and vital forms of life on this planet was destroyed for no better reasons than our desire to eradicate the Plains Indians and an insatiable lust for booty... and for blood.

❖ # 10
Wild Cats and Dogs

THE CATS

North America's Great Cat is the cougar—a tawny, long-tailed creature that can measure nine feet from tip of nose to tip of tail and weigh more than 200 pounds; and its frightful screams at mating time can be a source of terror to the uninitiated.

Before the arrival of Western man, the cougar (mountain lion in the West, puma in the South) inhabited the most extensive territory of any New World mammal, ranging from northern British Columbia and Yukon, east to Nova Scotia, and southward throughout the whole of the United States, Central America, and on to Patagonia at the southern tip of South America. The eastern race, often called painter (panther), roamed the forests of all Canada's Atlantic Provinces except Newfoundland, south to the Gulf of Mexico and Florida.

They were much feared in New England in early times. Higginson, in the 1620s, refers to them as lions, and William Wood, about 1634, wrote of them: "Concerning lions, I will not say I ever saw any myself, but some affirm that they have seen a lion at Cape Anne, which is not above six leagues from Boston. Some likewise, being lost in the woods, have heard such terrible roarings as have made them aghast, which must either be devils or lions ... Besides, Plymouth men have traded for lions' skins in former times [on those coasts]."

By 1720 it had become well known to the French, through their contact with the Indians. Charlevoix describes it under its Indian name of *carcajou*.

"The moose has other enemies besides the Indians ... The most terrible of all is the *Carcajou* or *Quincajou*, a kind of cat, with a tail so long that he twists it several times round his body ... As soon as this hunter comes up with the moose, he leaps upon him, and fastens upon his neck, about which he twists his long tail, and cuts his jugular. The moose has no means of shunning this disaster, but by flying to the water the moment he is seized ... [if the moose is successful] the carcajou, who cannot endure the water, quits his hold immediately ... This hunter too as he does not possess the faculty of smelling with the greatest acuteness, carries three foxes a hunting with him, which he sends on the discovery. The moment they have got scent of a moose, two of them place themselves by his side, and the third takes post behind him; and all three manage matters so well, by harassing the prey, that they compel him to go to the place where they have left the carcajou, with whom they afterwards settle about...dividing the prey. Another wile of the carcajou...is to climb upon a tree, where couched along some projecting branch, he waits till a moose passes, and leaps upon him...Under what [other] climate can we find brute animals, indued with so strong an instinct, and so forcibly inclined to industry, as the fox...and the carcajou?"

The reputed co-operation between carcajou and foxes may make Charlevoix seem credulous, but it is a fact that foxes regularly scavenge cougar kills.

Despite its ferocious reputation, the carcajou proved no match for European arms and wiles. It would run from a pack of dogs or even a single dog and frequently take refuge in a tree. Here it could easily be killed even with the primitive firearms of the seventeenth century. Professional cat hunters considered it cowardly, but it only wished to avoid conflict with men. That avoidance, however, proved impossible and the carcajou of the northeast—the painter of the southeast—was harassed and harried, usually with a bounty on its head, until it had nowhere to hide except such havens as the great swamps of Florida, a few enclaves in the Appalachians, and the enormous tangle of forests in Gaspé and New Brunswick.

The last Quebec carcajou was killed near Sorel in 1863 and, with its death, even the name was lost, eventually to reappear attached to the wolverine in northwestern Canada. The last cougar known from Ontario was killed in 1884. By the turn of the century it was believed to be extinct everywhere in eastern Canada and the United States, with the exception of Florida where a few still held out in the depths of the Everglades.[1]

After World War II a peculiar phenomenon began to manifest itself in eastern North America. Rumours began to be heard, at first few and widely scattered, but eventually mounting almost to a flood, of cougars reappearing from Georgia to New Brunswick. Although such reports now number in the hundreds, all except four remain unsubstantiated. Four cougars have actually been killed in the eastern region since about 1950; but three seem to have been strays from the Florida swamps, while the fourth was an escaped, semi-domesticated animal. Nevertheless, the wish to believe that the

---

[1] The Florida cougar is of a different race from the eastern cougar. As of 1984, it is thought that no more than two or three dozen Florida cougars still survive.

eastern cougar still exists is so strong that even otherwise sceptical scientists have been caught up by it.

Beginning in 1948, Bruce S. Wright, then director of the Northeastern Wildlife Station in New Brunswick, began investigating reputed cougar sightings, and he was still doing so up to his death in 1975. By then he had collected 300 reports and had even found what he believed to be the track of a cougar. In a book he published in 1959, Wright maintained that the eastern form of the great cat not only survived but might number as many as a hundred individuals, mostly in Maine and New Brunswick but extending west to Gaspé and east to Cape Breton Island.

I, for one, would give a great deal to see Wright's optimism vindicated. Yet, despite the animal's great size, a heavy annual traffic of hunters through its supposed territory, and a mushrooming of visual reports from, among other unlikely places, the outskirts of the city of Truro, the hard fact is that not a single cougar has been reported killed and no scrap of flesh, bone, or hide has been found in eastern Canada or Maine in this century. Most reluctantly, I have to conclude that the wish has been father to the thought, and that the great cat of the eastern forests is now a ghost.

In the Gaspé region about 1680, according to LeClercq, there occurred "three kinds of Wolves. [One of these] the *Loup Cervier* has a silvery fur and two little tufts of wholely black fur on its head. Its flesh is pretty good though rank to the taste. This animal is more fearful to the eye than savage in reality."

LeClercq's three kinds of "wolves" are a good example of the confusions encountered in reconstructing the natural history of this continent. While there were indeed three species of canines in the Gaspé, neither the *Loup Cervier* nor another of LeClercq's trio, the *Loup Marin*, belonged to the canine family at all. The *Loup Marin* is in fact a seal, while the *Loup Cervier* is the lynx.

The chunky, short-tailed, long-legged lynx was probably never common in southern parts. It ranged from the northern tier of the United States to the tree line in the Arctic. It was of only moderate interest to early fur traders whose European markets demanded short, densely haired pelts; nor does it seem to have initially aroused much animosity in European man, probably because it was so shy and nocturnal that men seldom encountered it or even knew it was about.

Then it fell victim to an absurdity of human categorization. English colonists, who had no name of their own for the creature, adopted the French Loup Cervier, but corrupted it to Lucifer or Lucifee. Soon, the old adage about giving a dog, or in this case, a cat, a bad name came true. The godly Puritans assumed that any animal called after the Prince of Darkness had to be an enemy of man; consequently, the Lucifer, now endowed with satanic qualities, joined the bobcat on the list of proscribed animals.

Although at first contact it seems to have been common along the eastern seaboard at least as far south as Chesapeake Bay, the Lucifee got such short shrift from the settlers that, by the mid-1800s, it had been exterminated from all but the most heavily forested portions of the northern United States. By then it had shed the name of Lucifer and was carrying the name originally given to its Eurasian relative, the lynx. But the removal of the devilish stigma brought no relief from human persecution, for its soft, pastel-coloured fur had become valuable over the centuries with the result that, by the end of the nineteenth century, it was being hunted commercially all across northern North America.

By the beginning of World War II it was virtually extinct in the United States, except for a few score individuals widely dispersed through northern New England. It was totally extinct in Prince Edward Island and so scarce in the other Canadian Maritime Provinces that only a handful could be trapped in any given year. This despite the fact that the price paid for lynx skins, even in the Depression era, ranged as high as $40.

Newfoundland was a special case. First mention of the lynx in the history of that province would appear to be a reference to the presence of "tigers" found there by the Corte Real brothers in 1500–01. By 1505, at least one live lynx from Newfoundland had been carried across the ocean as a gift for King Henry VII of England. Other references make it clear that the Lucifer or Luzarne, as it was sometimes called, was fairly common throughout Newfoundland until the nineteenth century, when it suddenly seemed to vanish. Its apparent disappearance was so striking that some biologists conclude it had never been in Newfoundland at all until the later part of the century, when lynx from Labrador crossed frozen Belle Isle Strait.

This misapprehension seems to have arisen from the current belief that the lynx is so dependent on the varying hare that it cannot exist without it, ergo, it could not have survived in Newfoundland before the introduction of that hare into the island in the 1880s. The truth is that, before the arrival of Europeans, the Newfoundland lynx (which had evolved into a separate subspecies) made a good living on the indigenous Arctic hare, and, to a lesser degree, on straying calves from the immense herds of caribou that roamed the island. It was the massive destruction of these two species by white men that nearly brought an end to the Newfoundland lynx and, by an ironic twist, it was the human introduction of the fecund varying hare that saved it from extinction.

The lynx has retained a hold in Newfoundland, but its fate elsewhere has been grim. Beginning about twenty years ago, lynx fur was elevated to the heights by the arbiters of fashion as a "superb natural fun fur." Lynx pelts immediately shot up in value. By the late 1970s a good pelt was worth $200 and the market was so avid that entrepreneurs were chartering aircraft to fly trappers into previously untouched country where, by the use of traps, snares, and poison, they swept enormous regions clean of lynx. The slaughter had become so extensive by 1982 that pelt "production" was in sharp decline. In accordance with economic law, this shortage sent the price up just as sharply. Thus, although the 1983 catch of Canadian lynx was just half of what it had been in 1982, the price per skin had soared to an average of $400–$500, with as much as $1,000 being paid for a single pelt.

So drastic has been the consequent collapse in lynx populations that Ontario is contemplating a closed season in 1985. In the eastern seaboard region, where it was once abundant, the lynx is now so rare as to have been declared a protected species in New Brunswick. It may still be hunted in Nova Scotia, assuming it can be found, but only a handful of pelts have been taken in that province during the past several years.

On Cape Breton Island, which according to the always-optimistic Nova Scotia Department of Lands and Forests supposedly harbours a "healthy Lynx breeding stock," I have only once seen a lynx track and have not been able to confirm a single sighting during the past three years. Trappers tell me that, to all intents and purposes, the species is extinct, not only in Cape Breton, but in the remainder of the province as well. It is commercially extinct *everywhere* in the eastern maritime region of North America, except possibly Labrador, and it is not in notably better shape across the continent to the westward.

At a weight of around twenty pounds, the stump-tailed bobcat was the smallest, and probably the most abundant, of the three wild cats initially inhabiting the region. Preferring a more southerly climate than the lynx, the bobcat ranged only as far north as the St. Lawrence River and the Gulf.

Its rather coarse and brittle fur was never worth much in the fur trade, but this did not save it from becoming the object of a vendetta waged by the invading Europeans who convinced themselves that the wild cat was an insatiable killer, not only of wild animals that men coveted, but of domestic stock as well.

As early as 1727, Massachusetts was paying a thirty-shilling bobcat bounty and, as late as the 1930s, was still offering a bounty of ten dollars. Similar treatment almost everywhere that the invaders settled eventually reduced the cat to vestigial numbers throughout most of its formerly wide-spread range, virtually extirpating it from the eastern portion of the continent except for the few forest sanctuaries that still endure in the eastern States and Canada's Maritime Provinces.

So secretive did it become as a result of centuries of persecution that it was not until the late 1960s that the existence of a relatively large bobcat population in the wilderness regions of central Nova Scotia was revealed as a result of a survey of fur-bearing animals conducted by the provincial Department of Lands and Forests. Once discovered, it was decided to "uti-lize this resource" as a means of attracting hunters to the province.

This led to the establishment of the World Bobcat Hunt, centred on the town of Truro where, in the words of one advertisement widely published in U.S. sportsmen's magazines, "there are always plenty of cats for your hounds to kill." The first World Bobcat Hunt was literally a howling success as something like 600 hounds, mainly from the eastern and central United States, were loosed in the Nova Scotian woods. Hunters followed the hounds in 4x4 trucks or all-terrain vehicles. Some of the more affluent ones used helicop-ters. Like most cats when pursued by hounds, bobcats tree readily. They can then easily be shot, but many hunters do not kill the animals outright, pre-ferring to disable them only enough so they will fall to the ground, where the hounds can tear them apart while still alive.

The highlight of the annual hunt is the suspension of a captured bobcat in a wire cage from a tree limb, while as many as a hundred frenzied hounds form a milling mob at the base of the tree. It is of interest to note that, while Nova Scotia's Department of Lands and Forests forbids the pri-vate possession of captive bobcats, its officers supply the ritual sacrifice for this event.

The Truro-centred hunt has been a tremendous success. During the win-ter of 1969–70, 1,729 bobcats were reportedly killed in Nova Scotia. By 1975–76, the kill had risen to 1,862, with an additional 752 slaughtered in nearby New Brunswick, mainly by sport hunters. However, the great days of the World Bobcat Hunt are now rapidly declining as the last stronghold of the bobcat in the eastern seaboard region is systematically destroyed...for fun and profit.

THE DOGS

Three wild members of the dog family inhabited the eastern seaboard region at first European contact, together with several kinds of domesticated dogs. Two of the wild kind have since disappeared, along with most of the aboriginal domestic ones, but—and this is a unique event—a new species has appeared and bids fair to making a niche for itself in a portion of the world where its cousins suffered annihilation at the hands of modern man.

Let us first look briefly at the domestic dogs. They included the so-called husky of the Inuit, several sorts of smallish hunting-cum-sled dogs belonging to mainland Indians, and a mysterious black water dog that seems to have been peculiar to Newfoundland.

The aboriginal husky could still be found on the Labrador coast as late as 1890. Photographs show it to have been similar to Arctic Eskimoan dogs, but rangier and not so heavily furred—as befitted an animal living in a more moderate climate. The disintegration of the human culture to which it belonged brought an end to the husky, too. Until the 1940s, some cross-bred relics of the breed existed at a few Labrador settlements such as Nain, where they still served a useful purpose as sled and pack animals. During the succeeding years they have been displaced by snowmobiles, until now only a few mangy and generally unwanted individuals remain, and they carry the blood of so many introduced canine strains as to make them unrecognizable.

The same story is to be told of the mainland Indian dogs, of which no apparent examples seem to have continued in existence after the early decades of this century. Only one of the three has managed to survive, albeit in modified form. The first mention of this remarkable creature that I can find appears in an account of the 1593 voyage of the *Marigold* to Cabot Strait, where her people met natives, "and their dogs, of colour blacke, not so bigge as a greyhound [which] followed them at their heels." Although historians claim that the Beothuks (the Newfoundland natives) did not possess dogs, I have found ample evidence that they did. Furthermore, when these were described, it was invariably as *black* dogs that bore no resemblance to the varieties possessed by mainland tribes.

What is quite certain is that the black, presumably aboriginal dog of Newfoundland is the most important ancestor of the breeds we know today as the Labrador, Newfoundland, and several other retrievers. Until as late as the 1950s, good examples of the type were still to be found in some remote Newfoundland outports where they were, and always had been, known simply as water dogs. Few, if any, still remain, but at least the main genetic elements of the Newfoundland water dog continue in existence, which is more than can be said of their one-time human associates, the Beothuk Indians, who were exterminated to the last man, woman, and child by Newfoundland settlers and fishermen.

Two species of fox inhabited the northeastern seaboard in the sixteenth century. The red fox, in both its red and black (or silver) colour phases, was abundant throughout the forested regions, and the available evidence suggests that the black was as common as the red. It is the only form mentioned by Parkhurst from Newfoundland in the 1570s. Champlain reported that walrus hunters on Sable Island around the turn of the century "captured a large number of very fine black foxes, the skins of which they carefully preserved." John Rose noted that foxes were abundant at Boston and that "some were perfect black." Even as late as 1780 in southern Labrador, Cartwright's catch of foxes for the year included sixteen silvers and twenty-eight cross (intermediates) to only nineteen reds. The black, or silver, pelt was highly valued then, as now, with the result that this colour phase has been almost extirpated from the remaining wild fox population of eastern North America. The red phase still hangs on throughout most of its original range but increasing demands for fox furs for the fun-fashion trade have greatly depleted its numbers in the past few years and it is now a comparative rarity in most places.

The smaller—it is not much larger than a good-sized cat—white fox has not done so well. Like the white bear, it is now reckoned to be solely an Arctic species and, in fact, is now officially called Arctic fox. Yet at first contact it was a common resident along the Gulf coast of Labrador and even in Newfoundland.

It, too, appeared in two colour phases—white and the so-called blue, which is actually grey. Parkhurst tells us that, in Newfoundland, "There be foxes, black, white and grey." The black we have already mentioned. The white could only have been the present species. The grey could have referred either to the "blue" phase in winter or to the summer coat of both, for the white fox of whatever colour undergoes a spring moult that leaves it clothed in dun-coloured, brown-to-greyish fur.

The white fox is distinguished by its insatiable curiosity and tameness toward men, which makes it extremely vulnerable. I knew a barren-land trapper in Keewatin who used to catch as many as 100 each winter without going more than a few score yards from his cabin. In early autumn, he would place several caribou carcasses around the perimeter of his "yard," just far enough away so that the stench as they rotted would not be intolerable. The odour would bring in white foxes, which in fall and winter are nomadic, from hundreds of square miles of tundra until dozens were feeding on the carrion. "They'd get underfoot like a bunch of cats, they was that tame," he told me. Then, in November or early December, when he considered their fur was prime, he would plant strychnine pellets in the carcasses and reap his harvest.

Destruction by fur traders overtook most of the aboriginal white fox population in the northeastern seaboard region, although, as late as 1779, Cartwright was still able to kill twenty-seven of them at Sandwich Bay—30 per cent of his total catch of all kinds of foxes for that year. Cartwright also noted that the white fox still bred at Sandwich Bay in his time. Even as late as 1895, according to A.P. Lowe, it was still "plentiful about Hamilton Inlet, but more rare southward to near the Strait of Belle Isle."

Some biologists assert that the white fox was never a true resident of the region, but only an occasional winter visitor driven to migrate south from the Arctic because of food shortage there. This repeats the official explanation of the aboriginal range of the white bear and the walrus and is equally fallacious, although there is no doubt that, at rare intervals, considerable southward movements of white foxes *have* taken place. The last time this happened was during the terribly severe winter of 1922–23, when numbers of the little animals reappeared along the southern Labrador coast and in northern Newfoundland after an absence of many decades.[2] However, these were not migrants in the proper sense—they were refugees who probably made no attempt to return to the Arctic with the advent of spring but remained near the Gulf and in Newfoundland until the last of them was trapped several years later. There is good reason to believe they might have succeeded in recolonizing their lost southern range, except for two factors. One was direct persecution by man. The other was a secondary result of modern man's destructiveness and probably is one of the reasons for their disappearance from the south in the first place.

To quote from Victor Cahalane's *Mammals of North America*, the blue foxes of the Pribilof Islands "feed in summer largely on birds and their eggs, especially [seabirds. Since these] live on the cliffs, the foxes climb about on almost sheer walls, hundreds of feet above the breakers…they frequently carry away both dead birds and their eggs and cache them…for feeding the growing pups. Despite this toll, the bird colonies are so huge that the foxes do not seem to have affected their hordes." White foxes in the eastern Canadian Arctic do the same thing still, as do red foxes in Newfoundland.

---

[2] At least one got as far south as Cape Breton, where it was trapped.

There can be little doubt but that southern white foxes depended heavily on seabird colonies during the summer, and that the destruction of most of these by modern man was a blow to their continuing survival.

It is at any rate a fact that the white fox has been extirpated from its former southern range and is now confined to Arctic and sub-Arctic regions, except for occasional individuals that drift south on the polar pack (accompanying white bears in a jackal role), only to find themselves aliens in an alien land, with little or no hope of surviving the guns and traps awaiting them there.

In a book that consists largely of epitaphs for animals that have been unable to survive the invasion of their world by Europeans, it is truly a relief to be able to document one success story.

"Little wolf" is a Plains Indian name for the animal we know as the coyote. In aboriginal times it was exclusively an animal of the West, being at its most abundant on the Great Plains, where it shared its territory with the grey wolf. But it was no secondary species. As time and death would prove, it was so adaptable that, long after the grey wolves had been exterminated, it continued to endure. In its struggle for survival against the ultimate killer, it first learned how to survive the destruction wrought upon it by poison, snare, trap, and gun, and then even began recouping its enormous losses. The following is another excerpt from Cahalane's book, written, be it noted, in 1947.

"The coyote is the garbage man, the health officer, the sanitary engineer and the exterminator. All this it does with no pay except bed and board...It puts a quick end to senile, wounded or starving creatures. One of the most potent checks on the rodent host, it keeps down crop and range damage and lessens the danger of epizootics. Throughout the ages it has helped to weed out the unfit and keep survivors alert. Largely due to it and other predators, the deer, the antelope and other hoofed mammals have evolved into swift, graceful, efficient animals. Were it not for [these predators] they would not only overpopulate and overeat their ranges, but would doubtless become lazy, fat and have cirrhosis of the liver.

"[Although] an estimated total of one hundred and twenty-five thousand coyotes are shot, trapped or poisoned each year in the United States, Canada and Alaska...due to their large and frequent litters, their cleverness and adaptability, they have spread and increased greatly in spite of such wide persecution...They have spread to the shore of the Arctic Ocean...and to the Pacific...Even localities as remote from their natural range as Maine and Florida are occasionally visited by coyotes. Periodically, 'strange doglike animals' are killed or trapped in the East, to become sensations in country newspapers. They are finally identified as 'brush wolves'.

"In spite of the coyote's shortcomings, it is a clever little pilferer at worst and often a useful, interesting member of the society of mammals. The West would not be the same without it. The plains and deserts would seem mute without its plaintive song. For better or for worse, I hope that the little wolf and its descendants will be with us always."

Cahalane's hopes are not shared by agriculturalists, sportsmen, game management experts, or politicians, most of whom harbour an irrational and abiding enmity toward the little wolf. I suspect this is at least partly because they see it not simply as a competitor, but as a creature that commits the most odious of crimes by successfully challenging our pretensions to dominion over all forms of life. If *they* had *their* way, the coyote would long since have become extinct. Its very survival, together with its ongoing occupation of vast reaches of the continent from which modern man has managed to eradicate most other predators, represents an intolerable affront.

The little wolf had reached Nova Scotia by the mid-1970s. In 1982, he crossed the man-made causeway into Cape Breton Island. The only Canadian provinces or territories where he is not yet to be found are Prince Edward Island and Newfoundland; and I would not like to bet that even these islands will remain forever free of him. To the south, the little wolf has reached the Atlantic coast all the way from Maine to Florida. And everywhere, despite our lethal enmity, he is digging in for the long haul.

The secret of his success seems to have eluded explanation, but I think I know what it is. Eastern specimens of the little wolf are noticeably larger and darker than their western relatives—to a degree that could hardly have been achieved through ordinary evolutionary processes during the mere century that has elapsed since the eastward spread began. However, it has long been known that coyotes breed freely with suitably sized domestic dogs. I strongly suspect that the brush wolf, as he is called by easterners, is the result of cross-breeding between the original coyote, the now nearly vanished timber wolf, and feral dogs; and that the little wolf of today is in effect a new species combining hybrid vigour with the insight into human behaviour that domestic dogs possess. If this is so, then the little wolf is succeeding because he is following that age-old precept: if you can't beat the bastards—join them.

Whatever the secret may be, I echo Cahalane's hopes for the tough, sagacious, and enduring little wolf, whose quavering midnight solo I heard in Cape Breton last summer for the first time since I left the western plains of my boyhood almost half a century ago.

Until about 10,000 years ago the wolf was second only to man as the most widespread and successful mammal in the entire northern hemisphere. In one or another of its many colour phases and subspecies *Canis lupus*—the grey wolf—was found from Japan through Asia, India, Europe, North Africa, and all of North America. Nowhere was it abundant in the sense of massive populations, for it lived much as did early man, in scattered familial groups or clans, each with its own hunting range, dispersed as far afield as the High Arctic islands, the swamps and jungles of the subtropics, the hardwood forests of the temperate zone, the searing plains of the Gobi Desert, and the towering ranges of the Alps, Himalayas, and Rockies.

There is extensive evidence that, far from being at enmity, wolves and hunting man not only tolerated one another but enjoyed something approaching symbiosis, whereby the life of each benefited the existence of the other. Wolf kills must often have served to feed struggling or starving human beings, and it is a well-established fact that overkills produced by the gradually evolving technology of human hunters were put to good use by wolves. As recently as the 1940s the caribou-culture Inuit of Canada's central Arctic actively encouraged wolves to live and den on the People's hunting grounds, believing that the big, wild dogs had the ability to "call" the migrating caribou. The wolves seem to have been happy to respond, since they benefited from surplus human kills.

After man began divesting himself of his hunting heritage to become a farmer or a herder dependent on domestic animals, he renounced his ancient empathy with the wolf and, in due course of time, came to perceive his one-time fellow hunter as an inveterate enemy. Civilized man eventually succeeded in totally extirpating the *real* wolf from his mind, substituting for it a contrived image, replete with evil aspects that generated almost pathological fear and hatred.

When European man began his conquest of the New World, wolves were omnipresent but were not at first considered of much consequence, probably because the early Europeans were not agriculturalists. Nor were they markedly "civilized." Anthony Parkhurst, from about 1574, mentions wolves almost incidentally. "I had almost forgotten to speak of the plenty of wolves." James Yonge, visiting Newfoundland in 1663, wrote equally casually of "the bears and wolves...with which this country abounds." As late as 1721, Denys de La Ronde, writing about Prince Edward Island, noted without apparent concern that "Wolves of great size abounded [there]."

Indeed, until about the middle of the eighteenth century, the intruders seem to have been relatively passive toward wolves except in those regions where settlement was proceeding. Explorers, fur trappers, even fishermen seemed neither to fear the animals nor to consider them a threat to life and limb. The fearsome legend of the all-devouring wolf, he of the slavering fangs and the blood-red eyes, came into existence on this continent only after Europeans settled down to "taming this wilderness and turning it into the Veritable Garden of Eden for Man's delight and use," which, presumably, it now is.

By about 1750, the transformation of the wolf in the New World from natural denizen to ravening monster whom, as New Englanders believed, "the Devil hath created to Plague Mankind" was well under way. It was accepted as a tenet of faith that the wilderness could not be "tamed," the New World "conquered," as long as the wolf roamed the woods and plains, tundra and mountain valleys. So began one of the most ruthless and deliberate wars of extirpation ever waged by modern man against a fellow creature.

In 1877, the Reverend Philip Tocque reported on the progress of this war in Newfoundland. "A few years ago these animals were rather common in the neighbourhood of St. John's...An Act was passed...the Wolf-killing Act [with] a reward of Five Pounds...In proportion as the [human] population increases so will the Monarch of the Newfoundland forest disappear... [until] its existence will no longer be known. The history of almost every nation bears proof that, in the same ratio as the empire of man has been enlarged, so has the animal kingdom been invaded and desolated. The history of Newfoundland bears evidence that some of the tenants of the ocean and the feathered tribes have [already] become extinct by the agency of the destroying hand of man."

The magnificent, almost pure white Newfoundland wolf, a distinct and unique subspecies of Arctic derivation, bore the prophetic name *Canis lupus beothucus*, to suggest its association with Newfoundland's aboriginal inhabitants, the Beothuk Indians. The white wolf was not long in joining its namesake tribe, as yet another extinction at the "destroying hand of man." The last known survivor was shot in 1911.

The story was essentially and remains the same everywhere on the continent. Spurred on by bounties and rewards, modern men using poison, trap, snare, and gun, together with new weapons provided by an enlightened technology including helicopters and fragmentation grenades, have waged and continue to wage war to the death against the wolf in a campaign that will evidently only cease with the extinction of the animal in North America, if not in the world.

As of 1984, *Canis lupus* has already been exterminated in Newfoundland, Prince Edward Island, Nova Scotia, New Brunswick, all of the southern portions of Ontario and Quebec, the Canadian Prairies and, effectively, Mexico and all of the United States south of the Canadian border with the exception of northeastern Minnesota and Michigan, where a few hundred survivors live in extreme jeopardy. From 1850 to 1900, bounty was paid on some *two million* wolves shot, trapped, or poisoned in the United States, exclusive of Alaska. During that period, a single "wolfer" equipped with a small sack of strychnine sulphate, ranging through territory after territory, could account for 500 wolves in a single season. Of the twenty-four subspecies and races of *Canis lupus* that inhabited North America at the beginning of the European conquest, seven are now totally extinct and most of the remainder are endangered.

The pros and cons of the wolf's reputation are complex. It must suffice to say here that the preponderance of independent scientific opinion agrees that the wolf serves a vital role in the well-being of its prey species; is no threat to human life; is responsible for only minute losses of domestic animals; and, for the most part, will not even live in proximity to human settlement and agricultural enterprises. We have doomed it to death, not for what it is, but for what we deliberately and mistakenly perceive it to be—the mythologized epitome of a savage killer, which is, in truth, the reflected image of ourself.

A recent example of the systematic destruction of wolves, once again using the discredited argument that we are helping "more desirable" species to flourish, has been taking place in British Columbia, with the cabinet minister responsible for conservation leading a war of extermination.

"These 'beautiful animals' may be pretty in a book, photo or a painting. They may be impressive in a zoo or in a contrived movie. In the bush under real conditions, they are one of the most dangerous, vicious, unrelenting killers in existence. Contrary to the Farley Mowatt [sic] version, they do not selectively kill. A pack of wolves will kill as many animals in a herd as they can, often tearing them open and leaving them to die slowly."

This condemnation of the wolf was made in November, 1983, by British Columbia's Minister of Environment, Tony Brummett. Brummett's electoral constituency includes the Peace River district in the northeastern corner of the province and embraces one of the last remaining areas of wilderness where the wolf has been able to maintain a foothold. The region centres on the town of Fort Nelson and is a paradise for big game and trophy-hunting sports, mainly from Japan, Germany, and the United States. The recreational pursuits of these wealthy ladies and gentlemen are of some financial benefit to Fort Nelson's motels, restaurants, and retail stores and are extremely lucrative for the several local guiding and outfitting establishments.

When, in mid-1983, Brummett (himself an avid hunter) was told that the ever-increasing flow of foreign sports was depleting the supply of game in the Peace River region, he was as disturbed as his constituents. Since it would have been politically inexpedient to reduce the level of human hunting, Brummett decided to eliminate man's only significant natural competitor for moose, bighorn sheep, caribou, and other trophy animals. This course of action also had the added advantage of deflecting public awareness away from the real culprits. In short, the situation would be rectified by making the wolf culprit and target, not only in the flesh but in the mind.

Brummett's first move was to have his departmental biologists assemble the requisite "studies" to justify an indictment against the Peace River wolves. These government employees then took upon themselves the roles of judge and jury and, having found the wolf guilty as charged, recommended the death penalty. Brummett thereupon directed Dr. John Elliott of the department's Fish and Wildlife Service, who was chief prosecutor against the wolf and also resident "wildlife manager" at Fort Nelson, to conduct the execution.

For political reasons it was determined that no public announcement of the program would be made and that no more than $30,000 of taxpayers' money would be committed to the cause. However, Elliott was not to be left short of funds. Arrangements were made by the British Columbia branch of the Canadian Wildlife Federation and the Northern B.C. Guides Association to provide additional funding to charter a helicopter with which Elliott could search out and destroy the wolf population of the North Peace region.

A word about the Canadian Wildlife Federation is called for at this juncture. Formed in the 1960s by hunting and fishing groups to represent their special interests, it must under no circumstances be confused (although such confusion seems suspiciously easy) either with the Canadian Wildlife Service—a federal government agency—or the Canadian Nature Federation—an affiliation of conservation and environmentalist groups. In its solicitations for funds and public support, the CWF proclaims it is devoted to "enhancing wildlife populations." What it does not explain is that this "enhancement" is, to a very considerable degree, intended to provide living targets to satisfy its sportsmen members.

A packet of pretty stamps depicting flowers, butterflies, and songbirds accompanying a solicitation for donations, which I recently received from the CWF, included this moving exhortation: "These stamps do a mighty job when you put one on every card, letter or package you send. They show a beautiful heritage we must all work together to protect. Use these stamps to remind others of the importance of wildlife, conservation and a healthy environment."

The British Columbia chapter's assistance in Dr. Elliott's wildlife "enhancement" program included collaboration with the Wyoming-based Foundation for North American Sheep, a kindred organization devoted to "enhancing" stocks of wild sheep for sporting purposes. Its president boasts that the foundation spent $800,000 in 1983, a "goodly portion" of which was used in Canada for wolf-killing, forest-burning, and other attempts to improve the prospects for sheep hunters. Some $200,000 of this went to support Dr. Elliott's and Mr. Brummett's wolf management program.

The Canadian Wildlife Federation also arranged a 1,000-ticket raffle, at $100 a ticket, to raise additional funds for Elliott's work. First prize in the raffle was a ten-day hunting safari to Zimbabwe, where the lucky winner would have the opportunity to shoot his fill of African animals.

Initially all these proceedings were conducted *in camera*, as it were. But in early January, word of what was to be done with the profits from the raffle leaked out and the pot began to bubble. An inquisitive reporter then discovered not only what Brummett planned to do, but that Dr. Elliott was already hard at work.

Sequestered at the ranch of one of the region's wealthiest sportsmen, who was also a munificent benefactor of the governing Social Credit Party that Brummett represented, Elliott was in command of a strike force consisting of a helicopter supported by several fixed-wing aircraft. The latter, owned and flown by "volunteers," fanned out over the wilderness, acting, as they merrily put it, like "air-borne hounds." When one of them spotted a wolf family, he would radio Elliott, whose helicopter would then be flown to the target point. While the light planes herded the wolves to prevent them from escaping, Elliott hovered over them and blazed away with automatic weapons at point-blank range. When convenient, the corpses were recovered and their skins—worth from $75 to $100 each—given to the volunteers as rewards for services rendered. About thirty-five wolves had been killed by the time the story was uncovered.

All hell broke loose as conservationists began to rally in protest. Elliott was summoned to Victoria, the provincial capital, where Brummett held a press conference. Calling the program a simple matter of "game management," the minister confirmed that its aim was "to 'enhance' the numbers of

145

animals for hunting." He compared it to raising livestock. "In agriculture we try and produce more animals so we can butcher more." Having then blandly claimed that his department was funding the entire program itself, he introduced Dr. Elliott. Simply and engagingly, Elliott explained that he was conducting a scientifically managed conservation program, whereby 80 per cent of the 500 wolves in the affected region would be "culled" in order to ensure the continuing good health of the big game population, *and of the wolves themselves*. Quoting facts and figures from his own studies, and others that reinforced his conclusions, Elliott seemed the epitome of the bright, young, dedicated scientist. Nevertheless, his "data base" was soon under assault as independent experts questioned both his methods and conclusions. The most devastating criticism was that no confirmation existed of Elliott's estimate of 500 wolves, of which he intended to kill 80 per cent. It was pointed out that this was an impossibly high population figure and that if Elliott did, in fact, find and kill anything like 400 wolves, he would have succeeded in wiping out the entire wolf population of a vast region.

Undaunted, Elliott flew back to continue his "enhancement" program—while Brummett took a holiday in Jamaica, perhaps hoping that the heat at home would subside in his absence. It did not. Protests against the wolf slaughter spread across Canada and the United States and on to Europe. In an effort to damp down the uproar, Brummett's department announced that, "for safety reasons," the area where the "cull" was taking place would henceforth be closed to reporters. The public furore eventually began to abate for lack of information on what was happening, but the kill continued.

Elliott was still engaged in his aerial war as late as April, by which time he had butchered 363 wolves. There is no reason to doubt that he had by then killed virtually *all* the wolves in the affected district.

The Canadian Wildlife Federation has reason for satisfaction, knowing as it must that the British Columbia Fish and Wildlife Service also poisoned, shot, or trapped some 400 additional wolves in other parts of the province during the winter of 1983–84. These "management" operations, together with commercial trapping and sport hunting, probably destroyed at least 1,400 of the "most dangerous, vicious, unrelenting killers in existence."

In the spring of 1984, Yukon Territory—British Columbia's neighbour to the north—began setting the stage for intensifying its own long-term program of "wolf management" by officially warning parents that the wolf threat had reached such proportions that children should not be allowed out after dark, even in the vicinity of the capital city of Whitehorse. Yukon wildlife scientists are now proposing to nullify this threat by a drastic escalation of their wolf control program. British Columbia's eastern neighbour, the province of Alberta, is also moving in the same direction. In a January, 1984, interview, biologist John Gunson, head of Alberta's Carnivore Management Unit, went on record as saying, "I don't see anything wrong with wolf control to enhance big game hunting. Wolves don't pay taxes, and people do...the problem is, if you want to take a great deal of big game, you have to do away with the wolves."

Alaska, too, has heard the same message. Biologists in that state have evolved a most sophisticated way to achieve "wolf management." Wolves, usually only one from a pack, or family, are live-trapped in summer and fitted with radio transmitter collars. Come winter, airborne hunters "cull" wolves simply by homing in on radio signals that lead them directly to the Judas animal and enable them to destroy the entire family to which it belongs. And in Minnesota, the only state in the lower forty-eight with a viable, if relict, wolf population, state and federal authorities abetted by hunter organizations are clearing the way to an open season on what the commissioner of Minnesota's Department of Natural Resources refers to as a "magnificent trophy animal."

As 1984 draws to a close, it is clear that a concerted effort is being made to apply a final solution to the "wolf problem" in those remaining regions where viable wolf populations still exist. There seems to be considerable likelihood that the attempt will be successful unless a massive protest can be mounted—one that will neutralize the unholy alliance of government game managers, self-serving politicos, and self-styled "conservation" organizations devoted to "enhancing" the supply of big game animals.

PART III

Fish out of Water

The familiar adage assures us that there are more fishes in the sea than ever came out of it. Indeed, there may have been a time when there was truth in this contention.

Not any more.

Ten years ago, Jacques Cousteau, speaking for those concerned about the future of the living seas, voiced his fear that about a third of the stuff of life in the world's oceans had already been destroyed through man's use of it, or his abuse of it. During the decade since, the situation has worsened. We are now facing the possibility that the seas may become virtual life-deserts in the not-far-distant future.

Fishes and marine invertebrates rarely strike a sympathetic chord in the human breast. Nevertheless, they comprise one of the most important skeins in the intricate weave of planetary life. It is only at the risk of undermining our own chances for survival that we can ignore what we have done, and are doing, to the sea-dwellers.

A second compelling reason for understanding the fate of the fishes has to do with truth-telling. During the past half-century, men who profit from the destruction of sea-life have been making increasingly vigorous efforts to escape the onus for laying waste the oceans, by blaming other animals. "Fish out of Water" puts the blame where it belongs, and describes something of the fate we have inflicted on marine animals in and about the Sea of Slaughter.

11
King Cod and the Regal Salmon

It is probably impossible for anyone now alive to comprehend the magnitude of fish life in the waters of the New World when the European invasion began. It may have been almost equally difficult for the early voyagers. According to the records they have left for us, they seem to have been overwhelmed by the glut of fishes.

In 1497, John Cabot set the tone by describing the Grand Banks as so "swarming with fish [that they] could be taken not only with a net but in baskets let down [and weighted] with a stone." On the lower St. Lawrence in 1535 Jacques Cartier reported that "This river...is the richest in every kind of fish that anyone remembers ever having seen or heard of; for from its mouth to its head you will find in their season the majority of the varieties of salt- and fresh-water fish...great numbers of mackerel, mullet, sea bass, tunnies, large eels...quantities of lampreys and salmon...[in the upper River] are many pike, trout, carp, bream and other fresh-water fish."

Captain John Smith was no less enthusiastic in extolling the fisheries of New England in 1614. "A little Boye might take of Cunners and Pinacks and such delicate fish at the ships sterne, more than six or ten men can eat in a daie; but with a casting Net, [he could take] thousands...Cod, Cuske, Halibut, Mackerell, Scate or such like, a man may take with a hooke and line what he will...no River where there is not plenty of Sturgeon or Salmon or both; all of which are to be had in abundance."

We round out the picture with a description of the Gulf of St. Lawrence about 1680: "Here also are seen prodigious quantities of all kinds of fish, Cod, Salmon, Herring, Trout, Bass, Mackerel, Flounder, Shad, Sturgeon, Pickerel, Oysters, Smelt, Skate, Whitefish..."

This chapter deals with the essence of industrial exploitation of life in the seas—with the several species the great commercial fisheries of the northwestern Atlantic were founded on, and which are now, after suffering 500 hundred years of ever-escalating human greed, running out their time.

Initially, cod was king; yet it was only the most valuable species in an entire group collectively known to those who catch them as groundfish. The story of what we have done to the groundfishes constitutes the first part of the chapter. The second deals with the baitfishes—small creatures that used to school in untold billions and upon which all the groundfishes and much other life in the seas ultimately depend. The chapter ends with an account of the destruction of one of the most celebrated of all North American fishes— the Atlantic salmon.

Early voyagers to the northeastern approaches of America encountered two kinds of land. One was high and dry, and they called it the Main. The other lay submerged beneath 30 to 150 fathoms of green waters, and they called it the Banks. The waters of the continental shelf from Cape Cod to Newfoundland form an aqueous pasture of unparalleled size and fecundity—a three-dimensional one with a volume sufficient to inundate the entire North American continent to a depth of a yard or more. In 1500, the life forms inhabiting these waters had a sheer mass unmatched anywhere in the world. This was the realm where cod was king.

The name Cabot used for Newfoundland in 1497 was Baccalaos, that being the one bestowed on it by Portuguese who had led the way. The word means, simply, land of cod. And Peter Martyr (from about 1516) tells us that "in the sea adjacent [to Newfoundland, Cabot] found so great a quantity... of great fish...called baccalaos...that at times they even stayed the passage of his ships."

The New World banks, and especially the Grand Banks lying to the eastward of Newfoundland, were a cod fisher's version of the Promised Land. By 1575, more than 300 French, Portuguese, and English fishing vessels were reaping a rich harvest there. Members of Sir Humphrey Gilbert's colonizing venture fairly babbled at the abundance of baccalieu. Cod, wrote one of the visitors, were present "in incredible abundance, whereby great gains grow to them that travel to these parts: the hook is no sooner thrown out but it is eftsoons drawn up with some goodly fish." To which one of his companions added, "We were becalmed a small time during which we laid out hook and lines to take Cod, and drew in, in less than two hours, fish so large and in such abundance that for many days after we fed on no other provision." A third summed it up: "Incredible quantity and no less variety of fishes in the seas [especially] Cod, which alone draweth many nations thither and is become the most famous fishing of the world."

Each new arrival on these fabulous fishing grounds found the same thing and had much the same reaction. When the *Grace* of Bristol sheltered at the island of St. Pierre in 1594, her people "laid the ship upon the lee, and in 2 houres space we tooke with our hooks 3 or 4 hundred great Cod for the provision of our ship." Charles Leigh, reconnoitring the Magdalen Islands in 1597, noted "About this Island there is as great an abundance of cods as is any place to be found. In a little more than an houre we caught with hookes 250 of them."

At the turn of the sixteenth century, as many as 650 vessels were catching thousands of tons of cod in New World waters, using only baited hooks and handlines. As John Mason, an English fishing skipper working out of a Newfoundland shore station, noted, "Cods are so thick by the shore that we hardly have been able to row a boat through them. I have killed of them with a Pike...Three men going to Sea in a boat, with some on shore to dress and dry them, in 30 days will commonly kill between 25 and thirty thousand, worth with the oyle arising from [their livers], 100 or 200 Pounds."

The slaughter was equally enormous elsewhere in the region. In Cape Breton and the Gulf, according to Nicolas Denys, "Scarcely an harbour [exists] where there are not several fishing vessels...taking every day 15,000 [to] 30,000 fish...this fish constitutes a kind of inexhaustible manna."

Near the end of the sixteenth century Richard Whitbourne, another fishing skipper, wrote that the average lading for any given ship tallied 125,000 cod. These were from virgin cod populations producing fish up to six or seven feet in length and weighing as much as 200 pounds, in contrast with today's average weight of about six pounds. In Whitbourne's time it was still in the fifteen- to twenty-pound range and the annual cod fishery in the northeastern approaches yielded about 368,000 tons.

By 1620 the cod fleet exceeded 1,000 vessels, many making two voyages annually: a summer one for dry cod and a winter trip from which the cod were carried back to Europe in pickle as "green fish." Yet, despite the enormous destruction, there was no apparent indication that cod stocks were diminishing. As the seventeenth century neared its end, travellers such as Baron Lahontan were still writing about the cod as if its population had no bounds.

"You can scarce imagine what quantities of Cod-fish were catched by our Seamen in the space of a quarter of an hour...the Hook was no sooner at the bottom than a Fish was catched...[the men] had nothing to do but to throw in, and take up without interruption...However, as we were so plentifully entertained at the cost of these Fishes, so such of them as continued in the Sea made sufficient reprisals upon the Corps of a Captain and several Soldiers, who dy'd of the Scurvy, and were thrown over-board."

The first hint that the destruction might be excessive (and it is a veiled hint) comes from Charlevoix in the 1720s. After first telling us that "the number of the cod seems to equal that of the grains of sand," he adds that "For more than two centuries there have been loaded with them [at the Grand Banks] from two to three hundred [French] ships annually, notwithstanding [which] the diminution is not perceivable. It might not, however, be amiss to discontinue this fishery from time to time [on the Grand Bank], the more so as the gulph of St. Lawrence [together with] the River for more than sixty leagues, the coasts of Acadia, those of...Cape Breton and of Newfoundland, are no less replenished with this fish than the great bank. These are true mines, which are more valuable, and require much less expense than those of Peru and Mexico." That Charlevoix was not exaggerating the value of the cod fishery is confirmed by the fact that, in 1747, 564 French vessels manned by 27,500 fishermen brought home codfish worth a million pounds sterling—a gigantic sum for those days.

At about this same time, New Englanders, who had by now depleted the lesser stocks of cod available on the southern banks, began moving into the northern fishery. They did so with such energy that, by 1783, over 600 American vessels were fishing the Gulf of St. Lawrence, mostly for cod, although they also caught immense quantities of herring. In that year, at least 1,500 ships of all nations were working the North American "cod mines" for all they were worth.

By 1800, English- and French-based vessels had become notably fewer, but Newfoundlanders, Canadians, and Americans more than made up the loss. In 1812, 1,600 fishing vessels, largely American, were in the Gulf, with as many more Newfoundland and Nova Scotia ships fishing the outer banks and the Atlantic coast of Labrador.

Those were the days of the great fleets of "white wings," when the sails of fishing schooners seemed to stretch from horizon to horizon. In addition to this vessel fishery, thousands of inshore men fished cod in small boats from every little cove and harbour. Vesselmen and shoremen alike still mostly fished in the old way with hooks and lines because "the glut of cod" was still so great that nothing more sophisticated was needed.

In 1876, John Rowan went aboard "a schooner cod-fishing close to shore...They were fishing in about three fathoms of water and we could see the bottom actually paved with codfish. I caught a dozen in about fifteen minutes; my next neighbour [a crewman] on the deck of the schooner, caught three times as many, grumbling all the time that it was the worst fishing season he had ever known."

Between 1899 and 1904, the annual catch of cod (and of haddock, which in the salt-fish business was treated as cod) approached a million tons. During those years, Newfoundland alone annually exported about 1,200,000 quintals of dry fish, representing about 400,000 tons of cod, live weight. By 1907, the Newfoundland catch had risen to nearly 430,000 tons; and there were then some 1,600 vessels, of many nationalities, fishing the Grand Banks.

But now there was a chill over the Banks—one that did not come from the almost perpetual fog. Cod were getting harder to catch, and every year it seemed to take a little longer to make up a voyage. At this juncture, nobody so much as breathed the possibility that the Banks were being over-fished. Instead, one of the age-old fisherman's explanations for a shortage was invoked: the cod had changed their ways and, temporarily, one hoped, gone somewhere else.

The early nineteenth-century discovery of immense schools of cod along the Labrador coast even as far north as Cape Chidley was seen as confirmation that the fish had indeed changed their grounds. In actual fact the Labrador cod comprised a distinct and, till then, virgin population. They did not stay that way for long. By 1845, 200 Newfoundland vessels were fishing "down north" and by 1880, up to 1,200. As many as 30,000 Newfoundlanders ("floaters" if they fished from anchored vessels, and "stationers" if they fished from shore bases) in 1880 were making almost 400,000 quintals of salt cod on the Labrador coast alone.

The Labrador cod soon went the way of all flesh. The catch steadily declined thereafter until, by mid-twentieth century, the once far-famed Labrador fishery collapsed. Attempts were again made to ascribe the disappearance of the Labrador fish to one of those mythical migrations. This time it did not wash. The fact was that King Cod was becoming scarce throughout the whole of his wide North Atlantic realm. In 1956, cod landings for Grand Banks/Newfoundland waters were down to 80,000 metric tonnes—about a fifth of what they had been only half-a-century earlier.

When a prey animal becomes scarce in nature, its predators normally decrease in numbers, too, permitting the prey an opportunity for recovery. Industrial man works in the opposite way. As cod became scarcer, so did pressure on the remaining stocks mount. New, bigger, more destructive ships came into service and the bottom trawl, which scours the bed of the ocean like a gigantic harrow, destroying spawn and other life, almost totally replaced older fishing methods. Scarcity brought ever-rising prices, which in turn attracted more and more fishermen. During the 1960s, fleets of big draggers and factory ships were coming to the Banks from a dozen European and Asian countries to engage in a killing frenzy over what remained of the cod populations. The result was that, between 1962 and 1967, cod landings increased until, in 1968, the catch topped two million tons. Soon thereafter, the whole northwest Atlantic cod fishery disintegrated for want of fish to catch.

Canada's extension of economic control to 200 miles offshore saved the cod in her waters from extinction. The stocks, which by conservative estimate had been reduced to less than 2 per cent of their aboriginal level, are now increasing, though at probably nowhere near the rate predicted by the statisticians whose task it is to justify government and fishing industry policies. Certainly the cod stock can never hope to regain even a semblance of its former substance so long as we continue the commercial annihilation of the baitfishes that are the cod's staff of life—a matter dealt with later in this chapter.

After the Second World War, the fishing business, which in the past had mainly been composed of small companies, began to exhibit symptoms of the gigantism that was sweeping the industrial world. By the 1960s it was largely in the hands of powerful cartels or national governments. Their reaction to the depredation of the once "inexhaustible" ranks of the cod was that of true devotees to the holy principle of the "bottom line." Instead of using their wealth, power, and influence to reduce and control the slaughter and so ensure a future for the cod fishery, they engaged in furious competition with one another to catch what cod were left. When not enough could be found to maintain "profitability," they quite literally spread their nets for whatever substitutes might serve to keep them in the black. The result was, and remains, an orgy of destruction on a scale unique in the long history of human predation in the seas.

Having seen what happened to the cod, let us look briefly at what has happened, and is happening, to the other major commercial fish species generically referred to as groundfish. Because the subject is so vast, I have restricted my exposition of it to the waters of Newfoundland and the Grand Banks where, however, the destruction has been typical of what has taken place almost everywhere.

Although never approaching cod in abundance the closely related haddock bore the first brunt of the generalized assault upon Atlantic groundfishes that began with the decline in cod stocks. By 1952, haddock, which had previously been a by-catch species (one taken more or less accidentally during the fishery for cod), was being fished at the rate of about 40,000 metric tonnes a year. At first it was the special prey of Portuguese and Spanish draggers. These vessels used such small mesh in their trawls that schools of young haddock were dragged to the surface along with their larger brethren. Since they were too small to be of any value, they were simply shovelled overboard—quite dead.

A pilot in the Royal Canadian Air Force who flew patrols over Canada's coastal waters in the 1950s has described for me what the haddock fishery looked like from the air.

"One morning we raised forty or fifty paired [two vessels towing one enormous trawl between them] Spanish draggers working Green Bank. It was a nice clear day and we could see them away off. What we couldn't understand was—some of them seemed to have a tail. It was shining in the sunlight like a streamer of floating silver paper a couple of miles long. We diverted to see what the devil it was, and when we came over them at about 2,000 feet, we saw it was dead fish. There must have been millions of them stretching out astern of each boat that had just hauled its net and was sorting the catch on deck. Undersized fish were going overside like confetti. It was actually kind of pretty, but our radio op, who was a Bluenoser from Lunenburg [a major Nova Scotian fishing port], was so pissed off he figured we ought to bomb the bastards. It was young haddock they were dumping, and what a bloody waste; but apparently that was the regular thing with the Spanish fleet."

In 1955, ships working the Grand Banks landed 104,000 tonnes of haddock—and probably killed and dumped that much again. Although everyone in the business knew what was happening, nobody did a thing about it. The useless massacre of young haddock continued unabated. By 1961 the draggers were only able to catch 79,000 tonnes and, soon thereafter, the haddock fishery collapsed. By 1969 it had been abandoned. A report issued by the Canadian government provides the epitaph.

"Most year classes [the young born in any given year] since 1955 have been complete failures. This, as well as heavy fishing pressure . . . has caused a reduction in haddock stocks to an extremely low level . . . there are no prospects for improvement in the immediate future."

Indeed, there were none; nor does there seem to be much of a prospect in the distant future either since, in 1984, haddock were still commercially extinct in Newfoundland/Grand Banks waters—and almost everywhere else as well.

The redfish is a large-eyed, deep-water fish that bears its young alive and is both slow-growing and slow to mature sexually. Hardly fished at all before 1953, it came under direct assault on the offshore banks in 1956 with landings of 77,000 tonnes. Marketed as ocean perch, it proved so profitable that entire segments of the multinational fishing fleet concentrated on it, landing 330,000 tonnes in the single year of 1959. This was followed by a predictable decline to landings of 82,000 tonnes in 1962. This fishery would soon have been exhausted had it not been for the introduction of new types of mid-water trawls and the discovery of a relatively untouched population in the Gulf of St. Lawrence. This precipitated a new massacre, which in its turn began to fail in the early 1970s for want of victims.

By that time almost all the larger and reproductively active redfish had been killed, leading Canada's foremost expert on the species, Dr. E.J. Sandeman, to predict that "prospects are poor for the next several years, and the redfish fishery is expected to decline."

A most accurate prediction. At the time of writing, the remaining redfish contribute only peripherally to the commercial fishery. There is little evidence of any significant recovery in its stocks.

Flatfish include several exploitable species of groundfish. The northwestern Atlantic forms that have suffered most, because they were most abundant, have been the enormous halibut, together with the sole-like plaice, yellowtail, and witch flounder.

All have been disastrously over-fished since about 1962, when it came their turn to fill the insatiable maws of draggers and factory ships. Before that date, they had been virtually ignored. The halibut, which could measure nine feet in length and weigh close to 1,000 pounds, was of only peripheral interest to the fisheries until recently. In earlier times it was even considered a nuisance because it would take cod bait and so waste the time and sometimes break the gear of cod fishermen. Lieutenant Chappell of the British Royal Navy, doing patrol duty on the Grand Banks in 1812, reported that "The fishermen of Newfoundland are much exasperated whenever an unfortunate halibut happens to seize their baits: they are frequently known in such cases to wreak their vengeance on the poor fish by thrusting a piece of wood through its gills and in that condition turning it adrift. The efforts which are made by the tortured fish to get its head beneath the water afford a high source of amusement."

Although, prior to 1960, some few halibut were landed by inshore fishermen from Newfoundland waters and sold either pickled or fully salted, it was not until 1963 that the species was attacked by the commercial fishing fleet. Catches began at about 220 tonnes in 1964 and leapt to at least 40,000 tonnes by 1970. Thereafter, as was ever the case, the catch declined until today the halibut has become a rarity in seas where it once abounded.

The several species of smaller flatfish in northern waters had no commercial value, and were not fished at all except for cod and lobster bait, prior to the post-Second World War development of effective mass-freezing techniques. Even as late as 1962, the total catch of all species of flatfish was under 33,000 tonnes, most of which was taken as a by-catch. In the following year, plaice was deliberately sought after, and yellowtail and witch flounder soon joined the list of exploitable species. By 1966, the catch of these three had topped 154,000 tonnes. The catastrophic decline that followed elicited these cautious comments from a Canadian fisheries biologist in 1976.

"The heavy exploitation of American Plaice on the Grand Bank has resulted in a sharp redaction in the catch per hour...There is every indication that the [yellowtail flounder] total removal levels [read: catch] will decline drastically in the immediate future...With the reduction of the previously unexploited stock biomass [of witch flounder] catch per hour has been greatly reduced."

All of which meant, in simple terms, that the flounder fishery was foundering.

And so it goes. Today, industry spokesmen and scientific advisers are extolling the potential profitability of a whole new range of species that might be fished in place of those that have been commercially exterminated. These include such deep-water and even abyssal species as the wolf fish, the porbeagle (a fancy name for the mackerel shark), and a small shark called the spiny dogfish. The thorny skate is also being touted, as are the grenadiers (otherwise known as rat-tails), which live as much as three-quarters-of-a-mile down in the black deeps. New fishing techniques will be required to "harvest" these "resources," but this should pose no problem to technological men who can travel to the moon and back. It will be interesting to see under what evocative names these species will be marketed.

At this point it would be well to look at one of the major justifications advanced to excuse the fishing industry's biocidal activities. This is the contention that the industry is *duty bound* to constantly increase its landings in order to improve the supply of protein for a human population, much of which lives on the edge of starvation.

This is blatant hypocrisy. In actual fact, the fishing industry of the developed nations, which is by far the largest and most destructive, achieves just the opposite result. Most of its production goes, not to starving peoples, but to those who are already the world's best fed, and who can afford high-priced food. In order to produce high-value (and high-profit) products, usually fillets, the Western fishing industry processes its catches in such a way that as much as 40 per cent of what *could* be used as human food is either completely wasted or is downgraded to make fish meal for animal feeds or fertilizer. On top of which, of course, there is the overriding fact that, by commercially exterminating species after species of the more nutritious and abundant fishes in the sea, the modern commercial fishing industry is actually guaranteeing an increased burden of starvation for the hungry hordes who fill the human future.

This is a new phenomenon. Until 1939, the bulk of the groundfish catch from the northwestern Atlantic was processed as salt fish, a product that preserved as much as 90 per cent of the edible portion of the catch and that was sold at a price affordable to impoverished peoples, for whom it provided a staple source of protein. Profit was certainly a central motive in the industry then, but it was not the all-embracing one it has since become.

Without doubt the most numerous fishes in the seas washing the eastern coasts of North America are still the smaller kinds collectively known as baitfishes. They acquired the name not so much because they provided bait for fishermen as because they were the basic food that sustained other sea animals ranging from sea trout through salmon, cod, halibut, and tuna all the way up the scale to seals, porpoises, and whales.

Baitfishes tend to live in gigantic schools. The best-known species in the northwestern Atlantic are squid, mackerel, herring, shad, smelt, gaspereau or alewife, and capelin. Mackerel are deep-sea breeders; herring and squid mostly spawn close inshore; some capelin spawn offshore on the banks while other populations lay their eggs on landward beaches; the remaining species ascend freshwater rivers and streams to lay their eggs.

Some indication of the prodigious abundance of the baitfishes can perhaps be derived from the following random observations spanning the period from 1600 to recent times:

"The late Monsieur de la Tour had a weir built in which were caught great numbers of these Gaspereaux which were salted down for winter. Sometimes they were caught in so great a quantity that he was obliged to break the weir and throw them into the sea, as otherwise they would have befouled the weir which would thus have been ruined."

"It is an astonishing sight to paddle down the Restigouche and see the farmers 'smelting'—scooping up the little fish in handnets. The amount they take is incredible and most of their potatoes spring from this fishy manure."

"Herring abound in countless shoals. Anyone not familiar with northern waters will suspect me of romancing when I say that I have seen 600 barrels taken in one sweep of a seine net. Often sufficient salt cannot be procured to save them and they are used as manure."

"An American schooner struck a school of mackerel...and before midnight, fishing with hook and line, the crew had 100 barrels caught...fish are destroyed and wasted in the most reckless manner, but the supply never fails. For a week in the spring, smelts run up all the rivers in an unceasing stream."

"Men scarce past middle life tell of seeing three hundred herring vessels off their shore at one time...of seeing Pleasant Bay so packed with herrings that men had only to dip them up until their vessel was full."

"When the capelin drove up on the beaches of Conception Bay to spawn we would stand up to our knees in a regular soup of them, scooping them out with buckets and filling the wagons until the horses could hardly haul them off the beaches. You would sink to your ankles in the sand, it was that spongy with capelin eggs. We took all we needed for bait and for to manure the gardens, and it was like we'd never touched them at all, they was so plenty."

"The run of squid was so heavy that the boats were filled with scoop nets instead of catching them with jiggers. At low tide so many got left behind that the foreshore was coated a foot deep and out a hundred paces from high water mark...one time they came in so strong the ones behind just forced the ones in front right out of the water and we had to shovel them clear of our boats and gear along the landwash."

"In the Potomac River the annual catch was 2,000,000 pounds of shad and 4,000,000 of alewives...As much as two million pounds of salted shad was shipped to the United States every year from the Bay of Fundy in the 1890s."

"In the spring of 1953 on a herring seiner in the Gulf of St. Lawrence we caught a *million* herring in a single set of the seine—a not unusual occurrence at that time."

Although smelt, shad, and alewives were savaged on their spawning runs as well as being ruinously netted at other seasons, this may not have been the deciding factor in the decline that has now brought them down to as low as 4 or 5 per cent of their former profusion. The ultimate blow seems to have been dealt by dams, diversions, pollution, and other man-made changes to their spawning grounds. In any event, none of these three species now exists in sufficient numbers to be a significant source of profit, and their former ability to sustain vast numbers of predacious fishes in the sea has vanished, too. One ray of light in an otherwise almost unrelievedly dark scene of devastation is to be found in current efforts by U.S. authorities to restore some of their shad rivers. Preliminary results seem good. One can but hope they will continue to improve.

Before the present century began, many of the commercially important fishes in our northeastern waters depended on herring, mackerel, and capelin as the mainstays of their existence. This natural toll was greatly intensified by a human catch made first for food, and then for bait, and finally for a variety of industrial products ranging from fish oil to imitation pearl lustre produced from herring scales. Nevertheless, all three species were still enormously abundant when, in the 1960s, new ways were found to profit from them on a previously unheard-of level of destruction.

First was the mass production of fish meal for animal feed and fertilizer. The species initially selected to fuel the ominously named reduction plants that sprang up along the northeastern seaboard was the herring.[1] Early in the 1960s, at about the same time the Newfoundland Industrial Development Service was concluding that local herring stocks were "under-utilized," the herring fishery on the Pacific coast of Canada was collapsing because of overfishing. In the words of the director of the IDS: "What could be more rational than to invite the unemployed British Columbia herring seiners to go to work for us?"

The first reduction plant was built on Newfoundland's south coast in 1965 and a single B.C. seiner made the long voyage around, through the Panama Canal, to test the waters, as it were. The test was eminently successful. By 1969, fifty of the biggest, most modern B.C. seiners were working the south and west Newfoundland coasts year-round, while half-a-dozen reduction plants filled the skies with black and oily smoke. Herring landings in Newfoundland, which had previously averaged less than 4,000 tons a year, shot up to 140,000 tons. Meanwhile, annual landings from the southern Gulf of St. Lawrence increased from 20,000 to 300,000 tons.

Then, in the early 1970s, herring began to disappear. Fisheries spokesmen reassuringly explained that the little fishes had probably altered their migration patterns but would undoubtedly return before too long. The

---

[1] The rationalization for fish meal production defies all logic. As animal food, about 100 pounds, live weight, of fish is required to produce one pound of beef. Two hundred pounds of fish meal used as fertilizer produces no more than three pounds of vegetable protein.

herring were not aware of these optimistic forecasts—for their once prodigious hosts have not returned as yet. There are those who doubt they ever will...or can.

The herring massacre was only one of several. During the 1960s, a mass fishery for mackerel began off southern New England to produce oil, fertilizer, and animal feed (including cat food). By 1972 it was landing the colossal amount of 390,000 tons a year, but shortly thereafter the mackerel mysteriously faded away. The slaughter off New England, together with several similar massacres in Canadian waters, has reduced the once-fabulous mackerel run up the northeast coast from Cape Cod to Labrador to an insignificant vestige of its former self.

In the 1960s Japanese seiners began pursuing offshore capelin on the Grand Banks. When word of this reached the Canadian Department of Fisheries, its mandarins concluded that capelin must be a money-maker and they thereupon decided to "develop a major capelin fishery." What had traditionally been an inshore fishery carried on by Newfoundland shoremen, with a catch of less than 10,000 tons a year, was now converted into an international offshore fishery with enormous quotas being granted to foreign as well as domestic fleets. The foreigners, it must be said, mostly used their catch for human food; the Canadians mostly poured theirs into the reduction plants. In 1976, the reported catch, which was almost certainly much lower than the real one, reached 370,000 tons. By the spring of 1978, the offshore capelin stocks had been effectively exhausted.

But not to worry. Inshore populations that spawned on Newfoundland beaches were still available for "development." These stocks are even now being decimated by Canadian companies, not to provide basic human food, or even fish meal, but to supply a luxury market. Although both sexes of capelin are seined in their millions, only the spawn from gravid females is processed, to be sold to the Japanese gourmet trade. The bulk of the catch is often simply dumped.

By 1983 most of the inshore capelin populations had been reduced to residual levels. Some biologists believe that this havoc has effectively blocked a recovery of groundfish stocks as well as administering what may well be a mortal blow to the few remaining large colonies of seabirds on Newfoundland's coasts—colonies that largely depend on capelin for their survival. Still other marine zoologists suspect that the mass destruction of baitfishes in general is seriously affecting the vitality of the remaining grey, harbour, and hood seal stocks together with several kinds of whales, all of which have been savagely depleted by man in recent years.

A few months ago, I asked a disaffected Fisheries biologist (of which there seems to be a growing number) what he thought about the industry practice of exhausting not only the populations of commercial fishes, but their feed stocks as well. Some of what he had to say in reply is unprintable, but the gist can be summed up in these words.

"Listen! For those bastards, there's no tomorrow. Or if there is, they'll have moved their money into something else, like maybe processing Third World human populations to make dog food. No matter what anyone in the industry, or in the Department tells you—there's just one thing on everybody's mind: make money...make as much as you can before the whole damn bottom drops out of ocean fisheries...The seas are dying, as if you didn't know."

If codfish be the plodding plebians of the sea (as viewed by human eyes), then Atlantic salmon are the glamorous aristocrats. Yet this has not mitigated against their destruction at our hands.

From 1865 to 1910, an *habitant* by the name of Napoleon Comeau was employed to guard the salmon in the rather inconsequential Godbout River on the north shore of the St. Lawrence estuary about 200 miles below Quebec. His employers were a handful of Montreal businessmen and politicos who had leased exclusive salmon fishing rights on the Godbout. Napoleon's task was to make sure that nobody and nothing took so much as a smolt from the waters that belonged to the self-styled "Lairds of the Godbout."

For forty-three years, he and his assistants waged war up and down the river and in the adjacent waters of the estuary against "Those base enemies of the regal salmon: white whales, porpoises, seals, bears, minks, otters, mergansers, kingfishers, ospreys and loons." The guardians also dealt harshly with any human poachers they might find, including the native Indians of the region whose ancestors had fished Godbout salmon for sustenance since time immemorial.

Comeau was not just a remorseless watchdog, he was also the faithful servant, cook, and guide to his beloved employers, of whom he (or his ghost writer) wrote: "Long may the Lairds of the Godbout enjoy their royal sport of matching their science and skill against the cunning, agility and strength of the kingly salmon."

A meticulous man, Comeau kept careful records of his Lairds' accomplishments. Although they only fished the river for two or three weeks in any given year, and seldom with more than six "rods," during Comeau's tenure they caught 14,560 salmon averaging eighteen pounds each, for a grand total of 258,000 pounds of the regal fish.

The 1903 season was typical. In two weeks, Messers John and James Manuel, James Law, and Colonel E.A. Whitehead killed 543 large salmon weighing a total of 6,334 pounds—of which about fifty pounds of each sportsman's catch was smoked so that he could take it back by boat to Montreal as proof of his prowess.[2] As for the rest of that three tons of "kingly salmon"—it was mostly left to rot in the Godbout valley where some of it served as bait to attract black bears, which were then trapped or shot to ensure that they would catch no living fish.

There is nothing unusual about this glimpse of sport fishermen in action. During the latter part of the nineteenth century and into the twentieth, more than 400 such salmon clubs fished the rivers of the northeastern seaboard from Maine to Labrador. Many held river leases giving them exclusive rights to kill the royal fish. Their members included the social, financial, military, and political elite of the continent together with distinguished, often aristo-cratic visitors from abroad. All killed salmon on a scale similar to that of the Lairds of the Godbout, or at least they did so until there were few salmon left. Yet, for all that, they were late corners to the salmon slaughter.

The earliest North American reference to Atlantic salmon is contained in the saga account of Leif Eriksson's voyage to Vinland in 995 when he over-wintered somewhere on the coast of Newfoundland. "There was no shortage of salmon there and these were larger salmon than they had ever seen before."

Not only were they larger, they existed in such multitudes that no mere description could do them justice. But consider this: at the time the European invasion of the Americas began, almost every river together with most minor streams emptying into the Atlantic from north-central Labrador to as far south as the Hudson, as well as those emptying into the St. Lawrence system as far west as Niagara Falls, was home to innumerable salmon tribes or clans. All members of each tribe were hatched and spent their youth in these home rivers, to which they returned to beget the next generation of their kind after spending the years of adolescence in the sea. By conservative estimate, at least 3,000 such salmon rivers provided several hundreds of thousands of spawning beds for an overall Atlantic salmon pop-ulation that may well have outnumbered that of the *several* salmon species found on the Pacific coast of North America.

---

[2] "Kill" is the verb traditionally used by both sport and commercial salmon fishermen.

Descriptions from early times can do little more than suggest the salmon's original abundance, yet they are impressive enough. Here is Nicolas Denys, writing of the Miramichi River in the early years of the seventeenth century. "So large a quantity of Salmon enters this river [that] at night one is unable to sleep, so great is the noise they make in falling upon the water after having thrown or darted themselves into the air [while] passing over the river flats...[Near Chedabucto Bay on Cape Breton Island] I found a little river which I have named Rivière au Saulmon...I made a cast of the seine net at its entrance where it took so great a quantity of Salmon that ten men could not haul it to land and...had it not broken, the Salmon would have carried it off. We had a boat full of them, the smallest three feet long...[On Baie Chaleur] there is found a little river with Salmon of extraordinary length, some have been taken of six feet in length." In the account of his travels around Nova Scotia, Prince Edward Island, New Brunswick, and the Gaspé, Denys lists dozens of such rivers and streams and comments in similar vein on the profusion of salmon in all of them.

John Smith reported that, in what would become New England, there was no river "where there is not plenty of salmon," a statement echoed by all the early English journalists. The French were equally impressed. Pierre Boucher, in about 1650, marvelled at the "many fine rivers abounding with fish, especially salmon; there are prodigious quantities of that fish there." The Sieur de Courtemanche, describing a journey along the north shore of the Gulf of St. Lawrence sometime around 1705, makes a litany out of the salmon rivers: "Muskware Bay, into which flow two rivers very rich with salmon...Washikuti Bay, equally rich in salmon...Etamamu River, full of salmon...Eskimo River, rich in salmon of extraordinary size...Blanc Sablon River, plenty of very good salmon."

This plethora was viewed as a noteworthy aspect of life in the New World, but not as something of any great commercial value until after 1700, when it was discovered that there was a market for salted salmon in Europe. Thereafter the kingly fish became an increasingly valuable article of commerce. Initially they were caught by blocking off spawning rivers with weirs, then forking the trapped fish ashore. Nets were later used to bar off river mouths although, in the early years, the salmon were so abundant, and so huge, that the nets often burst under the strain. On virgin rivers neither nets nor weirs were needed. In 1755, a New Englander named Atkins anchored his vessel in the mouth of a Labrador river and caught all the salmon he had salt to cure by having his crew stand in the shallows and gaff the great silvered fish as they swam by.

George Cartwright fished salmon for export in the 1770s from several southeast Labrador rivers. The run in White Bear River, he noted, was so thick "that a ball could not have been fired into the water without striking a salmon." He and a crew of three men killed 12,396 in one season on one river, and he lamented that he could and would have easily killed 30,000 if only he had not run out of salt with which to cure them. In 1799 he recorded, "In Eagle River we are killing 750 salmon a day and we would have killed more had we had more nets...I could have killed a thousand tierce alone at Paradise River, the fish averaging from 15 to 32 pounds apiece." A tierce was 300 pounds of salted fish, representing about 500 pounds of salmon, live weight. By the end of the eighteenth century, Newfoundland alone was exporting 5,000 tierce a year and it is estimated that the North American fishery was exporting annually in excess of 30 million pounds, live weight. In addition to this commercial catch, thousands upon endless thousands were every year killed locally for hog feed, to feed indentured workers, and to be spread upon the fields in lieu of manure.

By the beginning of the nineteenth century the salmon tide was noticeably ebbing in the more settled areas, not alone due to deliberate slaughter but also to the damming of rivers for millponds and to pollution from manufactories, especially tanneries and iron smelters. The results of this industrial destruction showed earliest along the eastern seaboard of the United States. "Previous to the separation from Maine," complained a Boston man in the 1820s, "large quantities of salmon were packed in Massachusetts; since 1818 none have been...The building of dams and manufacturing establishments...has almost annihilated them in this commonwealth."

The nineteenth century brought an enormous increase in commercial salmon fishing with the addition of canned and fresh fish to the old staples of smoked and salted salmon. By 1872, New Brunswick alone was every summer shipping 1,500,000 pounds of fresh salmon, packed in ice, to Boston and New York markets that could no longer obtain more than token amounts from the ravaged rivers of New England. And, by then, canned salmon was not only being shipped all over eastern and central North America but was going to Europe by the shipload. Here is a glimpse of the salmon canning business in Baie Chaleur in 1870.

"Salmon here are particularly large and fine. At the head of the bay they average 20 lbs in weight. The fishery is very important and lucrative...it lasts for two months and during that short period I have known one fisherman take 20,000 lbs of salmon...It would be hard to estimate the total amount exported from the bay, but it must be very large. The greatest part is tinned. One American firm puts up as much as 280,000 lbs here in a season. It is a pretty sight to see the fish coming to the cannery of a morning. Boat after boat discharges its load of silvery beauties fresh from the net. Sometimes whole boat loads will average 25 lbs each fish, and I have seen fish here up to 56 lbs in weight."

These developments were parallelled by the rapid growth of sport fishing, which, having received the imprimatur of the powerful and wealthy, became an activity to be aped by any socially pretentious person who could afford the cost of a split-cane rod. All of these factors together were inexorably diminishing the salmon tribes, although few cared to recognize the fact. One who did was John Rowan, a prescient English visitor to the Canadian seaboard in the 1870s.

"Thirty years ago, the salmon fishing in Nova Scotia was superb. But where nature is so bountiful in her gifts man rarely appreciates them. As with the forest, so with the fish. It would really seem as if Nova Scotians hate the salmon. Overfishing is bad enough, but to shut the fish out of the rivers is little better than insanity. Yet hundreds of miles of river, stream and lake are closed against the salmon by milldams, many of which are of no industrial value. By-and-by, when the forests have been destroyed and the rivers rendered barren, Canadians will spend large sums of money in, perhaps, fruitless efforts to bring back that which they could now so easily retain."

Rowan was an astute observer, though not always politic. "The most luxurious anglers are the Americans... Their rods, their reels, their flies are all works of art; expensive ones too, as they take care to inform you. They are always self-satisfied, always droll, always hospitable. They never go anywhere without pistols and champagne."

The turn of the century marked the beginning of the end for the Atlantic salmon in unmistakable ways. In 1898, the last known survivor of the millions that had once spawned in the rivers draining into Lake Ontario was netted near Toronto. By 1900 they were effectively extinct in Connecticut and Massachusetts and in most of the rivers of New Hampshire and Maine. Wherever chemical, metallurgical, or manufacturing industries dumped their wastes into nearby waters, salmon no longer swam. And a growing number of remote rivers along the north shore of the Gulf of St. Lawrence were now devoid of salmon because their spawning beds had been buried under rotting layers of sawdust, bark, and wood chips—the detritus from lumber mills and timber rafting. In all the waters to which salmon clans still clung, the assault by both sport and commercial fishermen grew ever fiercer as the spiral of exploitation tightened. As the fish became scarcer, so their value rose; they were hunted harder, and became scarcer, and their value rose...

Considering what they were enduring, and had endured, the mere fact of their ongoing survival was a miracle of vitality. However, it was not miracle enough to protect the fish of kings from the greed of men.

There is little need to detail the wasting of Atlantic salmon by mankind during the first half of the current century. It is enough to note that, despite some erratic gestures of protection (always too little and too late), the regal fish continued an inexorable slide toward extinction. While sportsmen and commercial fishermen squabbled in increasingly acrimonious terms over who would get what was left, modern technology unleashed two even more crushing blows against the remnant stocks.

During the late 1950s the United States Navy began sending submarines north under the Arctic ice, and one of them made a surprising discovery. Beneath the verges of the Baffin Bay pack it encountered gleaming hordes of large fishes that, after some confusion, were identified as Atlantic salmon. The discovery was particularly important because, until then, no one had known where Atlantic salmon spent their time once they departed from the continental coasts for their long sojourn at sea.

First to make capital of the discovery were the Danes, closely followed by the Norwegians. A fleet of deep-sea seiners and drift-netters was soon butchering salmon for the first time on their wintering ground. And it was not just North American salmon that died; the Baffin Bay ground was used by *all* surviving Atlantic salmon, including the remaining European tribes.

The North American tribes by this time were almost wholly restricted to Canadian waters. Now they were in double jeopardy. Between 1962 and 1982, the West Greenland winter fishery *reported* an annual catch of 2,000–3,000 tons, but it is known that the actual catch was at least 50 per cent higher than that. During this same period, Canadian fishermen running drift nets on the approach routes used by salmon bound for the spawning rivers, together with gill nets and traps at river mouths and along the shores, were landing about 2,000 tons a year. The combined destruction produced by this overkill of an already severely depleted species was in itself more than the salmon could bear. But it was not the only blow they had to suffer.

In the 1950s, forest industries and provincial and state governments along the northeastern seaboard began mass aerial spraying of insecticides. These lethal substances, initially including DDT, so poisoned salmon spawning rivers that entire year classes were wiped out. The ongoing use of pesticides, defoliants, and other chemicals continues to wreak ruin in salmon rivers, and their deadly effects are now being intensified by the invisible sintering down from the high skies of acid rain.

Acid rain, as anyone who reads must know, has already turned hundreds and perhaps thousands of lakes in northeastern America into virtually lifeless bodies of water. There is no doubt that, unless acid rain can soon be stopped and its effects reversed, fish life will become impossible in most of the remaining streams and rivers where salmon still attempt to spawn. Already twelve Nova Scotia salmon rivers have been lost to acid rain and many more are seriously threatened.

Meanwhile, in Canada, small armies of Quebec Provincial Police were recently sent to extinguish the rights of Micmac Indians to fish salmon in ancestral rivers, possession of which is claimed by industrial fishermen at the river mouths and by sport fishermen along the inland banks. However, while the Indians are being prevented from, as a spokesman of the sport fishing fraternity put it, "depriving themselves of a future full of salmon by their wasteful, haphazard and vicious use of nets," salmon have become so rare and sought-after that poaching is now a highly organized and efficient business throughout Nova Scotia, New Brunswick, and some regions of Quebec. Selling on the black market for as much as $10 a pound in 1983, the few remaining salmon are simply too valuable to be allowed to go on living.

Figures released by the federal government at the end of 1983 showed that the salmon population in one of the last and greatest of Canada's major salmon rivers, the Miramichi, had decreased by 34 per cent during that single year and by 87 per cent since the mid-1960s. Spawning runs in Canadian rivers were generally reduced by an average of 50 per cent, and the unofficial prognosis is that every salmon river south of Belle Isle Strait will be virtually empty of the regal fish before this decade ends.

There may be some exceptions. One such might be the Restigouche, where the exclusive Restigouche Salmon Club owns twenty-eight miles of river. Its members, who have included the Cabots of Boston, the Morgans, Whitneys, and Winthrops of New York, and at present includes such illustrious sportsmen as the chairman of Exxon, will perhaps be able to continue "enjoying their royal sport of matching their science and skill against the cunning, agility and strength of the kingly salmon." However, the fish they kill will probably be hand-raised to maturity on salmon farms maintained for the dual purpose of supplying gourmet appetites with luxury foods and of assisting the sporting fraternity to continue enjoying the sport of kings.

12
More Fish in the Sea?

Since Europeans first entered New World waters some of the creatures our forebears encountered have been almost entirely lost to memory or, at best, are remembered only as semi-mythical beings.

Of such is the unknown animal that gave rise to a number of early reports of mermaids and mermen, one of which is an eyewitness account by Richard Whitbourne. In 1610, he saw a "strange creature" swimming in St. John's harbour. He described it as having "strakes of hair down to the neck." It was certainly not a walrus, nor yet a seal—animals the old fisherman was fully familiar with. When it approached a boat manned by some of Whitbourne's men, they panicked and one of them "strooke it a full blow on the head." Even so it later approached some other boats. "Whether it were a Mermaide or no, I know not," Whitbourne wrote. "I leave it for others to judge." Josselyn described a triton or merman from Casco Bay in the 1670s, and even as late as the 1870s a missionary at the Strait of Belle Isle reported that a fisherman near St. John's Islands had netted a mermaid, which he preserved in salt to show the curious.

Although mermaids as such never existed, the sea mammals that gave rise to the idea assuredly did. They belong to a family called the sirenians, which includes the dugong and the manatees. Surviving sirenians are now found only in temperate to tropical waters, but until exterminated by train oil hunters in the 1760s (which was within thirty years of its discovery), a northern sirenian called Stellar's sea cow lived in the Bering Sea. Writing in his *Arctic Zoology*, published in 1784–87, the British naturalist Pennant thought that this animal or something similar might have "found its way through some northern inlet into the seas of Greenland; for Mr. Fabricus once discovered in that country the head of one, half consumed, with teeth exactly agreeing with those of [the manatee]."

A sirenian of such trusting habits as Whitbourne's mermaid would have had but little chance of surviving the European invaders. If one such did indeed exist in northeastern seaboard waters, it is now beyond even memory's recall.

Another and almost equally vulnerable sea animal that assuredly *did* exist in notable numbers seems to have been effectively exterminated before the eighteenth century began. On September 6, 1535, the vessels of Jacques Cartier's second expedition anchored under the lee of Île aux Coudres at Baie St-Paul in the St. Lawrence River. After noting the presence there of schools of white whales, Cartier's scribe added: "In this bay, and about this island there are inestimable numbers *de grande tortures*"—of great turtles. When Sir Humphrey Gilbert wrote a prospectus listing the rich marine resources of the northeastern seaboard, he named "Coddes, Salmons, Seals, Makerals, Tortoyses, Whales and Horsefishes." Brereton, visiting the New England coast in 1602, tells of finding "Tortoises" both on land and sea. The reference to land is almost certainly not to freshwater turtles, but to sea turtles coming up on the beaches to lay their eggs. About 1656 Du Creux, referring to the "Fish" of the Quebec region, included turtles, seals, and whales. Finally, Josselyn, in New England, not only listed five sorts of "Sea-Turtles," but watched from shipboard when "our men...hoisted the Shallop out and took divers Turtles, there being an infinite number of them all over the sea as far as we could ken."

By the end of the seventeenth century such observations were a thing of the past and, in our times, the appearance in any given year of a single sea turtle, usually a loggerhead or a leatherback, anywhere in the region is cause for much excitement. Such an occasion most often is a result of the unfortunate sea giant having been shot, or harpooned, and its massive corpse dragged ashore as a curiosity.

These are but two of the many probable losses the community of sea creatures sustained in times past. What follows are the stories of others that have suffered or are still suffering enormous depredations at our hands, and these creatures, too, may well be fated to join the mermaids and *les grandes tortures* in mythical obscurity.

As early as 1610, Champlain recognized three kinds of the armoured and ancient sturgeon in New World waters. One was the lake sturgeon, which was abundant in Lake Ontario and Lake Champlain and their drainage systems as well as in tidal waters of the St. Lawrence estuary. This was a big fish, ranging from four to eight feet long and often weighing 100 pounds.

The other two were salt-water fishes that spent their adult lives in the sea and only ascended rivers to spawn. The short-nosed variety was a small estuarine species, seldom exceeding three feet; but the sea sturgeon was enormous, some individuals weighing half a ton.

Pickled sturgeon meat had been a popular dish in Europe since ancient times, and by as early as 1520 French fishermen working New World waters were salting down quantities of sturgeon for the home market. At the same time, sturgeon provided a staple food for fishermen, early settlers, and native inhabitants alike. Sturgeon abounded everywhere. John Smith reported that no New England river was without it "in great plenty." Champlain noted that the "sea sturgeon were so abundant [in the territories of New France] that there might be sold in Germany, or other regions where this fish is much in demand, annually 100,000 livres worth."

Nicolas Denys gave it prominence in his listing of New World assets: "There are some of eight, ten, eleven and twelve feet in length and as thick in the body as Sheepe...the body is covered with scales of the size of a plate...Their flesh is as good as beef...That fish cometh to the entrance of rivers [and] leaps its own height above the water. It is taken with a harpoon...There are also smaller ones which are of another kind, but of better taste." Denys also noted that sturgeon swim bladders were an excellent source of isinglass, a clear, glue-like substance thought to be of great merit as a medicine.

During the 1630s, William Wood, in New England, wrote that "The sturgeons be all over the country, but the best catching of them is upon the shoals of Cape Cod and in the river of Merrimac where much is taken, pickled, and brought for England. Some of these be twelve, fourteen, eighteen foot long." A few decades later, Josselyn, writing about the same region, commented, "This Fish is here in great plenty and in some Rivers so numerous that it is hazardous for Canoes and the like light Vessels to pass to and fro."

About 1650, Pierre Boucher wrote of the lake sturgeon: "It is to be taken from Quebec [upstream]; and in all the great lakes there are great quantities of it...all large, of four, six and eight feet long; I have seen them taken in abundance in front of Montreal...it is very good when salted, and keeps for a long time."

Although the slaughter of all three species had been heavy into the early nineteenth century, sturgeon were so abundant and so fecund (each female laid up to three million eggs) that, until as late as 1850, they were still among the commonest fishes on the Atlantic seaboard. Then it was discovered that the eggs of the North American sturgeon could be converted into caviar of almost as good a quality as the Russian variety. At the same time a major market for industrial isinglass developed, while fresh sturgeon flesh was in increasing demand in large American cities. The combination was too much even for these prolific fishes to withstand.

Using nets, guns, harpoons, even bombs, fishermen attacked the spawning runs of the big sea sturgeon and its smaller cousins with such ferocity that, in 1890, the kill in the Delaware River alone amounted to more than 5 million pounds. As late as 1897, one group of fishermen was able to kill 335 large, spawning-run sturgeon in a single haul at Amaganset. This general massacre would not spare even enough gravid females to allow the species to propagate, and so the sturgeon began to disappear.

Although by the 1920s all three species had become, in the words of a Fisheries biologist, "as rare as they were extraordinary," nothing of any effect was done to save them. It is true that in recent years the few survivors have been given a measure of protection, but this has not compensated for the fact that many of their erstwhile spawning rivers and estuaries have become so polluted that their hatchlings cannot live.

Nobody knows how many sturgeon still remain alive in the northeastern region, but it is agreed that they represent no more than a fractional percentage of the ancestral multitudes that inhabited these waters before we came upon them.

Called *barse* by the early French, the striped bass was one of the more remarkable marine fishes found in the New World. Seldom swimming more than three or four miles offshore, and preferring to patrol the beaches where it chased its prey right into the foam, it originally ranged from the Gulf of St. Lawrence to Florida, ascending most major rivers and hundreds of minor ones in its spawning runs. A large, robust fish that often weighed fifty pounds (six-footers weighing 140 pounds were not uncommon), it was considered to be as good as or better eating than the Atlantic salmon. And it was present in unbelievable numbers.

It was manna from the seas for early settlers. Cartier commented on its "great numbers" at Quebec, and Champlain found it so abundant spawning in Bay of Fundy rivers that "entire ships could be loaded with it."

As for New England, here is what Captain John Smith had to say about it: "The Basse is an excellent Fish, both fresh and salte ... They are so large the head of one will give a good eater a dinner, for daintiness of diet they excell the Marybones of Beef. They are such multitudes that I have seene stopped in the river ... at one tyde as many as will bade a ship of 100 tonnes ... at the turning of the tyde [I] have seen such multitudes passe out of a pounde [net] that it seemed to me one might go over their backs drishod."

William Wood, in 1634, could hardly eulogize them enough. "The bass is one of the best fishes in the country and though men are soon wearied with other fish, yet are they never with bass; it is a delicate, fine, fat, fast fish having a bone in its head which contains a saucerful of marrow ... [he then describes the various ways bass were caught, all year long, ending with this description of netting them during the spring spawning run]...the English, at the top of an high water do cross the creeks with long seines or bass nets...and, the water ebbing...[the bass] are left on the dry ground, sometimes two or three thousand at a set, which are salted up against winter or distributed to such as...use them for [fertilizing] their ground."

In northern waters, the bass seem to have been smaller, or perhaps it was just that the destruction wrought upon them over the centuries left only a stunted remainder in modern times. At any rate, by 1870, John Rowan found them to be only about "20 and 30 lbs" in the St. John River: "Bass spearing is capital sport...a few miles above Fredericton on fine June evenings dozens of canoes may be seen darting about the broad surface of the river...pursuing shoals of bass which rise to the surface, plunge and roll, then dive. The canoes are paddled furiously and barbed spears or harpoons hurled into the midst of them...The striped bass are only killed for sport [on the St. John River, but]...in some Canadian rivers large quantities of bass are taken in scoop-nets through the ice. In the Miramichi alone, I am informed that over 100 tons have been taken in a winter." Rowan does not tell us to what use these fish were put but, from other sources, it appears they were used mainly for fertilizer.

John Cole in *Striper*, his 1978 book about the species, gives us an overview of the course of slaughter: "Who can ever measure the numbers taken by...the fleets that made landfall in the New World only to find the harbours writhing with the silver-sided splashings of the stripers?...And will there ever be any counting of the stripers netted in tidal coves, their gleaming carcasses...left by the thousands for colonial farmers to hoist to handbarrows for their trip to the corn fields and their burial there? And, as the nation grew, who ever tallied the bass taken by a growing commercial fishery that utilized hand lines, trot lines, line trawls, gill nets, stake nets, drift nets, runaround nets, seine nets, fyke nets, pound nets, trawl nets, scoop nets, trammel nets, and bag nets specially made to be slid under a river's winter ice to trap the bass as they crowded in giant schools near the bottom?...And who [can] tabulate the depredations of two centuries of recreational sport and meat fishing by individuals using hand lines...fishing from fifty-foot motor cruisers or wading in the surf?"

Because no one can answer these questions, there can never be a numerical accounting. But surely there should be a moral one for the decimation of the striped bass to what may already be the point of no return. Vanished now from the great majority of the rivers and from most of the coasts where it once abounded, its remnants are threatened, not so much by our overt actions as by the mindless manner in which we are turning the world of waters into a stew of death. Again, Cole tells the tale.

"After uncounted centuries as a presence on the east coast of this nation, the striped bass is dying. This fish, once so abundant it clogged river deltas... is being destroyed... There is no debate about the decline in striped bass populations. Annual surveys of bass reproduction in Chesapeake Bay and the Hudson River... tell the same story... These two bodies of water—which together are the nurseries for 99 percent of the [remaining] stripers of the northeast coast—have been increasingly unproductive each year.

"Why," asks Cole, "when the waters are cloudy with billions of eggs... why is there no surviving year class? Why does the creature's population decline until now the rivers and sea hold only a handful of old fish that gather each April for a sterile ritual of reproduction?"

He tells us why. It is because (and the evidence is irrefutable) the waters of the Hudson and of Chesapeake Bay, as is the case with most east-coast waters, have become so toxic with our industrial, domestic, and agricultural wastes that the fry of the striper, together with the young of countless other animals, simply do not survive. "Ten years from now," Cole says, "at its current rate of decline, the striped bass will no longer roam the inshore waters of the Atlantic... it will have vanished as a viable species."

The giant mackerel called bluefin tuna is one of the largest, most advanced, and unusual of all fishes. Capable of growing to a length of fourteen feet and a weight of 1,500 pounds, it is a compact mass of streamlined muscle of such superlative hydrodynamic design that it can swim at close to sixty miles an hour. In a sense, it is a "warm-blooded" fish since, almost alone of the finny kind, it can regulate its body temperature. The bluefin can manoeuvre in water with the effortless skill of a bird in air. There is probably nothing in the sea that can catch it... or escape it. Some modern biologists call it the superfish, but human recognition of its uniqueness goes back to the beginnings of history. Prehistoric cave painters evidently shared with the Mycenaean civilization of Crete an admiration for tuna amounting to awe.

Ancient sea-hunters killed tuna when they could, and other men continued to do so down through the ages; nevertheless, such is the vitality of the tuna that they easily held their own until little more than thirty years ago.

Western bluefins spawn in the Gulf of Mexico but range north in spring and summer at least as far as Newfoundland. Prior to 1939, only the younger members of the tribe, mostly two- to five-year-olds weighing from about ten to a hundred pounds, were fished commercially in North American waters. At a rate of a few hundred tons a year, the kill was small enough to be sustained. The giants, which could be as old as thirty-five years, were hardly fished at all and that only by the few who were wealthy enough to own or charter big motor launches from which they fished for sport with rod and reel.

But the 1950s saw the development of a new and deadly interest in the tuna tribes. Canned tuna meat was beginning to be popularized, both for human consumption on the world market and to feed the growing pet population belonging to affluent North Americans. So the commercial tuna-fishing effort rapidly increased, though still directed mostly against the younger fish. As for the old giants, upon whose survival and successful propagation the fate of the bluefin species rested, they became targets for an explosive growth in sport fishing that saw thousands of men and women who were now blessed with surplus income turn to trophy fishing as a recreation.

By 1960, more than 11,000 sports were going out in charter boats every year, hoping to hook and land "trophy" tuna beside which they could have their pictures taken. One of them set a world record in 1979 by landing a thirty-two-year-old, 1,500-pound bluefin in Nova Scotia waters. Its like has not been seen again and probably never will be.

During the peak years of the 1950s as many as 150,000 large bluefins were killed annually in the North Atlantic commercial fishery—but by 1973, the catch had fallen to 2,100. In 1955, the Norwegian fleet alone took 10,000 tons of smaller tuna; in 1973, it caught just over 100 individuals. In former years, Portuguese fishermen regularly killed 20,000 tuna a year in great net traps; in 1972, they caught *two* fish. One singularly enormous trap that has been operated in the Strait of Gibraltar since the sixth century caught 43,500 tuna as late as 1949; in 1982, its catch was 2,000 fish, all very small.

From the late 1950s, Japan offered the most lucrative market for tuna, which initially was bought from foreign fishing companies. However, with the perfecting of quick freezing and deep-sea freezer/fishing vessels, the Japanese moved into the fishery themselves. When the first U.S. tuna purse seiner *Silver Mink* (a marvel of technology) went into service in 1958 and quickly became the most successful fish killer ever launched until that time, Japanese, U.S., and multinational commercial fishing interests hurriedly followed her lead. They competed to build bigger, better, more efficient vessels that sought out tuna wherever they were to be found and killed them with fearful efficiency.

The ultimate tuna boat was *Zapata Pathfinder*—a 250-foot super-seiner under Panamanian registry that looked more like a Greek shipping magnate's private yacht than a working vessel. Valued at $10–$15 million, she had a satellite navigation system, carried her own helicopter for tuna spotting, and provided her captain with a suite of rooms embellished with a bar and lounge, a king-size bed, and gold-plated bathroom faucets. She was capable of catching, freezing, and stowing $5 million worth of tuna on a single voyage. She could earn her captain $250,000 a year, but how much she made in overall profits remains unknown, as do the identities of her owners, which are lost to view in overlapping and interlocking companies. Nevertheless, informed observers of the tuna fishery have estimated that *Zapata Pathfinder* probably returned 100 per cent profit on investment *every year* she operated. The magnitude of the carnage she and her sisters inflicted on the world's tuna population in the process of amassing these obscene profits was so great that, by the end of the 1970s, such super-seiners had fished themselves out of business.

In addition to building purse seiners, the Japanese made great strides in tuna long-lining, to the point where, by 1962, they were catching 400,000 tons of tuna a year. But by 1980 the entire Japanese fleet of 300 long-liners only managed to catch 4,000 tons of bluefin tuna.

The discovery, in the mid-1960s, that giant tuna were accumulating dangerous levels of mercury during their long lives as a result of pollution resulted in a ban on the sale of their flesh in most Western countries. For a time, conservationists hoped that the remaining giants might be spared to carry on the reproduction of their species. It was a faint hope. By 1966, tuna sport fishing had become so popular that 388 giants were caught and killed off Newfoundland alone that year. Since this was just recreational fishing, the enormous carcasses were mostly dumped overboard after the obligatory photographs had been taken.

By 1968, however, the Japanese gourmet market, fuelled by increasing national affluence, was developing an appetite for *jumbo magura*—the raw flesh of giant bluefin tuna. Undeterred by the mercury content (if indeed they even knew about it), Japanese epicures were eventually paying as much as $25 a pound for jumbo magura, and the North American "sport" fishery leapt at this opportunity to make windfall profits.

In 1974, charter-boat operators at North Lake, Prince Edward Island— the self-styled Tuna Capital of the World—helped their clients boat 578 giant bluefins, then sold most of the carcasses, quick-frozen, to Japan. Tuna guides and charter boatmen could hardly believe their golden luck. When

there were no "sports" to catch the big fish, they set tuna trawls—a procedure roughly commensurate, from a sporting point of view, with using baited
night lines in a trout pond.

In 1978, 3,000 giant tuna reached Japan for conversion into jumbo
magura, but by 1981 the Tuna Capital of the World was only able to catch
fifty-five. I was told at a sportsmen's motel in North Lake that year that the
bluefins "have changed their migration patterns, but are bound to return
soon." As this book goes to press they have not returned, and charter boatmen are selling their boats or trying desperately to find new ways to lure back
the sport-fishing enthusiasts—shark fishing, perhaps?

The jumbo magura business was so valuable that, in 1974, the Japanese
entrepreneurs who controlled it financed a unique "fish farm" in Nova Scotia
with the support and encouragement of Canada's Department of Fisheries.
This farm was permitted to net-trap all the giant tuna it could find in the
vicinity of St. Margarets Bay. The giants were then transferred to "feed lot"
underwater cages and there fattened with unlimited amounts of mackerel
until they reached prime weight and condition. They were then slaughtered,
iced, and flown to Japan. In 1974, fifty giant bluefins were so treated, but in
1977 nearly 1,000 were trapped, fattened, slaughtered, and sent off to titil-
late Japanese palates. The "farm" is now running out of stock. In the last few
years it has sometimes been unable to trap more than twenty of the great
fishes. Apparently they have gone elsewhere!

Many other members of the tuna family swim under the same dark
shadow. Marine biologists John and Mildred Teal wrote an epitaph for the
bluefin in their recent book, *The Sargasso Sea*: "The smaller bluefin tuna, the
medium five- to eight-year-olds and the small ones under five years, which
live in large schools, have been caught with line, bait and hooks in the eastern
Atlantic and with purse seines in the western Atlantic...Large commercial
catches are being taken even of very small bluefins weighing less than a kilo
each. Once the giants are gone the bluefin will disappear as a commercial
fish...The tuna's depletion is senseless, but we have never let this stand in
the way of overfishing for other profitmakers—whales, lobster and haddock."

Many other great North Atlantic fishes have suffered devastation. One of
these is the little-known swordfish. Nicolas Denys, in the early 1600s, wrote
of it: "The Swordfish is a fish as large as a cow, of six to eight feet in length...
it has upon its snout a sword...that is about three feet long, and about four
good inches wide...It is very good to eat in any manner. Its eyes are as large
as the fists."

Originally found on most fishing grounds off the northeastern coast, it was not much sought-after in early times. However, by about 1900 its tasty meat began to be popular in U.S. coastal states and, as refrigeration improved, came to be relished all across the continent as swordfish steak. Originally it was mostly taken by harpooning, but after World War II, with an ever-increasing demand, fishermen began catching it on long-lines. Never abundant, and slow to recoup its losses, it was depleted to the point of rarity by the early 1960s. Scientists then discovered that it contained such high concentrations of mercury and other toxic contaminants that it was dangerous for human beings to consume. It was therefore banned from the U.S., with the result that the fishery for it has been reduced to what a black market can absorb.

The effect of the massive accumulation of toxic chemicals on the surviving swordfish is not known, but it is to be assumed that what is deleterious to us can do the fish no good. At any rate, the numbers of swordfish apparently are still decreasing.

If it is possible to feel concern about the fate of a shark, then the following story should rouse at least some pity for an animal that has been savagely abused. The basking shark is a truly enormous animal—the second largest fish extant. Individuals measuring thirty-five feet in length and weighing an estimated fifteen tons have been killed. Basking sharks are as mysterious as they are huge. Almost nothing is known about them, except that they are completely inoffensive as far as man is concerned and like to go in schools, feeding on minute crustaceans and other forms of plankton they strain through their gill-rakers. A sluggish monster, this great creature takes its name from its habit of drifting slowly on the surface, back awash. This is a habit that has proved fatal to it in its contacts with modern man.

Although its flesh is of no value to us, its liver is. Weighing 1,000 pounds or more, the liver is rich in vitamins that can be extracted for human use. After World War II, it was so assiduously hunted for its liver in the eastern Atlantic as to have been virtually exterminated there. In colonial times, basking sharks were abundant in the Gulf of Maine, and thousands were killed off Cape Cod to produce liver oil for settlers' lamps. But the monster sharks have long since vanished from the eastern seaboard of the United States.

They were also abundant in eastern Canadian waters, where they were not seriously hunted. However, fishermen found them a nuisance since they sometimes became fouled in nets. In consequence, the Canadian Department of Fisheries declared war on them in the 1940s. (On the Pacific coast Fisheries protection vessels went after them first with harpoons. When these proved cumbersome and seldom fatal, rifle fire and even machine-gun fire were tried. However, bullets seemed to have little immediate effect on such enormous creatures, so the department devised an ingenious weapon— a pointed steel ram with a curved cutting edge honed to razor sharpness. Patrol boats fitted with this deadly device sought out schools of the great fishes and rammed them, one by one, either tearing them apart or, in some cases, cutting them in half. One Fisheries patrol vessel cut down eighteen of the giants in one day.)

Basking sharks have been so much reduced that it is now remarkable when as many as two dozen sightings are recorded in any given year along the northeastern seaboard of the continent.

In 1616, when Captain John Smith was extolling the virtues of New England—"You shall scarcely find any bay, shallow shore, or cove of sand where you may not take as many clams, or lobsters, or both as you pleasure,"—he was in fact describing the entire Atlantic littoral from Cape Hatteras to southern Labrador.

Some two dozen kinds of clams, oysters, mussels, scallops, and sea snails lived in shoal waters along the Atlantic seaboard, providing a seemingly inexhaustible smorgasbord of easily available food. It was a bounty of which native peoples freely availed themselves, as the grass-covered shell mounds that mark the sites of many of their coastal habitations still testify. European invaders, however, initially made only minor use of this largesse for food. Instead, they used it mainly as a source of bait for the cod fishery.

Oysters disappeared from salt-water lagoons along the west and south coasts of Newfoundland before the seventeenth century began. On the French island of Miquelon, thick layers of oyster shells lie at the bottom of mountainous accumulations of clam shells that were still being added to by bait-seeking fishermen when I stayed among them in the 1960s. But no living oyster has been found in Miquelon's enormous lagoon since time out of memory. The same holds true of the Magdalen Islands, where winter storms deposit windrows of oyster shells on the beaches, washed up from beds where no oysters still exist.

Shellfish biologists, pondering the disappearance of oysters from so much of their aboriginal North American range, have tended to attribute this to climatic changes. They do not seem to realize that the easily harvested oysters were used as commercial fish bait. Apart from the apparent idiocy of abusing what is now a luxury food in such a manner, they cannot see how such a slippery, watery creature could have been kept upon a hook. The answer is simple enough—the fishermen parboiled oysters, a trick they probably learned from Micmac Indians who still make oyster bait on occasion, considering it the most irresistible lure available.

The indefatigable Nicolas Denys gives us a mid-seventeenth-century glimpse of the munificence of the oyster beds in parts of Nova Scotia and New Brunswick where no oysters are now to be found. "From this cove [Port Mulgrave] there are lagoons of salt water in which are found good Oysters, which are very large, and of Mussels great abundance . . . here [at Havre Boucher] is found also an abundance of Oysters and Mussels . . . [at Antigonish] there are excellent Oysters and, at the entrance to the river on the left are still more of them . . . They are piled like rocks one over the other . . . [at Pictou are] Excellent Oysters, they are immense . . . Some are found there larger than a shoe . . . they are all very plump and good of taste . . ." And so it goes right around the southern Gulf coast to Gaspé. Once, they were abundant. Now, there are none, or almost none.

The profusion of oysters on Prince Edward Island was legendary, and they continue to survive there, although now much restricted and reduced in numbers. In Cape Breton's Bras d'Or Lake as many as thirty schooners at a time once baited with the shellfish at St. Patrick's Channel.

Oysters were but one source of shellfish bait. Clams and mussels served as well. Some nineteenth-century banking schooners loaded as much as ten tons of clams for a single voyage. The clams served a dual purpose: as ballast during the outward voyage, and as bait once the banks were reached. However, the inshore fishermen, inhabiting almost every nook and cranny along the cod coasts, did the most deadly damage. Shellfish bait was conveniently at hand, easy to dig or rake in any required quantity, easy to handle, much relished by the cod . . . and it was free.

Nor were the "hang-ashores"—colonists and settlers—behindhand in profligate destruction of shellfish. Herds of hogs were often turned onto the tidal flats to root out and fatten up on clams of all sizes and species. In 1848 the Indian commissioners for Nova Scotia indignantly reported that this practice had "consumed all the best shellfish on our whole shores." Farmers invaded the flats and shovelled mud, spawn, and adult clams into wagons and hauled the stuff off to their fields where it not only served to lime the ground but acted as manure as well.

Consumption for food did not become a major factor in the decimation of shellfish until late in the eighteenth century, by which time enormous quantities of oysters and clams, especially the cherrystone variety (young quahogs), were being shipped to towns and cities almost everywhere in Canada and the

United States. However, probably the deadliest blow of all was the incidental mistreatment of shellfish beds. It has been estimated that 80 per cent of those in existence in the sixteenth century between Cape Hatteras and Cape Cod have been effectively eliminated by domestic, industrial, and agricultural pollution; by tidal wetlands reclamation and land-fill projects; and by massive outflows of detritus resulting from human-induced erosion. As maritimers know all too well, even the beds that still remain are sometimes so heavily contaminated that shellfish from them are unfit or unsafe to eat.

One species failed to catch our acquisitive eye until the twentieth century. This was the scallop, an offshore animal that was enormously abundant on the more southerly fishing banks until as recently as the 1960s. It was not much sought after until this time, but since then has been fished with such intensity that, during the present decade, the catch has declined to the point where the entire scallop fishery is now in jeopardy. There is nothing in our recent history to give us reason to expect any lessening in the devastation of the scallops until they are commercially extinct. It is predicted that they will have reached this state by 1990.

When Anthony Parkhurst was on the east coast of Newfoundland in the latter part of the sixteenth century, he could "take up in less than half a day [with an eel spear] Lobsters sufficient to find 300 men for a day's meat." Charles Leigh, on the Cape Breton coast at about the same time, noted: "In this place are the greatest multitude of lobsters ever heard of; for we caught at one haul with a little draw net above 140." It was the same in the New England plantations in 1629, as reported by Higginson: "Lobsters [are so many] that the least boy in the Plantation may both catch and eat what he will of them. For my own part I cloyed with them, they were so great, and fat, and luscious. I have seen some myself that have weighed sixteen pound; but others...have had so great lobsters as weighed twenty-five pound." William Wood, writing of the same time and place, adds, "Their plenty makes them little esteemed and seldom eaten [except by the Indians who] get many of them every day for to baite their hooks withal and to eat when they can get no bass."

The use of lobsters for bait was something the newcomers could understand, and they took to that practice on a grand scale. Around 1720, inshore fishermen from Newfoundland to Cape Cod were in the habit of sending boys equipped with double-pronged fish forks to the shore at low tide, there to stab a day's supply of bait from amongst the lobsters sheltering under the sea wrack and in crevices between the rocks. Aaron Thomas, visiting Newfoundland about 1794, tells us: "Lobsters are in such plenty that they are used for Bait to catch the Codd Fish with...I went out in a small Boat to inform myself of the fact...I was not in the Boat more than Half an Hour during which time one man hooked fifty-nine Lobsters." Thomas also tells us that lobster was a sort of universal feed for settlers' livestock, including "Fowl, Cows, Ducks, Goats, Geese, Cats, Horses, Calves, Pigs, tame Sea Gulls [used for food], Sheep and Dogs...when I threw the Claw of a Lobster to a Cat, a Goat and a Hog would start after it...when the body of the Fish was chucked off, the Fowls, the Cows, and the Gulls and the Sheep would join in pursuit." This was common practice everywhere along the northeastern coasts. In fact, pigs were still being fattened on lobster in some remote regions of Newfoundland until as late as 1940.

Inshore fishermen were not alone in using lobster for bait. From as early as the 1760s, banking schoonermen regularly shipped tons of the crustaceans, and the practice continued until the middle of the nineteenth century. Ashore, many colonists and settlers refused to eat what they called "poor man's meat" but found a use for lobsters anyway. In 1852, a Canadian official noted, "Lobsters are everywhere found on the coasts...in such extraordinary numbers that they are used by the thousands to manure the land. Every potato field...is strewn with lobster shells, each potato hill being furnished with two, and perhaps three lobsters."

Lobsters were still considered commercially worthless in Nova Scotia as late as 1876 when John Rowan described the colonists killing the animals for fun. "On still summer nights, lobster spearing parties are the fashion among Halifax people. A birch-bark torch carried in the bow of the boat enables the spearer to see the lobsters crawling among the seaweed at the bottom." Killing lobsters was literally child's play. "I have seen two hundred lobsters taken in one tide by a couple of little boys wading about among the rocks armed with cod-hooks tied to sticks." Rowan also comments on their agricultural uses. "On one occasion, I saw several acres of potato ground manured with them. To give some idea of the little value put on lobsters, I may mention that they boil them for their pigs, but are ashamed to be seen eating lobster themselves. Lobster shells about a house are looked upon as signs of poverty and degradation."

What changed this attitude was the mid-nineteenth century discovery that lobster meat could be cheaply canned in giant steam cookers, and that there was a lucrative market for the resultant product, not only at home but in Europe, too. What then ensued has sometimes been referred to as the Lobster Klondike, though it was a gold rush of another kind.

Lobster factories sprang up along the New England coast in such profusion that it was said the smoke from their high chimneys competed with the fog in obscuring local landmarks—an exaggeration perhaps, but not such a far-fetched one. By the 1860s, there was hardly room for one more lobster factory on the American coast, and so the avid entrepreneurs began shoving north until their factories, reinforced by Canadian, British, and French plants, dotted the coasts of Newfoundland and Atlantic Canada from end to end. The example I have chosen to illustrate what followed is the west coast of Newfoundland.

The first factory was erected there in 1873. By 1888, twenty-six canneries were employing 1,100 fishermen, any two of which in their small boat would expect to catch as many as 1,000 lobsters a day, for which they received the scarcely munificent sum of $5. That year, the fishermen of Newfoundland's west coast delivered enough lobsters to fill 3 million one-pound cans.

The wastage was atrocious. Only meat from the tail and the two large claws was used. The bodies, many of them females festooned with spawn, were shovelled back into the sea where they washed up on the shores to produce a stench that could be smelled miles away. During the 1870s, it had taken, on average, only two lobsters to fill a can; as the slaughter mounted and the older and larger lobsters were destroyed, it took first three, then four, and finally as many as eight "little fish," which by then were all that could still be caught in any quantity.

By 1898, seventy canneries were fiercely competing with one another along the west coast, belching black-spruce smoke high into the skies from early spring until late autumn. By then, however, they only managed to produce a million cans among them. The lobster population was melting away. Four years later, production was down to 310,000 cans—about a tenth of what it had been in 1888.

Substantially the same sequence of events took place everywhere along the northeastern seaboard, except that in some regions—notably the southern New England states—the story ends with the virtual extinction of the lobster. The days when lobster was one of the most available and abundant animals along the Atlantic shores are long since at an end. From a peak of at least 140,000 tons in 1885, lobster landings in Canada and Newfoundland had plummeted to 43,000 tons by the early 1920s. By the 1970s, landings were down to about 20,000 tons.[1] Although this latter figure has doubled

---

[1] These figures are expressed as live weight. Production in 1885 was reported to have been 100 million one-pound cans, but a minimum of three pounds of live lobster was required to fill each can. The 1920s total is based on approximately 30 million cans plus about 5 million pounds sold live. Current catches are usually reported as live weight.

since then, some biologists believe current population levels are still perilously close to a disastrous crash should the death rate escalate, either due to increased human predation or to some accident of nature.

The lobster is, in fact, a classic case of a species precariously balanced between the desire of "resource managers" to placate their political and commercial masters with increased production and the need to preserve and even strengthen a perilously depleted population. Some men were aware of the danger as far back as the 1870s, when a far-sighted adviser to the Nova Scotia government recommended that the lobster fishery should be closed at least during the height of the spawning season. The suggestion was rejected by the provincial legislature, "probably [because] by making a closed season, the catch of lobsters, which is a source of considerable profit, would be greatly lessened, therefore they adopted the alternative of making it illegal to take undersize lobsters, or females in spawn. [However,] this law is not enforced, and the process of killing the bird that lays the golden eggs is being applied to the lobster fishery, as it is to the salmon fishery, and as it is to the lumbering business." Those comments, be it noted, were written 100 years ago, yet they remain as applicable as they ever were.

An analysis of the modern lobster fishery, by Harold Horwood, spotlights the danger: "As of 1982 Canadian lobster catches amounted to about 40,000,000 pounds annually, mainly one-pound lobsters; the larger ones being too scarce to be of statistical importance. The proportion of these one-pounders taken from the lobster population each year varies slightly, but 80% is close to average for the entire maritime region.

"Of the 20% of one-pounders which escape capture in any given year, a further 80% are taken the following year, as pound-and-a-half lobsters. *These are still too young to breed.* Indeed a female lobster has usually to escape being caught in three successive annual fisheries before she bears her first eggs. Consequently only *four out of every thousand* one-pound lobsters will, on the average, live to reproduce. But in some regions, sexual maturity is delayed yet another year, so that the egg-bearers are reduced to an average of *eight in every ten thousand.*

"On the basis of firm experimental evidence, lobster biologists believe that increasing the minimum size of lobsters that can be taken by 50% would, within five years, double the size of the Canadian lobster catch. The difficulty is that you have to sell the politicians on the plan, and they usually prefer to opt for short-term benefits which keep their constituents happy, rather than long-term ones.

"It would take only five years to double the lobster population and take the species out of danger...but who among those with the power to implement the plan really cares what happens five years hence?"

During preparation of this book I talked to marine scientists from three continents, experts who were in a position to speak freely and independently. All agreed that life in the sea is being diminished at a fearful and accelerating rate. Not only the larger forms are affected. Both fisheries strategists in the West and state planners in the East are now implementing ways to harvest plankton, the basic food upon which all animate life in the oceans ultimately depends. Plankton includes an enormous range of minute plants and animals, all of them tiny and many microscopic. Already Japan and the Soviet Union are spearheading what is intended to become a massive fishery for krill, a crustacean which, though only a few millimeters long, is amongst the bigger planktonic forms. Existing in nearly infinite numbers, krill provide the primary source of food for thousands of bigger creatures ranging through fish and seabirds all the way to the largest creature on Earth, the blue whale. Depletion of the "krill meadows" on the scale now being planned will result in intolerable damage to the populations of countless animals higher up on the food chain.

The probable long-term results of harvesting plankton on a major scale are so appalling that a senior scientist with Canada's Department of Fisheries and Oceans privately assured me that it could lead to the effective extinction of most kinds of fishes we have relied on in the past or which we might hope to exploit in the future.

"Although it would be an unimaginable disaster for marine life in general," he added, "it is probably the most rational approach to exploiting the food potential of the ocean. Its virtue is that it cuts out the middleman, as it were, allowing us to gather the proteins and other nutrients produced by plankton without the energy loss involved in having fishes, sea mammals, even birds, process and concentrate it for us first."

He concluded, rather ominously: "Will it happen, or is it just science fiction? Look at the record of our past successes with industrial fisheries. And don't ever underestimate what we can and will do if there's a good buck in it."

PART IV

Lost Giants of the Sea

Many historians are of the opinion that the cod fishery was the irresistible prime attraction that first drew Europe to the northeastern seaboard of America. Although true of the English and most of the French adventurers to a degree, early Portuguese, Spaniards, Basques, and Biscayan French all had something more than cod in view. That something was train oil, from marine animals.

Foreshadowing modern times, late fifteenth-century Europe found itself increasingly short of oil. In those days, it came mostly from rendering the fat of terrestrial animals or from vegetative sources. These were no longer equal to the demand. However, as many seafarers, particularly those from the Iberian peninsula, knew, seemingly limitless quantities of oil existed in the seas. Seals, walrus, and whales were all singularly well-endowed with oil-rich fat that could be readily rendered into train. As the sixteenth century began train became ever more valuable and in demand; and more and more ship-owners from southwestern Europe began to make its procurement their principal business.

Before the Sea of Slaughter became what we have made of it, it was the Sea of Whales. Thirty or forty million years ago, the progenitors of modern whales were secure in the womb of ocean to which their ancestors had returned after aeons of sojourning on land. Ages before the naked ape appeared, whales had become one of the most complex yet stable forms of life on the planet. Had it not been for the appearance of our kind, there is little doubt but that the whales would have remained the great presences dominating the seas that they still were when Europeans crossed the North Atlantic to possess the New World and its adjacent waters.

Many of these men came seeking train. The shocking history of what that avaricious pursuit meant to the whale nations makes other atrocities committed by modern man seem relatively mild.

13
The Better Sort

A bleak November sky broods over the Strait of Belle Isle while a sleet-laden nor'east gale howls across a gourd-shaped harbour on the northern coast. Bitter blasts rattle the red clay tiles that roof a score of wooden shanties crouched along a rocky shore. Wind whines through the rigging of several dimly seen anchored vessels before gusting out into the Strait over a mounded island that juts like a stopper in the harbour mouth.

The year is 1565, and the place is Buterus, so named by its Basque founders who come from Guipuzcoa and Viscaya in northern Spain. Buterus is only one of many similar settlements these men have established along the shores of the narrow waters separating the northern finger of Newfoundland from Labrador, but it is perhaps the largest.

Sleet slices horizontally across the harbour, dissipating the pervasive stench of rancid oil and rotting offal shrouding the settlement. The weather is so miserable that no man cares even to stick his head out of the window-less barracks where all hands huddle. So none is aware that the 500-ton *San Juan* has begun to drag. Having torn her anchors free of the bottom, the ponderous, high-sided carrack, laden to her marks with a cargo of barrelled oil and baled baleen, swings broadside to the gale and begins to pick up way, driving down into a smother of foam on the weather side of the island.

Nothing can stop her now. With a rending of oak on rock, she strikes. Then the storm takes her for its own, heeling her down until her rails are awash. Deep in the hold, heavy oil casks begin to break adrift and thunder to the lee side. She lurches, and rolls still farther, until she is lying on her beam ends and is flooding fore and aft. Slowly she begins to settle back and slips to her final resting place five fathoms down.

She lies there yet.

In the autumn of 1978, archaeologists discovered *San Juan's* remarkably well-preserved hulk at the bottom of Labrador's Red Bay. The place is so named because Newfoundland fishermen who settled it in the nineteenth century found the foreshore littered with soft red stones they supposed to be of natural origin, and which their children used as chalk for drawing pictures on the surrounding granite rocks. These new inhabitants had no way of knowing that the red stones were weathered fragments of clay tiles that had been carried across the Atlantic from Spain centuries earlier to roof cabins, sheds, and tryworks of which no recognizable traces still remained. They had no way of knowing that the bones of *San Juan* lay at the bottom of their harbour in company with the bones of thousands of great whales that had been butchered here to enrich men of another world, another time.

The Basques are a people shrouded in mystery. Descendants of a neolithic race who were never assimilated by the Indo-European invaders, they defied the changing ages within a bastion of rugged coasts and mountains at the western end of the Pyrenees. Here they remained as an enduring remnant of a forgotten epoch through some thousands of years after their erstwhile contemporaries elsewhere in Europe had been submerged and lost to view under successive waves of new peoples from the east.

Through the shadowed ages they had an abiding affinity with the sea. Consequently they entered historic times with an intimate knowledge of and feel for it and its inhabitants. An extraordinarily secretive and reclusive people, they continue to survive in, but not of, a world that has long tended to regard them and their incomprehensible language as uncouth and alien. Historians have only recently begun to realize how major was the role they played in the early exploitation of the seas; and that it was the Basques who lit the flame that was eventually to consume the mighty hosts of the whale nations.

Their war against Leviathan began at least 16,000 years ago, by which time the "strand-lopers" of the Bay of Biscay (Bay of the Basques) were actively whaling from small dugouts or skin-covered boats using bone- and flint-tipped harpoons and lances closely akin to those employed into our own times by such neolithic cultures as the Chukchee and the Inuit. Indeed, the very name "harpoon" is theirs, coming to us through the Spanish *arpon* from the Basque *arpoi*, which translates as "stone point."

For thousands of years they practised subsistence whaling directed at securing food for their own needs. However, as early as the fifth century A.D., the Biscayans began trading whale products for other peoples' goods, and by the tenth century they were making a good business of it. So the Basques became the first commercial whalers of record. They were to retain their supremacy as such through the succeeding 600 years.

The prehistoric Biscayans originally learned their trade in pursuit of a whale their descendants called *otta sotta*, the species we know as the grey whale. As whales go, it was rather small, up to forty-five feet in length and rarely weighing more than forty tons. An inshore whale by preference, it sometimes stayed so close to shore that its belly was on the bottom while its back was in the air. It bore its young during the winter in warm-water lagoons and bays. Spring sent it sculling north. By mid-summer, most otta sotta were probably cruising the icy waters of the Norwegian Sea and the upper reaches of the Baltic. In early autumn, they turned south again.

It is to be assumed that, in the beginning, only a few of the more courageous strand dwellers dared attack the lumbering behemoths as they wallowed through the surf of the Bay of Biscay on their spring and fall migrations; but as success attended those early efforts, the innovators were joined by others, and still others, until most Biscayan coastal communities were whaling regularly. They did so to such effect and through so many centuries that by as early as the fourteenth century, the otta sotta had been hunted to virtual extinction in European waters.

Its destruction did not bring an end to an enterprise that had become a way of life to the coastal-dwelling Basques. Foreshadowing modern precepts, they sought new targets. These they found in the whale known as *sardak baleac*—the herd whale, so-called because at certain seasons it gathered in huge schools. The sarda or, as we know it now, the black right whale was a giant, sixty to sixty-five feet long, weighing as much as seventy tons. Its thick coat of blubber could produce three times as much oil as the otta sotta, and it carried more and better whalebone (baleen). Although more of an offshore animal than the otta sotta, it too sought inshore shallows in which to mate and bear its young.

Initially the Basques hunted sarda as they had otta sotta, from marvellously swift and agile open boats. After a whale had been successfully harpooned and lanced to death, the carcass was towed for processing to the nearest of the scores of shore stations scattered along the Bay coast. However, this system limited the hunt to the three or four months of the year when sarda stayed close to land. As the European demand for whale products increased during the Middle Ages, the Basques began using small sailing vessels that could stay at sea for several days and range a hundred miles or more from shore. Although the corpses still had to be towed home for "cutting in," offshore whaling was such a success that vessels as large as 300 tuns were harrying sardas far at sea.

By 1450, a fleet of more than sixty Basque deep-sea whalers was seeking and killing sardas from the Azores all the way north to Iceland. They wrought such havoc that, before the new century began, the sarda, too, were verging on extinction in European waters. At this crucial juncture for the future of their whaling industry, the Basques became aware of a vast and previously untapped reservoir of "merchantable" whales in the far western reaches of the North Atlantic.

A prodigious effort of the imagination is required to visualize the variety and abundance of whales that swarmed in New World seas when the European conquest of the region began. It must have been at least comparable to the stunning plethora of whale life that abounded in the seas bordering Antarctica before twentieth-century whalers turned those waters red with blood.

Whales were so abundant on the northeastern seaboard and their presence was so all-pervasive that they posed problems for early voyagers. A record penned by an anonymous mariner of the mid-1500s complains that the worst risk to navigation in the *New Founde Land* was not fog, ice, or uncharted rocks—it was whales of such size and in such numbers that collision with them was an ever-present danger. In the early 1600s one French missionary reported testily that whales were still so numerous in the Gulf of St. Lawrence that "they became very tiresome to us and hindered our rest by their continuous movement and the noise of their spoutings."

When the *Mayflower* lay at anchor in Cape Cod Bay in 1620, her crew "every day saw whales plying hard by us; of which, in that place, if we had instruments and means to take them we might make a very rich return." Richard Mather, newly arrived in Massachusetts Bay in 1635, reported seeing "multitudes of great whales... spewing up water in the air like the smoke of chimneys and making the sea about them white and hoary... which [sight] now was grown ordinary and usual to behold." And as late as 1705, the Sieur de Courtemanche could still record that on the north shore of the Gulf of St. Lawrence, whales were "in such abundance that they came so close to the land they could be harpooned from the rocks."

At first contact the Gulf of St. Lawrence and the living waters overlying the continental shelf from Cape Cod to Labrador were among the foremost of the world's seas for their concentrations of marine mammals. Besides providing a haven for one of the planet's largest concentrations of walrus, they harboured untold numbers of seals of several species. Yet all of these were dwarfed into relative insignificance by the whale nations, which included almost every extant species of great whale together with many of the smaller kinds. It was not for nothing that some early Europeans referred to the northeastern approaches to the new continent as the Sea of Whales.

Although porpoises and dolphins are all members of the whale family, the word "whale" had a much narrower meaning in earlier times, when it was used to designate those sea giants that could be turned to commercial account. Thus "whales" included only those slow enough to be overtaken by sail or rowed boats; vulnerable to hand-held harpoons and lances, financially rewarding as to the amounts of oil and baleen they produced, and, finally, those that would float when dead. This last was vital since early whalers had no way of retrieving a whale that sank into the deeps. Nor could they keep a "sinking" whale on the surface while they flensed it or towed it to a shore station. Thus sixteenth-century Basques who built and manned Buterus and its fellow factories limited their activities to and recognized only four kinds of "whales." These they called the "better sort."

THE SARDA

When the first European vessel of the modern age thrust her blunt bows into New World waters, her people would have recognized the kinds that had once been the mainstay of Basque whalers—the otta sotta and the sardak baleac, or sarda.

If that first ship was not herself of Basque origin, it was at least inevitable that word of what her crew found would soon have reached the Basques. Certainly, by some time around 1500 their whaling ships were making the venturesome voyage across the wide reaches of the North Atlantic, and their harpooners were letting the blood of the western sarda nation.

The sarda, or black right whale, was a relatively easy as well as a rewarding victim despite its enormous size. Because its vast bulk had given it immunity from most natural predators it had not evolved defensive attitudes or weapons. Neither did it need nor have any great turn of speed. It fed by slowly plowing through the plankton pastures of the sea, forcing rivers of water past a fringed thicket of baleen, or whalebone, hanging from the roof of its huge maw, which filtered out a life-sustaining soup. And the baleen did this with such efficiency that the sarda was able to accumulate enormous quantities of surplus energy it stored as fat. This blubber blanket was so thick (as much as twenty inches) that it provided more than enough buoyancy to keep the body afloat even after death. It was so oil-rich that as much as 3,500 gallons of high-quality train could be rendered out of one individual. In every way, the sarda was one of the better sort, if not the best of them all.

The plankton-rich waters of the Sea of Whales were the sardas' main summering grounds. In late autumn they drifted slowly southward, congregating to breed in suitable bays south to Florida and the Gulf of Mexico. By the time they arrived in their wintering waters, they had accumulated such reserves of energy in blubber that they could comfortably afford to spend the long months until the return of spring bearing and nursing their young, courting and making love, without having to feed.

Late in March or early in April, the huge winter schools broke up into family-sized pods that began moving northward at a leisurely three or four knots. Grazing their way in the spring meadows of the offshore Banks, where the annual efflorescence of plankton was already turning the cold waters into a rich broth of life, most of the sardas eventually turned westward through either the Strait of Belle Isle or Cabot Strait into the Gulf of St. Lawrence, there to take advantage of a late-summer plankton bloom. Here, rotund and replete as summer ended, they again congregated in enormous schools that seem to have served some social need—a sort of whales' autumnal festival, perhaps—before beginning the slow drift south again.

Although there is no certainty as to just when the Basques first appeared on the North American scene, we do know that before Cartier made his well-publicized forays into the Gulf of St. Lawrence in 1534 and 1535, Buterus existed on French charts as *Hable de la Ballaine*—Whale Harbour; and the northwest tip of Newfoundland, the most significant landfall for ships inbound from Europe, already bore the name *Karpont*, a French corruption of the Basque *Cap Arpont*—Harpoon Cape. Furthermore, the municipal archives of Biarritz contain letters patent issued in 1511 authorizing French Basques to whale in the New World; and a number of references from other sources suggest a Basque presence in the Gulf as early as 1480. So we will probably not be far astray if we envisage salt-caked and sea-weary Basque caravels laboriously beating in toward the coasts of south Labrador, Newfoundland, and Cape Breton Island (which, incidentally, takes its name from the ancient Basque whaling port of Cap Breton) by the end of the fifteenth century.

They were soon to be found over the whole region. Current charts still preserve more than a score of names testifying to their widespread presence, and the mossed-over, wind-eroded, and sometimes sea-flooded remains of their shore stations are to be found as far westward as the mouth of the Saguenay River, a bare hundred miles from Quebec City.

Buterus itself seems to have been a typical Spanish Basque station. In any given summer it was home to as many as 1,000 men. Before dawn each day, scores of whaleboats under light sail, or propelled by oars if there was no breeze, dispersed in both directions along the coast, and out to seaward from it, until they formed an arc with a radius of ten or fifteen miles centred on Buterus. Then they waited for the light to quicken. All hands intently scanned the surrounding sea for the V-shaped double spout that bespoke the sarda. As soon as one was seen, hanging diaphanous in the morning air, two or three of the nearest boats converged on it. The harpooner took the head in each, and every crew rowed desperately, hoping to give its own harpooner the first throw.

The chosen victim normally reacted to the approaching boats with little more than amiable curiosity—until a harpoon flashed in the rays of the rising sun and the wickedly double-barbed iron drove through thick blubber deep into flesh below. The "struck fish" sounded, only to find itself tethered to the dragging weight of the boat above. When it surfaced to draw breath, it might be struck with a second and even a third harpoon. Panic and fear must have flooded the mind of a creature that, in all likelihood, had experienced neither before. There would have been agonizing pain as well, as the irons ripped and tore in the straining muscles.

After hours of titanic struggle, even the sarda's mighty strength would ebb. Then the boats closed in, driving the stricken animal under with thrusts of long, slim lances before it could fill its straining lungs. Mortally stabbed by lilliputians, the sarda at last rolled helpless on the surface. Its spout became a crimson fog. The sea about it swirled dark with blood. The mighty flukes lifted and fell in one last paroxysm, and life was gone.

With a haze of gulls already gathering over it, the glistening carcass was towed by two or three boats into Buterus harbour and moored to one of several barrel buoys a few hundred feet off the tryworks. Here it would lie in a pod of dead companions until the log slip-way on the beach was cleared of earlier corpses and it could be hauled up the greasy slope by capstan winches.[1]

Day long, night long, under the smoky glare of train oil torches, the butchers swarmed over the gargantuan carcasses, their cutting knives thrusting and shearing, while other men carried slabs of blubber to the tryworks threshold. Here the fat was minced into pieces small enough to fork into a row of sputtering, bubbling cauldrons heated by roaring fires, themselves fuelled with a ropy detritus of connective tissue fished out of the pots from time to time—the whale thus provided the fuel for its own immolation.

Having stripped the blubber from its body and hacked the baleen from its mouth, the whalers would trip the capstan brake allowing the naked corpse to slide back into the sea. It would still float, even though stripped of its fat, because the progress of internal decay swiftly produced such quanti-

---

[1] At stations where there was sufficient tide the carcasses were often simply grounded on the beach at high water and cut-in when the falling tide had left them high and dry.

ties of gas as to inflate the carcass into a monstrous, fetid balloon. Turned loose to the mercy of wind and tide, this enormity would join a host of similar putrescent horrors being vomited out of the score of bays where whalers worked. Most of these ghastly objects eventually drove ashore, adding their contributions to a charnel yard that stretched for hundreds of miles along the shores of the Grand Bay.

The Sieur de Courtemanche has left us a macabre glimpse of what those shores must have been like. In 1704, at the head of a small bay only a few miles from long-abandoned Buterus, he found "a quantity of bones cast up on the coast like sticks of wood, one on the other...there must have been, in our estimate, the remains of more than two or three thousand whales. In one place alone we counted ninety skulls of prodigious size."

Evidence of the scale of the slaughter remains into our times. An engineer engaged in building a highway up the west coast of Newfoundland in the 1960s told me that wherever his earth movers dug into beach gravel, they uncovered such masses of whale bones that portions of the roadbed were "constructed more of bones than stones." Skulls, he told me, "were a dime a dozen—some of them as big as a D-8 dozer." I examined some of these barrow pits soon after the road was completed and satisfied myself that the majority of the gargantuan remains were from the relatively recent past and were not the slow accumulation of the ages.

Sardas were so numerous in the Gulf during the first half of the sixteenth century that whaling was simply a matter of selecting and killing as many as could be dealt with, from what must have seemed an inexhaustible supply. The process was roughly analogous to taking cattle for slaughter from an immense holding pen. The limiting factor was not the number of whales available, but the ability of the factories to process them.

Buterus, which seems to have supported as many as three separate try-works, was only one of perhaps twenty stations ranged westward from the mouth of the Strait of Belle Isle along the north shore of the Gulf and into the St. Lawrence River as far as the Saguenay. Chaleur Bay and the Gaspé coast supported several more, as did the Magdalen Islands, Northumberland Strait, and the southern and eastern shores of Cape Breton. As many as a dozen factories blackened the skies over the south shore of Newfoundland. In all, there seem to have been forty to fifty in operation in and around the Sea of Whales at the peak of the Basque "fishery." Those to the north and east were worked mainly by Spanish Basques, those to the south and west by French Basques. Together they wrought havoc on the right whale nation.

It is possible to estimate the magnitude of the slaughter. We know that the crude tryworks of the sixteenth century yielded about 3,000 gallons, or twelve tuns, of train on average from each adult sarda and, at least initially, the harpooners disdained everything except adults, and large ones to boot. We also know the cargo capacity of Basque ships. These were of two sorts: caravels that brought men, boats, and gear out to the factories each spring and could carry home from 250 to 500 tuns of oil; and carracks, or sack ships, which sailed west in mid-summer for the sole purpose of transporting oil back to Europe. These early "tankers" were immense vessels for those times, some being capable of carrying nearly 1,000 tuns.

Sixteenth-century records indicate that the combined Basque whaling fleet ranged between forty and 120 vessels in any given year. Taking eighty as the median, and allotting to each an average lading of 350 tuns, we arrive at an annual toll of some 2,300 whales. But this by no means represented the total annual *mortality*. We must add at least 20 per cent to cover the loss of calves that starved to death when their mothers were killed and adults mortally wounded but not landed. An estimate of 2,500 whales a year during the peak period of the sarda slaughter (c. 1515–60) is probably conservative.

During the mid-portion of the sixteenth century, most of the train that fuelled the lamps of western Europe and provided raw materials for lubricants and soap-making, leather- and jute-processing, and even cooking oil, came from the sarda of the Sea of Whales. In addition, the western sarda provided most of the baleen, whose myriad uses included plumes for military helmets, clothing supports, stuffing for upholstery and mattresses, bristles for brushes, screening and sieve material, knife handles, horn spoons, and even springs to power mechanical toys and scientific instruments.

It was an immensely lucrative industry. In one good season at the Sea of Whales a Basque ship-owner could amortize his investment in ship and whaling gear, crew wages, supplies, and all other expenses, and show a healthy profit. It was not only good business, it was very big business. By 1570, the Basques had established their own independent consulates in many European countries solely to deal with the whaling trade. By then, their interwoven syndicates and companies had become the Exxon of their time.

Such was the magnitude of the slaughter that, by about 1570, the western sarda had been wasted to relic numbers. Time was running out for the sarda; but it was running out for the Spanish Basque whalers, too. In 1588, the Spanish Armada made its attempt on England and was largely destroyed in consequence. Amongst the scores of ships sent to the bottom by English cannon and fierce storms was the bulk of the Spanish Basque whaling fleet, conscripted to the service of King Philip and sacrificed to his ambition. The disaster was so overwhelming that the Spanish Basques never again returned to the Sea of Whales in strength.

The Armada debacle was followed by another and even more serious setback to Basque whaling in New World waters when, during the first decade of the seventeenth century, a fabulous new whaling ground was found in the icy seas around Spitzbergen. This discovery provided the genesis for a new whaling industry that soon eclipsed the fishery in the Sea of Whales and forever ended the age-old Basque monopoly.

As the main focus of the slaughter shifted eastward, the persecution of the western sarda nation eased. But it did not end. French Basques continued killing sardas, and so did increasing numbers of Norman and Breton fishermen who were turning the Gulf of St. Lawrence into a French lake. Furthermore, the migrating sardas were now coming under assault from New Englanders, who were developing a "Bay whaling" industry.

Although originally relying mainly on otta sotta, as we will shortly see, these English shoremen also killed the bigger and fatter sardas whenever they got the chance. As more and more of them turned to whaling, the sardas were denied sanctuary anywhere along the continental coast. Perhaps the survivors sought winter refuge around uninhabited islets and reefs in the West Indies and took to making their north and south passages farther and farther off the deadly North American shore. If so, it was of small avail because the New England bay whalers were extending their reach. By 1720, they were sailing out of sight of land in half-decked little sloops that could stay at sea three or four days. Although the crews of these swift little vessels killed sardas whenever they encountered them, by then both the otta sotta and the sarda had become so scarce that the New Englanders were switching the main thrust of their hunt to yet another kind of whale.

The Basques called this one *trumpa* and ranked it third of the four whales of the better sort. It became known to generations of Yankee whalers as the sperm. The sperm is an open-ocean mammal feeding at great depths on squid, and it seldom comes near land. Relatively easy to approach, it carries a blubber layer thick enough to keep it afloat after death and moderately good for making train. Because it is a toothed whale it has no baleen, but this deficiency was compensated for, in the whaler's view, by a unique substance, partly light oil and partly wax, carried in its head, which some early ignoramus thought was actually its sperm—hence the name, spermaceti. By any name, it was and remains extremely valuable as an ultra-fine lubricating oil. The sperm also produced another valuable substance, described by an early seventeenth-century writer in somewhat unprepossessing terms: "In this sort of whale is likewise found the Amber grease lying in the entrails and guts of the same, being of shape and colour like unto cowes dung." Despite its appearance, ambergris was such a precious medicinal and chemical substance, especially as a base for perfume, that as late as the nineteenth century it was literally worth its weight in gold.

The discovery of great numbers of sperms offshore drew the New England whalers seaward in such earnest that by 1730 they were sailing fully decked sloops and schooners south to Bermuda and north to the Grand Banks in pursuit of them. Since their vessels were initially too small to carry ship-borne tryworks, they at first killed sperms almost entirely for the few hundred gallons of spermaceti that could be baled out of the heads. One result of this horrendous wastage was that sometimes so many bloated sperm whale corpses floated abandoned on the fog-draped Grand Banks that they posed a hazard to transatlantic shipping. Another was that the trumpa tribe of the northeastern approaches was so severely reduced that for a time it all but disappeared.

In the process of destroying the trumpa, the New Englanders became true offshore whalers. By 1765, as many as 120 New England whaling vessels, now mostly equipped with tryworks, were "fishing" the Strait of Belle Isle, the Grand Banks, and the Gulf of St. Lawrence. By this time, most of the whales they were killing were humpbacks (which we will come to later); some were sperms, and a number were black right whales, which were always the preferred quarry when they could be found. During the same period, other New Englanders were sailing into southern waters searching for sperm whales, but killing every black right whale they encountered.

By the beginning of the nineteenth century, no more than a few thousand sardas remained alive in the entire length and breadth of the North Atlantic. For a few years, a group of perhaps 100 managed to conceal themselves in summertime in the wild fiords of southern Newfoundland. Here they were discovered by Newfoundland and American whalers in the 1820s; by 1850, only one lone individual—a cow—could be found and killed. None was reported subsequently in Gulf, Newfoundland, and Labrador waters for 100 years, although it appears that a few score, presumably made especially wary by the fate of the rest of their kind, still survived.

In 1889, a Norwegian steam whaler armed with the new and deadly explosive harpoon gun was ranging south of Iceland when she came upon a pod of the now almost legendary sarda. The catcher killed one of seven seen before bad weather saved the rest. The next year the rusty catcher came coursing back, found the remaining six members of the pod, and killed them all.

By 1900, the sarda was still known in life only to the men of a few scattered fishing hamlets on Long Island—men who still maintained the old tradition of whaling from open boats as their ancestors had done almost three centuries earlier. Once or twice a year, but sometimes not for several years, they still saw a right whale "in passage," and, if they were lucky, killed it.

The last such kill was made in 1918 from a steam seiner fishing for menhaden. The quarry was a female sarda and her calf northbound along the Long Island coast off Amaganset. One of the whalers, Everett Edwards, wrote an account of the incident in his biography, under the heading "A Pleasure Trip." I have condensed it.

"The last one that will ever be caught around here came along in the summer of 1918. It gave Bert and me the most expensive two days' sport we ever had for it was right in the middle of the fishing season. Bert had been fishing in the *Ocean View*; as morning broke he spied two whales just in back of the bar. He came ashore in a boat and just at sunrise I heard his voice under my bedroom window—'Ev—you want to go whalin'?'

"We rowed out and climbed aboard and caught up with the whales right opposite Egypt Beach. The whales must have heard the vessel's propellor for they started offshore. Soon one broke water square across the bow. Bert darted an exploding hand-harpoon at the big whale, which settled away deep as she could in that shoal water, then struck offshore. You could see her breaking water and spouting blood. Opposite Nepeague Life Saving Station we caught up with both whales. We had six or eight bombs. Bert, Felix and I took turns darting them from the bow of the steamer into whichever whale gave a chance, until the bombs were used up. After that we used a swordfish rig...the swordfish lance had a keg attached, so we could see it all the time.

"When the small whale seemed tired and began to quiet down I launched the dory to finish him with the handlance. When the young whale was nearly finished, the old one came alongside with her head out of water, plunging. Our old steward lanced that whale as slick as ever I saw a lance darted. But the lance-rope parted, and we lost that only lance we had in the big whale, which left the scene. Our little whale then came up dead.

"We followed the other whale which was spouting thick blood, offshore for another six miles. It was then nearly night so we returned to our little whale. It was towed to Promised Land docks. Crowds of people, many of whom had never seen a whale before in their lives came to view this unusual catch. We tried out about thirty barrels of oil, but never sold it. It had no market value any more."

The extermination of the sarda on both sides of the North Atlantic was now effectively completed; but there were other oceans and other tribes of the far-flung species the Yankee whalers called the black right or, below the equator, southern right.

Within a century of its birth, the New England pelagic whaling fleet had girded the earth, and amongst its global targets were those tribes of the sarda nation that swam in the South Atlantic, South and North Pacific, and Indian Oceans. Their destruction was carried out with such diligence and rapacity that between the years 1804 and 1817, more than 200,000 were killed, mainly around the coasts of South America. The devastation spread with such fury that within fifty years the black right whale had been almost exterminated world-over.

Something of the scope and nature of the carnage is summed up in a letter written by an anonymous Yankee whaling captain in 1852: "In the commencement of [black] right whaling the Brazil Banks was the only place of note...then came Tristan da Cunha, East Cape, Falkland Islands and Patagonia. These encompassed the entire South Atlantic. Full cargos were sometimes obtained in an incredibly short space of time. Whales were seen in great numbers—large pods [which had] gambolled unmolested for hundreds of years. The harpoon and lance soon made awful havoc of them and scattered the remainder...a few remain, as wild as the hunted deer. Can anyone believe they will ever again exist in such numbers? Or that they multiply as fast as they are destroyed?

"After the Southern [Atlantic] Ocean whales were cut up, the ships penetrated the Indian and South Pacific Oceans...I believe it is no more than twenty years since whaling began in either of these localities—but where now are the whales, at first found in great numbers? I think most whalemen will join in deciding that the better half have been killed and cut up long ago...Then came stories of large whales in large numbers in the North Pacific...and in a few years our ships swept entirely the broad Pacific and along the Kamchatka shores. They moved round Japan and there whales were found more numerous than ever. But the leviathans were driven from the bosom of the sea, their few scattered remnants running in terror."

By the early 1900s, the bloody saga was almost over for the great black right whales, which had been amongst the most numerous and widespread of the whale kind before becoming the object of human avarice. Almost over...but not quite. Scattered here and there on the immeasurable vastness of the oceanic world a few small pods and individuals continued to exist. They were so few and scattered it no longer paid to seek them out and hunt them down.

Yet, poised as they were on the verge of the abyss of extinction, they would receive no mercy. Wherever sardas were encountered by modern whalers, they were butchered. A typical example of the treatment meted out to them took place off the north coast of Newfoundland in 1951. A catcher with no licence to take right whales met a lone sarda and promptly killed it. When the incident was reported in the press, officials of the company explained that the catcher captain had merely made a slight mistake. The company processed the sarda and sold the products and was not even publicly reprimanded by the Canadian authorities.

Even after the International Whaling Commission finally placed the black right whale on the protected list, the killing continued. In 1962, a Japanese pelagic whaling fleet encountered the largest pod of right whales to have been seen for many decades, in the waters around the remote South Atlantic island of Tristan da Cunha. Despite the fact that Japan was a member of the IWC, the entire pod was butchered and processed on the spot. No punishment was meted out to those responsible for this abomination and, in fact, the IWC has never officially admitted that it happened.

To this day, non-members of the IWC, mostly using Japanese equipment and backed by Japanese capital, continue to kill right whales when they can find them. So do pirate whalers on the high seas, most of whose illicit products also go to Japan. As of 1984 the products of a single sixty-ton black right whale delivered in Japan are worth as much as $50,000.

The activities of these particular entrepreneurs are well described by Robert McNally in his book, *So Remorseless a Havoc*: "The pirate whalers are vessels of uncertain ownership and clouded registry that whale as they wish... The most notorious pirate whaler was the *Sierra*... Ownership of the *Sierra* was held by a South African through a corporation chartered in Liechtenstein, the flag was Cypriot, the master was Norwegian, and the label on the ship's frozen whale meat read 'Produce of Spain'.

"The *Sierra* killed with a cruelty appalling even in the brutal whaling business. To save as much meat as possible the *Sierra* used a barbed metal harpoon without an explosive grenade. Struck whales commonly took hours to die, bleeding slowly to death and disemboweling themselves in their struggles against the harpoon. When the whale died often only prime cuts were taken, meaning that a 40–50-ton animal died for the sake of 2 or 3 tons of meat. The *Sierra*, fortunately, no longer sails. An explosion [detonated by an anti-whaling organization] sent the ship to the bottom of Lisbon harbour in 1979. But there are now even more pirate whalers at sea following the *Sierra*'s bloody and destructive wake."

On August 31, 1981, cetologist and long-time friend of whales, Dr. Peter Beamish, saw an unfamiliar one surface in Newfoundland's Bonavista Bay. Beamish gives this account of what ensued:

"From the shore we saw an unidentified but very large whale just sounding. Quickly we launched our Zodiac and were afloat. We moved slowly out onto the Bay. Ten minutes had passed since the whale had dived. We stopped the engine. There was silence.

"Then, like a giant rock rising in the tide the animal slowly surfaced and blew, not ten feet from us. We were being directly looked at by it, and at the same time covered with spray from the 'blow'. Amazed and almost unbelieving we realized that here, swimming leisurely and freely beside us, was a solitary black right whale, one of the rarest animals on earth!

"Although the overwhelming feeling of delight and joy that filled me had to give way to the professional needs to photograph and record the details of the observation, the feeling of exhilaration I experienced will stay with me forever…We followed the whale slowly westward along the rocky coast and its behaviour was fearless toward us, and even appeared purposefully friendly. As darkness fell and we lost contact with it I felt a real sense of loss."

Through the succeeding two days, a fleet of boats and two aircraft tried, with the best of intentions, to find the whale again. They failed. Beamish thinks the lone sarda may have been seeking a dimly remembered ancestral summering ground and, having found it empty of its kind, pursued its lonely search elsewhere.

More and better news has followed upon Beamish's sighting. During 1982 and 1983 an aerial search revealed as many as seventy right whales summering in the Bay of Fundy region. And in May, 1984, it was announced that a further search had uncovered the whereabouts of a calving ground. Mindful of the pirate whalers, the researchers did not pinpoint the location, saying only that it was "somewhere" along the coasts of Georgia and Florida. Fifteen adult sardas were sighted, accompanied by four newborn calves.

It is uncertain whether these sightings indicate a resurgence in an almost extinct population or are simply the belated discovery of a remnant group. But it would appear that as many as a hundred sarda may still survive in the North Atlantic, together with another group of about equal size in the South Atlantic. A third group, the last in the North Pacific, is now thought to be extinct.

The northeastern seaboard is not yet quite devoid of the great creatures called *sardak baleac*, and that is a mercy to be thankful for. Yet their continuing existence remains at imminent risk unless we can give them meaningful protection. Apart from pirate whalers, they are endangered by modern shipping. One juvenile was killed near the New Jersey coast in 1983 when its tail was chopped off by the propeller of a vessel suspected to have been a high-speed warship. There is also concern that a combination of pollution and increased boat and vessel traffic may deny the whales the use of their last calving grounds. Nevertheless, some black right whales still live, and that is grounds for hope.

The Whale That Never Was

The grey whale of the Pacific coast of North America is today one of the best known of all whales. Its annual migration between the lagoons of Baja California and the Beaufort and Chukchi Seas takes it some 9,000 miles, for the most part within sight of land. Whale aficionados gather in their thousands on headlands and cliffs to watch with awe and admiration as the stately procession of great sea mammals makes its leisurely way past.

It was not always so.

When the Pacific tribe of the grey whale nation was discovered by American whalers in 1846, it had not previously suffered at the hands of modern man and its numbers were still legion. The whalers soon rectified that. During the next few decades, they slaughtered grey whales by the thousands, mostly in the lagoons along the Mexican coast where the females gathered in enormous schools to calve.

Because the lagoons were shallow and almost totally enclosed, the whalers had little need for harpoons and lances. Instead they relied mainly on cannons that fire explosive shells into the whales either from shore or from anchored whaling ships. There was no need to immediately secure the carcasses, as had to be done at sea, because almost every animal hit by a shell was doomed to die sooner or later either from loss of blood, damage to its internal organs, or massive infections—and, once dead, the body would remain available. Whaleboats had only to tour the lagoons at intervals, collecting the floating or stranded corpses and towing them to the tryworks. Here it was found that the victims were mostly female and either pregnant or else lactating, having recently given birth. The whalers did not bother the orphaned calves, which had no commercial value. They were left to die of starvation.

The massacre of grey whales in the lagoons was so thorough that, by 1895, the species was commercially extinct along the Pacific seaboard of North America. The plight of a sister tribe inhabiting Asiatic waters was little better. It was savaged by Korean whalers who had been quick to turn the technology developed by Western whalemen to their own advantage.

Nevertheless, some grey whales remained alive and, during the respite provided by the First World War, the species made a modest recovery. This did not escape the notice of whalers of the post-war period, now mostly using deep-sea whale catchers and factory ships. The slaughter began anew. By 1938, Norwegian, Japanese, and Korean catchers in the western Pacific had destroyed all but a handful of grey whales there. Norwegian and American catchers operating from U.S. and Canadian stations had not been quite so efficient, and as many as 2,000 whales may still have been alive at the beginning of World War II. After that war, grey whales had less value and the commercial attack on them in eastern Pacific waters began to wane. But science took up the slack. Between 1953 and 1969 Canada, the United States, and the Soviet Union licensed the killing of over 500 greys for scientific purposes. Three hundred sixteen were slaughtered to provide data for two scientists in the U.S. Fish and Wildlife Service so that they could produce a study grotesquely titled: *The Life History and Ecology of the Gray Whale*.

In the early 1970s the remnant Pacific grey whales were, belatedly as usual, granted protection by the International Whaling Commission. It was a short-lived respite. In 1978, under pressure from the Americans, Japanese, and Soviets, the surviving grey whales were stripped of their protected status.

Largely because of massive pressure exerted by great numbers of people who had seen a grey whale in life, this protection has since been returned to them, at least in eastern Pacific waters. If we have truly found enough compassion in us to spare the grey whale of North America's Pacific coast from extinction it will be some small measure of atonement for what we did to the sister tribe that once inhabited the waters off America's Atlantic coast.

Until quite recently, the existence of grey whales in the Atlantic in historic times was denied by many zoologists and some even now are reluctant to accept the evidence, not only that it was once an abundant species on both sides of that ocean, but that it flourished along North America's eastern coast until as late as the end of the seventeenth century. For these authorities, it remains the whale that never was.

In the mid-1800s some very large bones were found on the shores of a Swedish inlet. They were identified as being those of a whale, although of what species no one could tell because the grey whale was then totally unknown to science. Some considerable time later, when the Pacific grey came to the attention of naturalists, the correct correlation was made with the Swedish bones. Similar relics had meanwhile turned up in drained areas of the Zuider Zee, and it was established that grey whales must at one time have lived in European waters.

But how long ago? The experts concluded that, since nobody seemed to have any documentary evidence to show that such a whale had lived in European waters in historic times, it could only have been present in some remote prehistoric period. Consequently the bones were labelled "subfossils," implying an antiquity of several thousand years. Thus was the otta sotta, the favourite prey of Basque whalers until they exterminated it, relegated to historical oblivion. The same treatment has been meted out to the grey whale of the New World, despite the fact that there is more than enough evidence testifying to its presence and abundance in historic times.

To begin with, let us go back to 1611 when the Muscovy Company dispatched a vessel named *Mary Margaret* on a pioneering whaling voyage into the icy seas to the north of Europe. Because the English were tyros in the business, *Mary Margaret* shipped six skilled Basque harpoonists from St. Jean de Luz. In the Master's account of the voyage, we are told that part of their task was to instruct the English "how to tell the better sorts of whales from the worser, wherebye in their striking they may choose the good and leave the bad."

The various sorts are listed under their Basque names, and the fourth in order of "goodness" is called otta sotta. It is described as being "of the same colour as the Trumpa [sperm] having finnes [baleen] in its mouth all white, but not above halfe a yard long; being thicker than the Trumpa but not so long. He yeeldes the best oyle but not above 30 hogs heads."

This description fits the grey whale and no other known species. Moreover, since all the other chief kinds of large whales are accurately described and specifically named, there can be no doubt as to this identification. Yet by this date the Atlantic grey whale had long been extinct in European waters. How then to account for the Basque description of it as a species still of importance to whalers of the time? St. Jean de Luz, from which the harpooners hailed, was the major French Basque whaling port of that period, and we know that its whalers had been "fishing" almost exclusively on the northeastern seaboard of the New World for the better part of a century. It follows that one of the "better sort" they hunted there must have been the otta sotta.

In later times, when New Englanders first learned to go a-whaling, they called the earliest "fish" they took the scrag whale. The Honourable Paul Dudley, a naturalist and Chief Justice of Massachusetts in the 1740s, has left us the sole surviving description of this whale. "It is near a-kin to the

Fin-back, but, instead of a Fin upon his Back, the ridge of the Afterpart of his back is scragged with half a Dozen Knobs or Kuckles; he is near the Right Whale in figure [shape]...his bone [baleen] is white but won't split." Once again the description fits the otta sotta, and *only* the otta sotta.

That the scrag was widespread and well known along the eastern seaboard in early historic times is confirmed in my view by the presence on old charts of a number of features bearing the name. I have found forty-seven Scrag Islands, Scrag Rocks, Scrag Ledges, and Scrag Bays along the shores of Nova Scotia, the Gulf of Maine, and the American coastal states as far south as Georgia. Sag Harbor, once a famous whaling port and now a fashionable resort, was originally Scrag Harbor. The bestowing and the survival of so many examples of the name of a specific kind of whale is unique. It resulted from the fact that the grey whale was, and is, a shore-hugging animal and so would have been the whale most frequently observed, encountered, and, as we shall see, killed by early European settlers; and, before their arrival, by aboriginals.

The Algonkian people who lived there for uncounted generations called it *Nanticut*—the distant place, a name this sea-girt island outflung into the Atlantic near Cape Cod well deserved. Low-lying, windswept, and composed mostly of sand covered with a scanty soil upon which beach grasses and scrubby oaks and cedars grew, it seems an unprepossessing choice of a place to live. However, those who made it their home in ancient times did so not because of what the land had to offer but for the sustenance that came from the sea around it.

As the November Hunter's Moon began to wane, the people waited. Young men topped the high dunes on the northern shore to stare fixedly seaward into the scud of autumnal gales or into the brilliant glitter of occasional sunny days. In the village of bark-covered houses, men, women, and children took part in ceremonial dances and incantations intended to encourage and welcome the gift of life that they awaited.

One day, the watchers on the dunes beheld first one or two, then half-a-dozen, then a score of misty fountains rising from a sullen sea. These blew away like smoke, only to be renewed again and again until, by day's end, the whole seaward horizon was fretted with them. The southbound columns of the sea creature the Indians called *powdaree* had reached Nanticut at last.

For weeks to come, the long procession would stream by within sight of the island people. The marine mammoths surfaced, blew, rolled in the surging breakers on the shoals, and came close enough to the beaches so the watchers could see the sea-lice and barnacles mottling the dark, gleaming skin. But always, and inexorably, they kept their stately way toward the south.

They did not pass entirely unscathed. On the first fair-weather day following their appearance, clusters of canoes put off from the island beaches. Captain George Weymouth, explorer of the Maine coast in 1605, was an eye-witness of what then ensued.

"One special thing is their manner of killing the whale which they call powdare; and [they] will describe his form; and how he bloweth up the water; and that he is twelve fathoms long; that they go in company of their king with a multitude of their boats; and strike him with a bone made in a fashion of a harping iron, fastened to a rope; which they make great and strong of bark of trees; then all their boats come about him as he riseth above water, with their arrows they shoot him to death; when they have killed him and dragged him to shore they call all their chief lords together and sing a song of joy; and those chief lords, whom they call sagamores, divide the spoil and give to every man his share, which pieces are distributed, [and] they hang them up about their houses [to dry] for provisions."

The natives of Nantucket Island, as it is now called, were not the only ones who took a major part of their winter food from the powdaree. Many coastal tribes along the 7,000–8,000-mile migration route of the whales evidently did likewise. But considering the fearful risks involved in tackling forty-ton whales from bark canoes, there is little likelihood that any settlement killed more than one or two animals each season. One would have provided meat and fat enough, preserved by smoking and rendering, to feed two or three score people all winter through.

Leaving Nanticut behind, the river of grey whales, for such I believe the powdaree to be, forged slowly southward, moving perhaps thirty or forty miles a day and always staying close to the coast. By the end of December the head of the column might have been in the vicinity of the Florida Keys, but where it went from there is anybody's guess.

We do know that the by-then very pregnant cows would have been seeking shallow, warm waters spacious enough to allow free movement, but protected from storm seas. Such salt-water enclosures are to be found on the east Florida coast, but are especially abundant along the east, north, and western rim of the Gulf of Mexico, offering the whales an environment as hospitable as the Baja California lagoons. I conclude that this is where most of the powdaree calved and nursed their young.

In early February, the pods began to head northward toward the lush summer plankton grazing grounds. By mid-April, they would have been passing Nanticut again. Early May probably saw the head of the ponderous procession approaching the south coast of Newfoundland, then splitting into two streams, the one entering the Gulf of St. Lawrence through Cabot Strait and the Strait of Canso, the other veering eastward and then northward over the Grand Banks.

Where the northeast-bound powdaree went thereafter is also a mystery. If they followed a pattern similar to that of their Pacific cousins, they would have continued down the coast of Labrador, seeking shallow northern seas where the small, bottom-loving crustaceans that comprised their chief food multiplied in their billions. Their chosen pastures may have included the shoal regions of Hudson Bay (Foxe Basin in particular), as well as the banks off southern Iceland. While there is no concrete evidence attesting to their use of Hudson Bay, there *are* seventeenth-century reports of otta sotta in Icelandic waters.

Initially Basque whalers in the Gulf probably took small toll of the otta sotta. Although its blubber produced train of premium value, it yielded only about a third as much as could be rendered from a sarda and, as we shall see, even before the sarda had been devastated, the Basques had found an even more rewarding quarry in the bowhead whale. Nevertheless, the fact remains that the powdaree *did* vanish into limbo. Who sent it there?

The answer is to be found in a re-examination of the early history of Europeans in the eastern United States and in the elimination of errors that have become part of that history. All current accounts of what took place in New England during the early centuries correctly emphasize the importance of the whaling industry. However, they also state that the shore-based whaling that was the genesis of the industry was based on the black right whale—and this is simply wrong.

By the time the New Englanders began whaling in earnest in the mid-1600s the western sarda nation had already been so reduced that its survivors could not have sufficed to build an industry the size of the one that did emerge. It is also clear that the New England settlers were drawn into whaling by the abundance and availability of a whale that came so close inshore it could be attacked with success by people of limited seagoing pretensions and abilities. There is no doubt that these people learned whaling as the ancestors of the Basques had done, upon a "fish" that came to them, rather than vice versa.

The first recorded attempt at shore whaling on the eastern coasts of what is now the United States was made by a Hollander named de Vries who, in 1632, brought two vessels and crews to the New Netherlands—the Dutch settlement on Long Island Sound. Whales were abundant in the Sound and within a few days of their arrival, de Vries' men had killed seven in the enclosed waters of South Bay. What kind of whales were they? All seven together yielded only about 150 hogsheads of oil, whereas a single sarda of only average size would have yielded at least eighty hogsheads. de Vries' whales could hardly have been sarda. The yield from them is, however, compatible with what would be expected from the grey whale. Their productivity was a disappointment to de Vries, who complained that "The whale fishery is very expensive when only such meagre fish are caught." The upshot was that he gave up the American experiment and the Dutch made no further attempts to exploit the New World whale fishery, preferring to concentrate their efforts on the rapidly unfolding and immensely lucrative Arctic bowhead fishery instead.

If the local whales were but small fry to the Dutch, they nevertheless sufficed to fire the cupidity of the English settlers. In 1658, twenty English families led by Thomas Macy "purchased" Nantucket Island from its Indian owners, optimistically hoping to farm its scanty soil. Either that same year or in the following spring, the settlers discovered a whale swimming about in their shallow harbour. They promptly set upon it, but with such blundering incompetence that it took them three days to kill it. Nevertheless, having crudely rendered its oil, they realized that they were onto a good thing.

Obediah Macy, one of Thomas's descendants, tells us in his *History of Nantucket* that this first whale was a scrag, and that it was the kind the island natives had long been used to hunting. In truth, it was the Indians who here, as elsewhere along the coast, taught the English how to catch these whales. Furthermore, through most of the succeeding century, native whalers were employed (dragooned might be a better term) to do most of the actual killing that fed a mushrooming proliferation of shore factories.

By 1660, scrag whales were being killed by shoremen along much of their migration route between Nova Scotia and Florida. During the northern migration of 1669, Samuel Mavericke alone took thirteen off the east end of Long Island and noted they were so abundant that several were seen right in the harbour every day. In 1687, seven small factories along the Southampton and Easthampton beaches of Long Island tried out 2,148 barrels of oil, while 4,000 barrels were made on Long Island in 1707. A forty-six-barrel whale was considered a good catch, while thirty-six-barrel whales were the norm. A black right of average size, it should be remembered, yielded up to 160 barrels.

By 1725, only three-quarters of a century after the diligent New Englanders had begun killing them, the last days of the powdaree had come.

Although the English were not solely responsible for their destruction—French Basques whaling in the Gulf of St. Lawrence in the summer season undoubtedly killed their share as substitutes for the now all-but-vanished sarda—it was the New Englanders who doomed the powdaree.

In so doing, they found themselves forced to abandon their dependence on inshore whaling and to take to "ye deepes," as the *Boston News-Letter* of March 20, 1727, reported: "We hear from the Towne of the Cape [Cod] that the Whale-fishery amongst them having failed much this Winter, as it has done for several winters past, but having found a way of going to Sea upon that Business...they are now fitting out several Vessels to sail with all Expedition upon that dangerous design this Spring." These "several Vessels" were forerunners of the enormous and horrendously predatory Yankee deep-sea whaling fleet that would eventually scour all the oceans of the world in merciless pursuit of whales of many species.

Although the execution of the grey whale took place along much of the Atlantic seaboard of what is now the United States, by far the bloodiest destruction was committed in the Cape Cod and Long Island district, where extensive shoals lying athwart the whales' migration route made them especially vulnerable to boat whalers. Consequently, this region is fully entitled to its claim to being the cradle of the American whaling industry. It is also entitled to renown as the place that gave the impetus to the first major extinction to be perpetrated by Western man in North America...the first of many such.

BOWHEAD

During the autumn of 1947, I was in Churchill, Manitoba, the northern terminus of the Hudson Bay Railroad on the shore of the vast inland sea of the same name. The straggling little community was dominated by an enormous concrete grain elevator that towered like a misplaced skyscraper over a primeval world of rolling tundra and icy seas. Yet impressive as it was, my most vivid memory from that visit is of a giant of another sort.

One day when an easterly gale was blowing across the surging waters of the Bay, dusting the dim world in driven snow, I sought shelter in the bar of a hotel. I was nursing a beer when a red-faced fellow stomped into the place.

"Down to the gov'mint pier!" he yelled. "Seen it myself! Big as a goddamn boxcar! Bigger'n *two* of the buggers. You gotta see it, boys!"

Twenty minutes later the grain-loading pier jutting into the ice-rimmed harbour was crowded with most of the male residents of Churchill. I stood among them, parka hood pulled up against the freezing spindrift. Next to me, three Inuit hunched their shoulders. They were from Pond Inlet on distant Baffin Island and had been shipped south to be trained as truck drivers for an American radar base. I had met them before and found them morose and withdrawn, but now they could hardly contain their excitement. When I asked if they had seen the visitor who had drawn us to the pier, they exploded in words and gesticulations.

"Eeee! Yiss! *Arveq*—the Big One! Look there!"

The waters heaved and there it was, a glistening blue-black monster, massive as an upturned ship, looming through the storm-murk not a hundred feet from the concrete cliff on which we stood. It seemed at least as big as the sixty-foot tug moored to the pier. I heard a muffled *whoooooooffff* as twin, steamy jets spouted twenty feet into the air and blew down upon us, bringing a touch of warmth and a rank, fishy stink. The Inuit were beside themselves.

"Breathe well! Get strong! Go north! Take word of us!" they shouted.

The whale spouted three times, then sounded, seeming to roll down into the depths like the segment of a gigantic wheel. The snow was thickening and soon all things were hidden in a full-fledged blizzard. I never saw it again ... but he, or she, was unforgettable.

The still-ebullient Inuit joined me for a beer and we discussed the visitation. What we had seen, they told me, was the greatest being their world knew. In the days of their fathers, Arveq had been everywhere. "All the bays, all the passages—he come so many nobody can count." Then, they said, big ships had begun to appear off the Baffin coast and white men had begun killing the great whales. Now so few were left that the Pond Inlet people counted themselves lucky if they glimpsed one during the course of several years.

I count myself lucky, too. Arveq, or *Balaena mysticetus* as it is known to science; bearded whale, Greenland whale, Grand Bay whale, Arctic right, polar whale, or bowhead, as it was called by a succession of whalers, is now one of the rarest animals on earth, perhaps even rarer than its cousin the sarda.

A giant amongst giants, it attained lengths of over seventy feet and weights of as much as ninety tons, although in later days, after we had laid our doom upon it, few survived to reach fifty feet or sixty tons. Shaped rather like a gargantuan tadpole, its body was wrapped in the heaviest blanket of fat carried by any whale, sometimes two feet thick and capable of producing as much as 7,000 gallons of oil. In addition, it carried the biggest "head" of baleen of any whale—up to two tons of the horny substance.

Its size was such that even latter-day whalers were awed by it, as this nineteenth-century description attests: "Consider his mouth as having a 300 barrel capacity...nearly ten feet high, twice that in length, and more than fifteen feet wide. The lips are four feet thick. The lips and throat alone should yield 60 barrels of oil. When the creature feeds, his lips are spread as much as 30 feet apart and to obtain a single mouthful he strains the minuscule organisms that are his meal from a quarter of a mile of ocean. Barrels of blood more than 100 degrees warm pour through the massive pipes of his circulatory system, the largest a foot in diameter, driven by a heart as large as three barrels."

The prodigious quantities of whalebone and train oil obtainable from the bowhead made it by far the most valuable of whales and, in consequence, the most avidly and relentlessly pursued—once it had been discovered. But that discovery came surprisingly late in whaling history.

In summer the Greenland whales cruised bays and inlets from Franz Joseph Land in the eastern Barents Sea, west to Spitzbergen, northeast Greenland, Davis Strait, Baffin Bay, and the islands of Canada's eastern Arctic archipelago. When October began darkening the skies in high latitudes and pack ice began to spread and thicken over Arctic seas, these giants, bursting with blubber acquired during their summer plankton feasting, moved majestically southward. Those from the seas east of Greenland shaped their courses southwestward through Denmark Strait, between Iceland and Greenland. They did not migrate into European waters because had they gone in that direction they would have encountered warm tendrils of the Gulf Stream, and their super-insulating coats of blubber probably made them uncomfortable in water more than a few degrees above the freezing mark. After rounding Cape Farewell, I believe that many of the massed squadrons from the Greenland Sea continued southwest across the Labrador Sea and by late November had ridden the frigid Labrador Current to the mouth of the Strait of Belle Isle, through which they poured into the Gulf of St. Lawrence, there to spend the winter months. Meantime, companion multitudes that had summered in Davis Strait, Baffin Bay, and amongst the Arctic islands made their ways south to Hudson Strait or Fury and Hecla Strait and through one of these into Foxe Basin and Hudson Bay, where they would calve and breed in lanes of water kept open all winter long by fierce winds and powerful tidal currents.

Those wintering in the Gulf of St. Lawrence probably remained there until early March, by which time the females had given birth to their fifteen-foot offspring and mating had taken place. Then the passage north began, at first following the seaward edge of the vast tongue of ice that thrusts south down the Labrador coast in late winter. As summer progressed the spreading pods pushed north, east, and west, everywhere following the retreating pack or even penetrating deep within it to feed on the luxurious plankton bloom fostered by the effect of the sun's rays on melting sea ice. So the annual cycle made its round...a round that remained completely beyond the ken of European man until well into the sixteenth century.

The European discovery of the New World did not immediately reveal the existence of the polar whale because until about the mid-sixteenth century, most Europeans were summer visitors only. They had no taste for the North American winter, or for being storm-battered by autumnal gales in the roaring seas of the North Atlantic.

Nevertheless, it was inevitable that, sooner or later, some ships and crews would find themselves benighted, either through shipwreck or because they had been caught in harbour by an unseasonably early freeze. That misfortunes of this nature did overtake early Basque whalers in the Strait of Belle Isle is an historic fact. Probably most of the men so marooned perished miserably, but any whaler who managed to survive the bitter cold and the terrible attrition of scurvy, and then make his way home, would have had a tale to whet the appetite of any whaling syndicate.

He would have reported the presence of winter whales of prodigious size and numbers. We can gain some idea of the numbers involved by considering that it took the massed whaling might of Basques, English, Scots, Dutch, Germans, and Americans 350 years of intense and unremitting hunting to effectively exterminate the Greenland whale. The slaughter is reasonably well documented after about 1610, and my analysis of the records suggests that, at first contact, the North Atlantic population numbered as many as 150,000 individuals. If only a part of these spent the mid-winter months in the Gulf of St. Lawrence, the December flood of Greenland whales funnelling through the narrow neck between Newfoundland and Labrador would nevertheless have provided an unparalleled spectacle.

But did the Greenland whales really winter in the Gulf? Most authorities seem to have little or nothing to say about the matter. Typically, Dr. F. Banfield, in his recent *Mammals of Canada*, describes the southward migration of *Balaena mysticetus* as far as southeastern Baffin Island, after which those multitudes mysteriously vanish. The possibility that the Gulf might have been the goal of many of them, and that it could have given them the nursery and wintering grounds they needed, seems not to have been considered, perhaps because of a conviction gained from looking at the map that it lies too far south to be suitable for such "Arctic" animals as bowhead whales.

In truth it would have been as suitable to them as it was to such other nominally Arctic animals as the polar bear, walrus, and beluga whale, all of which were found there in abundance in earlier times. Although it becomes partially though never wholly ice-covered as winter progresses, this would have been no disadvantage to the polar whales, which would have welcomed the familiar presence of ice. Capable of remaining submerged for up to an hour while making passages from one lead of open water to another under the immensely heavy pack of the Arctic Ocean, they would have found no hindrance to free movement here; yet the drifting pack would have provided protection against heavy weather and big seas during the crucial period when the calves were being born. It should be remembered that the Greenland or bowhead was a cold-water animal and seldom if ever sought warm water, as did many other whales. The northern waters of the Gulf were eminently suitable since they were chilled by an offshoot of the Labrador Current entering through the Strait of Belle Isle. A comparison between the Gulf and the major wintering and calving ground of the Pacific tribe of bowhead whales in the Sea of Okhotsk reveals a range of similarities that strongly recommend the Gulf as an ideal wintering ground for North Atlantic bowheads.

Solid evidence has recently come to light as a result of excavations being undertaken in the boneyards surrounding ancient Basque whaling stations on the north shore of the Gulf. Intermingled with the remains of the sarda are quantities of bowhead bones.

A final point. In the list of the four whales of the "better sort" recorded by the Master of the *Mary Margaret*, the whale that stands first in excellence is, by its description, indubitably the bowhead; yet until the voyage of the *Mary Margaret*, neither the Basques nor anyone else had whaled in European Arctic waters where bowheads might have been encountered. How then did the Basques know about this whale, and why did they rank it so highly? The answer has to be that they knew it and hunted it in the Sea of Whales. Confirmation of this comes from the fact that the name by which it was first known to both French and English was Grand Bay whale—Grand Bay or *La Grande Baie* being the name given to the northern arm of the Gulf by sailors of these nations.

The pattern of whaling voyages to the northern Gulf exhibits significant changes during the 1560s. Whalers still sailed from Spanish ports as usual, aiming to pass through the Strait of Belle Isle early in July after the pack ice had cleared out of its narrow waters. On reaching their stations along the north shore, they began hunting sarda as they had done for close to half a century; but, whereas in former times the fleet had used to weigh anchor for home ports before the end of October (by which time the sarda had departed for the south), now the Basques lingered on. Not even white frosts at night and the onset of bitter warning winds out of the northwest could force them to depart. They waited, and they watched, even though the Sea of Whales now seemed devoid of prey.

November came. Scum ice began to form in the harbours, and still the Basques waited. Finally, lookouts on high ground at the easternmost station of Xateau—now Chateau Bay—staring out over the grey seas spotted the approaching vanguard of Grand Bay whales rolling south on the Labrador Current, breaching and blowing until the sky seemed filmed with frozen haze.

From station after station the whaleboats swarmed out to meet the oncoming armada. Braving razor-edged cat-ice, ice fogs, snow squalls, and freezing winds, the boatmen pressed their attacks with a frenzy that ignored everything except the urgency of killing. It was indeed a terrible urgency, for they had to complete the slaughter, make their oil, and depart quickly—or face a deathly winter, frozen in on Labrador's black coast.

The risk was real. In 1577, winter struck in early December and never relented thereafter until the following spring. Shore-ice made so quickly and so thickly that it trapped much of the Basque fleet in harbour. Something less than half seem to have escaped, perhaps by fleeing southwest into the Gulf, thence eastward through Cabot Strait into the Atlantic; however, for some twenty-five or thirty ships and more than 2,000 men, there was no escape. Through five interminable months they endured fearsome cold, near starvation, and, worst torment of all, the scourge of scurvy. Before spring freed their ships, 540 of them died. Although this was a singularly savage blow, it did not dull the whaling syndicates' appetite for gain; in 1578, an even larger than usual fleet returned to risk its men in the December gamble for the oil of the Grand Bay whale.[2]

As the slaughter of the western sarda slowed for want of victims, a new wave of destruction incarnadined the northern reaches of the Sea of Whales. Until the loss of their fleet in the Armada debacle of 1588, the Spanish Basques fished the Grand Bay whale with the ruthless singleness of purpose that lust for profit fires in men; and, when they were gone, their place was taken by the French Basques who, according to Champlain, were making

---

[2] During 1983, excavators at the Basque station at Red Bay uncovered the skeletons of scores of men, the reasons for whose deaths could not be determined. They may well have been scurvy victims.

200,000 livres worth of train a year during the first decades of the seventeenth century. However, as we have already seen, by then the great days of the Basque whaling monopoly were fast fading away.

The event that triggered the beginning of the end of that monopoly took place in 1607 when that doughty explorer, Henry Hudson, sailed into the virtually unknown Arctic seas seeking a passage around Asia leading to Cathay. Hudson coasted the polar pack for hundreds of miles, discovering the isolated island he called Hudson's Touches (Jan Mayen Island) and examining parts of the Spitzbergen archipelago. Although he failed to find what he sought, he reported "great store of whales" of enormous size that seemed to swarm everywhere in the Arctic seas.

News of this discovery spread rapidly through the business capitals of northwest Europe and ignited considerable excitement—if the reports were true, it appeared that a source of train oil at least equal to that dominated by the Basques in the Western Ocean had been found much closer to home. The upshot was that first the English and then the Dutch sent ships into the frozen north to investigate. By 1612, a new oil rush was under way.

At first the English dominated the new whaling grounds in what they vaguely called the Greenland Sea, which included all that portion of the Arctic Ocean lying between east Greenland and Novaya Zemlya. Then the Dutch came whaling in force. Skirmishes and even pitched battles were fought between the rivals in the bleak fiords of Spitzbergen. But this was as nothing to the war they waged together against the leviathan they would come to call the Greenland whale.

By 1622, the Dutch alone were sending 300 ships and 15,000 to 18,000 men to "fish" Spitzbergen's frigid waters, and had built a big summer settlement on one of the barren islands, which they appropriately named *Smeerenburg*—Blubbertown. The carcasses of as many as 1,500 Greenland whales were towed into its stinking harbour each season to be flensed and their blubber rendered. Countless more whales were killed and their oil rendered in temporary shore stations all around the archipelago by English and Dutch alike.

In a few years the resultant gush of train oil into European markets washed away the former Basque monopoly. Although some French Basques continued to whale in New World waters on a much-diminished scale, most either turned to fishing cod or hired themselves out as mercenary harpooners aboard Dutch and English ships fishing the new grounds in the Greenland Sea.

Although the Grand Bay whales now enjoyed something of a reprieve on their wintering grounds, the cold polar waters where they summered were reddening with their blood. By 1640, the Greenland or Grand Bay whale was being hunted across the whole sweep of the European Arctic. Soon the old tale was being told anew. As the hunt intensified, the numbers of available whales began to shrink and competition for what was left grew fiercer. In 1721, a century after the great Arctic slaughter had begun, 445 whaling ships of half-a-dozen nationalities scoured the Greenland Sea—and succeeded in killing an average of only two whales each. By 1763, the average was down to one whale per ship, and those that *were* being killed produced only two-thirds to half as much oil as had been rendered from the monsters originally found around Spitzbergen.

Whales are long-lived animals. Unmolested, a Greenland whale might have lived sixty years or so and, growing all the time, attained a length of seventy feet. By the time the seventeenth century ended few, if any, were being permitted such longevity. By 1770, a fifty-five-footer was considered a big whale, and the kill of ever younger and smaller whales from year to year was becoming the regular pattern. Eventually more than half the kill would consist of "nursery whales"—youngsters of the year, still nursing on their dams.

Having taken the cream of the big whales from the Greenland Sea, the Dutch began searching farther afield until some of their ships rounded Cape Farewell and entered Davis Strait. Here they found a virgin population of Greenland whales and the slaughter began anew. The Dutch tried to monopolize this new ground, but English whalers avidly followed the stench of oil and money westward. Meanwhile, the young but vigorous New England whaling industry had begun sniffing northward. About 1740, its whalers discovered the wintering grounds of the whale they christened "Bowhead," but at first they were frustrated in their attempts to exploit the find because the Gulf of St. Lawrence was still French territory and forbidden to the English. The New Englanders thereupon resorted to clandestine methods, seasonally and secretly reoccupying some of the old Basque stations and establishing new ones concealed in coves on the lower Labrador and the *Petit Nord* peninsula of Newfoundland.

Since French cod fishermen did not winter on these coasts, using them and their harbours only from June to October, the New Englanders had only to wait until the French fishing fleet departed for Europe before putting wintering whaling crews ashore, after which the mother ships sailed south to hunt for sperm whales in warmer waters. As early as possible the following spring the schooners headed north again, braving the south-flowing polar pack in order to pick up the wintering crews and their production of oil and baleen before the French fleet again arrived on the scene. The French authorities either did not realize what was happening or, possibly, they knew but were not overly concerned.

After the British expelled the French from the region in the 1760s the New Englanders—mostly New Bedford men—were able to whale openly. They increased the number of winter stations fishing bowheads and, not content with this, sent their whalers northward in the spring to range the edges of the Labrador pack and pick off laggards from the stream of migrants. These were mostly nursing females whose progress north was slowed by their calves. The cow bowheads were particularly vulnerable because they would not abandon their young, a fact that whalers learned early to exploit. When a cow with her accompanying calf was sighted the harpooners first attacked the calf, aiming to cripple it but not to kill it outright. They could then take their time slaughtering the mother.

When the American colonies went to war with Britain in 1775, their whalers were excluded from fishing the Sea of Whales, so many went north to compete with the English and the Dutch in Davis Strait.

They were not missed on the Labrador coast, where their behaviour had been less than civil. In 1772–73, Lieutenant Curtis of the Royal Navy was sent to the Strait of Belle Isle to investigate complaints against them and he reported that they were "lawless banditti, the cause of every quarrel between the Eskimos and the Europeans...they swarmed upon the coast like locusts and committed every kind of offence with malignant wantonness."

Their departure may have brought relief to the people of the region but it came too late to help the bowheads. By that time the Greenland whales had been so decimated on both their summer and winter grounds that only a few pods remained. By the turn of the century they had become so rare on the Labrador coast that the Inuit, who had long depended on killing the occasional one for subsistence and for whalebone to trade for European goods, were unable to do so anymore.

In 1766, the wealthy English naturalist Joseph Banks visited Chateau Bay, which had been one of the main whaling harbours on Belle Isle Strait since at least as early as 1535. Here he was told of a remarkable find. "Last year, in digging, an extraordinary discovery was made of a quantity of Whalebone [baleen] carefully and regularly buried...and so large that I have been told by those who saw it that as much was dug as, had it been sound, would have been worth £20,000...it is supposed to be Left here by the Danes who in their return from Groenland South about, touched upon this Coast and Left several Whaling Crews, tempted no doubt by the Large quantities of Whales Which Pass Every Year through the Straights of Bellisle into the Gulph of St. Lawrence. Here we are to suppose that the fortunate Crew who had taken this immense quantity of Bone fixed their habitation... till the Ships should return as usual where upon [under threat of] an attack by the Inland Indians they Buried the Bone for greater security and most Probably were cut off to a man, so that their Treasures remained untouched till chance directed us to them in their present decayed state."[3]

Banks' identification of the people responsible for this cache is surely mistaken. No Danes are known ever to have whaled the Labrador coast. Nor could the cache have been of any great age since, unlike true bone, baleen rots rather quickly after it is buried. This considerable treasure was most probably secreted by a New England wintering crew, whether against a possible native attack as Banks supposed, or, what is perhaps more likely, against discovery by French summer fishermen after the whalers' mother ship failed to return for them.

Toward the end of the eighteenth century the Dutch, having reaped untold millions of guilders from two centuries of butchery (between 1675 and 1721 alone they sold whale products worth 80 million guilders), abandoned what remained of the bowhead fishery to English, Scots, and Yankee whalers who were then competing fiercely in Davis Strait. However, the Americans did not long remain in those crowded waters.

In 1847 a Yankee whaler hunting down remnant black rights in the North Pacific entered the Sea of Okhotsk and "found an enormity of whales assembled there." They were of a kind unfamiliar to the Captain, who had never hunted in northern waters before, but when a Sag Harbor whaler went through Bering Strait two years later and found enormous numbers of these same whales, he recognized them as being close kin to the bowhead. Called polar whales at first, they were in fact true bowheads, but of a separate tribe that ranged the North Pacific and the Beaufort and Chukchi Seas in the Arctic Ocean.

The discovery of this previously untouched lode drew almost every American whaling vessel into those distant waters, where Yankee daring, ingenuity, skill, and, above all, cupidity initiated a carnage that would have awed the Dutch of Smeerenburg. It took the Americans just fifty years to effectively exterminate the Pacific bowhead. They were merciless, killing every individual they could, regardless of age, size, or sex. Indeed, some ships' crews made a business of taking calves, which yielded as little as ten

---

[3] Another observer estimated the quantity of baleen as forty-five tons, which would represent the take from twenty to thirty bowheads of average size.

barrels of oil and little or no baleen. In 1852 one of the Yankee captains described their activities in this wise:

"The great combined fleet moved northward toward the Pole, and there the ships of all [our] whaling ports are now, lending their united efforts to the destruction of the [Bowhead] whale, capturing even the young...The whales have diminished since I was first here two years ago...how can it be otherwise? Look at the immense fleet fishing from Cape Thaddeus to the [Bering] Straits! By day and by night the whale is chased and harassed... there could not have been less than three thousand polar whales killed last season, yet the average [quantity] of oil is only about half as great as it was two years ago. The fact speaks for itself and shows that it will not long be profitable to send ships to the Arctic."

The Captain may well have been right about the profitability of train oil, the value of which was already being undercut by petroleum; but there was still baleen. In the mid-nineteenth century, demand for it in the manufacture of such varied articles as whips, parasols, hats, suspenders, neck-stocks, canes, billiard table cushions, fishing rods, divining rods, tongue scrapers, etc., etc. seemed to be ever on the increase, and the price rocketed accordingly. By 1855, baleen was worth $2 a pound and double that ten years later. There followed an orgy of destruction during which thousands of bowheads were killed *solely* for their "bone."

Freed of the time-consuming and exhausting business of flensing carcasses and boiling down the blubber, the whalers were able to devote almost all their time to killing. Some ships brought home as much as twenty-five tons of baleen from a single voyage. This amount represented as many as thirty or more whales, for by then it was a rare bowhead which lived long enough to produce as much as a ton of bone.

By 1910 the Bering-Beaufort-Chukchi Sea tribe of bowheads was commercially and almost literally extinct. Its eastern relatives fared no better.

Even by as early as the first decades of the nineteenth century, whalers in the Greenland Sea, where the immolation of the bowhead had begun, were running out of victims. More and more vessels—mostly English at this period—were chasing fewer and smaller whales. Not having had time to learn caution, these adolescent animals were easily approached. In 1818, the grotesquely misnamed Hull whaler, *Cherub*, Captain Jackson commanding, got into several pods of these youngsters and a massacre ensued. At one point, *Cherub* had every corner, on deck and below, stuffed with blubber— and still had fourteen untouched corpses of young whales moored alongside. Eventually Jackson had to cut them loose and let them drift away with "very great distress at the loss occasioned therebye to the Owners." Jackson and his crew killed forty-seven nursery whales in that single season.

No form of mammalian life could long withstand this kind of attrition and the bowhead of the Greenland Sea was no exception. By the 1830s, the species was effectively extinct although a scattered handful may have survived into mid-century. Their executioners were, however, now exercising their bloody skills in what they called the Western Grounds.

Davis Strait had been fished since the middle of the seventeenth century, but, by 1810 bowheads were becoming scarce there and so the whalers pushed their luck toward the north. They shouldered into the dangerous pack ice of southern Baffin Bay, reached Disco Island on the west Greenland coast and, to their amazement, found open water in the northern reaches of Baffin Bay. In 1815 some of them crossed it to reach the shores of the Canadian Arctic archipelago, which they named West Land. Here they broke in upon the summering grounds of the last undevastated bowhead tribe in the Atlantic region.

An observer on the English whaler *Cumbrian* at Pond Inlet on Baffin Island in 1823 provided this vivid glimpse of the carnage that ensued: "We turned south along the land floe [and] along the floe edge lay the dead bodies of hundreds of flenched whales, and the air for miles around was tainted with the foetor which arose from such masses of putridity. Toward evening the numbers we came across were even increasing, and the effluvia which assailed our olfactories became almost intolerable." This, it is to be remembered, was in the refrigerated climate of the Arctic!

Cumbrian's crew killed twenty-three bowheads on this single voyage. The forty-one ships in company with her flensed more than 350 whales amongst them—and probably fatally wounded and lost another fifty.

Again, such havoc could not be sustained. In 1850 the whole of the British whaling fleet in Baffin Bay only managed to find and kill 218 bowheads, and from then on the kill waned dramatically for want of victims.

During the 1860s steam-auxiliary whalers largely replaced the old sailing ships. Most were Scottish, but by this time some American whalers were returning from the devastation they had wrought in the North Pacific. In 1863 two American steam whalers forced their way through the spring ice into Hudson Bay where they found "legions of whales...the north part of the Bay from Marble Island to Cape Fullerton was full of whales."

This was no new discovery. Since time immemorial these waters had provided wintering, calving, and mating grounds for the bowheads of Baffin Bay and the Arctic archipelago. As early as 1631 explorers had commented on their majestic presence there. One Hudson's Bay trader wrote in 1751: "There are such shoals of whales [in Hudson Bay] as is nowhere to be met with in the known world."

The Hudson's Bay Company, never an organization to miss an opportunity for profit, tried several times to start a bowhead fishery but always failed, primarily because the attempts were made by landsmen with no whaling experience. This was put to rights by the arrival of the Yankee whaling ships. For them, this was the last great whale bonanza—and they made the most of it. Between 1863 and 1885, 146 whaling voyages were made into the Bay, and a hundred of these overwintered or left wintering crews on shore. Since a single whale could yield $3,000 worth of oil and $15,000 worth of baleen, the competition amongst the whalers was ferocious, and the hunt was merciless.

The wintering whales congregated with their calves in open leads, particularly in the northwestern part of the Bay. Although they could not be easily reached by boat, they could be approached on foot along the ice edge. So instead of harpooning them, the hunters attacked with hand-held guns firing fragmentation bombs that inflicted terrible internal wounds. Unless instantly killed, a struck whale would sound beneath the ice and if and when it surfaced again it would often be in some distant lead beyond reach of the gunners. According to Inspector Moodie of the Royal Northwest Mounted Police, who witnessed the hunt during its final days, at least three-quarters of the bowheads shot with bomb guns were not recovered. It can be assumed that most perished later of their wounds.

This was destruction on such a scale that, by 1895, only a handful of whaling ships were still finding it worthwhile to "fish" in Hudson Bay. The last whaler departed those waters in 1908 with empty holds, having failed to find a single bowhead.

Ten Scots steam whalers ranged almost the whole perimeter of Baffin Bay during the summer of 1910 and managed to kill only eighteen whales between them. Since this was not enough for a paying trip, they tried to "make up the voyage" by killing whatever else came to hand. This included some 400 of the small whales known as beluga, 2,000 walrus, 250 polar bears, and 5,000 seals. However, not even this additional slaughter enabled them to turn a profit. The game was finished. By the time the human world plunged into its own orgy of self-destruction in 1914, the eastern bowhead was thought to be extinct.

That it was not entirely so was certainly no fault of the whalers. A few score bowheads had managed to evade destruction, but they were not left free from persecution. Between 1919 and 1976, more than forty recorded attacks were made on bowhead whales in Canadian eastern Arctic and west Greenland waters, some by natives on their own account, but more under the direction of white residents, including government officials and employees of trading companies. About half of the whales attacked were killed and most of the rest were wounded. There is no trustworthy indication that the tiny remaining remnant of a once-enormous whale nation is recovering. It may not even be holding its own.

A somewhat larger portion of the North Pacific tribe escaped the devastation. During a 1969 visit to Magadan on the shores of the Sea of Okhotsk, I was told by a Soviet cetologist that as many as 400 had been located by aerial surveys during the previous winter. His estimate of the total number of surviving North Pacific bowheads was no more than 2,000. However, he did not believe they were increasing because too many were being killed by the Aleuts and Inuit of northeastern Alaska.

Like their Chukotkan peers (and like some of the Inuit of the eastern Arctic), a number of Alaskan native communities hunted whales as a major part of their subsistence through many hundreds, if not thousands of years. But in pre-European times there was an abundance of whales, and the primitive hunting gear possessed by the natives ensured that this abundance could not be depleted by human predation. That has all changed now.

Today, when there are at most only a few thousand bowheads left alive in the world, native peoples in Alaska are hunting them more intensively than they have done for many years. They no longer do so primarily to obtain essential subsistence but more for sport and profit. They also use deadly weapons provided by modern technology. Instead of the ancestral skin-covered *umiaks* and hand-thrown harpoons, some native whalers now use fast powerboats, and all are armed with devastatingly destructive bomb guns and bomb-lances. Nor is it unusual for them to hire spotter planes to find and track the whales as they work their way through the leads in the pack to reach their summer feeding grounds in the Beaufort and Chukchi Seas.

The result has been, and continues to be, devastating to the surviving bowheads. Dr. Floyd Durham has spent many years studying the Alaskan "native" bowhead hunt and he reports that the "sinking loss" resulting from modern hunting methods and weapons is 80 per cent. During one period when he observed, thirty bowheads of all ages and sexes were struck by Inuit hunters, *and not one was recovered*. In 1973, he witnessed the successful killing of a fifty-foot bowhead female and her nursing calf. The dead female proved too much for the Inuit to handle, so they turned her adrift after removing only about 10 per cent of the blubber. Twenty-nine bowheads were landed in Alaska in 1977—but an additional eighty-four were lost after having been harpooned and/or bomb-lanced.

Canada and Greenland have now forbidden the killing of bowheads in their territorial waters under any conditions. Since the rediscovery of the wintering pods in the Sea of Okhotsk in the 1950s, the Soviets have given bowheads full protection. The United States, on the other hand, finds it expedient to permit the destruction in Alaskan waters to continue.

Environmentalists have recently become much exercised about the probable effect on the few remaining bowheads of oil and gas exploitation in Arctic waters. Within a few years a massive traffic of gigantic tankers through much of the bowheads' summering grounds is to be anticipated. More than a hundred wells are already pumping oil. An accident involving a wellhead blowout, or a tanker rupture, is more than a probability; it is a statistical certainty, and at least one such disaster is predicted to occur every ten years. Studies indicate that a major spill in ice-covered Arctic waters can be expected to wreak damage to the marine environment and its associated life forms greater by a factor of ten than that resulting from such southern disasters as the sinking of the *Torrey Canyon* or the recent gargantuan spill from a runaway well in the Gulf of Mexico.

The situation in which the surviving bowheads find themselves is tragically ironic. While modern man has given over the deliberate slaughtering of them, his industrial practices indirectly threaten their tenuous hold on life. What seems even sadder is that they are still being killed by native peoples, who have now become the bearers of Western cultural attitudes toward animate creation...and who no longer need the bowheads for their own survival.

❖ 14
Rorqual

By the latter part of the eighteenth century most of the "better sort" of whales had been extirpated from the northeastern approaches to America. Nevertheless, those waters still teemed with the several species early whalers termed "the worser sort" because they were generally too swift and agile to be caught; difficult or impossible to recover after death because they sank; or poor in oil compared to the right whales.

The worser sort included the largest animal ever to exist upon this planet—the blue whale. Exceptional blues may have reached a length of a hundred feet or more and weighed over a hundred tons. Today, there are probably few survivors over eighty feet. But then, there are few survivors.

Although a creature of almost unimaginable magnitude, the blue whale was and is a gentle giant. Its food consists of the small, shrimp-like krill it filters out of the water by means of a screen of 300–400 plates of baleen contained in its enormous mouth. Streamlined to perfection, it possesses a physical strength almost beyond belief. It drives its enormous bulk along at eight or nine knots while cruising, but can accelerate to twenty.

The blue is the most prominent member of a family known as the rorquals. The similarities between most rorquals are so striking that only recently have scientists agreed as to how the group should be divided. They include the blue, followed by the fin, fin-back, or finner, which reaches a length of about eighty feet; then come two almost identical species, sei and Bryde's, which range up to sixty feet; and, finally, the relatively "little" minke, at about thirty-five feet.

The rorquals represent the most recent (which is to say the most highly evolved) of all baleen whales. There is reason to suspect that their brain capacity does not lag far behind that of the human species, although it is most certainly not used for the purposes that we use ours. Before we laid our doom upon them, they were also the most abundant of the large whales.

Apart from size (and the size range of each species overlaps that of those above and below it) and colour, the several rorqual species are almost indistinguishable in life to the eye of the casual beholder. In fact, the minke acquired its current name when a Norwegian whaler by the name of Meincke mistook a near-at-hand pod of these smallish whales for a distant pod of blues. It was a mistake that gave the unfortunate fellow an undesired immortality.

The behaviour and life history of all the rorquals is also essentially similar, except that the blue restricts its diet to krill while the others may also eat such small fishes as capelin, sand lance, and herring when opportunity invites. All are long-lived animals, some attaining ages in excess of eighty years. All are exceptionally swift and graceful swimmers, the sei being capable of underwater speeds close to twenty-five knots. All are essentially wide-roaming creatures of the open sea, wintering in temperate to tropical waters and (except for Bryde's) migrating in spring to colder, even polar climes. Because of their supreme adaptation to the sea, they have no special need for protected nursery grounds and most bear their young in the open ocean. Many, however, close with the land during spring and summer to take advantage of the great abundance of food to be found on continental and inshore banks. In the days of their glory, they were notably gregarious, and highly visible in consequence. As late as the 1880s, congregations of finners numbering above 1,000 individuals were no uncommon sight. A Captain Milne, in command of a Cunard liner that sailed through such an assemblage in the North Atlantic in the 1880s, likened it to "a space of about half-a-county in dimension filled with railroad engines, all puffing steam as if their lives depended on it!"

As is the case with many close-knit families, the rorqual clan harbours an eccentric. This is the humpback, a creature not only singular in appearance but in behaviour, too. One of the most "playful" of animals, it has apparently undergone major physical modifications as a result of its predilection for complicated gyrations. The humpback is also famous for its virtuoso ability to compose and sing individual songs of considerable complexity and haunting quality.

Its somewhat dumpy body seems foreshortened in contrast to the exquisite streamlining of its fellow rorquals. Attaining a weight of some sixty tons and a length of fifty-five feet, the humpback boasts two greatly extended and very flexible front flippers used for balance and for propulsion, and as arms with which courting couples enthusiastically embrace and caress each other.

It lacks the purposeful drive and thrust of other rorquals, normally proceeding at a leisurely five or six knots, although it can reach a speed of ten or twelve. Its rotund form, slow speed, gregariousness, amiability, and liking for inshore waters, together with the fact that, unlike its relatives, it sometimes floats when killed, made it appear rather more like a right whale than a rorqual in the eyes of early whalers.

New England whalers sailing out of New Bedford seem to have been the first to conclude that the humpback could be commercially exploited. By as early as 1740 these men were sailing small schooners into Newfoundland waters chasing black rights, greys, bowheads, and sperms; but the rights and greys were becoming ever rarer; the bowhead did not frequent that region at all in summer; and the sperm was only to be found in useful numbers far off-shore. The New Englanders must have been frustrated, not to say infuriated, to find themselves surrounded by uncountable numbers of rorquals from which they could get no profit. We will probably never know which acquisitive skipper it was who concluded that at least one of the worser sort might prove to be an exception; but by about 1750, the entire fleet was hunting humpbacks when nothing better offered.

They hunted it despite the fact that in summer it was usually a "sinker." Vessels of those times had no mechanical devices capable of hauling such massive corpses back up to the surface of the sea; nor did they have the wherewithal to keep them afloat while towing the carcasses to a shore station or while flensing them alongside a ship. No matter. The New Bedford men depended on the whale itself to deliver its carcass into their hands by virtue of a phenomenon they called "blasting."

When any great whale dies its body temperature quickly begins to *rise*, not fall, as one might expect. This is because the heat produced by decomposition is retained inside the blubber-insulated body, which becomes a kind of pressure cooker. After two or three days the internal tissues actually do begin to cook, and putrefaction soon generates gas enough to make even a hundred-ton sunken whale grow buoyant and begin to rise through the water like a surfacing submarine. Such noisome corpses do not float indefinitely. Eventually they rupture, sometimes so explosively as to send gobbets of rotting tissue flying about like soft shrapnel. What remains then sinks again, and the second sinking is forever.

The New Englanders seldom attempted to get fast to a humpback with harpoon and rope. They preferred to lance it, using twelve- to fourteen-foot lances. Sometimes the lance thrusts were enough in themselves to mortally wound the animal. If not, subsequent infections would do the job. Having fled from its tormentors, the whale would sicken and die, sink to the bottom, putrefy, then "blast" to the surface again to drift at the vagaries of wind and tide. The whalers counted on spotting such "blasted" humpbacks, whether of their own killing or of another, in sufficient numbers to reward them for the trouble they had taken. A recovery rate of one humpback for every three they lanced was apparently considered an adequate return.

It was a hellishly wasteful business, but profitable. When English authorities assessed the potential of whaling grounds around the mouth of the Strait of Belle Isle a few years after the expulsion of the French, they found the fishery booming. In 1763, according to the report of the naval officer in charge of the survey, the whale fishery on the coasts of Labrador was employing 117 New England sloops and schooners each crewed by about a dozen men, who took 104 whales within thirty leagues of the mouth of the Strait. How many more they may have killed but failed to recover will never be known. By 1767, the New England whaling fleet in the Gulf of St. Lawrence and along the shores of southern Labrador, Newfoundland, and Nova Scotia amounted to 300 sloops and schooners manned by more than 4,000 whalers. While their first choice remained black right, sperm, and grey whales when they could find them, they were frequently constrained to "make up their voyages" with humpback oil.

Except for a brief hiatus during and just after the American Revolution, the Yankee slaughter in the Sea of Whales steadily increased in magnitude until shortly after the turn of the century. By then greys, rights, and St. Lawrence bowheads were all effectively extinct; the sperms of the northeastern approaches were almost destroyed, and humpbacks were so devastated that it no longer paid the Americans to continue hunting the "northern waters." About 1820 there was a partial lull in the carnage—a lull brought about solely by the fact that the better sort of whales had been exterminated or reduced to residual remnants and, as yet, the whalers had found no way to do the same to the bulk of the rorquals that continued to roam the seas in prodigious numbers.

The lull lasted for about fifty years, during which there was only relatively small-scale whaling in the Sea of Whales, mostly for humpbacks. One such operation was conducted by a Jersey company in Hermitage Bay on the south coast of Newfoundland. Its whalers annually landed some forty to sixty humpbacks, killed by whaleboats equipped with a new horror—the Greener's bomb-lance. This was an explosive grenade on the end of a metal shaft, fired from a smooth-bore tube. No line was attached since, in principal, the bomb-lance was intended to be used to give the *coup de grâce* to a whale that had already been harpooned. However, whalers used it as their prime weapon against the humpbacks, counting on killing enough whales with it so that a profitable percentage might be recovered after the blasted corpses surfaced. In fiord-like bays such as Hermitage, the recovery rate was rather better than off an open coast. Nevertheless, the Jersey whalers probably doomed two or three for every one they landed.

Although humpbacks continued to suffer, the rest of the rorquals remained beyond effective reach of human rapacity until, near the end of the nineteenth century, the most ruthless and inventive sea marauders of all time finally devised the means to doom not only the rorquals, but all surviving great whales everywhere on Earth. The new slaughter was set in motion by a genius in the arts of destruction, a Norwegian named Svend Foyn. A long-time seal and whale killer, Foyn felt so thwarted by his inability to profit from the abounding rorqual nations that he single-mindedly, not to say fanatically, devoted more than ten years of his life to discovering and perfecting a way to kill and to recover them. During the 1860s, he unveiled his tripartite answer to the rorqual problem.

The essence of it was a one-ton cannon that fired a massive harpoon deep into a whale's vitals. A fragmentation bomb in the nose of the harpoon then exploded, riddling the victim's guts with jagged chunks of shrapnel. The explosion also caused steel barbs concealed in the harpoon shaft to spring outward, firmly anchoring it and its attached rope in the whale's flesh.

The effect of this demoniac device on a living whale is well described by F.D. Ommanney, a cetologist with a latter-day Antarctic whaling expedition. "Our quarry broke surface [after having been harpooned] some five hundred yards away and began his silent, terrible death struggle. If whales could utter cries which could rend the heart, their deaths would be less dreadful than this losing battle which our whale was now engaged upon in silence broken only by the far-off screaming of sea birds. We could not even hear the thrashing of crimsoned foam as he writhed and plunged, spouting a bloody spray at first, then an upgushing, followed by a bubbling upwelling amid a spreading island of blood...the struggle ceased, the red foam subsided and we could see the body lying quite still. The birds busied themselves above and around it with shrill cries."

The second prong of Foyn's deadly trident was a small, swift, and highly manoeuvrable steam-powered vessel with a specially strengthened bow upon which the cannon was mounted. She was also fitted with an extremely powerful steam-winch and spring-pulley system that enabled her to play a harpooned whale as a sport fisherman might play a salmon, and to raise even a 100-ton dead whale from as deep as two miles down. Originally these boats were forthrightly called whale killers, but today they are known as whale *catchers* in deference to public sensibilities. The first killer boats were only fast enough to run down a cruising rorqual, but that was enough in the early days because the whales had not yet learned to flee the grim destroyers. With the passing years, the killer boats became larger, swifter, and more lethal in every way, some eventually being able to range as far as 400 miles from their shore base and overtake, kill, and tow home as many as a dozen of the largest and fastest rorquals.

The third element was simply a hollow metal tube thrust into the lungs or abdominal cavity of a dead whale after it had been hauled back to the surface. Through this tube compressed air or sometimes steam was injected, thereby inflating the corpse until it was buoyant enough to be towed to the factory.

Armed with Foyn's inventions, the Norwegians began to build what is admiringly referred to in commercial circles as the modern whaling industry. "Svend Foyn commenced full-scale operations on the Finnmark coast of Norway in 1880," one of his admirers tells us, "and his immediate success was followed by a crowd of catchers, each killing sometimes as many as five or six rorquals in a single day, rapidly depleting the northern grounds. The industry, however, was so profitable that the gallant Norwegians, having found a trade after their own hearts, set out to look for 'fresh fields and pastures new'."

Between 1880 and 1905, the Norwegians processed nearly 60,000 North Atlantic whales, mostly blues and finners. How many they actually *killed* during that quarter century can only be estimated, but considering the loss-to-landing ratios of those times a figure of 80,000 is probably conservative.

Toward the end of the nineteenth century, Norwegians seeking "fresh fields and pastures new" were doing so with such compulsive energy that their shore stations, each served by several of the deadly killer boats, had spread like a pox along almost every oceanic coast where whales were to be found in any numbers. One of the first regions they infested was the Sea of Whales.

In 1897, the Cabot Whaling Company was incorporated at St. John's, Newfoundland. Typical of its kind, it was a lethal mating of the avarice of local merchants with the predacious skills of the Norwegians. A shore station with the poetic name of Balaena was built at Hermitage Bay and began operating in 1898 with a single killer boat. That first season she landed forty-seven large rorquals. The following year she landed ninety-five. In 1900 her catch was 111, and in 1901 she was joined by a second killer and the two of them delivered 472 whales to the flensers at the station. In 1903, four killers worked out of Balaena and landed 850 large rorquals, almost equally divided between blues, finners, and humpbacks.

By 1905, twelve Norwegian/Newfoundland factories were engaged in the ever-escalating butchery. By 1911, twenty-six were or had been operating in the Gulf of St. Lawrence and along the Atlantic coast from south Labrador to Nova Scotia. The massacre of whales by swarms of killer boats was on a scale that makes the earlier slaughter in the Sea of Whales by Basques, French, and Americans pale before it.

In August of 1905, J.G. Millais, an English naturalist, artist, and self-styled sportsman, was invited to be the guest of the St. Lawrence Whaling Company's factory on Newfoundland's Burin Peninsula.

"The hunting steamer was to leave in the evening for a cruise so I made a few preparations and went aboard. The little steamers used in the pursuit of the Rorquals are vessels of about 100 tons burthen and 95 feet in length. They can steam fast—from twelve to fifteen knots—and can turn in their own length. Up in the bows is the heavy swivel gun which has back and front sights. The charge is half a pound of powder. The harpoon is four and a half feet long, furnished with a diamond-shaped head, which flies open when the time-fuse explodes. The main shaft has four iron flukes which are tied with string, and these open and anchor the main shaft in the whale on the explosion. The after part of this iron shaft is divided, and in this opening runs the iron ring to which is attached a strong manilla rope, two or three inches in diameter.

"The crew of the *St. Lawrence* consisted of—Captain Neilsen, who was also first gunner; a mate, Christian Johanessen; an engineer, and four seamen, each of whom could take any part, from shooting the whales to cooking the dinner. They were all Norwegians, and very cheery, modest fellows. I felt I would like to sail about the world amongst unvisited places, and hunt all kinds of wild beasts, with none but Norwegians as my companions. They are the best of all comrades, always good-natured, loving sport.

"During the night the captain decided to steam right out for the Greenbank [about 120 miles south of St. Lawrence]. The wind had fallen, and I was eating my breakfast and reading Dickens, when at 9 A.M. I heard the engines slow down, and knew that meant whales, so I ran on deck.

"It was a glorious morning, with bright sun and the sea like oil. Far ahead were two spouts of silvery spray, and as we approached I could see they were higher than those of Finbacks.

"'Yes, those are Blaa-hval' [Blue Whales], said Johanessen, 'and we shall kill to-day.'

"We were within three hundred yards of the larger of the two whales when it rolled over, showing its enormous tail, and disappeared for the 'big' dive.

"'That's a ninety-foot bull,' said the captain, as I stood beside the gun. His eyes glistened as he swayed the swivel to and fro to make sure that the engine of destruction worked well. Both whales were under the sea for a quarter of an hour by my watch, and then burst up about a quarter of a mile ahead, throwing a cloud of spray thirty feet into the air.

"'Full speed ahead and then 'safte'" [slowly], and we ran up to within fifty yards of the rolling slate monsters, which were now travelling fast, though not wild. When a shot seemed imminent they both disappeared from view… The captain and I were gazing fixedly into the green and clear depths when far away down beneath the water I saw a great copper-grey form rising rapidly right underneath the ship. The captain signalled with his hand to the man at the wheel on the bridge, turning the vessel off a point just as the ghostly form of the whale, growing larger and larger every moment until it seemed as big as the ship, burst on the surface beside us, and broke the water within ten yards. In a moment we were drenched in blinding spray as the whale spouted in our faces. I turned my arm to protect my camera and to click the shutter as the captain fired his gun. The latter planted the harpoon fairly in the great creature's lungs.

"'Fast!' yelled the cook, who had rushed on deck brandishing a kettle of potatoes in one hand. Crimson flecks of blood floating on the emerald sea alone told us of the success of the shot. There was a lull of silence. Nothing was heard except the flop, flop of the line as it rolled slowly out, and the movement of the men as they ran quietly to their posts beside the steam-winch and the line-coil down below.

"'Was that a death-shot?' I asked the captain.

"'Don't know, sir,' he answered; 'I think it will run a bit.'

"It was so. The line at first slowly dribbled out, and then it began to go faster and faster, until it rushed from the bow at such speed that I thought it would catch fire.

"'He's going to travel now,' said Neilsen, pulling me away from the smoking rope. 'You must not stand there. If the rope breaks you might get killed.'

"We repaired to the bridge to get a better view.

"'Two lines gone now' [about 500 yards], said my companion. 'I fear I hit him too far back.'

"At this moment all eyes were riveted on a great commotion in the sea about 500 yards away. The next instant the whale appeared, rolling and fighting on the surface. It lashed the sea into white spume with its flippers and raised its head frequently right out of the water, opening its immense jaws. The leviathan of the deep was fighting hard with death, but the harpoon had penetrated its vitals, and its struggles only lasted about two minutes. Soon it grew weaker and weaker, until, casting forth a thin spout of red blood, it threw up its tail and sank in one mighty swirl.

"The first operation in raising the dead whale from the bottom is to take in the slack line. This is done by one man mounting the rigging and placing the rope over a strong running pulley, which receives play by means of a powerful spring concealed in the hold of the ship. At first all is easy, and then the line receives a tremendous strain as it lifts the carcase from the depths.

"The winch is set in motion, and with each rise of the ship we notice the 'give' of the line and the utility of the spring which prevents the strain being either sudden or excessive.

"For half-an-hour the powerful steam reel goes pounding on until the finer line of the gun rope comes up over the side. Then looking down you see the yellow grey ghost appear far below in the limpid depths. In another moment the mystery has developed into form, and the great Blue Whale comes floating to the surface, with the hilt of the harpoon buried in its side.

"Johanessen now passes a rope over the tail whilst I make some colour sketches and notes immediately after death—an important point for the artist, as whales lose their rich colour very rapidly.

"The rope on the tail is attached to a strong chain which loops round the huge member and fastens it securely to the bows of the ship. The flukes of the tail are now cut off. We decide to look for another whale, so the carcase must be set afloat. To achieve this it is necessary to blow it up with steam. This is effected by driving a sharp hollow spear into the stomach; to this is attached a long rubber hose pipe which connects with the engines of the ship. The whale is then blown up with steam. As soon as a sufficient quantity has entered the iron pipe is withdrawn and the hole plugged with tow.

"A long harpoon, on the top of which floats the Norwegian flag, is now fixed to the carcase, and the floating whale is cut adrift. The ensign can be seen twenty miles away on a fine day."

Millais also gives us the only contemporary account of the blue whale in life, as well as death, in the eastern approaches to America.

"It is distinguished from other Rorquals by its superior size and rich colour. All the upper part is a rich zinc-blue, the lower a dark blue-gray...in March and April large numbers approach the [southern entrance to the] Gulf of St. Lawrence just keeping outside the drifting ice. Here the main body separates, one gathering going right up the [St. Lawrence] estuary as the ice breaks up, the other turning east along the south coast of Newfoundland.

"The Blue Whale travels in search of food at the rate of about eight miles an hour, but when frightened, travelling, or struck by a harpoon, it can go at twenty knots, a speed which it can maintain for a long period. In feeding on a bank of 'kril', it swims on its side, erects a fin, and gives a sudden movement of 'full-speed ahead'; at the same moment the vast mouth is opened and slowly closed, encompassing about twenty barrels of shrimps. As the mouth closes the water is forced outwards, and may be seen rushing in a white stream from the sides of the baleen, whilst the food remains resting on the inside of the 'plates', to be swallowed at leisure. All the Rorquals feed in this manner, and I have seen a large Finback rolling round and round the steamer, taking in its huge mouthfuls with evident satisfaction, and caring as little for our presence as if we were not there at all—in fact it seemed a miracle that he could avoid striking the vessel with his great jaws.

"The Blue Whale generally remains under water during his great dive, according to my watch, for ten to twenty minutes. On reaching the surface he 'blows', sending up a spout of air and steam to a height of from 20 to 30 feet...Then he makes a series of from eight to twelve short dives on the surface, occupying four minutes...It is during the time the whale is making these short dives on the surface that the steam whaler races in and endeavours to get the shot. When struck by the harpoon and its bursting charge, the great Blue Whale often dives at once and sinks to the bottom of the sea. Frequently it rushes off at high speed, and then, coming to the surface, dies after a short 'flurry'. Sometimes, however, when the whale is hit too far back or near and under the backbone (in which case the bomb does not explode), a long and difficult chase, protracted for hours, ensues. On the whole this is a fairly tame whale, and not considered dangerous, if ordinary precautions are observed. The value is from £100 to £150.

"This species is possessed of greater strength and staying power than any whale, and some exciting experiences have fallen to the lot of the whalers engaged in its chase. The most remarkable and protracted hunt on record was experienced by the steamer *Puma* in 1903.

"The *Puma* spied and 'struck' a large Blue Whale, six miles from Placentia, at nine o'clock in the morning. The animal immediately became 'wild', and it was found impossible to get near enough to fire another harpoon into it, as it came on to blow hard. For the entire day it towed the steamer, with engines at half-speed astern, at a rate of six knots. Towards evening a second rope was made fast to the stern of the vessel and attached to the first line, now 'out' one mile. The steamer then turned about and put on full-speed ahead. This seemed to incense the whale, which put forth all its strength, and dragged the whole of the after part of the vessel under water, flooding the after cabin and part of the engine-room. The stern rope was immediately cut with an axe and the danger averted. All through the night the gallant whale dragged the steamer, with the dead weight of two miles of rope, and the engines going half-speed astern, and at 9 A.M. the following morning the monster seemed to be as lively and powerful as ever. At 10 A.M., however, its strength seemed to decrease, and at 11 it was wallowing on the surface, where, at 12.30, it was finally lanced by the captain. This great fight occupied twenty-eight hours, the whale having dragged the steamer a distance of thirty miles to Cape St. Mary."

Because of its immense size and the consequent amount of oil that could be extracted from it—a large individual could yield as much as 3,000 gallons—the blue was at first the prime quarry of the Norwegians in the Sea of Whales. They went after it with such ferocious competence that even as late as 1905 their fleet had been able to slaughter 265 blues in a single season, but by 1908 a much larger fleet could only find and kill a mere thirty-six. To all intents and purposes, the blue was commercially extinct in the Sea of Whales by then, so the Norwegians began to hunt finners and what remained of the humpbacks. Millais recorded the following poignant vignette of the Norwegian humpback hunt.

"The whales exhibit unusual attachment to their young, and will stand by and endeavour to defend them even if seriously wounded. This affection is reciprocated by the calf...Captain Neilsen was hunting in Hermitage Bay when he came up to a huge cow Humpback and her calf. After getting 'fast' to the mother and seeing that she was exhausted Captain Neilsen gave the order to lower away the boat for the purposes of lancing. However when the boat approached the wounded whale, the young one kept moving around the body of the mother and getting between the boat and its prey. Every time the mate endeavoured to lance, the calf intervened and, by holding its tail toward the boat and smashing it down whenever they approached, kept the stabber at bay for half-an-hour. Finally the boat had to be recalled for fear of an accident, and a fresh harpoon was fired into the mother, causing death. The faithful calf now came and lay alongside the body of its dead mother, where it was badly lanced but not killed. Owing to its position it was found impossible to kill it [with a lance] so a harpoon was fired into it."

With the blue whale almost gone and the humpback close behind it, the fin whale took the brunt of the ongoing destruction. The indefatigable Millais has left us this account of how the finbacks died.

"About six o'clock in the evening we encountered the fringe of the main herd of Finbacks, which were spouting in all directions. We pursued whale after whale, but all seemed wild except one monster which refused to leave the side of the vessel, and in consequence could not be shot at. At last the mate got a shot at 7 P.M., and missed. He was much crestfallen, and retired to the galley to enjoy the healing balm of coffee and potatoes. At 7.30 it was bitterly cold when Captain Stokken again stood beside the gun, and we were in full pursuit of a large female Finback that seemed tamer than the rest. Eventually in its final 'roll' the whale raised itself about ten yards from the gun, and the whaler tipping the muzzle downwards fired and struck the quarry under the backbone.

"At first the Finback was rather quiet, and then it began to run, the strong line rushing out at a speed of about 15 knots. When some two miles of rope had gone over the bow I turned to Captain Stokken, and said:

"'How much line have you got?'

"'About three mile,' was the curt reply.

"'But when that three miles goes, what then?'

"'Oh, well,' was the imperturbable answer, 'then I check line, and we see which is strongest, whale or rope.'

"In the course of a minute the captain gave the order to check the line. The strain now became terrific, the two-inch rope straining and groaning as if it would burst. At the same moment the little steamer leaped forward, pulled over the seas at about twelve miles an hour. There was a feeling of intense exhilaration as we rushed northwards, the spray flying from our bows as the ship leapt from crest to crest in the heavy swell. I have enjoyed the rushes of gallant thirty and even forty-pound salmon in heavy water on the Tay, the supreme moments in an angler's life, but that was mere child's play to the intense excitement which we now experienced during the next three hours. To be in tow of a wild whale is something to experience and remember to one's dying day. You feel that you are alive, and that you are there with the sport of kings. No wonder the Norwegians are full of life, and the men, from the captain to the cook, run to their several tasks with eyes and hearts aflame. This is a trade which will stir the blood of the dullest clod, and to men who are one and all the finest seamen in the world, it is the very life and essence of the Viking nature.

"Three hours of this fierce race went on, and the gallant Finback was as fresh as ever when the captain gave the order, 'Quarter-speed astern'. Another tremendous strain on the rope, the churning of the backward-driving screw, and our speed was at once reduced to 10 knots. It was marvellous the strength of the animal. The minutes and even the hours fled by, still the great cetacean held on its northward course without a check. Three hours went by; then came the order, 'Half-speed astern', and we were down to 6 knots, the vessel and the whale still fighting the battle for the mastery. In another hour the whale showed visible signs of weakening, when 'Full-speed astern' brought matters to a standstill. The machinery of man and the natural strength of the beast still worried on for another hour, and then we saw the steamer moving backwards; the whale was done, and could pull no more.

"The rope was then slackened, hoisted on to a 'giving' pulley, and then wound on to the powerful steam winch, which, acting like the fisherman's reel, at once began to 'take in'. Nothing was heard for another hour but the monotonous throb of the engine, and grind of the winch, until at last on the crest of a wave, about 300 yards to windward, was seen the great Finback, rolling over and over, spouting continuously, but so tired that it was unable to drag or dive.

"The captain now gave the order, 'Lower away to lance'. There was a fairly heavy sea running, and yet I never saw anything more smartly done than the way in which those Norwegians flung their light 'pram' into the water and jumped in from the bulwarks. Other men were ready with the oars, which they handed to the two rowers, whilst the mate seized the long 15-foot 'killing' lance, and the small party rowed rapidly away toward the whale.

"Hans Andersen, the mate, stood up in the stern, holding his long lance, as the men rowed slowly up to the leviathan. Then the rowers turned the boat round, and backed it in towards their prey. At times they were lost in the great swell, and then they would appear apparently beside the sea-monster, whose pathetic rolling was at once changed into spasmodic life. The whale, churning the water, now righted itself, and at once turned on its attackers, who retreated at full-speed. Now on one side and now on another, the plucky mate tried to approach and bring off his death-thrust, but all to no avail. Every time the exhausted cetacean had just enough strength left to carry the war into the enemy's country, and to turn the tables on its opponents. Mist and darkness were rolling up, the sea was rising, and still the duel of attack and defence went on. At last darkness hid the combatants from view, when Stokken turned to me and said:

"'This very wild whale. Must give him another shot, or Andersen will get hurt.' He reached up and blew the steam whistle three times as a signal for the boat to return. In a few minutes Andersen's cheerful face was looking up at us, the lance held high and streaming with blood.

"'Ha, so you stab him,' said Stokken.

"'Ja, just as you blow the whistle,' replied the mate, with a smile. The pram and its occupants were soon aboard, and the whale rolled in and lashed alongside by the tail. The chase had lasted seven hours."

So the great rorquals disappeared from Newfoundland waters—not fleeing to some distant sanctuary as apologists for their absence insisted—but into the trypots, pressure cookers, and fish-meal plants of the whaling industry.

The outbreak of the First World War brought a respite of sorts while men concentrated their destructive energies on each other. The big rorquals of the northwest Atlantic were by then in desperate need of respite. Since the beginning of the Norwegian onslaught in 1898, more than 1,700 blues, 6,000 finners, and 1,200 humpbacks had been "harvested" in the Sea of Whales. These numbers, be it remembered, only represent whales delivered to the factories. They take no account of those fatally injured, of calves that died of starvation after the deaths of their mothers, or of those that perished as a result of wound-induced infections.

If I stress this latter point, it is because whales appear to be singularly susceptible to terrestrial bacteria and viruses, against which they seem to have little if any natural immunity. This constitutes a mortality factor seldom mentioned in discussions of whaling practice and usually ignored in official statistics purporting to represent the damage inflicted by whalers. However, the whalers themselves have been well aware of the infection factor and have used it to their own advantage since earliest times.

As far back as the ninth century Norwegian fiordsmen were driving pods of minkes into the inner reaches of long fiords, then barring off escape with nets. The trapped animals were attacked, not with spears or lances, but by firing crossbow bolts into them—very special bolts that had been deliberately dipped in vats of putrid meat. The organisms introduced into the whale by this "innoculation" were so virulent that the infected minke would die within three or four days, its bloated body a seething mass of gangrene and septicaemia. Meat from such corpses was, of course, useless, but the blubber was unimpaired and was rendered to produce lamp oil, whale-oil tar, and other such products. Sei whales were still being killed in fiords near Bergen by what was essentially the same barbarous method until early in the twentieth century.[1]

By 1908, having ravaged the great rorquals on both sides of the North Atlantic, packs of Norwegian killer boats were swarming across the equator into the South Atlantic. From there they soon found their ways into the Pacific, then into the Indian Ocean. Shore stations sprang up behind them

---

[1] An earlier book of mine, A Whale for the Killing (1972), describes the death of a large female fin whale from septicaemia after she became trapped in a small lagoon on the south coast of Newfoundland where she was used as a target for rifle fire.

and the stench of megadeath spread like a miasma. The havoc the killers wrought on the whales of the tropical and temperate oceans was of a previously unimaginable enormity. It included the virtual obliteration within a few brief years of the remaining southern black right whales, a devastating massacre of previously untouched tribes of humpbacks, and the near extinction of grey whales in the North Pacific.

It was not enough. The Norwegian whaling industry had become a modern Moloch whose appetite was insatiable—and unrelenting. And there was still one major ocean left to ravage. The killer fleet ranged even farther south until, off the tip of South America, it found whales in such multitudes as had not been seen since the first Basques sailed into the Sea of Whales 400 or more years earlier.

By 1912, sixty-two killer boats were steaming out of shore bases on the Falkland and South Orkney Islands, scouring the nearby waters with such rapacity that, in the summer of that year, they delivered more than 20,000 whale carcasses to the factories. About 80 per cent of these were humpbacks, the rest a mixture of right whales, blues, and finners.

Because the whales were so incredibly abundant, individual catchers could easily kill a dozen or more in a single day. And because they *could*— they often *did*. One catcher out of the Falklands killed thirty-seven whales between dawn and dusk. The corpses were flagged, then cast adrift to be picked up when the killer boat had finished her butchery and was ready to return to the factory. That is, they were picked up if they could still be found. All too often they were never seen again, having been lost in darkness or in fog, or carried away by wind and current. When we take into account losses from this cause alone, together with the usual mortality suffered by wounded whales and orphaned calves, the true magnitude of the slaughter begins to boggle the imagination.

Processing was as wasteful as killing. Because there was a glut of corpses, the flensers only stripped off the thicker back and belly blubber whereupon, as Ommanney tells us, "the *skrotts*, as the carcasses were called, were cast adrift in the harbour. They floated ashore to rot on the beaches and to this day [1971] Deception Harbour in the South Shetlands and many of the bays and inlets of South Georgia are edged with ramparts of bleached bones, skulls, jaws, backbones and ribs, memorials to the greed and folly of mankind."

The stench of these harbours was legendary. But as the manager of a latter-day American whaling station defiantly proclaimed: "Who the hell gives a damn! That's the stink of money and it sure smells good to me."

It smelled so good to the Norwegians that, just after World War I, a few of their bigger killer boats pushed yet farther south to explore the possibilities of even more profitable slaughter. When they came within sight of the permanent ice pack of the Antarctic Ocean they discovered what Herman Melville, of *Moby Dick* fame, had believed would forever remain an inviolable refuge where "The whales can at last resort to the Polar citadels, and diving under the ultimate glassy barriers and walls there, come up among icy fields and floes; and in a charmed circle of everlasting December, bid defiance to all pursuit from man."

That last resort was one no longer. When the returned catcher captains reported having found rorquals in such numbers as to be almost astronomical, neither the Antarctic Ocean's remoteness from shore bases nor the white hostility of its climate could suffice to protect the whales from man's remorseless avarice.

Initially, distance was a problem. Shore factories could not be established on the ice of the frozen continent itself, and the island bases were a long way north. However, in 1925, a Captain Sorlle of Vestfold, Norway, displayed the genius for destruction of a Svend Foyn and invented the ultimate weapon with which to convert what remained of the world's great whales into hard cash.

He invented the pelagic factory ship—a very large vessel designed to operate in the open ocean, fitted with a gaping hole in the stern and a ramp up which whales could be winched into a combined floating abattoir and processing plant. Even the first of these ships was big enough and rugged enough to "work" whales at sea in almost any weather, and it could be stored for voyages of six months or more. Each factory ship became the nucleus of a fleet grimly comparable in composition to a naval task force. It included a pack of killers of new and even more terrible potential, buoy boats to mark the corpses, tugs to haul them to the factory, and freighter-tankers to resupply the fleet at sea, after which they would carry the accumulated whale products from the factory ships to distant markets.

Even Sorlle's rudimentary prototype was able to penetrate southward to near the edge of the Antarctic pack, and later versions ranged the whole of the Antarctic Ocean, killing and processing rorquals and such other whales as might be found on a twenty-four-hour-a-day assembly line basis. There was now no place left on earth where whales could escape the fate we had ordained for them.

The ensuing massacre (and there is no other word for it) remains without parallel in the history of man's exploitation of other living beings. It will probably never be surpassed, if only because no other such an enormous aggregation of large animals still exists upon this planet.

In 1931, only six years after the first voyage of the first factory ship, forty-one such ships serviced by 232 killer boats were savaging the Antarctic rorquals. They flew the flags of the several nations whose businessmen had rushed to gain a share of this lucrative enterprise. Among them were the U.S., Norway, Great Britain, Japan, Panama, Argentina, Germany, and Holland; but it was the Norwegians who dominated the shambles, either on their own behalf or by means of the crews and ships they provided on hire and charter.

That year, 40,200 rorquals, mostly blues, were ripped apart in the floating knackers' yards...and the cold seas of the distant south ran dark with blood.

It was a banner year for the whaling industry and for the men who sat in board rooms in London, Tokyo, Oslo, New York, and other bastions of civilization. One factory ship, the nobly named *Sir James Clark Ross*, docked at New York after a six-month Antarctic voyage with a cargo consisting in part of 18,000 tons of whale oil worth just over $2.5 million.

A good time for whalers.

An evil time for whales.

Between 1904 and 1939 well over 2,000,000 great whales died the death prescribed for them by modern business practices.

By 1915, the last Norwegian killer boat had abandoned the wasted Sea of Whales to join in the South Atlantic carnage. The surviving North Atlantic whales were not, however, safe from death-dealing men. As the U-boat menace mounted in the Atlantic, the Allies launched more and more anti-submarine vessels until several hundred lean and lethal destroyers were committed to battle against equally deadly mechanical whales. But green crews for the destroyers needed training and, man being what he is, it was decided that an effective way to hone the killer skills would be to practise these on living whales. Unofficial reports suggest that some thousands of whales were killed in consequence. Most were victims of naval gunfire, but others were imploded into shapeless masses when they were used as targets for depth-charge training. There is also at least one known case of destroyers using whales as targets for ramming practice. Probably as many or more whales died in "accidental" encounters when they were mistaken for enemy submarines; but no one kept a record of how many whales were sacrificed to the cause of Victory at Sea.

When the Armistice brought an end to the military murder of men and whales, the commercial whalers hastened back to work. Although the major assault was directed at the South Atlantic and Antarctic rorquals, the wartime discovery that train oil could be processed into a prime ingredient in margarine so escalated its value that even the remnant populations of rorquals in the North Atlantic became attractive quarry. Thus, between 1923 and 1930, three Norwegian stations again worked the coasts of northern Newfoundland and southern Labrador for a landed kill of 153 blues, 2,026 finners, 199 humpbacks, 43 seis, and 94 sperm whales.

Profits were small compared to those of the southern fishery, but by making greater use of each whale they were kept at a satisfactory level. After trying all the oil out of the blubber, the residue, including meat, bones, and guts, was dried to produce fertilizer—manure as it was called. In a paraphrase of the age-old farmer's joke, a Newfoundland partner in the Hawkes Harbour whaling plant told the *St. John's Evening Telegram*: "We put every inch of the whale to profit, except the spout."

Nevertheless, when the Depression struck in 1929, profits fell below acceptable levels; so, from 1930 until 1935, there was another brief hiatus in whaling in the Sea of Whales. However, in 1936, two stations reopened, one in Labrador, the other in northern Newfoundland, and one or both remained active until 1949. During that period, they were able to kill and land 1,100 finners, 40 blues, and 47 humpbacks.

Figures have but small impact on the imagination, but perhaps these will have more significance if we think of the whales involved as being equivalent in biomass to some 12,000 elephants—or a mountain of flesh, fat, guts, and bone weighing considerably more than the liner *Queen Elizabeth*. Small as this local butchery may have been by comparison with what was happening in the Antarctic, it was by no means a negligible slaughter.

The cataclysmic advent of World War II afflicted the few remaining North Atlantic rorquals with even worse horrors than they had endured during World War I. Corvettes, destroyers, and frigates, eventually numbering in the thousands, prowled the dark waters of the Western Ocean and they were much more lethal than their ancestors had been twenty-five years earlier. Sonar, for the detection of underwater objects, together with a wide range of new weapons not only made them deadly hunters of submarines but, more or less incidentally, of whales, whose sonar echoes were often indistinguishable from those of submarines. As the war at sea grew fiercer, the drifting carcasses of bombed or depth-charged whales became a familiar sight to the crews of naval and merchant ships alike.

This military massacre did not cease with war's end. Beginning in the mid-1940s, U.S. naval aircraft flying out of their leased base at Argentia, Newfoundland, regularly used whales as training targets, attacking them with machine-gun and cannon fire, rockets, depth charges, and bombs. When this came to light in 1957, as a result of an investigation by Harold Horwood of the St. *John's Evening Telegram*, the naval authorities appeared baffled by and even indignant at the resulting public outcry. Having pointed out that all navies routinely practised gunnery and anti-submarine warfare on marine animals, they questioned the logic and even the motives of those who would condemn such an eminently practical procedure. Large whales, they pointed out, not only provided excellent simulacra of enemy submarines, they cost the taxpayer absolutely nothing. Surely, the naval brass concluded, the death of a few whales was a small price to pay for helping to preserve our freedom.[2]

Advances in the arts of war had another and even more disastrous effect on the whales. When the Antarctic whalers went back to work in 1946, they were armed with a panoply of new weapons. These included sophisticated communications systems, sonar, radar, new navigational equipment, and electronic devices to disorient, scare, and confuse the whales. Spotter aircraft or helicopters operating from immense new floating factories (some of which displaced 30,000 tons) were combined with ex-naval corvettes and frigates converted to whale killers. The largest of these were 700-ton vessels of 3,000 horsepower, capable of making thirty knots and armed with harpoon guns of formidable efficacy. The overall combination ensured that any whale that came within the wide-ranging ken of a pelagic fleet now stood no more than a fractional chance of escaping death. What followed was annihilation.

By the end of the 1940s, some twenty to twenty-five pelagic fleets were annually killing 25,000 to 30,000 whales, mostly blues, from an Antarctic whale population that had already been reduced to less than half its initial size. By 1950, the Antarctic blues, which had originally numbered between a quarter and half a million, were all but gone and the killer fleets had shifted their attentions to the finners. By 1955, it was estimated that no more than 100,000 Antarctic finners remained from an original population in excess of

---

[2] During the 1960s U.S. naval units stationed in Iceland boasted of carrying out target practice on orcas (killer whales) using aircraft and surface vessels. Although the excuse given for this atrocity was that it was done to benefit Icelandic fishermen, there was no scientific or economic justification for it. It is believed that several hundred whales—by no means all of them orcas—were killed in this "exercise."

three-quarters of a million; and in the following year, the whalers landed 25,289 fin whales—about a quarter of what was left.

Although even the statistics released by the whaling industry during the late 1950s made it brutally clear that the great whales everywhere on earth were entering upon their final days, no steps were taken to reduce the slaughter. Multinational corporations as well as national interests from the U.S., Great Britain, Norway, Holland, Japan, and the Soviet Union made it abundantly clear that they were not only determined to continue the carnage, but intended to increase the scale of the bloodletting. As one discouraged conservationist expressed it: "They clearly felt the whales were just too valuable to be allowed to live."

The voice of mercy, or even of sanity, was not often heard speaking out on behalf of whales during those years. To the contrary, the world was treated to a spate of novels, non-fiction, and even feature films that not only justified but *glorified* the continuing slaughter, at the same time praising the heroic qualities of the whale killers and the financial acumen of the whaling entrepreneurs.

Equally revolting was the prostitution of science to justify the holocaust. In 1946, the countries most actively engaged in whaling formed the International Whaling Commission, which they claimed was dedicated to the protection of whale stocks and to the regulation of the industry through scientific management. A surprising number of scientists were prevailed upon to lend themselves and their reputations to creating and maintaining a most unsavoury subterfuge.

From its inception, the IWC has been little more than a smoke screen created by corporate industry with the full support of national governments and justified by subservient science, under cover of which the world's whale populations have been systematically destroyed. A detailed account of its evasions, outright lies, queasy morality, and abuse of science is beyond the scope of this book, but those who can stomach the unpalatable details are invited to read Robert McNally's *So Remorseless a Havoc*.

McNally summarizes the sham of self-serving interests policing themselves in the following terms: "A cliché of liberal ideology has it that an entrepreneur profiting from a resource will strive to protect that resource in order to make profits over the long run. Thus, the argument continues, market forces contribute to the preservation of the environment. This may be good corporate public relations, but the whaling capitalist cares not a fig whether there will be whales in the sea in fifty or a hundred years. His sole concern is whether the whales will last long enough for him ... He will keep on killing as long as some gain can be had . . . Market forces provide no check to extinction; they actually contribute to it. Greed preserves only itself."

One of my friends and neighbours when I lived in Burgeo, Newfoundland, was "Uncle" Art Baggs, who had been a fisherman on the sou'west coast since the 1890s. He remembered meeting his first whales at the age of eight, when he accompanied his father in a four-oared dory to the offshore cod fishery at the Penguin Islands.

"'Twas a winter fishery them times, and hard enough. The Penguins lies twenty miles offshore . . . nothin' more'n a mess of reefs and sunkers . . . we'd row out there on a Monday and stay till we finished up our grub . . .

"They was t'ousands of the biggest kind of whales on the coast them times. Companies of 'em would be fishing herrings at the Penguins whilst we was fishing cod. Times we'd be the only boat, but they whales made it seem as we was in the middle of a girt big fleet. They never hurted we and we never hurted they. Many's the time a right girt bull would spout so close you could have spit baccy juice down his vent. Me old Dad claimed they'd do it a-purpose; a kind of joke, you understand."

It was during the winter of 1913 that Arthur witnessed the disappearance of the great whales.

"Back about 1900 they Norway fellows built a blubber factory eastward of Cape La Hune. They called it Balaena and, me son, it were some dirty place! They had two or three little steamers with harpoon guns, and they was never idle. Most days each of 'em would tow in a couple of sulphur-bottoms [blues] or finners and the shoremen would cut 'em up some quick. No trouble to smell that place ten miles away.

"And floating whales! When they got the most of the blubber off, they turned 'em loose, the meat all black, and them all blasted up so high they nigh floated out of the water. Some days when I been jigging off shore 'twas like a whole new kit of islands had growed there overnight. Five or ten in sight at once and each one with t'ousands of gulls hangin' over it like a cloud.

"'Twas a hard winter for weather and I never got out to the Penguin Islands as much as in a good year, but when I was there I hardly see a whale. Then, come February, one morning when 'twas right frosty and nary a pick of wind, I was workin' a trawl near the Offer Rock when I heared this girt big sound. It kind of shivered the dory.

"I turned me head and there was the biggest finner I ever see. He looked nigh as big as the coastal steamer. He was right on top of the water and blowin' hard, and every time he blowed, the blood went twenty feet into the air...I could see there was a hole into his back big enough to drop a puncheon into.

"Now I got to say I was a mite feared...I was tryin' to slip me oars twixt the t'ole pins, quiet like, when he began to come straight for I. Was nothin' to be done but grab the oar to fend him off, but he never come that close. He hauled off and sounded and I never saw he again...no, nor any of his like, for fifty year."

During the mid-1950s, to the astonishment of most of the younger fishermen, who had never seen a great whale before, some fin whales reappeared along the sou'west coast. A pod of half a dozen even took to wintering amongst the Burgeo islands. Arthur was delighted to welcome them back again, and when my wife and I came to Burgeo in 1962, he showed them to us with proprietary pleasure.

These resident finners fed on herring in the runs and channels between the islands and each winter through the next five years from December into March I could look out the seaward windows of our house almost any day and see them spouting high puffs of hoary mist into the cold air. Unmolested by human beings, they were quite fearless, allowing power dories and even big herring seiners to approach within a few yards. In the course of the years, I became almost as familiar with them as if they had been cattle-beasts in a neighbouring field, but by far the most spectacular view I ever had was on a fine July day in 1964.

The pilot of a Beaver float plane was taking my wife and me joy-riding along the towering, rock-ribbed coast to the eastward of Burgeo. It was a cloudless afternoon and the cold waters below us were unusually transparent. As we crossed the broad mouth of one of the fiords, our pilot unexpectedly banked the plane and put her into a shallow dive. When he levelled out at less than a hundred feet we were flying parallel to a pod of six fin whales.

There were in line abreast, swimming only a few feet below the surface and, as seamen say, making a passage under forced draft. We estimated their speed at nearly twenty knots. The pilot throttled back almost to a stall and we circled them. They were as clearly visible as if they had been in air. Their mighty flukes which, unlike the tails of fish, work vertically instead of horizontally, swept lazily up and down with what seemed to be a completely effortless beat. There was no accompanying turbulence and the overall effect was of six exquisitely streamlined bodies hovering in the green sea and seeming to undulate just perceptibly as if they were composed of something more subtle and responsive than mere flesh and bone.

They were beautiful.

About ten minutes after we met them, the whales surfaced as one, blew several times, then sounded while still moving at full speed. This time they went deep, shimmering and diminishing in our view as if they were sliding down some unseen chute into the abyssal depths.

We had no way of knowing that they and their rorqual fellows were about to be plunged into much darker depths.

The reappearance of finners on the sou'west coast was due to the fact that—unlike the northern waters of the Sea of Whales, in which they had been more or less continuously hunted for fifty years—the waters *south* of Newfoundland had provided something of a haven for the rorqual tribes since the closing of the Balaena factory in 1914.[3]

Female rorquals of the larger species do not become sexually mature until they are several years old and can then produce only a single offspring every two to four years. Because of this, those species that had been reduced to near the vanishing point were not able to gain much from the half-century reprieve. However, because a fair number of finners had survived the pre-World War I massacre, they had been able to increase their numbers to perhaps as many as 3,000 by the early 1960s. The southern portion of the Sea of Whales also harboured some sperms and humpbacks, together with a population of seis and minkes that had never been fished commercially.

By 1960, the heyday of whaling in the Antarctic was over. The blues were gone. The finners were fast disappearing. It was clear that switching to the much smaller seis would not satisfy the gargantuan appetite of the pelagic fleets for long. By 1963, many of the factory ships had already been laid up or converted to other work. There was, however, no peacetime role for the killer boats, except for those few sold to Third World countries to serve as naval gunboats. Nevertheless, as both the Norwegians and Japanese were aware, such small pockets of marketable whales as existed here and there in remote corners of the world's oceans could still be turned to good account before the last killer boat had to be sold to the breakers' yard for scrap.

In the winter of 1963–64, an Antarctic killer named *Thorarinn* tossed

---

[3] In 1945, a Norwegian/Newfoundland consortium reopened the old factory at Hawkes Harbour in Labrador, and in 1947, the Olsen Whaling and Sealing Company began operations at Williamsport in northern Newfoundland. Subject to no controls of any kind, these companies whaled with such ruthlessness that, by 1951, the waters that could be swept by their fleet of killer boats had been "cleaned out." By then the two factories had processed 3,721 finners together with several hundred "other whales," and had reaped an estimated return on their investments in excess of 900 per cent.

and thrust her way across the cold wastes of the North Atlantic. Her destination was Blandford, Nova Scotia. Before her arrival, she hauled down her Norwegian flag and hoisted the Canadian ensign in token of the fact that she would henceforth be working for a nominally Canadian company.

Thorarinn was a 200-foot, 800-ton, 2,000-horsepower diesel-electric killing machine, whose 90 mm harpoon gun mounted high on her destroyer bow had already taken the lives of thousands of great whales in southern waters. She could range 300 miles from base, kill and take in tow eight or nine big whales, return them to shore, and be off again within a few hours on a new sweep of destruction.

Manned by seasoned Norwegian whalers, *Thorarinn*, and a sister ship that joined her a little later, belonged to the misleadingly named Karlsen Shipping Company. As we shall later see, this organization was headed by a Norwegian named Karl Karlsen, who arrived in Canada shortly after the end of World War II to establish a business based on killing harp seals and exporting their skins to Norway. The business flourished and the company constructed an extensive plant at the little village of Blandford. Sometime in the early 1960s, the company became aware of the presence of the resurgent finner population and of the untouched seis and minkes in the southern portion of the Sea of Whales. The rest is bloody history.

Between 1964 and 1972, Karl Karlsen's plant at Blandford legally processed 1,573 fin whales, 840 seis, 94 sperms, and even 45 of the little minkes. In addition, it processed three illegally killed blue whales together with a number of finners under the legal size. In no case was the company punished for breaking Canadian laws.

The products of the factory included select frozen whale "beef" and "bacon" for the gourmet Japanese market; marine oil (the new name for whale oil), which was mainly used in making margarine and as a base for cosmetics; bone meal for fertilizer; and, not least, large quantities of low-grade meat and offal for pet food markets in Europe and in North America.

The Karlsen organization was not long left to reap the benefits from this last whale bonanza all to itself. The stink of dead whales, and of money, soon reached other "harvesters of the seas." In 1965, a Norwegian-manned "small whale" operation at Dildo, Newfoundland, which had been established to kill minke and pilot whales in co-operation with a Japanese company called Kyokuyo Hogei, went to work on the larger rorquals. It was followed in 1967 by the Japanese Taiyo Gyogyo Company, in association with Newfoundland's largest fish processor, Fisheries Products Limited, which reopened the old whaling plant at Williamsport.

251

Canada welcomed this new exploitation of her resources with open arms, proclaiming it to be the beginning of an enduring Canadian (sic) fishery that would bring great economic benefits to the maritime regions. To ensure that such would indeed be the case, the federal Department of Fisheries announced that the new industry would be closely supervised and rationally managed on such sound scientific principles as Maximum Sustainable Yield, whereby only the surplus whale population would be "harvested."

As was to be anticipated, there was no effective supervision and no real effort was made to regulate the hunt. The scientific basis for management that was adopted worked, not for the ongoing survival of the whales but to legitimize and even encourage their depletion to extinction. Canada, all on her own, chose to play the sleazy International Whaling Commission tune... one more time.

From 1964 until 1967, no restraints were placed on the whalers as to the number or kinds of rorquals they could kill. In 1967 they were finally forbidden to kill blues and humpbacks, which were almost effectively extinct in any case, and were given a finback quota determined by Fisheries scientists on the basis of the estimated Maximum Sustainable Yield of a local population that had been scientifically calculated to number between 7,000 and 10,000.

This first quota allowed the killing of 800 finners, but the best efforts of three whaling companies produced only 748 fin corpses. Perhaps, the scientists concluded, the quota might be a little high. They lowered it to 700 for 1968. This time, the whalers managed to fill it, but only just. Still a bit high perhaps? In 1969, it came down to 600 but the whalers only managed to land 576. Down it came again—to 470—yet the whalers were able to kill only 418. In 1972, the quota went down—to 360—and this time, by dint of Herculean efforts, the killer boats managed to meet it.

Now the experts reworked their data and concluded that the original fin whale stock must actually have been on the order of 3,000, not 10,000. They thereupon proposed a 1973 quota of 143 finners, presumably on the assumption that all of the original 3,000 were still alive and busily reproducing their kind.

The whalers could have told them otherwise. Having processed 4,000 finners, 900 seis, 123 sperms, 46 humpbacks, at least three blues, and one black right (together with hundreds of smaller whales) during the preceding eight years, and having probably killed, but failed to recover, an additional several hundred, they were running out of whales.

The "promising new Canadian whale fishery" of a Department of Fisheries' press release was in trouble. In the spring of 1972, in response to a query of mine about its prospects addressed to what had by then become the Fisheries Branch of a quaintly named department called Environment Canada, I received the following reply.

"The market conditions in the future, coupled with the limited availability of whales off our Atlantic coast, could make it uneconomic for the Canadian [sic] stations to continue to operate. The current policy of the Department is to permit a limited Canadian whaling activity based on sustainable annual yields estimated from the available scientific evidence."

In the autumn of 1972, I had a meeting with the Minister of the Environment, the Honourable Jack Davis, in my capacity as president of the Canadian branch of Operation Jonah, one of several international organizations working toward a general moratorium on commercial whaling. Davis was not only surprisingly sympathetic, he was actively encouraging. In fact, he as good as promised that Canada would make an end to commercial whaling in her territorial waters before the year was out. I left his office feeling euphoric. My delight was slightly dampened by a conversation with one of the minister's senior officials who, as I recall his words, had this to say.

"You came at a good time. Karlsen is about ready to close down for lack of whales; but naturally, he'd prefer for us to close him down. That way we'd have to provide compensation and also look after his shore people. The Japanese? No way do they want out. Not until there isn't a damn whale left alive. But yes, you'll likely get your ban."

At the end of 1972 the ban was duly promulgated, but it was initially limited to "large whales" in the Atlantic region. It was vague even as to exactly which species were to be protected. The door was left open for the future killing of whales whose populations could be considered "commercially viable." As we shall see in the next chapter, these included not only the minke, but pilot and white whales as well.

Imposition of the ban did not sit well with many bureaucrats, nor with some scientists. The latter may have been disgruntled because the ban would deny them specimens for dissection and examination, without which they could not amass the material on which many of the "papers" so essential to scientific advancement had been based.[4] Fisheries mandarins were displeased because it was, and remains, department policy that Canada's

---

[4] Between 1969 and 1971, Fisheries issued special permits allowing east-coast whalers to "take" seventy of the by then protected Atlantic humpbacks, in the interests of scientific inquiry. Forty-one were killed before the "take" was stopped on the strong recommendation of one departmental cetologist, who vigorously disagreed with the policy.

marine resources should be exploited to the fullest extent possible. Furthermore (as we shall see in Part V), it was established policy to seek the elimination of all marine mammals that might be competitive with the commercial fishery, either directly or indirectly. A number of whales and porpoises had been so stigmatized. The bureaucrats saw even a limited ban as interference with the department's internal dogma, and at the same time viewed the ban as a dangerous precedent for the future. They did what they could to subvert it.

During the late 1970s, one departmental expert claimed to have detected a notable recovery in the numbers of fin whales and to have established that exploitable stocks of seis were still available in Canadian waters. Despite the fact that another Fisheries scientist denied these claims, "an initiative" was taken to have the ban rescinded so that a Japanese whaling company could again begin "harvesting an otherwise under-utilized resource." However, word of what was afoot was leaked by a whale sympathizer and the likelihood of massive public condemnation made the proposal politically inexpedient, at least for the nonce. In 1980, the department once more tested the water by orchestrating the complaints of Newfoundland fishermen to the effect that whales were causing intolerable damage to nets and cod-traps, and therefore should be "controlled." But by then public opinion had swung so strongly to the side of the whales that a proposed whale control project, to be undertaken through a Japanese-financed commercial "harvest," had to be shelved.

Equally revealing of the attitude of the mandarins is the fact that, until 1982, Fisheries nominated a Canadian commissioner to the International Whaling Commission who was one of a small, intractable minority that for ten years stubbornly refused to accept a United Nations General Assembly recommendation for a worldwide moratorium on commercial whaling.

Attitudes and actions such as these inevitably give rise to scepticism about the validity and use of scientific data and the objectivity (if not the honesty) underlying government and industry policies for the "management" of marine life. Because the Canadian ban on killing rorquals *has* remained in place, small numbers of finners have returned to the sou'west coast of Newfoundland and the Gulf. Family pods of humpbacks once again range from Cape Cod to southern Labrador. Perhaps as many as three dozen blue whales are now to be found in northeastern seaboard waters. Minkes and seis disport themselves in the Bay of Fundy and up the St. Lawrence as far as the Saguenay.

While the ban remains in place there is hope for the surviving rorquals.

Yet those that are alive today are hardly more than a token remnant of the legions of their kind which, together with the vanished multitudes of black rights, bowheads, greys, belugas, and smaller whales, once made the north-western waters of the Atlantic Ocean truly deserving of the name—the Sea of Whales.

15
The Little Whales

In the spring of 1954, my father and I sailed his sturdy old ketch from Montreal downriver into the Gulf of St. Lawrence, bound for the Atlantic via the narrow Canso Strait. This was the last year the Gut, as the Strait is familiarly known, permitted free passage. A nearby mountain of granite was being demolished to form a massive causeway linking Cape Breton Island with the Nova Scotia mainland. By the time we approached it there remained a gap of only a hundred feet through which the tidal waters of the Atlantic were forced to funnel. They did so in a torrent that thundered and foamed in such fierce restraint that no vessel could have surmounted it.

We anchored to await slack water. It was a sweet morning with a soft green light suffusing the new-leafing forests on both sides of the Gut. I was looking with some awe at the roaring cataract when the curling lip of angry water began to sprout gleaming ebony eruptions. These came and went so rapidly I could not tell what they were. I stood up to see better and at that moment a dozen white-bellied, brown torpedoes, each the size of a small man, broke the surface alongside, curved four or five feet into the air, then plunged back into the water as smoothly as hot bullets passing through butter.

They were harbour porpoises, one of the smallest members of the whale kind. As I watched, fascinated, more and more of them debouched through the roaring gap and fell to circling in the calm backwater where we lay. Suddenly a group of about twenty turned abruptly east and headed back into the fury of falling water.

Even Atlantic salmon, most expert of all white-water fishes, would have been hard put to mount that monstrous cascade and I expected the little whales to be flung back from it in utter confusion. Instead they accelerated as if propelled by rockets, hit the downfall, vanished for a moment, and then were airborne, curving cleanly over the lip of the overflow and plunging into the swift but smooth waters beyond. And then—and this dumbfounded me—they turned in one sleek movement and plunged back down the chute.

I watched, enthralled, as group after group shot up the cascade, circled swiftly, and ran down again. Only as the tide began to turn, and the power of the waterfall waned, did they lose interest. The game was over. Pod by pod they began to drift westward toward the exit from the Gut.

PORPOISE

More than sixty species of porpoises and dolphins (the designations are generally interchangeable) inhabit the world's oceans together with a few freshwater lakes and rivers. The majority of those living in the northeastern approaches to America are pelagic, but some species, including the harbour porpoise, prefer inshore waters where, through unnumbered centuries, they were familiar to native tribes of the Atlantic littoral who hunted them for food.

Porpoises were very much in evidence in early historic times. Jacques Cartier commented on their abundance in the Gulf in the mid-1530s. Roberval reported "great store of porpoises" in the lower reaches of the St. Lawrence in 1542. In 1605, Champlain noted that they were "in such abundance [along the coasts of Acadia] that I can guarantee there was never a day or night during which we did not see and hear more than a thousand porpoises pass alongside our pinnace." Nicolas Denys wrote of the *poursille*, as it was called in French: "It goes always in large bands and is found everywhere in the sea. They go near the land following the bait [fishes]. They are good to eat. Black puddings and chitterlings are made from their tripes; its head is better than mutton, though not so good as that of veal."

So long as they were only killed in small numbers for food, whether by natives or Europeans, their populations remained unaffected. However, as the great whales became scarcer, it was inevitable that the little whales would catch the cold and calculating eye of commerce.

Commercial killing of porpoises for oil seems to have begun in the Cape Hatteras region as early as 1780. Thereafter increasing numbers of shoremen assaulted the porpoise schools from small boats, blazing away at them with smoothbore guns. Although the recovery rate was as low as one brought to land for every ten or a dozen fired upon, the little whales were so numerous that even with this colossal rate of wastage, hunting them was a paying proposition.

By the 1820s, hundreds of fishing communities from the Carolinas to Labrador were "fishing" porpoise, often as an adjunct to other fisheries. Some places, however, made such enterprises their main business. Net fisheries at Cape Cod and Grand Manan regularly took many thousands; and even more thousands were destroyed in drives by small boats resulting in strandings of entire herds that were then speared to death and their thin coats of blubber stripped off and sent to the trypots.

The history of the nineteenth-century porpoise fishery along the north shore of the Gulf of St. Lawrence is representative of what took place along the whole northeastern seaboard. By the 1870s, each of twelve major net fisheries in the Gulf was killing from 500 to 1,000 porpoises a year. In addition, many independent fishermen took a hand in the business. Napoleon Comeau has left us a description of how it was done in the 1880s. "Two good men in a canoe with first-rate rifles could if the weather was right get from 50 to 100 in a season. Porpoise oil was worth 75–80 cents a gallon. Only the fat was cut off and the bodies abandoned. They littered the beach for miles and the stench was indescribable."

The slaughter was maintained until early in the twentieth century and the inshore porpoises might well have been harried to regional extinction had not the increasing cheapness and availability of petroleum eroded the value of train oil in the early decades of the new century.

The commercial hunt had all but ended by 1914, but to this day porpoises are still shot by fishermen who believe the little whales not only compete with them for fishes but destroy their gear as well.[1] Furthermore, in recent years as many as 2,000 porpoises and dolphins have been killed annually as an unwanted by-catch of the Atlantic salmon driftnet and the Gulf mackerel fishery; further hundreds die in the new and deadly monofilament cod nets and traps. Additional hundreds perish from gunshot wounds inflicted by sportsmen who pursue the animals with fast motorboats in order to enjoy, in the words of one such, "good target practice at moving targets and get rid of vermin at the same time."

Although I have too often found their bullet-punctured bodies on the beaches of the Gulf and of Nova Scotia, I have encountered living porpoises all too seldom during the past thirty years. Most memorable was a summer evening in the open roadstead of Miquelon, in the St. Pierre archipelago off southeast Newfoundland. I was sitting alone on the fishermen's wharf keeping anchor watch on my schooner. The setting sun on my back grew warm, and I decided to strip off and have a swim. The water was frigid and I was about to turn back when a swirling of water to seaward caught my attention—and held it, riveted! Heading directly at me were two dozen scimitar-shaped dorsal fins slicing through the rose-tinted sunset sea in line ahead, at breakneck speed.

---

[1] A new fishery opened in Passamaquoddy Bay in the Bay of Fundy during the 1970s to supply feed to mink ranchers in the region. No figures are available, but it is believed that large numbers of porpoises have perished in consequence.

Almost paralyzed with fear, for my first thought was that I was under attack by sharks, I trod water. On they came, like great torpedoes. Then they were on me—alternately shooting past on either side, and so close I imagined I could feel the slick caress of their sleek bodies.

By then I knew what they were, having recognized their porpoise faces and the black-and-tan colours of the white-sided dolphin. Fear went from me and I waited in wonder as the school circled and returned, still moving at flank speed. This time the leader shot bodily out of the water and curved over my head like an enormous projectile, while his or her followers repeated the alternating passage past me. Then they were gone. I swam back to the pierhead and waited on it until full dark, but they did not return. They had, as seamen would say, made their signal—and departed.

The last time I saw living porpoises was in 1976. It was spring again and this time I was crossing the Canso causeway in a car. Approaching the eastern terminus of the canal through which all marine traffic in the Gut must now pass, I saw a group of people intently watching something in the water. I got out my binoculars and swept the nearby surface of the Strait. And there they were again—the sleek, swift little whales I had first encountered near this same spot twenty-two years earlier.

There were only seven of them this time and they were not slicing through the water with the explosive vim I had once marvelled at. They circled slowly, seemingly undecided, some fifty yards from the closed lock gate. As I watched and wondered, the lock master came out of his control room and joined me. He was an old acquaintance and, after exchanging greetings, I asked what the porpoises were up to, and did he see them often?

"Nope. Not no more. When the Gut was closed off they come in from seaward next summer by the hundreds—they and big herds of potheads [pilot whales] and even a few big whales, yes, and just millions and millions of herring and mackerel. But, of course, nothing could get through. The big whales turned around and went off to sea but the porpoises stuck it out till August. They'd come and go—like they would come back every few days to see was the way clear yet. One time a bunch came right into the lock when the eastern gate was open and I had half a mind to lock them on through, except the supervisor might have raised hell if I had.

"After that they never come back for years and years. But a couple years ago a bunch about this size showed up. Could be the same crowd. I don't know. Nor I don't know what they got in mind; but they sure seem to be waiting for something, don't they now?" He paused and glanced down the Gut toward the smoke-belching new industries built after the causeway was completed. "Anyhow, I hope those sons-a-bitching playboys with the speed-boats leave them be this time. Last year they chased them all one weekend and I hear they shot a couple—just for the hell of it."

Whether harbour porpoises and their several cousins will ever again swim in the Sea of Whales in anything other than token numbers remains a moot question. Although the outright kill by mankind has been much reduced, it appears that we are now attacking them indirectly and uninten-tionally through massive pollution of the seas. Extremely high concentrations of toxic chemicals have been found in the bodies of harbour porpoises from Nova Scotia and New Brunswick waters, and this affliction would seem to be worsening with time.

BELUGA

Several other kinds of small whales once lived in great abundance in the Sea of Whales. One of the most attractive was a creamy-white creature that reached a length of about seventeen feet and weighed up to a ton. Intensely sociable, it gathered in schools composed of hundreds of individuals. It was possessed of a voice clearly audible to human beings, which led to the name sea canary being bestowed on it by early whalers. It is known to us as the white whale or, more commonly, beluga.

The beluga is categorized as an Arctic species because in our times it sur-vives in significant numbers *only* in the Arctic. This was not always the case. When Cartier reached the upper estuary of the St. Lawrence in 1535, he found the waters teeming with "a species of fish which none of us had ever seen before...the body and head white as snow. There are a very large num-ber in this river. The [Indians] call them *Adhothuys* and told us they are very good to eat." In 1650, Pierre Boucher found the white whales all the way from the mouth of the Saguenay to the present site of Montreal. "One sees extraordinary numbers of them between Tadoussac and Quebec, leaping about in the River; they are very long and large and at least a barrel of oil may be reckoned on to be got from each." Champlain also commented on the "great numbers of white porpoises in the river" and noted that their oil was excellent and fetched a goodly price.

So did their skins, from which a good grade of morocco leather was manu-factured. Consequently, from as early as 1610 onwards, French colonists killed white whales in ever-increasing numbers. Beluga "fishing" sites were among the most sought-after perquisites in New France, and the early seigneurial grants along the river usually included specific and exclusive rights to fish for porpoises of all the several kinds, but especially for the white variety.

A special ordinance issued by the Intendant of New France in 1710 created a monopoly of the white porpoise fishery for six landowners at Rivière Ouelle; and an ordinance authorizing another such monopoly at Pointe aux Iroquois stated that it was "the King's will that as many such fisheries as possible be established in this country." The King's will was obeyed so enthusiastically that by mid-century there were at least eight white whale companies operating between Pointe des Monts and Île aux Coudres. Between them they seem to have killed several thousand beluga every year.

Indians of the St. Lawrence had been aware since time immemorial of a faculty of the white porpoises that remained unknown to science until late in the present century. This was the ability of the little whales to "see" their way through murky waters by using a form of echo location. Prehistoric Indians had discovered that interference with this system disoriented the animals and made them easier prey. They put their knowledge to especially effective use at Isle aux Coudres, where enormous schools of beluga swam upstream on the rising tide in pursuit of the baitfishes that comprised their principal food, returning downstream again on the ebb.

Once the whales had passed to the westward of the island, the Indians paddled out to the shoal ground surrounding the place and planted long lines of thin, resilient wands spaced several feet apart. Each line was angled slightly and terminated at the shore of the island. When the tide began to ebb at full force, its powerful current made the wands vibrate, generating what amounted to a wall of high frequency sound that the eastbound whales evidently interpreted as an impenetrable or at least dangerous obstacle. In their efforts to avoid it, some would swing toward the island and into the rapidly shoaling water over the mud flats. Here they were met by men braced waist-deep in the flood who harpooned them.

This ingenious system had supplied the Indians with the meat and oil they needed through untold generations; but it was not productive enough to satisfy the French. They wanted a means to slaughter the animals *en masse*. The one they devised for porpoises in general, but especially for the white porpoise, is described by Charlevoix in the 1720s.

"When the tide is out they plant, pretty near each other in the mud or sand, stout poles to which they tie nets in the form of a pouch...in such a manner that, when the fish has once passed through it, he cannot find his way out again...When the flood comes, these fishes, which give chase to herrings which always make toward the shore [and] which they are extremely fond of, are entangled in the nets where they are kept prisoners. In proportion as the tide ebbs you have the pleasure of seeing their confusion and fruitless struggles to escape. In a word they are left high and dry, and in such numbers that they are sometimes heaped upon one another...it is affirmed that some have been found to weigh three thousand pounds."

As I have noted, most cetologists are emphatic that the beluga is an Arctic species and that those found in the Gulf represent no more than a "small disjunct population that is probably a relic of a past colder period." In fact, the beluga of the Gulf originally comprised one of the largest single populations of their species extant. Nor were they narrowly limited to the St. Lawrence estuary. In 1670, Josselyn recorded the presence in New England of "the Sea-hare, as big as a Grampus [the orca, or killer whale] and as white as a sheet. There hath been of them in Blackpoint-Harbour, and some way up the river, though we could never take any of them, several have shot slugs at them but lost their labour." Nicolas Denys reported them amongst the porpoises of Cape Breton Island and Chaleur Bay. "Those which come near the land are of two kinds. The larger are all white, almost the size of a Cow...they yield plenty of oil." In the 1720s, Charlevoix recorded seeing "many of them on the coasts of Acadia in the Bay of Fundy." Even as late as 1876, the English traveller John Rowan wrote: "White porpoises visit the Bay [Chaleur] in considerable numbers...I am told one of these fish will yield oil to the value of $100." Rowan also reported them from the coasts of Cape Breton Island. The Micmacs fished them, along with other porpoises, from ancient times until the nineteenth century in the Bay of Fundy; and Dr. A.W.F. Banfield believed that a tiny remnant population might still have been in existence there as late as the 1970s, although this seems dubious. In short, the white whale was evidently at home almost everywhere in and around the Sea of Whales.

The large scale commercial fishery on the northwest shore of the Gulf estuary, and upstream at least as far as Île aux Coudres, continued without serious interruption until almost the middle of the twentieth century. It ended for the usual sorry reason. Not enough white whales remained to turn a profit.

That it had been well worthwhile in its time is clear. As late as the 1870s, 500 beluga were net-trapped during a single tide at Rivière Ouelle, and through the rest of the century that single station, which had been in continuous operation since as early as 1700, killed an average of 1,500 every year. However, by 1900 the kill had so far outrun the supply that only the factory at Rivière Ouelle and another on Île aux Coudres remained. The Île aux Coudres plant was closed in 1927, but the one at Rivière Ouelle continued in operation until 1944, by which time it was only able to kill a few score whales even in a good season.

What is singularly disgusting about those final years is that the fishery would probably have collapsed at least a decade earlier than it did, with the likelihood that enough beluga might have survived to maintain a viable population—had not the government of Quebec intervened. In 1932, Quebec began paying a bounty of $45 (a very large sum in the Depression years) for every white whale killed in provincial waters. The public excuse for this bloody largesse was the canard that beluga were destroying the salmon fishery. The real, but hidden reason for the bounty was to provide a subsidy to the Rivière Ouelle whaling company so that it could continue to function for a few more years.

Because salmon were indeed becoming scarce where they had once abounded, the official stigmatization of the white whale as the chief culprit turned every man's hand against it. Even after the termination of bounty payments, commercial fishermen, sportsmen, and sporting guides alike continued to make it their business to shoot every white whale they could. A questionnaire circulated amongst fishermen on the north shore in 1955 indicated that as many as 2,000 white whales may have been killed during the previous decade under the pretext that they were salmon-poaching vermin. In 1974, Jean Laurin, a graduate biology student studying what was left of the Gulf belugas (he estimated that no more than 1,000 then remained alive), encountered gunners on the cliffs overlooking coves frequented by the little whales, taking pot shots at them whenever they surfaced. When Laurin tried to put an end to this senseless persecution, he was rebuffed both by federal and provincial authorities, each of which claimed that the *other* had jurisdiction over the matter and so refused to take any action to protect the whales.

Not all governments have treated the white whales so shabbily. Odd as it may seem to those unfamiliar with its geography, Manitoba harbours a white whale population. The pods are strung out along the west coast of Hudson Bay where, through more than 200 years, they were commercially hunted by the Hudson's Bay Company. That fishery went into decline early in the twentieth century as a result of the falling value of marine oils but was revived after World War II by a new breed of entrepreneurs. These developed a lucrative business killing belugas in the estuary of the Churchill River, a major calving and nursery ground, and shipping the meat a thousand and more miles south by rail to the Prairies where it was sold for mink feed. Between 1949 and 1960, more than 5,000 beluga were processed at Churchill for this trade. Nearly as many more seem to have been killed but either not recovered or abandoned when the small packing plant was unable to handle them.

I witnessed that sanguinary slaughter on three separate occasions during the 1950s. Big freight canoes driven by outboard engines and manned by hunters, mostly armed with old .303 military rifles firing hard-nosed bullets, criss-crossed the shoal waters of the estuary which were alive with hundreds of white whales. According to the season, the targets included pregnant females, nursing females, and calves. If a volley proved quickly fatal to a beluga, it was gaffed and towed ashore; however, if it was only wounded it would usually escape. With so many other targets available, the gunners seldom wasted time and energy pursuing cripples.

On one occasion I watched three gunners in two canoes fire at least sixty rounds into a dense school of perhaps thirty whales that had been driven into such shoal water that they could not fully submerge. Although this fusillade was delivered at point-blank range, only two corpses were recovered.

The market for mink food collapsed during the early 1960s for reasons that will become apparent later in this chapter. Nothing daunted, the Churchill whalers then began canning *muktuk*—the whale's thick, inner skin—as an exotic snack to be sold to the kind of people who serve chocolate-covered bees at cocktail parties. This abomination ended in 1970 when it was discovered that Hudson Bay belugas were so contaminated with mercury—a pollution by-product of mining and pulp mill operations on the rivers leading into the Bay—that they were unfit for human consumption. Not to be discouraged, the operators of the Churchill fishery sought other ways to profit from whale killing. One of these involved using the *outer* skin of white whales as a material from which leather for the high-fashion trade could be manufactured. But by far the most appalling stroke of entrepreneurial ingenuity was an attempt to make the white whales central to a form of northern tourism—not as creatures to be seen and admired in life, but as targets for sport hunters.

In 1973, I received a glossy, illustrated flier extolling the pleasures to be had from shooting belugas—*Adventure and Excitement in a Thrilling Chase to Catch a Two-Ton Monster of the Sea*. This sent me posthaste to Manitoba and the office of the provincial Premier, Edward Schreyer. I put the case for the whales to him and he promised an immediate investigation. Shortly thereafter his New Democratic government banned the further killing of belugas in Manitoba waters for commerce or for sport. This was a unilateral decision taken despite the fact that the federal government of Canada, which claims jurisdiction over all sea mammals, refused to recognize such a ban; and despite the fact that it was denounced within the province as unwarranted interference with free enterprise.

Schreyer's enlightened action has benefited both the beluga and the people of Churchill. The white whale population in Churchill's vicinity has increased since 1973 and hundreds of nature-watchers journey there each summer to see the sea canaries in life. More local people and businesses draw more profit from this new approach than ever they did during the years when Churchill harbour ran red with the blood of butchered whales.

The story of the white whales in the Gulf has no such happy ending. In the summer of 1973, two remarkable women, Leone Pippard and Heather Malcolm, volunteered to help Project Jonah in its attempts to save what was left of the whale tribes in Canadian waters. Pippard and Malcolm undertook to study the belugas of the Gulf to obtain data from which a campaign for their preservation could be developed. To that end they spent several summers living in a camper truck near the mouth of the Saguenay River, devoting their waking hours to observing the whales. Their efforts were derided by some doctrinaire scientists, one of whom, Pippard remembers, "laughed in our faces when we told him we were going to learn something about white whales. He said we'd learn as much by going home and having six kids each."

Although there was much evidence of previous abundance—one old man told Pippard that in his youth the whales had been "as many as the whitecaps on the St. Lawrence River"—by 1975 the subjects of the study seemed very hard to find. When the women undertook a census, they found to their dismay that fewer than 350 belugas remained and that their numbers were evidently still shrinking year by year. Pippard produced a report for the federally sponsored Committee on the Status of Endangered Wildlife in Canada, and, in June of 1983, had the satisfaction of seeing it accepted. In the meantime the survivors of the St. Lawrence belugas had been granted nominal protection from hunting as of 1979, but the efficacy of that protection was then, and still remains, in some doubt.

When I attempted to find out why this last pathetic remnant of a ravaged species had for so long been refused our help, the official answer I got was chillingly revealing. "An extinct population that was of no real value anyhow is one that will give us no future problems and cause no pain. Furthermore, the niche vacated by such a species can usually be filled by another that *will* contribute to human welfare and prosperity."

Certainly the federal Department of Fisheries and Oceans does not seem overly optimistic about the Gulf belugas' ultimate survival. It currently predicts that "at the present rate of decline the [white] whales could disappear from the St. Lawrence in as little as two years." One wonders which species the department would prefer to fill that vacant niche.

NARWHAL

A close companion of the beluga in Arctic and sub-Arctic waters is the narwhal, noted for the male's immensely long single tusk, which gave it the name sea unicorn. Although as late as the 1860s it was regularly seen by Inuit, and sometimes killed by them as far south as mid-Labrador, it has since vanished from those waters. Its story is as grim as that of the other threatened species of small whales. Totally extirpated from European Arctic regions, where it once seems to have been common, it is now found only in west Greenland waters and in the eastern Canadian Arctic. Here it suffers such heavy predation from native hunters (mainly for its tusk, which is worth up to $50 a pound to curio collectors and to apothecaries in Oriental countries) that its remaining population, thought to be less than 20,000, is steadily shrinking toward the point of no return.

CHANEY JOHN

One of the most remarkable of the small whales is also one of the least understood. A deep-water species, its western clans winter off the coasts of Nova Scotia and New England, migrate across the Grand Banks, and summer as far north as the ice edge. For the most part, they live their lives unseen by man, and until less than a century ago unmolested by him. For some now-forgotten reason, nineteenth-century British whalers, who were their first human enemies, named them Chaney Johns. Today, we know them by the unlovely name of bottlenose whale.

Chaney John is a toothed whale, of the same family as porpoises and dolphins, but can grow to thirty-five feet in length and weigh as much as eight tons. Its food consists mainly of squid taken at great depths. Extremely strong and energetic, it may be the champion mammalian diver of the world. There is a record of a harpooned individual taking out three-quarters of a mile of line in what appeared to be a vertical dive and surfacing *two hours later* in almost the same spot, still full of life.

Although abundant in northern waters during the summer, Chaney John was of little potential value to whalers, prior to the 1870s and the advent of the harpoon gun, because, as well as being hard to kill, it was a "sinker." Nevertheless, it was of at least peripheral interest, as witness this account by Fridtjof Nansen cruising off the east Greenland coast.

"We saw numbers of bottlenose whales, often lying quite still in front of the bow or in our wake. Herd after herd bore right down upon the ship, then went round her and inspected us from every point of view.

"I regret to say that we made several attempts to shoot them with our express-rifles; but they took no notice. Then we decided to fire a volley.

"Three bottlenoses were heading straight for us; they came up astern, and one of them stopped and lay motionless about 20 yards away from the ship. The gunners stood together on the half-deck aft. Counting up to three we all blazed away, but the whale lifted his tail high in the air, lashed the water with it, and disappeared. Some blubber which it left floating on the surface was much appreciated by the gulls.

"The whale did not worry itself much about our bullets, apparently, for we afterwards saw it swimming along quite gamely with the others. We knew it was the same one by the gulls which gathered on the water wherever it had been, no doubt finding blood and blubber there.

"The captain suggested that it might be interesting to lower a boat and see how near we could get to them. This was accordingly done and we rowed towards one or two whales which were lying quite still. We were able to approach so near that we could almost touch them with our oars. Then suddenly they lifted their tails in the air, brought them down with a whack that drenched the boat with spray, and disappeared. Presently they came up again close to us, swam round the boat and had a good look at us from every point of view, then lay just under the surface of the sea, turning on one side to watch us with their small eyes.

"Once the captain laid hold of the tail of one of them with the boat-hook. The whale heaved up its tail, brought it down with a splash, and dived. If we rowed on a bit they followed, half a dozen of them at once swimming alongside of us, now a little in front, now a little behind, but always quite close to us; they were evidently extremely inquisitive.

"I cannot deny that we wished we had possessed some sort of instrument to fasten on to these big fellows, for they would have been sporting steeds to drive, as Markussen once discovered when he 'harnessed' one of them. He told us the story himself on board the 'Viking'.

"'I couldn't bear seeing all this blubber going a-begging year after year in the sea round my ship', he related. 'Well, one fine day I saw a lot of bottlenoses about. So I rigged up a boat with a harpoon, and took three whale-lines to be on the safe side...Well, we soon fell in with a fine fellow who came up right ahead of the boat. When I stuck the harpoon into him, he made a hell of a splash and then sounded; the line ran out so fast that you could smell burning...The first line ran out, and the second soon followed; then he started on the third line, and it ran out every bit as fast as the other two had done.

"'When he had taken the lot of it he pulled the boat under too, straight on without a stop; down it went, and left us behind kicking about in the water.

"'The men yelled like the devil—they couldn't swim; but I told 'em to stow it, and gave each of 'em an oar to hang on to.

"'As luck would have it the "Vega" had steam up, and could come at once and haul us out.

"'But them fish are the very devil to stay under water. Though the sea was like glass and we kept a sharp look-out from the crow's nest all day in the hope of seeing our boat, neither boat nor fish did we ever see again. He certainly didn't come up anywhere between us and the horizon.

"'I felt pretty sore at losing such a good boat.

"'Well I wasn't going to risk another boat, but I thought I'd be even with him all the same. Next year I took some petroleum casks with me. I rigged up three of these casks, fixing them on to three new whale-lines, and laid them all ready at the bottom of the boat.

"'Then we started out again. Well, I made fast to a fish, and down he went in the same way. The first line ran right out and we chucked the first cask overboard. But he pulled it on down with him full pelt as before, without stopping a moment. Then the second line ran out, and we chucked the second cask into the water, but it just went after the first and disappeared in the same non-stop fashion; while the third line went running out as fast as though we hadn't had any casks at all.

"'At length we chucked the last cask overboard; but I'll be hanged if it didn't go under every bit as quick as the others. So we'd lost the whale and the lines and the casks, and we never saw them again. This whale didn't come up anywhere within sight either, so far as we could make out.

"'Who'd have thought the old fish had so much go in him? Anyway, I gave him up after that.'"

About 1877, with the bowhead almost gone, some Scots whalers working the northwestern grounds began killing Chaney Johns using bomb-lances and grenades. As Nansen had discovered, their friendliness and curiosity made them easy targets. Moreover, they were bound by extraordinarily strong family ties and would not abandon a wounded member of the pod, as Captain David Gray, the first Scot to hunt them, found:

"They are gregarious in their habits, going in herds of from four to ten, although many different herds are frequently in sight at the same time. The adult males very often go by themselves; but young bulls, cows and calves, with an old male as a leader, are sometimes seen together.

"They are very unsuspicious, coming close alongside the ship, round about and underneath the boats, until their curiosity is satisfied. The herd never leaves a wounded companion so long as it is alive; but they desert it immediately when dead; and if another can be harpooned before the previous struck one is killed, we often capture the whole herd, frequently taking ten, and on one occasion fifteen, before our hold over them was lost."

In 1882, Gray, commanding the Dundee whaler *Eclipse*, killed 203 Chaney Johns off northern Labrador. Thereafter they became increasingly sought after, particularly by Norwegian whalers newly equipped with Svend Foyn's terrible harpoon gun. By 1891, seventy Norwegian killer boats were hunting them. Every year thereafter until early in the twentieth century, the Norwegians landed an average of 2,000 and "struck" and lost a great many more. The cumulative destruction was so enormous that by 1920 the whalers could only find and kill 200–300. At this point the "fishery" was abandoned as being insufficiently rewarding.

That the Chaney Johns had not been totally exterminated was due to the dispersal of the few survivors over such a vast waste of ocean that whalers could no longer find them in worthwhile numbers. They, however, could find each other and during the next half-century their pods began to grow again. Given sufficient time they might eventually have recovered something approaching their former abundance—but that was not to be.

As we have seen, during the 1920s and 1930s, Norwegian whalers turned their fatal attention to the titanic slaughter of great whales in southern waters. However, as that massacre reached its bloody climax and began to wane from lack of victims, more and more Norwegians returned to hunting "second-string" whales in waters nearer home. Although the minke (soon to be discussed) was chief amongst these, the awesomely efficient Norwegians discovered that some few Chaney Johns were again available in western waters and began killing them as well. World War II did not bring a halt to Norwegian whaling, which continued under the aegis of the Germans; but it did limit it to home waters with the result that, being a pelagic species, few Chaney Johns were caught. But when that war ended, Norwegian whalers began going deep-sea again.

Equipped with a new generation of extremely fast and efficient small-whale killers, they carried death and destruction first to Scottish waters, thence ever westward to the Faeroes, Iceland, Greenland, and the northeastern approaches to America. Along the way they devastated the few remaining pods of Chaney Johns.

In 1962, I went aboard one of their small-whale catchers in Thurso harbour in northern Scotland. The skipper, who was also the gunner of his seventy-foot killer, cheerfully explained the nature of his business.

"We are just a meat shop, you might call us," he said with a laugh. "We fit out from Bergen and just keep going west 'til we find whales. Minkes is best for us, bottlenose is next, but if we don't get enough of them, there is always killers and potheads [orcas and pilot whales].

"After the whale is struck with our nice 50-mm gun, we bring him alongside. If he is not too big we haul him on deck. If not, we put a sling around him to keep him steady, then the lads go overboard with spiked boots and cutting knives. We don't have too much refrigerated stowage space, you understand, so we mostly just cut out the prime cuts: steaks, sirloins, roasts. The rest? Well, the sharks got to have their suppers too."

I asked about the market for meat and was told that minke commanded a very good price in Norway, where some people preferred it to beef, but that bottlenose was only fit for pet food. When the kill was greater than the home market could absorb, the frozen meat was shipped to the apparently insatiable Japanese.

The second depredation visited on the Chaney John was less severe than the first only because there were far fewer whales to kill. It was, however, more thorough and has resulted in the near elimination of the species in the North Atlantic. Between 1962 and 1967, Karl Karlsen's fleet operating out of Blandford, Nova Scotia, killed eighty-seven Chaney Johns, but met with no more during the remaining five years the station was in operation. Between 1969 and 1971, long-range whaling vessels from Norway patrolling through the seas off the Canadian Atlantic coast mainly after minkes killed about 400 bottlenose whales as an incidental catch, but by 1972 they were only able to find and kill seventeen. In later years, they could find none.

In the opinion of one Canadian cetologist, Chaney John may be destined to become the second whale species, after the Atlantic grey whale, to become extinct at the hands of man, this despite the fact that, since 1977, the North Atlantic bottlenose has had "provisional protected status" under International Whaling Commission regulations.

MINKE

"Small-whale quartet" is the name given, half humorously perhaps, by cetologists and fisheries management experts to the group that includes the bottlenose, orca, pilot, and minke whales. Of the four, the minke has been and still remains the most important to Norwegian whalers, the chief exploiters of the quartet.

The thirty-foot, ten-ton minke is, it will be remembered, a rorqual—the smallest member of that family. Whale scientists, who are notoriously conservative about such matters, concede that as late as the 1950s it numbered better than a quarter of a million in southern seas and probably more than 100,000 in the North Atlantic. It had suffered only slightly from commercial whaling before World War II because it was relatively small, but after men finished with the human slaughter the minke's turn came.

A group of Norwegian businessmen arrived in Newfoundland in 1946 with a proposal to establish a small-whale fishery there. They were greeted with open arms and within the year had built a modern processing plant, Arctic Fisheries, near the village of South Dildo in Trinity Bay—a mighty arm of the sea that for centuries had been renowned for its plethora of whales. Supplied by two ultra-modern killer boats, the plant was designed to produce marine oil for the margarine trade and frozen meat to be sold in Europe and Japan. In later years, Arctic Fisheries operated with Japanese affiliations, killing large whales as well as small, but at first it concentrated on the small-whale quartet. Orcas and bottlenoses proved scarce but an abundance of minkes and pilots made up for that. Because minkes were individually much larger and therefore more valuable than pilots, they were the first choice of the killer boats.

Between 1947 and 1972, the company processed slightly more than 1,000 minkes. Yet, although typical of its kind, the Dildo operation represented a mere drop in the bloody bucket of worldwide minke exploitation. Norwegian "small quartet" whalers ranging the North Atlantic landed 16,000 minkes between 1953 and 1957. Thereafter, the annual yield began to decline until by 1975 the catch was down to a mere 1,800. It continues to decline as the last remnants of the eastern North Atlantic minkes are hauled up on the greasy decks of Norwegian processing vessels.

A numerical assessment of the total kill is difficult to arrive at, but since some of the Norwegian boats are known to have had loss rates of 80 per cent, and considering that the reported landings between 1939 and 1975 totalled nearly 75,000, the death tally for the North Atlantic minke tribes must by now be well over 100,000.

The North Atlantic is not the only current minke killing ground of note. In 1969, Antarctic pelagic whaling fleets began taking minkes in lieu of the larger species that by then had mostly been extirpated in southern waters. During the succeeding three years Norwegian, Japanese, and Soviet Antarctic factory ships processed nearly 20,000 minkes. This was the beginning of the last hurrah for whaling in the far south. When it concludes, as it will soon if for no other reason than a lack of whales, peace will return to those cold and distant seas—but it will be the peace of the dead and the departed.

In the Sea of Whales the commercial massacre has ended. It is now possible for dedicated whale watchers in the right places, at the right seasons, to see there some of the last survivors of the minke kind. If we can forbear from turning on them once again, the minke may yet escape the vortex of extinction.

THE PILOT

About 1592, a cartographer named Petrus Plancius drew a map of *Nova Francia* and the New World. Like many maps of that era it was illustrated with vignettes of life. One such is a lively and detailed picture of whaling on the east coast of Newfoundland.

The scene is the foot of a deep bay. The foreground is filled with rowboats, each carrying two men. This flotilla has just completed driving a school of small whales onto a gently sloping beach and, while some of the boatmen attack the stranded animals with lance-like darts, others on shore are already at work stripping off the blubber. In the distance, a tryworks sends a great coil of black smoke into the sky. The whales, not much larger than the boats, have bulbous, protruding foreheads. Considering their size and circumstances they can only be identified as pilot whales. And this picture could, with some small variations, equally well represent a scene from several thousand years ago; or from the 1950s.

The sleek, black pilot is gregarious, living in schools or clans containing up to several hundreds of individuals of all ages and both sexes. Growing to twenty feet in length, and weighing two to three tons, they sport elegant dove-grey throat patches, long and flexible front flippers, and watermelon-sized, oil-filled bulges on their foreheads. This peculiar but not unattractive feature, which serves as part of the animal's echo-location equipment, gives rise to the inelegant name of pothead, especially in vogue in Newfoundland.

Its chief food is a small squid that schools in almost unimaginable numbers. These squid live in the deeps well away from shore throughout most of the year, and there the pilots pursue them, diving into darkness to depths perhaps as great as those achieved by Chaney John. However, during the summer the squid strike in to shore to mate and lay their eggs, coming right up to the landwash and sometimes even entering brackish lagoons and freshwater streams. The pilots fearlessly venture after them and, in so doing, expose themselves to the terrible danger of stranding.

Accidental strandings most frequently take place when the little whales chase squid into shallow, murky waters. Perhaps due to sickness, or to some physical disability, the leader sometimes seems unable to use his or her echo-sounding sense, and so, becoming aurally as well as visually blind, goes aground. A grounded whale is usually powerless to help itself and the pilot is no exception. The rest of the clan, being strongly conditioned to follow its "pilot," as well as to assist one of its kind in trouble, tends to close in. In the chaos that ensues, an entire clan can strand itself. If the tide is rising, or if there is a sufficiently high sea breaking, some may escape. Otherwise, they die.

In prehistoric times, such accidents must have been spectacularly rewarding to shoreside scavengers, including man. Eventually our ancestors realized that they had no need to wait passively for such gifts from the gods but could arrange for them to happen on a regular basis. So the whale drive was born.

When a clan of pilots swept into a fiord or dead-end bay in northern Europe, following the squid, a rabble of skin boats or dugouts would put out from shore and attempt to bar the whales' avenue of escape. Men beat on hollow logs, howled and shrieked, pounded the gunwales with paddles, and churned the water into foam. Later generations added trumpets, horns, and bells.

The purpose of this din was to panic the whales into heedless flight toward shore. The noise also tended to disrupt their delicate sonar sense, thus masking the dangers posed by the shoals ahead until it was too late to turn back. Once the driven whales were wallowing helplessly in the shallows, the boats would push in amongst them; hunters stabbing ferociously with spears, lances, even swords, attempting to immobilize as many of the creatures as they could.

Exploitation of North American pilot whales by Europeans must have begun early in the sixteenth century since, by the time of Petrius Plancius, it had become sufficiently important to warrant its advertisement on his map. By the eighteenth century it had become a traditional seasonal occupation for fishermen living in the deep bays of the northeast coast of Newfoundland and at other suitable drive sites as far south as Cape Cod. Some Newfoundlanders found a way to make extra profit from it by substituting pothead oil for the more valuable seal oil and selling it to the rapacious St. John's merchants—a classic case of the biter being bit.

So long as it remained localized and small in scale, this fishery posed no major threat to the continued existence of a species that evidently mustered on the order of 60,000 members in Newfoundland waters alone. Until the middle of the twentieth century the annual kill over the whole of the northeastern approaches seems seldom to have exceeded 2,000, except for a few years in the 1880s when a drive fishery on the Cape Cod beaches accounted for that many every season. Even the latter-day Norwegian small-whale fishery did no great damage initially, since it only killed pilots when nothing better was at hand.

In the 1950s, that all changed.

Newfoundland, it will be remembered, joined Canada in 1949. The man who claims personal credit for this confederation and who became the first Premier of Canada's tenth province is Joseph Smallwood, a one-time labour organizer who, by 1950, had been transformed into a born-again believer in entrepreneurial capitalism. Smallwood was determined to industrialize Newfoundland and, to this end, sent emissaries to scour the Western world with offers of financial assistance, free land, tax benefits, and any manner of other inducements that might persuade new enterprises to come to Newfoundland. Perhaps the most seductive inducement was the offer of a free hand to "develop" Newfoundland's natural resources.

Amongst those who descended on the island with schemes ranging from building a machine-gun arsenal to a condom factory was one representing mainland mink ranchers. He explained to Smallwood that the mink industry, then largely based in the western provinces, where a combination of the right climate and access to the cheap meat of wild horses had made it immensely profitable, was facing difficulties. The wild horses had almost all been converted into mink feed and the ranchers were forced to buy beluga meat, which had to be shipped all the way from Churchill at great cost. The proposal was that the mink industry relocate in Newfoundland and thereby make that province a world centre for the production of luxury furs.

Smallwood was much enamoured of the idea, which certainly had more glamour attached to it than did the condom plant. When he inquired what would be wanted from the province, he was told it would suffice if Newfoundland paid the costs of moving the ranchers east, provided free land, subsidized the construction of new ranches, and provided an unlimited supply of meat for mink feed. Although Smallwood was only too happy to acquiesce, he was somewhat uncertain about the meat supply. Where would that come from? Ah, said the representative, from a source that is presently doing nobody any good, not earning a penny for Canada: namely, the pilot whale.

Splendid, said Smallwood. Bring on the mink!

Since Newfoundland was now part of Canada and its marine resources therefore came under the jurisdiction of the federal government, Ottawa had to be consulted. The federal Department of Fisheries enthusiastically embraced the proposal. It also instructed its scientific experts to assess pilot whale "stocks" and draw up a management program for "harvesting" them.

Everything was now going swimmingly. The only problem was how best to "harvest" the whales. Happily, the owners of the Dildo whale processing plant proved most co-operative.

The chosen method of destruction proved to be an innovative combination of old and new. During slack intervals when the three killer boats then supplying Arctic Fisheries were not harpooning humpbacks, finners, seis, and minkes, they carried out sweeps of Trinity Bay, locating pilot clans—sometimes seven or eight of them—at distances of as much as thirty miles from Dildo. Through the skilful use of ultrasonic underwater transmitters, combined with deafening engine and propeller noises to confuse and terrorize the whales, the killer boats would herd the pilots toward the foot of Trinity Bay.

Three killing beaches had been selected there, adjacent to the outports of New Harbour, Chapel Arm, and Old Shop. Having been alerted that a drive was starting, fishermen from these places would stand by at sea in a variegated collection of trap skiffs, power dories, long-liners, and outboard-engined "sporting" boats. Radio contact kept everyone informed of what was happening, and when the knife-edged bows of the killer boats foamed into view, boatmen and shoremen alike were ready to receive the pilot clans, which by then had disintegrated into a disoriented and exhausted mob fleeing in panic from it knew not what.

About a mile off the chosen beach, the killers "delivered" the results of the round-up to the fishermen, whose boats now formed a curved line of "beaters" behind the whales. In the words of a journalist hired to write a publicity handout for the federal Department of Fisheries: "This is perhaps the most thrilling phase of the hunt, certainly the most noisy. Coursing back and forth behind the potheads the boatriders create a cacophonous din—beating on drums, slapping oars in the water, throwing stones, yelling and halooing—with the staccato noise of the open exhaust motors overriding all...the drive continues into the shallow water at the edge of the beach where the struggling whales stir up blinding mud and silt...the whales are killed by lancing."

The killing was not quite as clean and easy as described. Individual whales might be stabbed scores of times, often by boys ten years of age and upwards using knives lashed to sticks. It was no surprise to the blood-drenched butchers on the beach to discover that some of the whales they were cutting up were still alive. Almost completely immobilized by their own weight, such unfortunate victims could only flex their flukes in agony as cutting spades sliced through their flesh.

What was even worse was the practice of holding live whales on the beach. When so many had been stranded that the flensers could not deal with them, the surplus animals were sometimes "preserved alive" by hauling them clear of high-tide mark with tractors or teams of horses and left high and dry. During cool and cloudy weather they might endure for as much as three or four days, dying by inches, before the butchers finally got around to them.

The first season of this new fishery—the summer of 1951—was a smashing success. The fact that only two mink farms had yet been established in Newfoundland, and neither had freezing or meat storage facilities, did not detract from that success. By summer's end, at least 3,100 pilot whales had been slaughtered on the beaches near Dildo—and mostly left to rot. Meat was removed from less than a hundred corpses, and much of even this went bad before it could be used by the mink ranchers.

All that was salvageable from this colossal shambles was several hundred gallons of the light and viscous oil found in the melon on the pilot's head. This oil is very stable at a wide range of temperatures and, like that of the sperm whale, commands a premium price for use as a lubricant in fine instruments and in guided and ballistic missiles.

The situation had improved by 1955. Construction of a freezing plant in which whale meat could be stored, together with the installation of a "corral" of buoyed netting in which the surplus animals from a drive could be held alive until "taken to the beaches for processing on an assembly line basis," at least reduced the wastage. It did not reduce the scale of the destruction. This had increased with each passing year until, in 1956, it reached the astounding total of *10,000 pilot whales in that single season.*

The mink industry was now flourishing and had become so lucrative that the Premier himself became part-owner of a ranch. Women of fashion and wealth all over the civilized world were wearing the latest pastel shades of mutant mink from Newfoundland. Unfortunately, even though the fur farms had expanded by leaps and bounds they could not begin to use anything like the quantity of pilot whales that were now being slaughtered. Nevertheless, the overkill was considered justifiable because of the increased production of melon oil.

It seemed that the pilot whale had found its place and purpose in the human scheme of life. Then things began to go askew. In 1957 the killers were only able to butcher 7,800 whales; and thereafter the size of the pilot herd mysteriously declined until, by 1964, only 3,000 could be landed. However, according to experts of the Department of Fisheries, the decrease was apparent rather than real. It was probably due, they explained, not to over-harvesting, but to temporary alterations in the migratory patterns of the pilot whales' chief prey, the squid, brought about by "changed hydrographic factors." The experts predicted that the squid would soon return and bring the whales. Meantime, it was suggested, why not feed the mink on minkes? This play on words was considered amusing enough to warrant its publication in a staid research bulletin devoted to population dynamics.

In due course, the squid (which do tend to be cyclic) did return. But the great clans of pilot whales did not. They could not—because they had been destroyed. In a single decade, *more than 48,000 of them had died on the beaches of Trinity Bay*. One would have thought that, with this figure in hand, Fisheries management experts and their scientific advisers might have reached the logical conclusion and called a halt to the massacre before it was too late. That they did not do so may seem inexplicable; nevertheless, it is a fact.

In 1967, the total kill went down to 739. By 1971, it was down to six!

By then the pilot whale clans that had once enlivened the waters of Newfoundland and, in migration, the seas as far south as Cape Cod, had been virtually exterminated—not by accident or by miscalculation, but with deliberation, in the name of that most holy of modern icons, the gross god Profit.

No one was even taken to task for this horrendous bloodletting, this massive act of biocide, perhaps because it took place in one of the world's more "advanced" nations, where such crimes can readily be rationalized on the basis of economic determinism. Yet if an emergent African country were to slaughter some 60,000 elephants simply to supply the luxury trade with ivory, we can be sure such an act would be loudly denounced by us as a barbarous outrage.

There is an epilogue. Having been responsible for the depletion of wild horse herds in Alberta, beluga whales at Churchill, and the near extinction of pilot whales in Newfoundland, the mink ranchers again began to experience difficulties maintaining an adequate level of profits. For a while they fed their animals on minke meat, but when that whale, too, was reduced to near the vanishing point, they were forced by lack of any other available mammalian substitutes to switch to fish. Such a diet proved incapable of producing the quality of fur demanded by discerning women, and so the Great Newfoundland Mink Bubble burst—pricked, as it were, by the phallus of unbridled greed.

So ends the story of how the Sea of Whales became a Sea of Slaughter as, one by one, from the greatest to the least, each in turn according to its monetary worth, the several cetacean nations perished in a roaring holocaust fuelled by human avarice.

Now that there are no longer enough of them remaining to be of any significant commercial value, the fires that consumed their kinds are burning down. But it is unlikely—our instincts being what they are—that even the far-flung scattering of survivors will ever be secure from our rapacity unless, and until, they receive worldwide protection.

Surely this is the least that we can do to make atonement for the evil we have done to them.

And it *was* evil—of that, make no mistake.

PART V

Finfeet

Two great families of mammals have made the seas their homes. Whales are one. The other I call finfeet. It is composed of seals, walrus, and related swimmers whose hind feet have been modified into fins, or flippers. Compared to whales, finfeet are latecomers to the oceanic world; but they have nevertheless lived there for a much longer time than recognizable human beings have existed on this planet.

Finfeet are, and always have been, much better known to us than whales because most have retained close ties with the terrestrial world. The names we have given them testify to the sense of familiarity we feel: sea horse, sea cow, sea wolf, sea elephant, sea lion; these are but a few examples.

When the first European adventurers sailed into the northwestern approaches to the New World they found the seas thronged with finfeet, including those of five major kinds. One of these was the massive walrus. Two others, grey and harbour seals, lived in close association along all the coasts and were permanent residents, bearing their young on beaches and islands. The two remaining major species, harp and hood seals, lived, and still do, in a world apart. In summer, they range the High Arctic seas. In winter and well into spring, they form enormous aggregations in the Gulf of St. Lawrence and just to the north of Newfoundland, where they bear their young on the drifting world of the pack ice. These are the ice seals, and they seldom voluntarily come on land.

The abundance of finfeet in aboriginal times must have been truly astounding. The ice seals alone could not have numbered less than 10 million.

All five species became grist to the mill of human greed as Europeans set about the exploitation of the northeastern seaboard. One was totally extirpated; another so reduced in numbers that, for a time, it was believed to be extinct in North America. The remaining three suffered and continue to suffer such depredation at human hands that, if no halt is made, it may well prove fatal to their survival.

There are those in authority—men entrusted by our society to husband "our animal resources"—who are, as we shall see, committed to just such ultimate destruction of the finfeet kind.

16
Sea Tuskers

All islands are imbued with mystery, but few so darkly as Sable Island. Cast adrift in the thunder of the Atlantic a hundred miles off the Nova Scotian coast, it is a new-moon sliver of shining sand where no dry land has any right to be. Unseen shoals curve for many miles beyond its crescent tips, forming twin scythes that have reaped a full share of men and ships and earning the island its grim sobriquet: Graveyard of the North Atlantic.

Such is its dark side, yet when our European forebears first glimpsed its shifting shores it was a bright haven of fecund life. Here is how it might have seemed in the discovery years at the beginning of the 1500s.

It is a June day and the high sky is streaked with tendrils of cirrus cloud. A puffy nor'east breeze tells of dirty weather in the offing but, for the moment, the sun burns brazenly over this nameless island where no man has ever walked.

A milky beach hones its edge in the heavy roll of the unquiet ocean; but this gleaming scimitar is discoloured here and there by rough-textured patches, each of which is several acres in extent. Closer examination reveals that they are composed of thousands of immense, cylindrical creatures crowded so close to one another that they appear to be almost a single entity. Most are sprawled lethargically on their backs in a state of sun-drugged apathy, careless that their exposed bellies are beginning to glow a warning shade of pink.

Goggle-eyed faces, spiky whiskers, deep-wrinkled cheeks and jowls seem faintly reminiscent of a multitude of Colonel Blimps—except that each, no matter what its age or sex, carries a down-curving pair of gleaming, ivory tusks. Those gracing the 3,000-pound bulls are as long as a man's forearm and wrist-thick at the base. They glitter in the sunlight, imparting to their ponderous owners an aura of primal power suggestive of fearsome possibilities should they be roused to rage. These are walrus, tuskers of the sea.

Formidable as they may seem, there is nevertheless something endearing about these lumpen beings packing the long sweep of beach like middle-aged human holiday-makers. Perhaps it is that they are so patently enjoying life. Not all are lolling on the sands. Just beyond the roaring breakers, herds of cows lave sunburnt hides while keeping alert eyes on youngsters, sporting in the surf.

Once waterborne, these creatures are transformed into sleek and sinuous masters of another element from which, were it not for the requirements of calving and the joys of sex and sunbathing, they would have no cause ever to depart. Water is their true medium, and has been since their ancestors rejected life upon the land uncounted millions of years ago.

Measuring up to fourteen feet in length, superbly muscled, clad in a hide as tough as a suit of armour, the adults fear nothing in the oceanic world. Gregarious and amiable except when roused in defence of kith and kin, they live harmoniously as one of several far-flung tribes of the walrus nation, which in those times existed in untold numbers as far south as Cape Cod on the Atlantic shores of North America, and the Queen Charlotte Islands on the Pacific side. Plunging effortlessly through the deeps, feeding on beds of oysters, mussels, clams, and giant sea snails, or lolling in satisfied repletion on sunswept beaches, they lived an enviable life.

That is how things were with the sea tuskers some 500 years past when European man first came upon them.

A few years ago, in the museum of the Arctic and Antarctic Institute in Leningrad, I was handed an intricately carved and ancient piece of heavy bone. The Chukotkan archaeologist who was my host was playing guessing games. What did I think the object was?

"Ivory?" I hazarded. "Maybe elephant tusk...or maybe mammoth?"

"Ivory, yes. The hilt of a sword from excavations in Astrakhan on the old trade route to Persia. Fifth century, perhaps. But it is *morse*...the walrus, as you say. And did you know that in those far-off times the morse's tusks were more valuable than elephant ivory?"

I had not known, and was intrigued. So my friend showed me a ninth-century account of a Muscovite prince captured by Tatars whose ransom was set at 114 pounds of gold...or an equal weight in walrus tusks. I learned that, from well before Christ's birth until as late as A.D. 1600, walrus ivory was one of civilization's most valued and sought-after commodities. Compact and easily portable, the tusks were used as currency in their natural "ingot" state or were worked into precious and ornamental objects.

"The tooth of the morse," mused my companion, "was white gold in northern Europe and much of Asia through more than 2,000 years. How strange that such a monster should have been so great a source of wealth."

Ivory was not the only value to be derived from walrus. Inch-thick leather from the hides of old bulls is so tough it will deflect a musket-ball and offers better protection against cutting and thrusting weapons than bronze. Consequently it was the first and most expensive choice of shield makers and their warrior customers through many centuries.

The hide had other uses. A narrow strip cut spirally from a single skin would yield a rope an inch in section and as much as 100 yards in length. When treated with walrus oil, such a rope became as flexible and durable as contemporary ropes of vegetable fibre, and a good deal stronger. Walrus-hide rope early became and long remained preferred cordage and rigging for northern ships.

These same ships depended on still another walrus product: a tar-like substance produced by evaporating boiled walrus oil. This sticky black stuff was used to seal a vessel's seams and to protect her planking from the inroads of the ship-worm. The first known European vessel to complete the crossing of the North Atlantic Ocean, a *knorr* sailed by the Icelandic merchant Bjarni Herjolfsson to Newfoundland in 985, was almost certainly rigged with hvalross (whale horse) rope and sealed with hvalross tar.

Northerners were not the only men to make use of the animal. Bones found in Neolithic middens laid down in dim antiquity testify to its one-time presence as far south as the Bay of Biscay, and it seems to have still been present in the English Channel as late as the second century A.D. However, as men increased in number and improved their killing skills, the toll they took of the walrus became so heavy that the tuskers gradually vanished from more southern waters. The last Baltic walrus was killed in the seventh century and, during the succeeding hundred years, tusk and hide hunters harried it to extinction in the North Sea and around the sea-girt Faeroe, Orkney, and Shetland Islands. In the ninth century, a Norwegian adventurer named Octher reported that hvalross were hardly to be found south of North Cape, Europe's polar promontory. As they grew rarer they increased in value and so were hunted harder, to such effect that by the late tenth century not even Norwegian kings could find enough walrus hide to cover the wooden shields ranged along the gunwales of their dragon-headed longships.

By the thirteenth century, hvalross of mainland Europe survived only amongst the ice fogs of the Barents Sea in the Russian Arctic. They were already becoming legendary. A clerical chronicler of those times wrote of them: "Toward [those] northern parts there are huge great fish as big as elephants which are called Morsi or Russ-morsi, perhaps from their sharp biting; for if they see any man on the sea-shore, and can catch him, they come suddenly upon him and rend him with their teeth...these fish have heads fashioned like to an Oxe and hair growing as thick as straw...They will raise themselves by their Teeth, as by ladders, to the very tops of Rocks that they may feed on the Dewie grass...They fall very fast asleep upon the Rocks, then Fisher-men make all the haste they can, and begin at the Tail and part the Skin from the Fat, and into this that is parted they put very strong cords and fasten them on the rugged Rocks or Trees. Then they throw stones at his head out of a Sling to raise him and compel him to descend, therebye stripping off the greater part of the Skin, which is fastened to the Ropes. He being therebye exhausted, fearful and half dead, he is made a rich prey, especially for his Teeth, that are very precious among the Scythians, the Moscovites, Russians and Tartars."

Although the European walrus tribe had been reduced to little more than the stuff out of which fantastic tales are woven, walrus ivory and hides continued to appear in continental markets where they commanded ever-escalating prices. But these goods came from sources so distant they were themselves semi-mythical.

The mysterious island of Thule, which had loomed dimly on the western horizon of Europe for hundreds of years before the Christian era began, was colonized by the wide-ranging Vikings early in the ninth century. In Iceland, as they named it, they found a vast population of hvalross that they turned into white gold with such rapacity that the supply soon began to fail. So they fared farther afield into the western and northern mists to discover new tribes of walrus on the island continent of Greenland. After A.D. 1000, it was mainly from this outpost on the outer edge of the known world that hvalross products continued to reach European markets.

However, the Greenland walrus hunters, clinging precariously to the western rim of Europe's carousel, were unable to survive a deteriorating climate that brought an onslaught of great storms and plunging temperatures. Their settlements waned and died, and in the late 1400s the trickle of hvalross products into Europe finally failed. It was at this juncture that Europe discovered the walrus multitudes of the Western Ocean.

Who made the discovery remains unknown. Perhaps it was the Portuguese brothers Gaspar and Miguel Corte Real who in 1501 and 1502 explored the coastal waters of the northeastern seaboard of America. At any rate, a certain Pedro Reinal who sailed with them made a sea chart that shows an island called Santa Cruz lying off the Nova Scotia coast. Santa Cruz is Sable Island, and whoever found it could not have failed to note the legions of walrus for whom that curving strip of sand was home.

The twenty-mile-long island rises from the centre of Sable Island

Bank, an immense submerged plateau remarkable not only for its abundant stocks of fish but for the quantities of molluscs that encrust its underwater pastures. Few shellfish beds anywhere can equal these. But one other that can do so (we will look at it later) is known to have still supported 100,000 walrus as late as the middle of the eighteenth century. We can reasonably conclude that Sable Island and its surrounding banks were home to at least that many. Early vessels passing close to the island would perforce have sailed through an ocean crowded with sleek behemoths whose tusks glistened wetly as they raised huge heads to stare in fearless wonder at the intruders.

The discovery of Sable Island's walrus legions meant the unveiling of a train oil bonanza as productive of avarice in those times as the North Sea and Alaskan oil fields have been in ours. And exploitation of it was undertaken with comparable energy . . . and ruthlessness.

Because the approach to Sable was exceedingly dangerous except during rare intervals of calm, and because it offered no harbours where ships could lie secure from storm, the walrus "fishery" there was fraught with risks. No matter. Ships sailed for Sable hoping to reach the island in May or early June when the greatest part of the walrus population would be hauled out on the beaches to whelp. The outward voyage might take a month or more through storm and fog, and even when the low loom of Sable's dunes was sighted, the sea-weary vessels might be forced to beat back and forth in imminent peril for days on end, awaiting a respite in the weather during which small boats could run the gamut of the roaring breakers to land the hunters and their gear. Once that was accomplished, the ships would make all haste away from the raging surf, steering for safe harbours on the mainland coasts where the crews could spend the balance of the summer fishing cod.

Those who landed on Sable would have found themselves immersed in a veritable stew of life. The surrounding waters teemed with walrus, seals, porpoises, and whales. The sky resounded to the endless flight of seabirds. A salt-water lagoon stretching down the centre of the island was alive with ducks whose nests, half-hidden under tufts of dune grass, were so numerous a man could scarcely pick his way amongst them. Lobsters, clams, herring, and mackerel swarmed in the lagoon and along the outer shores. Profligate life abounded in and over this island for, until the coming of Europeans, it had never known the hard and bloody hand of man.

Not that it was inhospitable to humankind. It harboured none of the biting flies that were the curse of the mainland of the New World. Fresh water was obtainable from rain-water ponds. Although no trees grew, a millennium's collection of driftwood lay windrowed above storm-tide level. The weather could be rough, but summer temperatures were equitable and the sun often shone. Blackberries, cranberries, and wild peas abounded. Life for a summer-time visitor to Sable in the early days could have been something of an idyll. But for those who came to it for walrus oil, life was the way of death.

Iron-headed mauls and axes, double-handed stabbing spears, flensing knives, clay bricks, copper cauldrons, bundles of oaken staves, and willow withes were the major items amongst the gear perilously ferried ashore. The cauldrons were set up over firepits dug in the sand and lined with bricks. Coopers assembled staves and withes into train oil casks. Shack tents of sail-cloth and driftwood sprouted in the sparse shelter of the dunes.

All was hurriedly made ready and then the fishing masters led their gangs down to the beaches—to those long, sun-gleaming beaches densely packed as far as the eye could see with serried ranks of walrus.

No first-hand description of how the slaughter was conducted during the long-ago years on Sable now exists, but we have an account from Bear Island, 300 miles north of Norway, where in 1603 a previously unknown tribe of European walrus was discovered by a far-roaming ship of the English Muscovy Company. The author of this account of what followed was a crew-man named Jonas Poole.

"We saw a sandie Bay in which we came to anchor. We had not furled our Sayles but we saw many Morses swimming by our ship and heard withall so huge a noyse of roaring as if there had been a hundred Lions. It seemed very strange to see such a multitude of Monsters of the Sea lye like Hogges in heapes [upon the beach]."

To see them was one thing. To kill them, quite another. These men knew next to nothing about the morse and were frankly frightened of it.

"In the end we shot at them, not knowing whether they could runne swiftly and seize upon us or no."

However, the guns of those times proved largely ineffective against the massive skulls and armoured hides.

"Some, when they were wounded in the flesh, would but looke up and lye down again. And some would goe into the Sea with five or sixe shots in them, they are of such incredible strength. When all our ball shot was spent we would blow their eyes out with bird shot, and then come on the blind side of them and, with our Carpenter's axe, cleave their heads. But for all that we could doe we killed but fifteen."

The ivory and oil from those fifteen walrus proved quite enough to whet the appetite of the Muscovy Company, and the crews that were sent out to make a killing the following year had seemingly been briefed on how the job was done in the New World.

"The year before we slew with shot, not thinking that a Javelin could pierce their skinnes, which we now found contrary, if it be well handled; otherwise a man may thrust with all his force and not enter; or if he does he shall spoyle his Lance upon their bones; or they will strike with their forefeet and bend a Lance and break it."

Getting the feel of the job now, Poole's crew killed about 400 walrus and sailed home with eleven tuns of oil (about 2,300 gallons) and several casks of tusks. By the next year they had become professionals. One day Jonas Poole, in charge of a gang of eleven men, made his way along the shore of a walrus beach, dropping off a man every twenty yards or so until he met the leader of a similar group coming the other way, and so "enclosed the Morses that none of them should get into the Sea."

The line of hunters then turned inland, stabbing every walrus within reach in the throat or belly; killing some but wounding more, and causing such a panic that the great beasts humped frantically away from their one hope of refuge, in the sea, until overtaken by thrusting blades and swinging axes.

"Before six hours were ended we had slayne about six or eight hundred Beasts...For ten days we plied our business very hard and took in two and twenty tuns of the Oyle of the Morses and three hogsheads of their Teeth."

Within the space of eight seasons after Poole's first visit the estimated 10,000–20,000 walrus of Bear Island had been so reduced that the few survivors were no longer worth the hunting. By contrast, the Sable Island herd was initially so vast that it was able to sustain a lucrative annual fishery through almost two centuries.

A few decades after the first visits of the Portuguese, Sable temporarily slipped from their control to become the source of unspecified "rich merchandise" for one Jean Ango, a powerful sea lord of Le Havre who sent several expeditions to it between 1510 and 1515. Thereafter, João Alvares Fagundes, a Portuguese merchant-adventurer, reclaimed the island and held it until the late 1580s, when the French once more seized it.

Sable's new French "owner" was a Breton entrepreneur grandiloquently called Troilus de La Roche, Marquis de la Roche-Mesgouez. His chief associate was a sea captain named Chefd'ostel, and their mutual enterprise affords a revealing glimpse of the kind of men who were engaged in the "discovery" of the New World, and of how they operated.

In exchange for his sworn promise to discover, occupy, and settle the whole northeastern coast of the new continent on behalf of the King of

France and to lead its heathen savages to God, La Roche received letters patent from Henry of Navarre appointing him Viceroy and Lieutenant General over the territories of Canada, Newfoundland, Labrador, Norumbega, and, especially and significantly, Isle de Sable.

Mere promises of great deeds to be done would hardly have sufficed to procure such a munificent grant. The evidence indicates that it was acquired by massive bribery. By the time La Roche got his patent, he was almost broke. Undaunted, he used his new powers as Viceroy to assume custody of a number of convicts from Breton and Norman jails, ostensibly to make colonists in the New World of them. In fact, he proceeded to sell them their freedom in France for hard cash. The scheme worked so well that he did it again, this time obtaining 250 prisoners. Of these he retained forty who were described as "the sweepings of the gutter" and gave "the better sort" their liberty...in exchange for enough gold to equip his expedition.

The fleet intended for his grand accomplishment consisted of two small fishing smacks. Into the black, stinking hold of one went forty shackled "colonists," kept in order by the muskets of ten mercenaries. Oddly enough, the Viceroy did not direct his course to the vast mainland of his new possessions. Instead he sailed to Sable Island where, as soon as the weather permitted, he set ashore his "colonists," their guards and overseers, and meagre stores. La Roche and Chefd'ostel *then* sailed to the mainland coast, where they probably made a summer fishing voyage for cod, returning in the autumn direct to France. There the Viceroy brazenly announced that he had been prevented from planting a settlement anywhere other than on Sable because the weather had been unsuitable! In truth, the whole thing had been a most successful scam, by virtue of which La Roche obtained his object—exclusive title to Sable Island and its riches in train oil and ivory.

The worth of his little Eldorado can be judged from the fact that the French government was then paying a subsidy of one *écu* on every barrel of train unloaded in a French port, and, by the time of his death in 1606, La Roche had earned some 24,000 *écus* on this subsidy alone. Since the fat of from two to four walrus (depending on size and season) was required to make a barrel of oil, La Roche's slaves presumably must have killed something on the order of 50,000 walrus, plus an unknown number of seals, during the eight years he held the monopoly of Sable Island.

Chefd'ostel normally visited the "colony" every year to pick up cargo and leave supplies. He failed to do so in 1602. During the ensuing winter the convicts revolted, killing their guards and overseers. When Chefd'ostel returned in 1603, he is said to have found only eleven convicts still alive, though it seems as likely that he and his tough Breton crew hunted down and slaughtered the bulk of the slaves in revenge.

That the mutineers had indeed been brutally treated is evident from the sequel. When, filthy dirty, manacled, and still clad in homemade sealskin clothing, the eleven were brought before King Henry for punishment, he was so moved by the account they gave of their suffering that he not only freed them, he awarded each man fifty *écus* in compensation. The reaction of La Roche and Chefd'ostel to this act of benevolence is not recorded.

La Roche's successors maintained the French monopoly until about 1630, after which they were forced to share Sable's wealth with English fishermen-colonists from Massachusetts Bay. These made no attempt to establish shore factories, contenting themselves with raiding the beaches and the French stations. One such raid in 1641 yielded 400 pairs of tusks, which sold in Boston for the modern equivalent of $10,000. Walrus ivory was still white gold, and the New Englanders were out to get their share. Apart from raids on Sable, they scoured their own walrus beaches (which seem to have stretched south as far as Cape Cod) to such effect that by about 1700 the species seems to have been exterminated south of Nova Scotia. The last walrus recorded as being killed in Massachusetts Bay, in 1754, was probably a straggler from farther north.

Not even the immense herds that had originally frequented Sable Island Bank could forever survive such unbridled rapacity. Sometime between 1680 and 1710, there came a spring when the curving sweep of Sable's beaches held no more of the great creatures that had once drawn themselves up on the warm sands in their countless thousands. Nor would their living presence ever be known there again.

For a century thereafter, Sable lay shrouded in half-legendary obscurity, dreaded and avoided by mariners until, early in the nineteenth century, lighthouses and a lifesaving crew were established on it. Thereafter, lonely riders patrolling the empty beaches on half-wild ponies sometimes came across walrus skeletons newly exposed by the ever-shifting sands. But the massive bones seemed so antediluvian that they were thought to belong to an era long before Europeans first crossed the Western Ocean.

Buried in Sable's sands, the teeming legions of the past were also buried out of memory. Recent histories make little or no mention of the nation of tusked creatures that once lived there, or of how and why it perished. Nevertheless Sable is once again looming large in our view. Gigantic drilling rigs, both on and off the island, are plunging their steel proboscises deep into the ocean floor, seeking what the Portuguese first found there almost 500 years ago...the wealth derived from oil.

Sable's walrus tribe was immense but still only an outlying colony of a nation whose real heartland lay in the Gulf of St. Lawrence. The southern portion of that inland sea is dominated by a roughly circular basin some 200 miles in diameter, bounded on the east by Cape Breton Island, on the south by Prince Edward Island and Northumberland Strait, and on the west by the Gaspé Peninsula. The Magdalen Island archipelago rises almost from its centre.

The basin's shallow waters contain a rich mix of oceanic currents, combined with the great outflow of nutrient-laden fresh water from the St. Lawrence River and the Great Lakes system. In its aboriginal state it possessed some of the world's most productive shellfish pastures, populated by stellar multitudes of oysters, soft-shelled clams, bar clams, quahogs, razor clams, scallops, moon snails, cockles, and other succulent molluscs that together offered an almost inexhaustible supply of prime walrus food. Furthermore, the surrounding shores held hundreds upon hundreds of miles of sandy beaches with space enough for uncountable multitudes of sea tuskers to mate, calve, or simply snooze under the summer sun.

But was it possible that an animal we now know only as an inhabitant of frigid polar seas could once have dwelt in these waters more than 1,300 miles south of the Arctic Circle, and less than 400 miles north of the city of New York? It was possible, and it was so; for this was the heartland of the western Atlantic walrus nation.

Spanish Basques seem to have been the first Europeans to have struck at that heartland, as early as the first decade of the sixteenth century; but men of other nations quickly followed. Around 1519, the same João Fagundes who fished for walrus on Sable Island made an exploratory voyage into the Gulf. What follows is my reconstruction of that region as he might have seen it then.

Having entered the Gulf through either Cabot Strait or Canso Strait, his high-pooped caravel makes her way slowly westward through Northumberland Strait with the solidly forested coasts of Nova Scotia, then New Brunswick, slipping away to port. To starboard lie the beaches and red-ochre mudbanks of Prince Edward Island. And everywhere—on land, in air, and in the waters—life abounds.

The strait surges with billions of herring and mackerel schooling so tightly as to form almost solid masses of living flesh. Seabirds wheel and dive into this stew in dense formations. Feeding cod rise from the bottom in such mighty phalanxes that their assaults upon the baitfish make the surface roil as if from an underwater eruption. Grey seals in their thousands watch, dark-eyed, as the ship slips past. Pods of whales, both great and small, cruise in such numbers that the caravel has sometimes to give way before them.

Yet what is of most interest to Fagundes are the legions of walrus clustered on the beaches, sandspits, and muddy shoals or surging up around the slow-moving vessel until their staring heads seem as ubiquitous as stumps in a clear-cut forest.

As the caravel passes out of the strait and opens the southern lip of Chaleur Bay, the walrus clans grow even more numerous. They are hauled out so thickly on the low-lying islands of Shippegan and Miscou that their somnolent bodies blacken acres of yellow sand and green grass.

Now the pilot steers south of east into the open waters of the great basin. After a day's sail, the lookout picks up a number of low, hazed humps on the horizon. As the ship draws closer these resolve themselves into a string of wooded islands faced with red sandstone cliffs and linked to one another by seemingly endless miles of glittering white beaches. This is the Magdalen Island archipelago, and here Fagundes would have looked upon the central core of the western walrus nation.

The Magdalens include nine major islands, seven of which are linked by broad beaches that enclose extensive salt-water lagoons. The interlocked group is forty miles long, and its seaward-facing beaches, together with those ringing the lagoons, total more than 120 miles in length. Separated from the nearest mainland by sixty miles of open water, the Magdalens, like Sable, seem not to have been occupied by pre-European men. This fact, together with the combination of sheltered lagoons, grassy meadows, wooded hills, and endless beaches set in the midst of a life-filled sea, made it a paradise for waterfowl and sea mammals such as can hardly have been matched elsewhere in the Northern Hemisphere.

The walrus clearly found it so. A conservative estimate indicates that the Central Gulf herd numbered at least a quarter of a million individuals when Europeans first came upon it. Or, to put it in terms that would have been particularly meaningful to the invaders, something more than 300,000 tons of living flesh...and fat.

Although the Magdalens seem to have been firmly in Basque hands at the time of Fagundes' visit, lucrative opportunities remained to be claimed by him elsewhere. In 1521, he formed a company of merchants in his home town of Vianna, under a charter from King Manuel that licensed the syndicate to exploit eight specific localities in the New World. All were islands or island groups, and the five that can still be identified with reasonable certainty all harboured major walrus rookeries. These were the Île Madame complex in Cape Breton's Chedabucto Bay, St-Pierre et Miquelon and the Ramea/Burgeo archipelago on the south coast of Newfoundland, Sable Island, and Prince Edward Island. Although no mention is made in the charter of the actual resources to be exploited (as was usual, for reasons of commercial secrecy), it *is* stated that one of the enterprises envisaged was a soap factory. We also know that at about this time the supremacy of olive oil in soap-making was being challenged by train oil—in particular by walrus oil. There can be but little doubt that walrus were intended to provide the major profits to the syndicate.

Fagundes established a year-round lodgement on Prince Edward Island, the first-known European attempt at settlement in North America since Norse days. French sources blame Indians for its destruction a decade or so later, but the indications are that the natives were being saddled with the blame for bloody deeds perpetrated by Europeans. Suspicion points strongly to the French themselves, as they began aggressively encroaching on Portuguese and Spanish Basque "white gold mines" in the Gulf.

I believe that French interest in the Beast of the Great Teeth, as early Breton mariners called the walrus, was a major motivation for Jacques Cartier's famous voyages to the Gulf in 1534 and 1535. It is at any rate a fact that he reconnoitred many of the major walrus rookeries and, shortly thereafter, his fellow Bretons were forcibly dispossessing the Portuguese of them. Well before 1570, the French had engrossed the rookeries on Northumberland Strait, at St-Pierre et Miquelon, on Prince Edward Island, and in Bay Chaleur, and had firmly established themselves on the Magdalens as well. By 1580, that rich archipelago had become the fiefdom of two of Cartier's nephews. In 1591, they licensed it to another St. Malo entrepreneur, La Court de Pré-Ravillon, for the stated purpose of fishing what had by then come to be known as *vaches marins*.

It was in this year that the English belatedly became aware of the riches that could be obtained from sea cows in the New World. Early in September, the Bristol privateer *Pleasure* was cruising off the Scilly Isles when her lookout spotted the topsails of two vessels making for the English Channel. *Pleasure* bore down, overhauled the smaller one, captured her, and took her into Plymouth.

She turned out to be the *Bonaventure*, belonging to La Court de Pré-Ravillon, homeward-bound from some place in the Western Ocean unknown to her captors but which her Master called *les Isles de Rames*.

These were the Magdalens, and English interest took instant fire when it was discovered that *Bonaventure* was laden with "40 tunnes of trayne oyell" together with great quantities of "hydes and teeth," the produce from 1,500 sea cows killed by her crew that summer. The cargo was valued at £1,500, a considerable fortune in those times.

Under interrogation her Master revealed that "The Island...is about 20 leagues about, and some part is flat and shoal: and the fish cometh on the shores to do their kind in April, May and June by numbers thousands; which fish is very big and hath two great teeth; and the skinne of them is like Buffe leather; and they will not go away from their yonge ones. The yonge ones are as good meat as Veal. And with the bellies of five of the said fishes they make a hogshead of Traine; which Traine is very sweet, which if it will make sope, the king of Spayne may burn some of his olive trees."

To which that indefatigable chronicler of English voyaging, Richard Hakluyt, added: "These beasts are as big as Oxen...the hides big as any Oxe hide...the leather dressers take them to be excellent good to make light targets [shields]...the teeth have been solde in England to the comb and knife makers at 8 groats and 3 shillings the pound, whereas the best [elephant] Ivory is sold for halfe of that...One M. Alexander Woodson of Bristol...a skilful Phisition, showed me one of these beasts' teeth [from *Bonaventure*] and assured me that he had made a tryall of it in ministering medicine to his patients and found it as sovereigne [a remedy] against poyson as any Unicornes horne."

Having caught the scent, the English were in a fever to seize a share of sea cow wealth; but none knew the whereabouts of the treasure isle. This difficulty was resolved by hiring a French Basque pilot, Stevan de Bocall, to guide two ships to the islands in the spring of 1592. One reached its destination only to find "all the fit places and harbours...to be forestalled and taken up by the Bretons of St. Malo and the [French] Basks of Saint John de Luz." The vessel's Master did not dare try to force an entry and so returned home empty-handed. Bocall piloted another voyage in the following year, but again was shut out. Finally, in 1597, a consortium of London merchants fitted out two heavily armed ships, *Chancewell* and *Hopewell*, and sent them to seize the Rames, drive out the French, and plant a permanent settlement there. What follows is a shortened version of the account written by *Hopewell*'s Master, Captain Leigh.

"The 14th [of June] we came to the Island of Birds [part of the Magdalen group] and saw great store of Morsses or Sea Oxen which were asleep upon the rocks; but when we approached neare unto them with our boats they cast themselves into the sea and pursued us with such furie that we were glad to flee from them. The 18th we came to the Isle of Rames and approaching neare unto the harbour of Halobalino sent our great boats in, which found 4 ships. Namely two of Saint Malo and two Basques of Sibiburo. Whereupon we presently [sailed *Hopewell*] into harborough and requested them, for our better security, peaceably to deliver up their powder and munitions.

"They would not consent thereunto: whereupon we sent the boat, well-manned, to fetch their powder and munitions. When [our men] came aboard the saide ships, which were moored together, they were resisted by force of arms, but quickly they got the victorie; which done they fell presently to pillaging the Baskes.

"Afterwards our ship's company fell into a mutiny and more than half of them resolved to carry one of those ships away. But they were prevented by the aid which the saide ships received from their countrymen in the other harboroughs. For the next morning very earley they gathered together at least 200 Frenchmen and Bretons who had planted upon the shore 3 pieces of Ordinance and had prepared themselves to fight with us, [and] so soone as we had discerned them, gave the onset upon us with at least an hundred small shot. There were also in readiness to assault us, about three hundred Savages." Indians had been brought by the French from the mainland to do the dirty work of the walrus slaughter.

For Captain Leigh it was now a case of turnabout having become fair play. When the French seized two men he sent ashore to parley, he was forced to ransom them with the powder and shot he had stolen. He did so with great protestations that his intentions had been strictly honourable. Nobody believed him. When he tried to leave the harbour, the French refused to release the anchor he had placed on the beach for his shore line, and he was forced to cut the cable. He then tried to fumble his way over the bar but went aground and had to stay on the shoal until dawn awaiting a high tide, terrified that the "Savages" would attack in darkness. When he finally got clear, the French on the beach ironically cheered him off.

Leigh's voyage marked the end, for nearly two centuries, of English attempts to enter the Gulf walrus fishery, not so much because of French resistance as because, as we have seen, in the first decade of the seventeenth century they found walrus of their own at Bear Island, and later at Spitzbergen.

Throughout the seventeenth century and well into the eighteenth, the Gulf remained essentially a French lake, with the walrus fishery as one of the most lucrative enterprises there. Permanent factories with over-wintering crews were established on the Magdalens and on Miscou Island. Summer walrus stations kept the trypots bubbling along Northumberland Strait; on the coasts of Prince Edward Island; on Anticosti Island; at Cow Head (originally Sea Cow Head), Port au Choix, and St. George's Bay on the west coast of Newfoundland; at the Mingan Islands and in Seven Islands Bay on the north shore of the Gulf; and even as far up the St. Lawrence River as Île aux Coudres, within sixty miles of the present city of Quebec. In addition, rookeries on the Atlantic coast and islands of Nova Scotia and Newfoundland were regularly ravaged. So profitable was this bloody business that Samuel de Champlain valued the sea cow and associated seal fisheries of New France at half a million *livres* a year—a livre being roughly equivalent to an English pound, or a month's pay for a working man.

Year by year the slaughter mounted in intensity...toward the inevitable conclusion. The course of the sea cow's destruction can be charted by the progressive elimination of the rookeries. All those along the St. Lawrence River had disappeared by 1680. Those on the north shore of the Gulf saw no more walrus after 1704. By 1710, Sable Island had only the bones of sea cows still to show, and the same was evidently true of all the Atlantic coastal rookeries from the Strait of Belle Isle south to the limits of the walrus's breeding range.

The ravaged tribes of the heartland alone survived into the first half of the 1700s. But at midpoint in that century, a visitor to Miscou Island found only bones remaining "in such numbers as to form artificial sea beaches... the murdered sea horses having left a more enduring monument than their murderers."

When the first English governor of Prince Edward Island took up his duties after the conquest of Canada in 1763, one of his prime concerns was the preservation of the sea cow fishery. He was too late. The tide had already run out for the vast colonies that had once populated the north shore beaches, and no mere governor could reverse it.

The one remaining foothold of the western Atlantic walrus nation was now the Magdalen Islands. In 1765, Lieutenant Haldiman, a young Royal Navy officer, was sent to the archipelago to investigate the sea cow fishery. His report is the only extant account of how the slaughter was and had been conducted in the Gulf. I have condensed and edited it somewhat.

"The places where the Sea Cows are killed are called *Echouries* [and consist of] a space of from one to six hundred feet frontage on the water, running back to the top of a sandbank which is a natural slope, sometimes so steep it is astonishing how so unwieldy an animal could ever get to the top.

"The method of taking the Sea Cows is as follows. When a great number are assembled below the bank they are followed by others coming out of the sea who, in order to get room, give those in front of them a small push with their tusks. These last are pushed on by more following them until the sea cows farthest from the water are driven over the bank, and so far inland that even the latest arrivals have room to rest; and they usually sleep if not disturbed.

"The Echouries being full, or containing so many that the hunters can cut off the retreat of three or four hundred; ten or twelve men prepare themselves at dusk with poles about twelve feet long. The attack is made during the night, and the principal thing to be observed is the wind which must always blow from the animals, to prevent the hunters being discovered.

"When they have approached along the beach to within three or four hundred yards of the Echourie, five men are detached with poles. These creep on hands and knees until they are close to the flank of the herd and to seaward of the high sandbank on top of which most of the sea cows lie. The reason for this is that if those cows farthest inland had the least apprehension they would all turn and retire toward the water. In which case, so far from being able to stop them, it would be great good fortune if the men saved themselves from being pressed to death or being drowned.

"Being now ready to begin the attack, the first man gives the Cow in front of him a gentle strike with the end of his pole upon the buttocks, imitating as much as possible the push they give each other. So he proceeds in the same manner with the next Cow counterfeiting the stroke of the tusks and making it advance up the beach while another of his comrades secures him from harm from the Cows to seaward of him.

"So they continue to the other side of the Echourie, having by this means made a passage which they call the *cut*. All this time they have observed the utmost silence, but now they begin to halloo and make the greatest noise possible to frighten and alarm the Sea Cows, and as a signal to their comrades to come and assist them. All the men now range themselves along the Cut, driving and beating the Cows to prevent them from falling back toward the sea. Those Cows which turn back from the top of the bank are prevented from escaping by those the men are belabouring toward them, and the collision of the two groups forms a bank of bodies twenty feet high and upwards.

"The men keep exercising their poles until the beasts are quite fatigued and give up the attempt to escape, after which they are divided into parties of thirty or forty Cows which are driven to a place, generally a mile inland from the Echouries, where they are killed and the fat taken off."

Haldiman's description of a cut is technically adequate, but lacks atmosphere. We must add the thunder of the surf foamed by escaping walrus and the roaring of hundreds of panic-stricken behemoths trapped on the beach. We must visualize the scene in an obscure and windy darkness lighted only toward the end by the red flare of torches. We must imagine the sensations of the men making the cut, crawling on hands and knees and all too well aware that at any instant they may be crushed beneath a black avalanche of flesh and bone. We must see them slipping and cursing in the manure-soaked sand, frantically pounding the heads and bodies of the sea cows, leaping out of the way of one and thrusting with puny human strength at yet another.

Human casualties did occur, although few records were kept of the unfortunates who died in distant places so that the oil vats and the money bags of Europe would be filled. One old *Madelinot* remembers hearing his grandfather tell of an occasion when the wind changed just as the hunters were crawling through the herd. Seven men were crushed, gored, or swept into the sea with broken legs and arms to drown.

Because it was possible to make as many as four cuts at a given echourie in a single season, and because of the sea cow's excellent sense of smell, it was essential that the actual slaughter take place at least a mile from the echourie itself so that the stench of rotting flesh would not keep the surviving walrus off the beaches. As Haldiman tells us, this was achieved by driving the animals to a sufficiently distant killing ground. Despite their immense strength, the walrus quickly became exhausted as they were forced to hump laboriously over dry land and soft sand. Though clubbed and goaded by human beings, and savaged by dogs, four or five hours could be required for them to drag themselves that long death mile. Calves that had survived the mêlée on the echourie usually died en route. It did not matter. They were too poor in oil to be of value, although an occasional one might provide the killers with fresh meat. By the time the driven beasts reached the abattoir they were incapable of resistance. They dropped their heads and lay quiescent, their only sound the stentorious breathing of exhaustion.

Once removed from the carcass, the blubber tended to "waste" or liquefy, allowing the precious oil to sink into the ground, so individual walrus were killed only as there was room for their fat in the trypots. But even with two pots boiling twenty-four hours a day, it took many days to render all the blubber from a single cut. During this time, the sun that had tempted the sea cows onto the beaches in the first place became their implacable tormentor. It burned down relentlessly until even their thick hides cooked and split, letting rivulets of blood and oil run down their heaving flanks. No drink was available and so, as their life fluids trickled away, thirst became an ultimate agony.

Eventually someone would give them their quietus. In Haldiman's time, this was done by firing a one-inch diameter iron ball from a muzzleloader into the cow's head. Frequently this only stunned the animal. No matter. The hide was stripped off even if the beast still lived. Then the blubber layer, which in autumn would be at least six inches thick, was sliced clear and forked into the bubbling vats. The naked carcass was left to lie where it was until eventually it, together with hundreds of attendant corpses, rotted down into the fouled and greasy sand, leaving behind only a colossal stench and acres of stained bones.

In earlier times the tusks had been carefully hacked out of the skulls, but by 1760 they were being largely ignored. A massive influx of elephant ivory into Europe from Africa and India had finally rendered walrus ivory relatively valueless. In the 1800s, a Magdalen Island merchant offered one cent apiece for every sizable walrus tusk that could still be found on the islands. Before that summer ended, the *Madelinots* had collected more than *two tons* of ivory from the old killing grounds. However, the merchant was then unable to find a market for this one-time treasure and was reduced to shipping it out as ballast in one of his schooners.

By 1760, changing European markets had also made walrus hides hardly worth the trouble of preparing them. Oil was now entirely the thing. In 1767, the oil derived from an average spring walrus fetched the equivalent of $20 (1984 value) while that from a fat, fall bull could go as high as $60. But before the next decade ended, the price had doubled! The noose imposed by human avarice was tightening in time-honoured style.

As the value of their oil rose, so were the walrus even more pitilessly butchered; and as the slaughter burgeoned, so did their numbers fall. But the value of their oil increased with their increasing rarity. The spiral tightened with every turn; and extinction lay at its centre.

The *coup de grâce* was delivered in 1762 when the British government gave two Bostonians, a Mr. Thompson and a Colonel Gridley, the monopoly of the walrus fishery at the Magdalens and in neighbouring waters. Gridley first visited the islands during the final years of the war with France, possibly accompanying Vice Admiral Molineux Shuldan, who took a British squadron there and was astounded to behold "seven or eight thousand walrus on each of the Island's echouries." What the astute Gridley saw was thousands of pounds sterling to fill the pockets of himself and his friends; and by 1765 he had every reason to know for a fact that what Lieutenant Haldiman had written in his report of that year was marvellously true: "The Magdalens seem to be superior to any place in North America for the taking of the Sea Cow. Their numbers are incredible, amounting, upon as true a computation as can be made, to 100,000 or upwards."

During its first year on the islands, Gridley's crew was only large enough to work three of the eleven traditional Magdalen echouries; nevertheless they killed some 25,000 walrus and made over 1,000 barrels of oil. The following year he imported twenty Acadian French families who had formerly been walrus hunters on Prince Edward Island and in Northumberland Strait.

Between 1767 and 1774 his firm exported walrus oil to Europe through St. John's, Newfoundland, to a declared value of nearly £11,000, or about a quarter of a million 1984 dollars. No records exist of how much was shipped via New England ports.

Gridley and Thompson had their Eldorado, but they were not left in sole possession of it. Following on the conquest of New France, predatory fleets of New England schooners had begun swarming into the Gulf to see what they could find. And they soon found the sea cows. Being rugged upholders of the principles of free enterprise, they were not intimidated by Gridley's monopoly, and so they not only harried the walrus in the waters around the Magdalens but raided the echouries, too.

"New England vessels approach close to shore and frequently shoot at the walrus near the Echouries, sometimes through ignorance and sometimes through mischievous design," wrote Haldiman. "The Master of one sloop, observing the coast of Brion Island to be well stocked with Sea Cows, made use of every method he could think of to capture them, but without success, till at length he hit on the unfortunate resolution of shooting at them from the banks behind the Echouries. In consequence, he made 18–20 barrels of oil to share among as many men, and the Cows abandoned that Echourie and have never resorted there since."

By 1774, as many as 100 New England vessels were fishing the Magdalen waters, mainly for herring and cod but taking walrus whenever they got the chance; and doing so, as the aggrieved owners of the island reported, "in a reckless and barbarous way...driving them away and preventing them from breeding." The schooner hunt *was* singularly wasteful. Of every dozen animals shot while in the water, only one or two would be recovered, most of the rest surviving as cripples if they were lucky, or dying later, according to the severity of their wounds.

Faced with the competition of the schooner men, Gridley redoubled his own efforts to get what remained to be got, hiring or dragooning more labour until he had fifty Acadian families as well as a lawless crew of New England "wharf rats" working for him. What followed was bloody massacre. In 1780 four cuts on one beach alone yielded 2,400 walrus.

In 1798, Captain Crofton of the Royal Navy was sent to the Magdalens by the governor of Newfoundland to investigate rumours that the sea cows were being perilously depleted. Crofton's report was brief, and final: "I am extremely sorry to acquaint you that the Sea Cow fishery on these islands is totally annihilated."

Two years later, on a fine spring morning at the beginning of the nineteenth century, some Acadians had gone to the beach at La Bassin in the south part of the Magdalens to dig clams for cod bait. A hundred yards off the empty echourie a massive head suddenly reared out of the heaving surf. The men straightened from their digging and stared seaward at a *vache marin* whose gleaming tusks seemed longer than any they had ever seen before. Holding its position rock-solid in the breakers, it seemed to return their stares with such intensity that some of the men became uneasy. Then it submerged.

None of its kind has ever again been seen in the one-time heartland of the vanished nation.

After 1800 no resident walrus existed anywhere south of the Strait of Belle Isle, and precious few remained alive even on the Labrador coast to the northward. An anonymous official reporting in the Sessional Papers of the Quebec government in mid-century had this to say about their disappearance.

"They used to be found basking in the sun and breathing at their ease on the sandy beaches of the Gulf. But first the French, then the English and Americans waged as bitter a war against them that at the commencement of this century they were almost totally destroyed...they are now hardly ever to be met with except on the Labrador coast, in Hudson's Straits and Hudson's Bay...Their tusks are often found buried in the sand of the shores of the River and Gulf of St. Lawrence. These are the last remains of those animals whose spoils have helped to build up many fortunes. But the indifference and want of foresight of governments, and the cupidity of merchants, have caused their total disappearance."

There was now no respite for walrus anywhere. During the latter part of the nineteenth century even those living in far northern waters came under attack as British and American whalers, having swept the Arctic seas almost clean of merchantable whales, turned guns and harpoons against any and all other creatures whose corpses could return some profit. Of these, the walrus was first choice.

Walrus hides had once again become of value, as raw material from which bicycle seats were made. There was even a renewed demand for tusk ivory in the manufacture of expensive toilet accessories for wealthy women. And train oil continued to rise in price. The result was that some whalers started going north especially for walrus. In 1897, having scoured the Spitzbergen archipelago clean of whales as well as walrus, the British ventured east to discover a previously untouched tribe in remote Franz Joseph Land. Within ten years, they had wiped it out. In Greenland, so Oliver Goldsmith in his *Animated Nature* tells us, "the whale-fishers have been known to kill 300 or 400 [walrus] at a time and...along those shores bones are seen lying in prodigious quantities, sacrificed to those who sought them only for the purposes of avarice and luxury."

In North America's eastern Arctic things were as bad or worse. Between 1868 and 1873, whalers in that region landed an average of 60,000 walrus a year, with a recovery rate of about one in four when shot at sea. This massacre was parallelled in the western Arctic, particularly in the Bering, Chukchi, and Beaufort Seas where, between 1869 and 1874, Yankee whalers landed an estimated 150,000 sea cows out of perhaps double that number killed, for a production of 40,000 barrels of oil.

This carnage brought starvation to native northern peoples who depended on walrus as a staple food. These unfortunates found an advocate in a New England whaler named Captain Baker who had once been wrecked on the Alaskan coast and had survived only because the Eskimos succoured him and his crew.

"I wish to say to the ship agents and owners in New Bedford that the wholesale butchery of the walrus pursued by nearly all their ships will surely end in the extermination of the races of natives who rely upon these animals...although to abandon an enterprise that in one season alone yielded 10,000 barrels of oil, for the sake of the Esquimaux, may seem preposterous and meet with derision and contempt...But let them who deride it see the misery entailed by this unjust wrong...I feel quite sure that a business that can last not much longer anyway will be condemned by every prompting of humanity that ever actuated the heart of a Christian."

Captain Baker was a cockeyed optimist. Nothing could deflect the whalemen and the good burghers from the pursuit of profits. Their own records show that, by 1920, they had slaughtered between two and three *million* sea cows and had reduced the Pacific walrus nation to a few tens of thousands. Nobody kept any records of the consequent loss of life amongst the native peoples of the northern coasts. Their agonies were irrelevant.

The massacre of northern walrus was not limited to commercial exploitation. From about 1890 until well into the 1920s, millionaire American and European sport hunters ranged the eastern Arctic all the way from Spitzbergen to Ellesmere Island on private "scientific expeditions," which in reality were nothing more than highly competitive attempts to kill more northern animals than anyone else had ever done before. These gentlemen kept careful records of the destruction wrought by their expensive guns, and walrus provided one of their prime targets. One proud sportsman who visited the northwest Greenland coast was able to tally eighty-four bull walrus, twenty cows, and "a number of youngsters" in his game book during a single three-week period. As he admitted, he had probably killed a great many more, but the ethics of good sportsmanship had prevented him from claiming any whose deaths had not been indisputably confirmed.

When the European invasion of North America began, the region that would become eastern Canada and the northeastern United States had a resident walrus population numbering no less than three-quarters of a million. At least another quarter million inhabited the adjacent seas to the northward. By 1972, the total walrus population of eastern North America may have numbered between 5,000 and 10,000, entirely restricted to Arctic and Subarctic waters. Although officially protected, their numbers are still being depleted, primarily for their tusks, which are now much in vogue again both as expensive souvenirs and as raw material for craft carving. In 1981, many tons of illegal North American walrus ivory entered international markets where it was selling for up to $150 a pound. U.S. Federal Wildlife Service agents in Alaska seized *10,000 pounds* of tusks in a single day. This much ivory required the destruction of a minimum of 750 adult walrus. So many headless walrus have recently washed up on the Siberian coast opposite Alaska that the Soviet Union has filed a formal complaint with the U.S. State Department against the ongoing massacre.

Nevertheless, the outlook for the survival of the walrus is not totally bleak. For whatever reasons, the Soviets have given effective protection to their remaining morse, and to such effect that the species is beginning to recover at least a shadow of its lost numbers both in the Barents Sea and in the East Siberian Sea. The Wrangell Island tribe, which was reduced to the verge of extinction by Russian and Yankee hunters early in the twentieth century, has now, under absolute protection, increased to nearly 70,000 individuals, a figure that Soviet biologists think may be close to the aboriginal number. And even in Alaskan waters, despite "headhunting" for ivory, there has been some recovery.

But in non-Arctic waters it has mostly become bones.

Old bones!

Near the village of Old Harry, on Coffin Island in the Magdalen group, is a place still called Sea Cow Path. It is a natural gully leading inland through the shifting dunes from the magnificent East Cape beaches (which once hosted the largest echouries in the archipelago) to a bowl-shaped depression a quarter of a mile in diameter. Once dry, this basin is now shallowly flooded by the waters of an adjacent lagoon.

One sunlit summer day I splashed my way across its length and breadth, walking—not on sand—but on a bed of bones. I dug a test pit at low tide and at a depth of three feet was still shovelling through crumbling brown bones in a stinking matrix of black muck. These were the mortal remains of thousands of sea cows for whom this place had been the end of the path that bears their name.

Later I rested on the slope of a nearby dune. A great blue heron paced the shore of the lagoon. Distant gulls mewed in the white spindrift on the empty ocean beach. The sweet smell of balsam from a nearby woods was a benison and a delight. Idly I sifted hot sand through my fingers...felt something......took it in my hand. It was a corroded iron musket ball, the size of a small plum. It lay heavy in my palm...and the scene before me wavered. Changed. And darkened.

Sable plumes of greasy smoke rolled high into a pallid sky from roaring fires under blackened vats whose contents bubbled noisomely. The hot air swirled about me, filling my nostrils with a sickly stench blended from hundreds of tons of rotting flesh, old blood, and rancid oil. My ears were assailed by the strident screaming of thousands of gulls and the raucous outcries of hundreds of ravens intermingling to form a living, piebald shroud that shifted, spread, and reformed over the mountain of death filling the depression at my feet. Half-clad children, lean men, bent women, glistening with sweat and oil and grimed by the choking smoke, chopped, hacked, and sliced reeking strips of blubber from flayed corpses that still shivered and writhed with the last ebbing of life. A musket bellowed. The birds lifted momentarily, screaming and wheeling, then settled back to feed...

Rust from the musket ball flaked in my hand. The heron launched itself into the stiff and laboured flight of its kind and bore off over the dunes toward the sea—toward the empty reaches of La Grande Echourie, where the last cut was made.

17
Dotars and Horseheads

In 1949, Dean Fisher, a young Fisheries researcher, made a discovery of the kind every field biologist dreams about. Employed by the federal government of Canada to study salmon in New Brunswick's Miramichi River, Fisher was investigating relationships between salmon and harbour seals. Choosing a hot August day of the sort that tempts seals ashore to lounge on the sandbars of the river mouth, Fisher proceeded to make a count of the recumbent animals through his binoculars.

Almost at once he noticed occasional seals of enormous size—far larger than harbour seals had any right to be. Puzzled, he worked his way closer, focused on one of the monsters, and realized with near incredulity that he was looking at an animal that had been unreported for so long that some biologists believed it to be extinct in North America.

The creature Fisher officially rediscovered that summer day is known to science as the grey seal. Early French arrivals in the New World called it *loup marin*, not because of any presumed wolfish nature but because of its haunting cries, which sound eerily like the distant baying of wolves. Since it was visibly the most abundant seal, this name soon came to be used in a generic sense, applied to all seal species. Thereafter both French and English called the present species by the distinctive name of horsehead because of the characteristic equine profile of the males. It is still best known by this name, which is the one I shall generally use.

Of the several kinds of seals frequenting the northwestern approaches when the European invasion began, four were pre-eminent: hood, harp, harbour, and horsehead by name. Although hoods and harps were the most numerous, they were of small importance to the human newcomers, being present only during winter and early spring and even then mostly staying so far offshore as to be seldom seen. Horseheads and harbour seals, on the other hand, lived year-round in astonishing profusion almost everywhere along the northeastern coasts of the continent.

The horsehead is by far the larger of these two; an old male may be as much as eight feet in length and weigh 800 pounds. Although females average only about seven feet, they still seem enormous compared to the harbour seal, in which species neither sex exceeds five feet or weighs more than an average human being.

Gregarious and polygamous, horseheads used to gather in January and February in enormous numbers on myriad islands and even mainland beaches from Labrador to Cape Hatteras, there to whelp and breed. Some of these colonies were so large that, as late as the mid-1600s, the lupine howling from them could be heard several miles away.

They tended to keep together during the balance of the year as well, forming large, convivial companies of up to several hundred individuals fishing together in inshore waters and hauling out to sun themselves in somnolent mobs on bars in salt-water lagoons and at river mouths. This was a preference they shared with their gigantic relative, the walrus. They even shared the same whelping grounds, although at different seasons.

Harbour seals, called common seals in Europe or dotars in Newfoundland (the name I prefer), now survive mostly in small family groups. Originally they seem to have been more sociable and their colonies were scattered in bays, estuaries, and inlets from the Carolinas north into Arctic regions. They also made themselves at home in fresh water. Prior to 1800 a colony actually lived in Lake Ontario, wintering below the great cataracts of the upper St. Lawrence River. What was probably the last member of this now-vanished band was killed at Cape Vincent on the south shore of the lake in 1824. Dotars undoubtedly inhabited many of the larger rivers draining into the Atlantic, too; but the European invaders soon hunted them out of these. Their current predilection for wide dispersal and their secretive and isolated breeding habits seem to be relatively recent adaptations, forced on them by the predation of modern man.

Jacques Cartier's anonymous scribe provides the earliest direct reference to the horsehead. While Cartier's second expedition was coasting the northwest corner of the Gulf of St. Lawrence in 1535, some of his men rowed into the sandy estuary of what is now the Moisie River to investigate a certain "fish, in appearance like unto horses...we saw a great number of these fishes in this river," which Cartier named Rivière de Chevaulx. Further west, at the mouth of the Pentecost River, the expedition found "Large numbers of sea horses" and we are told that more were seen all the way west to the Indian village at the present site of Quebec City.

Cartier's scribe also noted the presence of another and smaller seal, which was evidently the dotar; but it was the sea horse that most interested the St. Malo entrepreneur. He would have been quick to realize that the oil from such huge, blubber-encased creatures offered a rich opportunity for profit.

As we have seen, one of the most valuable products from the northeastern portion of the New World during the early centuries of European exploitation was train oil. Some of those seeking it concentrated their efforts on whaling, and some on walrus hunting—enterprises that required considerable skill and large investments. Seal hunting required neither. Seals could be killed by the merest tyro, yet their oil could make a modest fortune for anyone who could scratch together a ship, a crew, and a trypot. Furthermore, seal hides were also of considerable worth.[1]

The little dotar was at first ignored because of its small size and relatively low yield. Even as late as 1630, Nicolas Denys noted: "there is scarce anybody but the Indians who make war on them." Their time would come. Meanwhile, the horsehead was the seal nonpareil.

When Sir Humphrey Gilbert was touting his colonizing venture in 1580, he issued a brochure listing *horsefishes* among the prime exploitable resources in the new lands. A brief account of the voyage of the English ship *Marigold*, in 1593, makes a point of remarking that the expedition found "great store of seals," particularly on the west coast of Cape Breton Island, where a remnant population of horseheads still remains. The port books of Southampton tell us that, by 1610, an annual seal fishery was being conducted in Newfoundland during the summer season, when no other species except horseheads and dotars would have been available. A few years earlier, while exploring southern Nova Scotia and the Fundy and Maine coasts, Samuel de Champlain noted numerous islands "completely covered with seals" and heard of others where Indians killed seal pups in wintertime. Both references must have been to horseheads.

One of the earliest commercial ventures of New England colonists was sealing, and they pursued it with the efficacy that was to make their descendants legendary. They took to raiding the long string of horsehead breeding islands off their coasts during the pupping season, slaughtering all the young and as many adults as they could get. So ruthless were they that they soon eliminated the horsehead as a profitable commodity on their own coasts.

---

[1] Even the Spaniards, with the riches of the West Indies and Mexico at their disposal, did not disdain the profits to be made from seals. Within a decade after Columbus's first voyage they were butchering the confiding monk seal in the Caribbean to make train, and their successors continued to do so with such rapacity that today this species of monk seal is extinct.

They then sailed north, and by mid-seventeenth century Nicolas Denys was complaining bitterly of their incursions into his Magdalen Island fiefdom where horseheads were to be found in the great lagoons in tens of thousands. Denys intimated that he had devised a new and more effective way to fish them there; but, being a properly cautious merchant, he refrained from committing the details to print.

The French, who were the first permanent European residents of southern Nova Scotia, were as voracious as the New Englanders, as Denys makes clear in his account of the horsehead fishery. "[The seals] come for their lying-in about the month of February...and take position on the islands, where they give birth...Monsieur d'Aunay sends men from Port Royal with longboats to make a fishery of them. The men surround the islands, armed with strong clubs; the fathers and mothers flee into the sea and the young, which are trying to follow, are stopped, being given a blow with the club on the nose of which they die...Few young ones save themselves...There are days on which there have been killed as many as six, seven and eight hundred...Three or four young ones are required to make a barrel of oil, which is as good to eat when fresh, and as good for burning as olive oil."

The Sieur de Diereville witnessed a similar slaughter in Acadia at the end of the seventeenth century and was moved to pen a poem about it. Apart from the archaic language, it might have been written by a seal-hunt observer of today. It ends:

> The Hunters, armed with heavy clubs,
> Advance upon the Isle, and by the noise
> They make, affright the Creatures, which
> By flight into the Sea, seek an escape
> From those upon their slaughter bent...
> It matters not which course they take,
> All are struck down upon the way;
> Fathers and Mothers, little Ones...
> Upon them all, blows fall like hail;
> If well directed, one upon the nose
> Suffices and the deed is done. But
> The beast still lives, for by the blow
> It is but shorn of consciousness;
> And sometimes so, within an hour's space,
> Five or six hundred are laid low.

Abundant as they must have been along the Atlantic coast, horseheads were even more so in the Gulf of St. Lawrence where they provided a year-round fishery for French settlers who sequestered ancient Indian sealing places for their own use. The memory of one such is still preserved in the Micmac name Ashnotogun, The Place We Bar the Passage (in order to catch seals).

Charlevoix provides a description of this fishery. "It is the custom of this animal to enter the rivers with the rising tide. When the fishermen have found out such rivers, to which great numbers of seals resort, they enclose them with stakes and nets leaving only a small opening for the seals to enter. As soon as it is high tide they shut this opening so that when the tide goes out the fishes remain a-dry, and are easily dispatched...I have been told of a sailor who having one day surprised a vast herd of them...with his comrades killed to the number of nine hundred of them."

By the mid-seventeenth century, settlers in New France had improved on the Indian methods and were building seal weirs in the mighty St. Lawrence River itself, siting them at strategic points where horseheads passed close to shore. The returns from this fishery were so great that possession of a site was almost as good as being able to coin one's own currency.

However, by the turn of the century unbridled slaughter on the river had so depleted the horseheads there that sealers were forced to seek new killing grounds. Some pressed eastward along the north shore of the Gulf. A memoir of a reconnaissance of this Côte du Nord, conducted in 1705 by the Sieur de Courtemanche from Anticosti Island almost to Belle Isle Strait, describes what was still a virgin coast insofar as non-native sealers were concerned. As such, the memoir provides us with some rare glimpses of the horsehead nation in its original state: "[Washikuti Bay], equally rich as other places in seals. [Caribou River], needless to repeat seals...are very abundant at this place. [Etamamu River], the seals are in greater abundance than at any other place previously referred to. [Netagamu River], there is such an abundance of seals that herds of them may be seen on the points of the islands as well as on the rocks. [From there to Grand Mescatina], all the islands abound with seals. [At Ha Ha Bay], I killed 200 seals with muskets in two days."

The fact that this journey was made in summer, taken together with the habits of the animals described, makes it certain that these were not harp or hood seal, but horseheads with, no doubt, an admixture of dotars. In 1705, they must have swarmed upon the north shore of the Gulf in tens of thousands.

Together with the walrus, horseheads had a number of special rallying places where enormous aggregations gathered during the summer months. These included some of the beaches near Cape Cod together with Sable, Miquelon, Miscou, Prince Edward, and the Magdalen Islands, all of which possessed shoal lagoons, sandy beaches, and rich, adjacent fishing grounds. Early Europeans viewed such massive concentrations as God-given reservoirs of oil wealth and treated them accordingly. At first the walrus bore the brunt of the assault but as they were exterminated at rookery after rookery in the southerly portion of their range, horseheads replaced them in the trypots until, by 1750, most of the summer gatherings of the big seals had been so savagely depleted as to leave only vestiges of their former selves.

There were some exceptions. Sable Island's scimitar of sand was too distant and dangerous to be easily reached in the small craft used by most sealers, and so its great central lagoon (which was then still open to the sea) was described as still containing a "multitude" of seals in the 1750s. Miscou Island, where as many as a hundred Micmac families had gathered every autumn since antiquity to obtain their winter supply of seal meat and fat, still supported a respectable horsehead population. However, the largest remaining aggregation was probably on the Magdalens.

An English naval officer sent there in 1765 to evaluate the walrus fishery found other things to note as well: "Although no regular method of taking seals has yet been attempted here, it is probable that it might turn out to advantage, particularly in the lagoon betwixt Haywood and Jupiter Harbours, a situation very commodious for laying nets and where there is frequently seen two or three thousand at one time, embayed and playing or sleeping upon the shoals."

Throughout the latter part of the eighteenth century, the demand for train oil kept growing and the consequent destruction of walrus and whales increased the burden on the seals of providing oil. By the 1780s, horseheads were being so sought after that a Nova Scotian named Jesse Lawrence built a permanent factory on Sable Island so he and his men could seal during the pupping season, when foul weather frequently prevented ships from landing there. Lawrence was not long left to enjoy this profitable enterprise in peace. The long-nosed merchants of Massachusetts got wind of it and dispatched schooners to Sable as soon as spring weather would permit. The Yankee crews not only killed all the seals they could find, they looted Lawrence's station, pirated the store of oil and hides he had accumulated during the winter, and eventually drove him off the island.

Law and order of a sort arrived on Sable in the 1820s when the colonial government of Nova Scotia built two lighthouses there together with a life-saving station. This humanitarian act brought no relief to the seals. By 1829, according to Thomas Haliburton, lightkeepers and lifesavers had all become keen sealers, and the island had ceased to be a summer rendezvous for horseheads, "although the seals still resort to the island...for the purpose of whelping." Haliburton graphically describes how the keepers killed adults on the whelping ground. "Each person is armed with a club 5 or 6 feet in length...the butt being transfixed with a piece of steel, one end of which is shaped like a spike, and the other formed into a blade...the party rushes in between the seals and the water and commences the attack...each man selects one and strikes it on the head several blows with the steel spike. He then applies the blade in the same manner and repeats the blows until the animal is brought to the ground...When driven off [the nursery beaches]... they disappear until the ensuing year."

The treatment of horseheads on the Magdalens followed much the same pattern; except that those islands had long since been settled by fishing folk who, having been brought there to hunt walrus, turned easily to slaughtering seals. By 1790, each of the several communities had its own tryworks and the seal hunt had become the islanders' most lucrative occupation. They also killed the migratory harp and hood seals when they could get them, and dotars, too; however, through many decades, the Magdalen seal fishery was mainly based on horseheads, which could be killed in quantity year-round in the lagoons and on the beaches. There was an additional winter slaughter at the rookeries, where pups and females were butchered so ruthlessly that soon only the off-lying and frequently unapproachable Bird Rocks and Deadman Island remained of the many former whelping grounds.

By early in the 1800s, oil from a large horsehead was worth $7 or $8—a good week's pay for those times—and, in consequence, the hunt for them was becoming ever more intense. In the single year of 1848, 21,000 gallons of seal oil, almost all of it made from horseheads, was shipped out of the Magdalens alone.

By the 1860s, the species had been extirpated from much of its former range. The ferocious law of supply and demand was having its baleful effect—the rarer the animals became, the more hotly they were harried, and the more their oil was worth. Oil from an average-sized horsehead on the Côte du Nord in 1886 was worth $11 to $12, and the skin an additional $1.50.

There is little doubt that the horsehead would have followed the walrus into extinction on the northeastern seaboard had it not been supplanted by the unfortunate harp seal as the prime prey of the oilers. By the middle of the nineteenth century, the slaughter of the latter species had come to engross the efforts of all except a scattering of individual sealers. Horseheads were still killed when opportunity offered, but the few survivors had by then become so wary and were so dispersed that active pursuit of them was hardly worthwhile. So, as the twentieth century began, they faded into fortunate obscurity.

The question of how many horseheads existed at first European contact cannot be answered with any degree of certainty. Nevertheless, a searching examination of all the sources—maps, charts, written accounts, and the memories of old maritimers—convinces me that something over 200 whelping rookeries originally existed between Cape Hatteras in the south and Hamilton Inlet on the Labrador coast and that the total horsehead population probably totalled between 750,000 and 1,000,000. Some of these rookeries were still producing 2,000 pups a year as late as the 1850s, and it was largely due to their systematic despoilation that the horsehead so nearly perished, a fact that has not been lost on the new breed of "natural resource managers" who now hold the ultimate fate of the horsehead in their hands.

During the early centuries of the European invasion, the little dotar was luckier than its large relative. Because of its small size, low oil yield, and more scattered distribution, it escaped major commercial exploitation. But it did not go unscathed. As more and more Europeans came to fish and live along the Atlantic coast, the dotar was increasingly hunted to provide food, household oil, and skins for boots and clothing. Furthermore, it suffered the eventual loss of many of the coves and inlets where it had once lived and bred in relative security. Finally, when train soared to golden values, fishermen and small-scale sealers began hunting it for cash. In 1895, for example, a certain Captain Farquhar took a crew to Sable Island where, during a summer-long massacre, he so decimated the dotars there that the species virtually disappeared from Sable for a decade.

Dotars still occupied, if sparsely, most of their original range when the twentieth century began. By then, fossil oil gushing from wells on land had begun replacing train for most industrial purposes and an ensuing drop in the value of seal oil promised a new lease on life, not only to the dotars, but to the few horsehead survivors as well.

It was not to be. Now that these two species were no longer seen as a *source* of profits, human perception of them changed and they began to be perceived as a *threat* to profits. By early in the twentieth century, the once-astronomical profusion of Atlantic salmon was diminishing so rapidly under the pressure of the enormous carnage visited upon it that fishing interests belatedly began to be alarmed. Soon they were bringing powerful pressure to bear on provincial and federal politicians to take measures to halt the decline—so long, of course, as there was no interference with the God-given rights of the fishing industry and of wealthy and influential sport fishermen to continue killing all the salmon they themselves desired.

The politicians did as they so often do: they ordered their minions to find an appropriate villain to blame for the salmon crisis—preferably one that could be savaged with impunity, while absolving the real culprits of any responsibility for the consequences of their greed.

The dotar came conveniently to hand. Seals were already stigmatized as competitors to fishermen, and the public had no need to know what government experts knew full well: that dotars seldom eat free-swimming salmon, if only because it is difficult to catch such swift and agile prey.

In 1927, the federal government of Canada officially condemned the dotars as pernicious and destructive vermin; charged them with wreaking havoc on the salmon; and placed a bounty on their heads. The initial $5 bounty was, for its time, very generous, being more than a dotar had ever been worth commercially. In order to collect it a hunter had only to bring the "muzzle" of a seal to a Fisheries warden or other local official. Most of these gentlemen were quite unable to ascertain whether the bloody lump of fur and gristle submitted to them was the nose of a dotar or that of some other species. In consequence, the bounty hunters were soon killing any and all seals, including whatever remnants of the horsehead nation they could find.

The war on dotars turned most able-bodied male coastal dwellers into bounty hunters, either as a rewarding pastime or as a serious means of increasing their incomes. The onset of the Great Depression, and the economic misery it inflicted on east-coast fishermen, gave even greater impetus to what soon became a general anti-seal crusade. The results were devastating for the seals. By 1939 extensive stretches of the Canadian and adjacent U.S. coastline had been so denuded that some fishermen were actually complaining they could no longer find a seal to kill for the table.

Nevertheless, a scattering of both species did manage to survive in the more remote and isolated regions until the onset of World War II gave them a breathing and a breeding space. They made the most of the interlude, and by 1945 there may have been as many as 2,000–3,000 horseheads in existence together with some tens of thousands of dotars, and both species were attempting to recolonize their ancestral ranges.

This was not to be allowed. If there had ever been any thought given to ending the unholy war against the seals, it came to nothing in view of the political fact that east-coast fishermen had come to regard the seal bounty as a kind of permanent subsidy. To take it from them would have been to risk losing votes. So, not only was it retained, it was doubled. However, the $10 payment was made dependent on presentation of a dotar lower jaw—a change deemed necessary by the discovery that some enterprising bounty hunters had for years been manufacturing seal muzzles from other seal parts. An unanticipated result followed from this change. Because the jaw of an adult horsehead was recognizably larger than that of a dotar, adult horseheads ceased to be of interest to bounty hunters and the horsehead population continued slowly to increase.

Dean Fisher's 1949 rediscovery of the horsehead was not greeted with delight by the mandarins of the Department of Fisheries in Ottawa. And the further discovery during the succeeding two decades that horseheads were actually becoming more numerous brought consternation. As an employee of the department remembers: "It was a bit of a shocker. We'd written the grey seal off and figured the harbour seal was on the way out, which was what the industry was after. The grey comeback posed a problem. It took a while before we found the solution."

It is a fine, crisp February day in the here and now. A big helicopter hovers above a rocky islet set in a glittering expanse of fragmented sea ice a few miles off the Nova Scotia coast. Scattered across the dark rock, more than a hundred ivory-white seal pups stare in dumb amazement at the thundering apparition hanging over them. From their places beside the pups and from steaming leads between the offshore floes, the gleaming heads of scores of parent horseheads rear back in apprehension.

The helicopter slides down its shaft of air and lands. Doors are flung open. Bulking huge in military-style parkas, several men leap to the frozen ground, led by two uniformed officers of Environment Canada's proud Conservation and Protection Branch. All six are armed either with heavy-calibre rifles or "regulation" sealing clubs.

They spread out rapidly, running to get between the seals and the ice-rimmed shore. Mother seals hump nervously toward the frozen sea, turn back toward their mewing pups, then mill in indecision until the staccato roar of rifle fire sends them into sudden panic. A barrage of soft-nosed bullets slams into passive flesh. Some wounded females break through to the shore, lurch convulsively into the leads, and vanish into the dark depths. Others die upon the islet—some still suckling their young.

The pups have little enough time to react to the crimsoning of their small world. A new sound intrudes itself between the now-scattered rifle shots—a sodden *thuck .. thuck .. thuck ..* a sickening mallet-into-melon kind of sound, as club-wielding officers and hired sealers methodically smash the skulls of every pup they can find.

The operation is conducted with precision and dispatch by men well-practised at their trade. Hidden from the public eye, they have been conducting such search-and-destroy missions against horsehead rookeries since 1967. Every year since then, just two months before the internationally infamous slaughter of harp seals in Canadian waters begins, these employees of the federal government of Canada have been busy waging a secret war of extermination against the horsehead seal. They do the job on behalf of what is now the Department of Fisheries and Oceans. They are part of the "solution" to the problem posed by the return of the grey seal from the brink of extinction.

Only five significant horsehead breeding rookeries survive in all of North America, and all come under Canadian jurisdiction. They are on Amet, Camp, and Hut Islands along the coasts of Nova Scotia; on offshore Sable Island; and on the pack ice that gathers in Northumberland Strait. This latter site seems to be a new development, the result of desperate efforts by seals that once bred on islands off the west Cape Breton coast to find a whelping place that will not be turned into a charnel yard by the Conservation and Protection Branch. A recent rookery on Deadman Island in the Magdalen archipelago has now been virtually exterminated. There is a relic breeding population of grey seals in the Muskeget Island area near Cape Cod, but only eleven pups have been recorded since 1964.

In 1981, I visited Hut Island, off the south coast of Cape Breton, and found its barren surface carpeted with seal bones and decaying carcasses. Most were the remains of horsehead pups, but many were those of adults, presumably nursing females. All had died at the practised hands or under the direction of Conservation and Protection officers who have visited Hut Island every winter for the past seventeen years and have destroyed virtually every pup born there during that time. With one exception, the same scene of mayhem has been repeated annually at all the other rookeries up to and including 1983, although the one on the shifting ice of Northumberland Strait has occasionally escaped detection by spotting planes and helicopters.

Only on Sable, a hundred miles out to sea, has a horsehead colony been permitted to bear and rear its young in relative security. Relative, because even this remote site is disrupted at whelping time by government biologists who for many years branded all the pups they could catch and are still tagging them. Mortality amongst the pups from shock, infection, or due to abandonment by their mothers has been high; but this is not all the Sable colony has had to endure. Additional pups and adults are regularly killed to provide scientific specimens. Up to the spring of 1984, 865 horseheads had been "taken" for scientific purposes.

The Sable colony is permitted to survive partly because it serves as a research laboratory where scientists can accumulate data for the publications upon which their fames and fortunes largely depend. However, the island also happens to loom large in the public eye because of finds of natural gas in its vicinity and because of its famous herd of wild horses. The kind of secret butchery visited on the other horsehead rookeries could not easily be concealed on Sable and would be sure to provoke a furious outcry from conservationists. Still, such a prospect may not be of great moment to the Fisheries and Oceans potentates who have now authorized a "controlled cull" of the horseheads on the island at some as yet unspecified date, presumably at a time when public attention is directed elsewhere.

The rationale for this projected action is that the seal population on Sable is increasing. No recognition is made of the fact that the increase is more apparent than real, resulting in part at least from the arrival on Sable's beaches of many adults that have been forced to abandon their mainland rookeries under pain of death.

"Controlled cull" is surely one of the most abhorrent of the newspeak phrases devised by "wildlife and resource managers" in order to conceal the true intentions of their political and commercial masters. As applied to the horsehead, it is a revoltingly cynical deception, since it actually means an *uncontrolled* slaughter directed to the effective extirpation of the species in Canadian waters. A perusal of Fisheries and Oceans' own internal statistics makes this grimly clear. Since the beginning of the "controlled cull" in 1967, I calculate that at least 90 per cent of all horsehead pups known to have been born outside of Sable have been butchered by the quaintly named Conservation and Protection Branch. Between 1967 and 1983, more than 16,000 pups and 4,000 associated adults were admittedly destroyed in raids on the rookeries.

The reality behind the deception is so atrocious as to challenge credulity. How could an agency of a civilized government engage in such a blatant attempt at biocide? What good or useful purpose could it possibly serve?

When I asked the Department of Fisheries and Oceans for an explanation, the essence of the reply contained this chilling statement couched in the new jargon: "Seals inhibit the maximization of fisheries growth potential, adversely affecting rational harvesting of these natural resources and the maximization of a healthy economy. Such negative-flow factors must be dealt with by scientifically validated management programmes such as the one we are engaged in."

In support of what amounts to a writ of execution, three specific charges are laid against the horsehead by Fisheries and Oceans. First: they are extremely destructive of the gear and catches of inshore fishermen. Second: they eat tremendous quantities of fishes that would otherwise be harvested by commercial fishermen. Third: they spread a parasite known as the cod-worm, which reduces the retail value of cod fillets and imposes a heavy burden on the fishing industry. Not only are all these charges specious in the extreme, they are for the most part patently untrue. Let us examine them one by one.

Fishing is and always has been a risk enterprise. Fishermen expect to lose gear and calculate accordingly. However, the actual damage done to catches and gear by *all* species of seals in Canadian Atlantic waters amounts to less than 1 per cent of losses sustained from storms, passing ships, malicious damage, sharks, even jellyfish that clog nets so that they are swept away by powerful tidal streams.

On the basis of data that are themselves suspect, the department asserts that horseheads consume 50,000 metric tonnes (1980 figures) of valuable fishes every year, or 10 per cent of the half-a-million tonnes taken by Canadian east-coast fishermen. Analysis of this charge demonstrates that less than 20,000 tonnes of the consumption *attributed* to horseheads (but by no means proven) is of species of even marginal commercial value. Furthermore, the presumed tonnage represents *live* weight—the weight of the *whole* fish—while the figure for the commercial catch is based on *processed* weight—only that portion of the fish that is packaged for sale. The live weight taken by Canadian commercial fishermen in 1980 was approximately 1.2 million tonnes. The percentage of commercially valuable fish eaten by the seals can therefore be no more than 1.6 per cent.

Statistics are sometimes designed to lie, and that these figures from Fisheries and Oceans were so designed is established by a statement that Dr. Arthur Mansfield and Brian Beck, senior marine biologists with the department, published in the Technical Report of the Fisheries Research Board of Canada. "The [available] data suggests that the two largest commercial fisheries, those for herring and cod, suffer little competition from the grey seal."

The final charge has to do with the fact that the life of the threadlike cod-worm is lived partly in the digestive tracts of seals (and some other animals) and partly in the muscular tissue of cod. The worm itself does not present a health problem to man. It does pose a cosmetic problem, but one with which fish-plant owners have long known how to deal. Operators inspect the cod fillets using a process similar to candling eggs and remove the worms.

Just how heavy an economic burden this imposes on the $2-billion Canadian fishing industry can be judged from the fact that, in 1978, the thirty major east-coast plants employed a grand total of sixty-five people, mostly women and mostly part-time, to deal with the cod-worm problem. I might add that these sixty-five jobs were, and remain, desperately needed in the chronically underemployed eastern provinces of Canada.

Nor is this all. The prestigious Marine Mammal Committee of the International Council for the Exploration of the Sea, meeting in Denmark in 1979, considered all available evidence on the cod-worm problem and concluded: "We are unable to say whether a reduction in the [cod-worm] infection of cod would result from a reduction in seal numbers."

Fisheries and Oceans directs much the same set of charges against the harp, hood, and dotar seals. However, the latter can no longer pose any conceivable threat to the well-being of the Canadian economy. Between 1926 and 1954, the dotar population was reduced by the bounty hunt from an estimated 200,000 to less than 30,000. Not content with even this massive destruction, Fisheries doubled the bounty, with the result that, by 1976, according to government biologists, fewer than 12,700 dotars still survived in eastern Canadian waters. Most of these held to their precarious existence on lonely stretches of coast uninhabited by men who either fished—or voted.

In 1976, after a half century of "management," the federal authorities decided that the destruction of the species had been effectively achieved and that the bounty no longer served any physical or political purpose, since hardly anyone was bothering to hunt the few remaining and now very wary dotars. However, by a stunning coincidence, they simultaneously concluded that the "controlled cull" of horseheads was not depleting *that* species fast enough; so, instead of being cancelled, the bounty was switched from the one species to the other.

This switch provided no chance of recuperation for the dotars since most bounty-paying officials could not tell the difference between the jawbone of a young horsehead and an adult dotar. Furthermore, the new bounty had been enriched to $25. Such largesse brought the hunters back out in droves to take part in a revived and general slaughter of both species.

The jaws of 584 horseheads and an unreported number of dotars were turned in for bounty during 1976; but this figure represents as little as a fifth of the actual kill. As the mandarins of Fisheries and Oceans are fully aware, one of the advantages of employing the bounty system against seals is that, for every one shot and recovered, several more sink to the bottom dead or later die of wounds. In July, 1976, department employees interviewed eighteen fishermen who reported that of 111 seals shot at and presumed wounded or killed, only 13 per cent were recovered. These deaths do not, of course, appear in the official statistics; but it is obvious that the bounty paid in 1976 represented the destruction of at least 1,500 and perhaps as many as 2,000 horseheads.

Although the bounty-engendered kill increased in each of the years 1977 and 1978, this was not enough to satisfy the Minister of Fisheries and Oceans. In 1979 the bounty was doubled, to $50 for each adult seal. To whet the appetites of hunters even more, an additional $10 was paid if the seal had been branded and a *further* $50 if the corpse bore a tag. In that year, more than 3,000 horseheads were slaughtered in what had become a perverse lottery of death.

If the hunters were to be selected as expert and responsible marksmen, the carnage might not be quite so appalling, but they are not. Although the department piously insists that only "bona fide fishermen who have suffered financial loss from seals" are permitted to shoot them, the truth is that any resident of the Maritime Provinces old enough to carry a gun can be a bounty hunter. Any Nova Scotian, for example, need only buy a non-commercial fishing permit, for $5, in order to validate an additional $1 permit to carry and use a rifle for seal hunting throughout the year. Hundreds do this, hunting for pleasure as well as profit. They shoot *every* seal they find, of whatever species, for the sport of it—and on the chance that it may be a horsehead. Since they are empowered to use rifles even during the closed seasons for other game, they take advantage of the opportunity to practise their skills on dolphins, whales, eider ducks, and even—I have seen this myself—on tuna.

In 1979, I tried to persuade Fisheries and Oceans to withdraw the bounty, citing some of the abuses connected with it. I was told the matter was under review. The following year I submitted a detailed report of demonstrable biocide against the seals to the man responsible for it—the Honourable Roméo LeBlanc, Minister of Fisheries and Oceans. *Four months* later, he replied to the effect that both he and his scientific advisers were satisfied there was no cause for concern. He concluded his letter with this remarkable statement: "Our policy is to build the stocks of harvestable fish and marine mammals to levels which will permit regular but controlled catches by Canadians while ensuring the well-being of these valuable resources. It has never been the Department's intent to do otherwise."

The cumulative destruction resulting from payment of blood money to hunters, begun in 1976, together with the "cull" at the rookeries, has now resulted in the deaths of at least 50,000 horseheads (and some thousands of dotars). It is somewhat difficult to comprehend how the "well-being" of these particular "valuable resources" is being ensured.

At the annual meeting of the International Convention on Trade in Endangered Species held in Europe in the spring of 1981, the spokesman for France pointed out that both grey and harbour seals were in trouble, world-over. He proposed that they both be listed in Appendix II of the Convention, which is designed "to avoid utilization incompatible with the survival of a species."

Canada refused to support the resolution.

This was at least consistent. Canada had long since refused to join the United States, which extended full protection to both dotars and horseheads as early as 1972. Now LeBlanc chose to implement the 1981 recommendations of the Canadian Atlantic Fisheries Scientific Advisory Committee. This ponderously named group has as its chief though undeclared raison d'être the furthering of government policies. Its proposal was: "As a short term strategy, aimed at either stabilizing or further reducing the grey seal population, between 8,000 and 10,000 animals [should] be killed for [each of] the next two years."

Fisheries and Oceans made every effort to carry out this recommendation. Yet, although 1,846 horseheads were "culled" at the rookeries in 1982, and the record number of 2,690 (1,627 pups and 927 adult females) in 1983, the target remained elusive. The truth was there were not that many grey seals in existence in mainland coastal waters. Had the "cull" been extended to Sable, that last refuge of the horseheads, the committee's goal might more nearly have been achieved.

There is no doubt that it was the intention of Mr. LeBlanc's department to visit the Conservation and Protection death squads on Sable's rookeries. But, considering the problems Fisheries and Oceans was then having in defending the "cull" of harp and hood seals in the face of mounting international protest (a matter dealt with in the following chapters), discretion as to the slaughter of seals on Sable was accounted the better part of valour—for the moment anyway.

Since 1981, I have been conducting annual assessments of dotar and horse-head populations in representative parts of eastern Canada. Places I am unable to visit in person are surveyed for me by competent naturalists. What follows is a representative sampling.

During visits to the Grand Barachois on the island of Miquelon reaching back to the late 1950s, I have seen as many as 300 horseheads and dotars, mostly the former, gathered together during their mid-summer convocations. In 1983 four observers were able to find no more than 100 seals of both species during two days of observation, and some of these were probably counted twice. There has been and still is a brisk trade in the jaws of horse-heads illegally killed on this French island and smuggled into Newfoundland or Nova Scotia where bounty is paid, no questions asked.

I summered on the Magdalen Islands during the 1960s and early 1970s and spent many hours watching horseheads there. In the early sixties they were more or less unmolested and were so tolerant of human beings that, on one occasion, I was able to approach a herd indolently sunbathing on a beach by swimming toward them and then crawling up on shore while pre-tending to be a seal myself. It was a somewhat chastening experience to find myself almost cheek by jowl with thirty or so adult horseheads who, at that close range, bulked gigantic in my timorous view. When a low-flying aircraft spooked them and sent the herd galumphing into the sea, I was momentarily terrified, not of being bitten, but of being flattened as by a herd of steam-rollers. However, they avoided my prone body with deliberate ease.

When I first saw the Magdalens, the horsehead population there num-bered several hundred and was slowly increasing. Introduction of the bounty and application of the "cull" has now virtually wiped them out in an orgy of destruction that disgusted Jacques Cousteau when he visited the archipel-ago in 1979.

Complaints by tourists about the stench from seal carcasses on the beaches of Prince Edward Island have been commonplace for several years. One stretch of beach became so unsafe for human visitors, because of rico-cheting bullets fired at seals, that the federal authorities, under pressure from the island's tourist board, were forced to forbid bounty hunting there during the tourist season. Nevertheless, our most recent survey recorded only nineteen horseheads and two dotars along nearly 100 miles of the island's beaches—and five of these were dead, of bullet wounds.

Micmac Indians used to gather every autumn throughout most of the last century on Miscou Island to hunt seals for food and clothing. Grey seals were still common there in 1965. During a recent visit by one of my confreres, not a single seal was to be found. He was told by local fishermen that "about a dozen" had been killed the previous year, but they were now so scarce that nobody bothered to go after them.

During the past several years I have lived on the southeast coast of Cape Breton Island. When I first went there, it was not unusual to see twenty or thirty horseheads from the window of my house on almost any given summer day. Now I count myself lucky to see two or three alive in any given month.

And yet...

On January 26, 1984, the Toronto *Globe and Mail* published an article headed: "Seals Making Comeback, Scientists Believe." It contained the following assertions: "Fisheries researchers agree there are more seals today than in the recent past. 'The population of grey seals has increased dramatically' in the past 10 or 15 years, said Wayne Stobo, a [federal government] expert on grey and harbour seals...as human killing declined, the number of sharks also apparently dropped in northern Atlantic waters, Mr. Stobo said. So seal populations are growing...Fisheries officials are under increasing pressure to cull herds to regulate seal populations, said Dan Goodman, senior policy planning advisor of the Department of Fisheries and Oceans. Estimates of the total population of grey seals range between 30,000 and 60,000..."

When governments lie, they do so with conviction. Of the many scientists specializing in seals with whom I have talked, none believes there are more seals alive today than in the recent or the distant past. Not one considers sharks a major or even significant predator on seals in North Atlantic waters. Not even the most optimistic believes the grey seal population in Canadian waters exceeds 30,000, and some estimate less than half of that. One wryly suggested that Mr. Goodman may have been "absent-mindedly" thinking of the entire existing world population of the species!

Occasional rays of light penetrate the murk. In July of 1983 the Parliamentary Committee on Seals and Sealing, an official advisory body to Fisheries and Oceans, recommended to Pierre de Bané, LeBlanc's successor, "that the culling of grey seals be stopped, since the committee sees no reason or justification for continuing the cull. This is in addition to our reiteration that the bounty system is inhumane and useless as a control technique."

This blunt recommendation, coupled with the disastrous consequences to Canada of the massive anti-harp sealing campaign of that year, seems to have had some effect. Early in 1984 the department announced that only 300 pups would be "culled" this year. However, the cessation of mass slaughter at the rookeries is *only* for this one year. It is no more than a tactical move that does not alter the overriding strategy of extinction that the Department of Fisheries and Oceans continues to pursue. And the bounty kill will continue as before. Furthermore, there is reason to believe that, in southern New Brunswick, it has been unofficially expanded to include dotars once again.

A carefully orchestrated attempt is being made, nominally by "independent" fishermen's organizations, to have the bounty increased. Other proposals, which I believe originate with Fisheries and Oceans, are now being publicly reflected back to it. They include the suggestion that Canada do as Ireland has done and sell grey seal hunting safaris to foreign sportsmen. East-coast fishing organizations are also clamouring for a "public seal hunt." Special prizes will be awarded to the good citizens who make the largest "score" (read: kill), and a festival will be held to celebrate those who have "helped Canada get rid of this growing threat to our fisheries."

The shape of things intended is clearly revealed in a Canadian Press release dated May 14, 1984.

"Seal Cull Urgent, Ottawa Told. The Nova Scotia and federal Governments have held discussions for several months on a possible cull of grey seals, according to provincial Fisheries Minister John Leefe.

"Mr. Leefe said on Friday the seals are eating about 1.5-million tonnes of cod off the East Coast annually and spreading a parasite which reduces the value of the fish. Because of the sealworm infestation, *processors have refused to buy cod caught near Sable Island, a major breeding grounds for grey seals.* [Italics mine]

"Mr. Leefe said the Nova Scotia Government wants a kill organized quickly but Ottawa is unwilling because it fears adverse publicity. Commercial seal hunts off Newfoundland and Quebec have resulted in campaigns by anti-sealing groups to have consumers in Britain and the United States boycott Canadian products.

"'Ottawa and four Atlantic provinces should take part in the cull,' Mr. Leefe said.

"He said Ottawa 'would be delighted' if the Nova Scotia Government dealt with the problem unilaterally but that the province doesn't have the power to do so. The grey seal population, estimated at a few thousand 20 years ago, now has increased to about 100,000, Mr. Leefe said."

It seems brutally apparent that the continuing survival of dotars and horse-heads in Canadian waters will depend, not on enlightened and honest policies applied by government departments and their patrons and lackeys, but on such independent conservation organizations such as may take up the battle on behalf of the grey seal.

18
Death on Ice (Old Style)

Now it is to be told that the ships of Karlsefni coasted southward with Snorri and Bjarni and their people. They journeyed a long time until they came to a river which flowed into a pond and thence into the sea. They settled above the shore of the pond and remained there all that winter.

One morning after spring arrived, a great number of skin boats came rowing from the south. They were so numerous it looked as if charcoal had been scattered on the sea. The two parties came together and began to barter.

Some of the Norse cattle were near and the bull ran out of the woods and began to bellow. This terrified the Skraelings and they raced to their boats and rowed away. For three weeks nothing more was seen of them, then a great multitude was discovered coming from the south. Thereupon Karlsefni and his men took red shields and displayed them. The Skraelings sprang from their boats, and they met and fought together.

Freydis Eriksdottir came out of doors and seeing that Karlsefni and the men were fleeing she tried to join them but could not keep up since she was pregnant. Then she saw a dead man before her, naked sword beside him. Freydis snatched it up and as the Skraelings came close she let fall her shift and slapped her breasts with the naked blade. Seeing this the Skraelings were frightened and ran to their boats and rowed away.

It now seemed clear to Karlsefni and his people that though this was an attractive country their lives there would be filled with fear and turmoil because of the Skraelings and so they decided to leave. They sailed north along the coast and surprised five Skraelings dressed in skin doublets asleep near the sea, and they put them to death.

This paraphrased and shortened version of an old Norse saga describes an event that took place about the year 1000 when a Norse expedition from Greenland tried to establish itself on the west coast of Newfoundland. The attempt failed because of conflict with a native people whom the Norse called *Skraelingar*. For almost a thousand years thereafter, the identity of these people remained a mystery.

Now we know they were not Indians, as might have been expected, but an Eskimoan people of the so-called Dorset culture who had been drawn from the High Arctic to make their homes in the relatively temperate Gulf of St. Lawrence region for the same reason that had attracted many northern animals such as the bowhead whale, beluga, walrus, and white bear— because it was a place that met their needs.

The Skraelings were seal hunters, and what brought them to the Gulf and held them there was the unimaginable multitude of seals that inhabited the neighbouring waters—and, in particular, the species known to us as the harp seal, with which their culture was inextricably entwined.

Skraelings lived and prospered on all the coasts of North America adjacent to the seas wherein the harp abounded. Around Baffin Bay basin, on both sides of Davis Strait, among the eastern islands of the Canadian Arctic archipelago, south along the Labrador, and into the Gulf of St. Lawrence at least as far as Cabot Strait, their places of habitation can still be found. The sites are easily identified by characteristic microlithic stone implements found in midden heaps, but especially by the composition of the middens themselves, which consist mainly of decayed organic material and bones of seals. Some middens, such as those at Englee, Port au Choix, and Cape Ray in Newfoundland, are so vast and their greasy black layers of long-decayed seal offal so thickly impregnated with seal bones that they convey the impression of titanic butchery. But that is an illusion due to the telescoping of time. These accumulations are the product of as many as eight or nine centuries of subsistence hunting by generation after generation of people for whom the harp seal was the staff of life.

The adult harp is of moderate size as seals go, averaging about 300 pounds in weight and five and a half feet in length, roughly midway between the little dotar and the massive horsehead. It is pre-eminently an ice seal, spending much of its life on or close to the broken floes of the drifting pack. A superb swimmer, it can dive to at least 600 feet and make long passages underwater, or under ice, remaining submerged for as long as half an hour.

The harp nation is composed of three distinct parts. One lives in the White and Barents Seas to the north of Europe, the second in the Greenland Sea east of that great island, while the third and largest inhabits the waters of the northwest Atlantic. This tribe, the one with which we are most concerned, summers as far north as Hall Basin, within 400 miles of the North Pole, but whelps off northeast Newfoundland and in the Gulf of St. Lawrence. During the cycle of one annual migration its members must travel 5,000 miles or more.

These western harps begin their autumnal migration a few weeks before the Arctic seas begin to congeal, streaming south in companies of thousands and tens of thousands to form an almost unbroken procession down the coast of Labrador—a procession that once was composed of several million individuals. By late November the leading companies have reached the Strait of Belle Isle, and here the river splits. The mightiest stream passes through the Strait and heads west along the north shore of the Gulf. Some conception of its magnitude can be gained from the observation of a French trader who watched the harps pass the northern tip of Newfoundland in the autumn of 1760. He reported that they filled the sea from shore to horizon for ten days and nights. At one time this stream flowed as far west as Isle aux Coudres, only a few score miles short of Quebec City, though what is left of it today seldom gets beyond the Saguenay.

From the Strait of Belle Isle, the other river seems to flow southeast-ward—and disappears. Some biologists believe it reaches the Grand Banks, where its members disperse and spend the winter, but there is no sure evidence for this. Perhaps the most likely explanation is that the swift-swimming seals loop around eastern Newfoundland and enter the Gulf through Cabot Strait. Thereafter, I suspect, they make their way northward up the west coast of Newfoundland where, once, they brought the gift of life to the Skraeling settlements that waited for them there.

But this is mostly speculation. It is a salutary thought that even in these days of electronic eyes and ears, and in seas full of working fishing vessels, the whereabouts of the mighty mass of the harp herds still remain essentially unknown from January through to the latter part of February.

During the winter months a titanic tongue of polar pack as much as 100 miles in width thrusts southward in the grip of the Labrador Current until, by mid-February, its offshoots are clogging the shores of northeastern Newfoundland and pushing through Belle Isle Strait to meet and mingle with winter ice born in the Gulf.

To the untutored human eye this world of grinding, shifting pans and floes, lifting, splintering, and raftering in the ocean swell, swept by bliz-zards, gales, and fog, has the aspect of a white and desolate desert, seemingly the very anathema of life. Yet it is in this realm of frozen chaos that, as February ends and March storms in, the teeming legions of the harp seal reappear.

Flying low over the pack on a rare sunny day in mid-February, one sees nothing but a glittering empty wasteland except, perhaps, that here and there in open leads one catches a glimpse of animation as pale sunlight gleams from the wet backs of a few porpoising seals. Several days later, a miracle seems to have taken place.

From a light plane cruising at 1,500 feet on a late February day in 1968, I looked down upon an endless vista of ice that was clotted, clustered, and speckled with whelping seals in such quantity that the biologist flying with me could only shrug when I asked how many he thought there were.

Even with the help of aerial photography, scientists can only roughly estimate the number of individuals in a major harp seal whelping patch. The working figure generally used is 3,000–4,000 adults per square mile, mostly female, together with nearly as many pups, depending on how far advanced the whelping is. There is *no* way of counting the males, which are generally in the water or under it. To make things even more difficult, the area occupied by the patch can itself be only roughly estimated. Although the heart of the one we flew over that day seemed to be about twelve miles long and at least six wide, amorphous strings and tongues of seals spread outward from it in all directions like the pseudopods of some gigantic amoeba. Our estimate, which was little better than a guess, was that this patch perhaps held half a million seals.

Yet it was as nothing to the size of those that once existed.

In the spring of 1844, more than 100 Newfoundland sealing ships worked a whelping patch off the southeast coast of Labrador, the main portion of which was at least fifty miles long and twenty broad. At a most conservative estimate that one patch contained more than 5,000,000 seals. What is known for *certain* is that the sealers landed approximately 740,000 pelts, the vast majority of which were stripped from newborn pups.

Western harp seals whelp in two well-separated regions: on the ice fields drifting off northeastern Newfoundland, which area is known as the Front, and in the Gulf. There are generally two well-defined patches at the Front and two or more in the Gulf. At each patch, the males linger in frolicking companies in open leads or rest companionably on the edge of the pans, while the females disperse across the ice plain, each claiming her own space on which to bear and nurture her single pup.

A description of the newborn pup, or whitecoat as it is called, is probably superfluous since its image has appeared so often that there can be few people who are not now familiar with it. This big-eyed, cuddlesome creature has become the ultimate symbol for those who are convinced that man must put a check-rein on his ruinous abuse of animate creation and, as such, it is by no means badly chosen.

It remains a whitecoat for only about two weeks. Then it is left to fend for itself when its mother, who has fed it such generous quantities of creamy milk that the pup has not only more than tripled in weight but has acquired a two-inch layer of fat, abandons it and goes off to mate with the attendant males. Now the soft, luxuriant white fur begins to shed. At this stage the pup is called a raggedy-jacket. In several days the moult is complete, leaving the youngster in a mottled coat of silvery-grey. Called a beater now, the pup makes its first venture into the water at the age of five to six weeks, soon teaches itself to swim, and begins learning how to make a living from the sea, meanwhile subsisting on its reserves of fat and protein.

As spring progresses, the adult seals, duty done and pleasure taken, form a second series of enormous aggregations, called moulting patches. For days and even weeks, the harp multitudes remain in close company, hauling out in black-and-silver multitudes to sun themselves, shed their coats, and, we can believe, socialize. This is the annual harp seal festival, celebrated at the end of the breeding year before a new cycle begins.

Toward the end of April, as the great ice tongue begins to dissolve under the influence of the spring sun, the festival ends and the adults begin the long journey back to Arctic seas. A month or two behind them come hordes of beaters, travelling individually and apparently with only an inner voice to guide them in their solitary passage to the ancestral summering grounds.

Basque whalers were probably the earliest Europeans to become aware of the existence of the harp nation of the west, having seen the migrating companies come pouring through Belle Isle Strait during those winters when the whalers were forced to harbour in the New World.

The first European *sealers* seem to have been the French colonists who began settling along the lower St. Lawrence River valley in the mid-seventeenth century. Initially, as we have seen, they preyed upon the horsehead, but as more settlers spread eastward down the shores of the great estuary, they began to encounter a different kind of seal, one that appeared in January in almost inconceivable numbers.

Since these silvery animals with their distinctive black caps and dark saddle patches shaped rather like harps never entered river mouths or hauled out on shore or off-lying rocks as did dotars and horseheads, the only way to hunt them seemed to be by gunning from small boats. The combination of ineffective muskets and ice-filled waters not only made this unproductive but exceedingly dangerous. Nevertheless, some considered it worth the risk, since each of these seals was so thickly layered with fat that it could yield almost as much oil as a much larger horsehead. So they were highly prized by the colonists, who called them *loup-marin brasseur* in distinction to the original loup marin, or horsehead.

The incredible abundance but relative untouchability of the loup-marin brasseur must have caused much frustration until, at last, the French found a way to slaughter them en masse. During the first half of the seventeenth century, some adventurer exploring eastward into terra incognita along the north shore of the Gulf encountered those most accomplished of all sealers, the Inuit. In those times, Inuit wintered at least as far west as Anticosti Island, subsisting primarily on seals, of which the harp was their principal quarry. Having no guns, they took it by means of nets woven of sealskin thongs set across narrow runs between coastal islands.

The French were always quick to learn hunting skills from native peoples and, in short order, were making and setting sealing nets themselves. This net fishery soon became so financially rewarding that the authorities in Quebec and Paris were kept busy selling new seigneuries. By 1700 these stretched as far east as the Mingan Islands, and in every case the wording of the grants clearly indicates that a local monopoly of the seal fishery was the most valuable right embodied in them.

Expansion farther eastward was halted, not by any shortage of seals but because the French had roused the enmity of the Inuit by associating themselves and their interests with various Indian tribes. The hostility that followed had grown so intense and bloody that neither French *nor* Indians dared winter on the Gulf coast east of Mingan until early in the eighteenth century.

A way around this was found by coming at it from the other end. The region around the Strait of Belle Isle had for long been dominated by cod fishermen from France and, although there had been bloody clashes with the Inuit there as well, French wintering parties could hold their own by retreating at need into the security of wooden blockhouses defended by ships' cannon. So, in 1689, two seigneuries, principally engaged in sealing, were established to encompass the whole of the Labrador and Newfoundland coasts bordering the Strait.

By then the harp seal fishery had become so lucrative that the French rallied their Indian allies and began waging a successful war of extermination against the Inuit for control of the Côte du Nord. By 1720, a string of seigneuries stretched from Tadoussac all along the north shore right to Belle Isle, then north along Labrador's Atlantic coast as far as Hamilton Inlet. Additional sealing stations also sprang up along the west coast of Newfoundland at some of the very sites once occupied by the vanished Skraelings.

The nature of the fishery had altered and become more complex as the French grew increasingly familiar with their quarry's annual cycle. To the eastward of Anticosti there were now two sealing seasons: one in early winter when the herds came pouring through the Strait and headed west along the Côte du Nord, and a second during the spring after the adults began making their ways northward to the moulting patches. Nets had changed, too. Instead of relying solely on mesh nets to entangle and drown the seals, pound nets were also being used. These soon grew to such size and complexity that it required up to a dozen men to operate one. By raising and lowering door panels with winches operated from shore, it was possible to trap entire companies of migrating seals, which could then be killed at leisure.

By the mid-eighteenth century, hundreds of men from the settlements of New France were engaged in harp sealing and the colony was exporting as much as 500 tons of seal oil every year, a quantity requiring an annual kill of some 20,000 adult seals. There was so much pressure to expand this money-minting enterprise as rapidly as possible that one contemporary visitor to New France felt compelled to register a warning.

"It is questionable whether it would be in the interests of the Colony to multiply the seal fisheries...on the contrary it is logical to conclude that too great a number of the same would lead in a shorter space of time to the destruction of this species of animal. They only produce one cub a year; the fishing takes place in springtime which is the season of breeding, or in the autumn at which time the females are pregnant and, in consequence a large number could not be caught without destroying the species and risking the exhaustion of this fishery."

Predictably, this opinion was ignored. In fact, the urge to kill as many seals as possible was being inflamed by the emergence of competition. Early in the eighteenth century, English settlers from eastern Newfoundland, who had been used to sailing their small craft to the north coast to engage in a summer fishery for cod and salmon, discovered what the French were up to on the Petit Nord (the Great Northern Peninsula of Newfoundland) and themselves began harp sealing. Soon they were establishing permanent settlements around Fogo and in Notre Dame Bay, from which they could seal in winter and fish cod and salmon in summer.

The English even added a new twist to the business. Having discovered that hordes of beaters and sub-adults, which they called bedlamers (a corruption of *bêtes de la mer*), haunted the northern bays in spring for some weeks after the adults had departed, they took to swatching (gunning from small rowing craft) for them amongst the thinning floes.

Such was the success attending both swatching and netting that, as early as 1738, the few scattered inhabitants of Fogo Island alone were shipping oil and skins valued at £1,200, the produce from more than 7,000 seals killed each year. Now the die was truly cast. Having become aware of the money to be made from the harp fishery, the English hastened to make it uniquely, and bloodily, their own.

At this stage, French and English sealers alike had no conception of the true size of the harp nation and knew little enough about the creature itself. For a long time they did not even realize that bedlamers and beaters were of the harp species. And they knew nothing about what the seals did when out of sight of land. The drifting world of the ice fields seemed so hostile that they avoided exploration of it. As long as this heartland of the ice seals remained sacrosanct, human predation, massive as it seemed to those engaged in it, could occur only on the periphery where it had small effect upon the nation as a whole. But this was a situation that, given accidents of fate coupled with the nature of the human beast, could not endure for long.

Very early one spring near the middle of the eighteenth century (it may have been in 1743), a prolonged period of unseasonably warm weather accompanied by heavy rains prematurely weakened the great ice tongue that thrusts down the Labrador coast to provide the floating fields whereon the largest part of the harp nation bears its young. By the time the million or more gravid females reached the fields, the floes had become so shrunken, dispersed, and rotten that the seals could find no proper place to whelp. Yet their time was on them and so, in desperation, they hauled out on any ice that would bear their weight; and there they pupped, not in the usual gigantic patches but scattered like chaff across thousands of miles of disintegrating floes.

A day or two after the mass whelping had taken place, a nor'easter came howling over the region. Seas quickly built to mountainous size in the open ocean outside the pack and, rolling in under the floes, began heaving them into wild and vertiginous motion until they were crashing into and crushing each other. Numbers of new-born whitecoats, and not a few of their mothers, were crushed, and many of the remainder of the pups, unable to swim as yet, were swept away and drowned. Those that remained alive found themselves on isolated fragments of swiftly disintegrating floes, inexorably driven south by wind and current. In mid-March, this ice began piling up along the western coast of Bonavista Bay, freighted with tens of thousands of pups.

A handful of English fishermen had already established a permanent foothold on that rocky and reef-strewn shore in order to be on hand to hunt for adult harps in winter and beaters in the spring. They were dismayed when the bay filled up with ice until it stretched so far from shore they could no longer see open water. Unless and until it blew out to sea again, there could be no boat hunting. It must have been at this juncture that some daring fellow ventured out onto the grinding chaos, perhaps because he thought he saw some sign of life, and found a scattering of small white seals.

Within hours every able-bodied person was scrambling across the dangerously uncertain pack. Before the wind hauled southerly and the ice slackened and drove offshore, they had dragged the bloody sculps (skins with the fat attached) of thousands of young seals back to land where the thick layers of blubber were peeled away and consigned to the trypots, there to produce many barrels of high-grade train oil.

It is recorded that the Bonavista people did not even realize what manner of beast it was they were slaughtering until someone noticed a whitecoat being suckled by a mother harp and drew the obvious conclusion.

There have been a number of such "Whitecoat Springs," each of which became a milestone in the history of Newfoundland. In 1773, the whelping ice piled into Notre Dame Bay allowing fishermen there to slay 50,000 pups. In 1843, the pack jammed into Trinity and Conception Bays, enabling the landsmen to slaughter an estimated 80,000. But the most sanguine massacre of all took place in 1861, when 60,000 embayed whitecoats were killed in Hamilton Inlet together with 150,000 more in Bonavista Bay. In 1872, even the townees of St. John's were able to swarm out on the ice beyond the harbour mouth and butcher nearly 100,000 pups.

The trouble with windfalls such as these was that they only happened at intervals of roughly twenty years. It was inevitable that, with the gleam of this white gold to light the way, Newfoundlanders should have gone looking for the mother lode.

At the time the search began, the fishermen knew only that the seals pupped somewhere on the illimitable waste of ice to the northward. Although they had no idea how distant the nurseries might be, as early as the 1770s some began probing the southern fringes of the vast ice fields in the open boats they normally used for the cod fishery. When these proved too awkward and too fragile to be forced in amongst floes or hauled across intervening pans, they developed light, clinker-built punts, which could be hauled over the ice by a two-man crew. These ice-skiffs were designed primarily for swatching beaters but, as time went by, the sealers took them farther and farther into the pack, thereby acquiring skill in the precarious business of ice navigation.

Finally, in 1789, a group of these ice hunters encountered a small whelping patch, which had drifted well to the south of where it should normally have been. During the next few days, the men of a fleet of ice-skiffs sculped 25,000 whitecoats and the drive to find what was already being referred to as the "main patch" received fresh impetus.

With the growth of experience, these tough and implacable seafarers had come to realize that the main patch could probably not be reached except with vessels strong enough to brave the pack and big enough to shelter crews from bitter temperatures and killing blizzards. So they developed the reinforced shallop, or bully-boat: a bluff-bowed, extremely strong little vessel of about forty tons, decked fore and aft, yawl-rigged, and capable of crowding a crew of a dozen sealers.

The bullies could stay out for a week or two, which was about as long as even these weather-hardened men could endure. However, although the bullies could be worked thirty or forty leagues into the loose ice fringing the central pack and could scavenge stray pockets of whitecoats that had been whelped outside the main patch, they could not reach Eldorado.

Bigger boats were built to look for it. By 1802, fifty-foot, fully-decked schooners, double-planked against the ice, were sailing north. Although the main patch continued to elude them, they made fortunes anyway. In the spring of 1804, 149 bullies and schooners sailed from the northern bays and, though they got few whitecoats, they swatched 73,000 beaters and old harps. The net fishery that year yielded an additional 40,000.

From its beginnings, the search for the main patch had been expensive in terms of lives and vessels lost. But in 1817 a ferocious storm of the kind that sometimes devastated the whelping patches brought desolation to many a northern outport. The sealers landed only 50,000 sculps that year and paid a fearful price. At least twenty-five vessels were crushed and lost in the pack, taking nearly 200 men to icy deaths.

Those who survived were not intimidated. Bigger and stronger vessels pressed ever deeper into the great ice tongue until, in 1819, they finally found what they were looking for. The ice that year was singularly open, and prevailing northeast winds had drifted the main patch to within 100 miles of the Newfoundland coast. Here it was discovered by sealers in a new kind of vessel: 100-ton ice-strengthened brigantines each carrying fifty to sixty men. This opening act in a drama of ongoing slaughter seems to have gone unrecorded. Thus the eyewitness report of a Professor J.B. Jukes, who in 1840 went to the main patch in the brigantine *Topaz*, will have to serve. I have abbreviated it somewhat.

"We passed through some loose ice on which the young seals were scattered, and nearly all hands went overboard, slaying, skinning and hauling. We then got into a lake of open water and sent out five punts. [The men of] these joined those already on the ice, the crews dragging either the whole seals or their sculps to the punts which brought them on board. In this way, when it became too dark to do any more, we found we had got 300 seals on board and the deck was one great shambles.

"When piled in a heap together, the young seals looked like so many lambs and when from out of the bloody and dirty mass of carcasses one poor wretch, still alive, would lift up its face and begin to flounder about, I could stand it no longer and, arming myself with a handspike, I proceeded to knock on the head and put out of their misery all in whom I saw signs of life . . . One of the men hooked up a young seal with his gaff. Its cries were precisely like those of a young child in the extremity of agony and distress, something between shrieks and convulsive sobbings . . . I saw one poor wretch skinned while yet alive, and the body writhing in blood after being stripped of its pelt . . . the vision of [another] writhing its snow-white woolly body with its head bathed in blood, through which it was vainly endeavouring to see and breathe, really haunted my dreams.

"The next day, as soon as it was light, all hands went overboard on the ice and were employed in slaughtering young seals in all directions. The young seals lie dispersed, basking in the sun. Six or eight may sometimes be seen within a space of twenty yards square. The men, armed with a gaff and a hauling rope slung over their shoulders, whenever they find a seal, strike it a blow on the head. Having killed, or at least stunned all they see, they sculp them. Fastening the gaff in a bundle of sculps, they then haul it away over the ice to the vessel. Six pelts is reckoned a very heavy load to drag over the rough and broken ice, leaping from pan to pan, and they generally contrive to keep two or three together to assist at bad places or to pull those out who fall in the water.

"I stayed on board to help the captain and cook hoist in the pelts as they were brought alongside. By twelve o'clock, we stood more than knee deep in warm seal-skins, all blood and fat. By night the decks were covered in many places the full height of the rail.

"As the men came aboard they snatched a hasty moment to drink a bowl of tea or eat a piece of biscuit and butter; and as the sweat was dripping from their faces, and the hands and bodies were reeking with blood and fat, and they spread the butter with their thumbs and wiped their faces with their hands, they took both the liquids and solids mingled with blood. Still, there was a bustle and excitement that did not permit the fancy to dwell on the disagreeables, and after this hearty refreshment the men would hurry off in search of new victims: besides every pelt was worth a dollar!

"During this time hundreds of old seals were popping up their heads in the leads and holes among the ice, anxiously looking for their young. Occasionally one would hurry across a pan in search of the snow-white darling she had left, and which she could no longer recognize in the bloody and broken carcass that alone remained of it. I fired at these old ones with my rifle from the deck but without success, as unless the ball hits them in the head, it is a great chance whether it touch any vital part.

"That evening the sun set most gloriously across the bright expanse of snow, now stained with many a bloody spot and the ensanguined trail which marked the footsteps of the intruders."

Topaz returned from her voyage freighted to her marks with between 4,000 and 5,000 sculps. But the vessels that in 1819 first found the main patch brought back nearly 150,000 whitecoats, bringing the total landings for that "bumper year" to 280,000 harp seals, young and old! The fires that would consume the harp nation were now flaming high.

A digression must be made here to deal with a misconception that has been of great service to those responsible for the recent "management" of the seal herds: namely, that the number of seals *destroyed* has always been, and remains, essentially the same as the number of sculps *landed*. Even in the net fishery this assumption is untrue, since a very large percentage of netted seals are pregnant females, the death of each of which represents two lives lost.

As applied to the gun fishery, it is also false. Prior to the breeding season, when they are still fat but not fully buoyant, at least half the adult harp seals killed in open water will sink before they can be recovered. In addition, most of those hit are only wounded and will dive and not be seen again. Of those adults killed outright in the water *after* the breeding season, when the fat reserves of both sexes have largely been exhausted, as many as four out of five will sink and so be lost.

Beaters more than a month old are mostly hunted in open water and are seldom fat enough to float. The current recovery rate by hunters using modern rifles is probably no more than one of every six or seven hit. The rate of loss for bedlamers is lower than that for fully adult animals, because bedlamers suffer little fat depletion and so retain considerable buoyancy; nevertheless the sinking loss is heavy. It is also high in the eastern Canadian

Arctic and west Greenland where, in the 1940s, native hunters annually landed as many as 20,000 harps killed in the water—but lost as many as seven out of every ten they shot. In recent years landings in these regions have ominously declined to about 7,000 a year.

The gun kill of harp seals on the ice itself is equally wasteful. Seals shot at the ice edge, which is where the males congregate during the whelping season and where both sexes gather while moulting, *must* be killed outright if they are to be recovered. Even then, muscular spasms plunge a good many into the sea where the corpses sink into the depths. But instant kills are hard to achieve. Even such a staunch proponent of sealing as Newfoundlander Captain Abraham Kean, who went to the ice sixty-seven springs and is credited with landing more than a million seal sculps (a feat for which he was awarded the Order of the British Empire), admitted that his men had to kill at least three adult seals on ice for every one they recovered. Dr. Harry Lillie, who went to the Front ice in the late 1950s, reported that only one seal was recovered for every five shot by the Newfoundland sealers he accompanied. During April of 1968 I went to the Front in a Norwegian ship under charter to Canadian government scientists who were collecting specimens from the moulting patch. Their seals were shot for them by experienced Norwegian sealers, yet the recovery rate was only one of every five seals hit. There remains the loss entailed in the whitecoat slaughter; but this we shall examine in succeeding pages.

In the meantime, it should be clear enough that landings are *not* and never have been synonymous with killings—a fact to be born in mind as you read on.

After 1819, Newfoundland went mad for seals. Although still vigorous, the net and swatching fishery of the outport dwellers was overshadowed and almost lost to view in the frenzied efforts of merchants and ship-owners in St. John's, and a handful of major towns in Trinity and Conception Bays, to exploit the main patch. They went about it with a single-mindedness that only unadulterated greed can induce. New vessels began coming off the ways at such a rate that, by 1830, nearly 600 brigantines, barques, and schooners were together carrying nearly 14,000 Newfoundland sealers to the ice each spring—a number that probably represented most of the able-bodied men of the northern coasts.

What followed was unregenerate carnage with no quarter given. Considering that oil was the prime objective (whitecoat skins themselves were worth very little at this period), the sealers might, in their own best interests, have been expected to refrain from killing pups until these had attained their greatest weight of fat at between ten days and two weeks of age. They might also have been expected to spare the females, at least until they had borne their young and nursed them to "commercial maturity."

They did neither.

Urged furiously forward by his vessel's owner, every sealing captain sought to be first to reach the main patch. The result was that the fleet sailed earlier and earlier each year, until it was arriving in the region where the patch was expected to form as much as two weeks *before* the females began to give birth. With nothing else to occupy them, the sealers waged war against adult harps as these clustered in the leads or hauled up on the floe edge. The indiscriminate slaughter that ensued resulted in the loss of uncounted tens of thousands of adult females and, not only of the pups they carried in their wombs, but of all the pups they might have produced during the remainder of their lives.

Females that did manage to whelp got no better treatment. Competition between ships' crews was so ferocious that men would be sent out on the ice to butcher pups only a day or two old rather than risk letting them fall into someone else's hands. To compensate for the loss of fat entailed by this barbaric (and idiotic) practice, the men would club or shoot all females they encountered, whether whelping, about to whelp, or nursing young.

"Never leave nothin' to the Devil" was the watchword of the individual sealer, whose own pitifully small returns were based on the lay or percentage system, and, therefore, on his ship obtaining the absolute maximum amount of fat. In consequence, each sealer did his best to ensure that the "devils" in the surrounding vessels would have to sail home "clean," or at least with only a poor "showing of fat" in their holds.

Yet another and equally destructive consequence of the ruthless rivalry was the system of "panning" sculps. Instead of encouraging each sealer to drag his own tow back to the ship after every "rally," captains divided their crews into battle groups whose task was to cover as much of the ice field as swiftly as possible. Some men in each group were to do the sculping, which they did almost on the run. Others gathered the steaming pelts from each area of slaughter, stacked them into a pile on some convenient floe, marked them with a company flag atop a bamboo pole, then hurried on. Such groups might travel miles during ten or twelve hours on the ice, leaving a glaring trail of blood to mark their passage from one pile of sculps on to the next.

Theoretically, the mother ship would push along as close as possible on the sealers' heels, bruising a passage through the floes or being towed through by her working crew, and picking up each pan of sculps as she came abreast of it. In practice, even latter-day steam-powered sealers, built as ice-breakers, often found the task impossible. In 1897 five steam sealers at the main patch abandoned some 60,000 panned sculps they could not reach; while in 1904, the steamer *Erik* alone abandoned eighty-six pans that together held about 19,000 sculps. In the days of sail, sealing ships frequently lost half their pans, and it was not unusual for them to fail to pick up any if the men had been working distant ice when a storm came down. Such losses were considered no great matter. There were always lots more white-coats waiting to be killed.

Not only pans were lost; ships were, too. Vessels were sunk when the ice set tight and crushed their hulls and, when they went down, they often took thousands of seal sculps with them. None of this was of any great consequence to the Captains of Industry who controlled and directed the seal hunt from their counting houses in Newfoundland towns and English cities. The profits being made were so enormous that such losses constituted no more than a negligible nuisance.

From 1819 to 1829, the annual average *landed* catch was just under 300,000 sculps; but when the unrecorded kill is calculated we find that the slaughter must have been destroying at least 500,000 seals a year. In 1830, some 558 vessels went to the Front, returning with 559,000 sculps. The following spring saw the landings rise to at least 686,000 (one authority gives the catch that year as 743,735). The smaller of these two figures indicates a real kill in excess of a million seals. The consuming fire of human greed was roaring now.

Harp seals have so far engrossed this chapter; but theirs was not the only seal nation in the world of floating ice. They shared that realm in evident amity with a larger species known to sealers as the hood—a name derived from an inflatable sac carried by each adult male on the front of his head.

If harps can be thought of as urbanites of the ice, living by preference in dense concentrations, then hoods constitute a kind of rural population. Usually their breeding patches are composed of dispersed and distinct families, each consisting of a male, female, and single pup. The patches are located by preference on the chaotic surface of old polar pack, which is much thicker and rougher than the relatively flat and fragile first-year ice that is the usual choice of the harp nation.

Hoods are monogamous in any given year, intensely territorial, and fiercely protective of their young. Neither sex will flee an enemy. If a sealer approaches too closely, one or both adult hoods may go for him. Since a male hood can be more than eight feet long, weigh 800–900 pounds, is equipped with teeth a wolf might envy, and can hump his vast bulk over the ice about as fast as a man can run, he poses no mean threat. Nevertheless, hoods are no match for modern sealers, as Dr. Wilfred Grenfell tells us.

"[The hood] seal displays great strength, courage and affection in defending its young and I have seen a whole family die together. Four men with wooden seal bats did the killing, but not before the male had caught one club in his mouth and cleared his enemies off the pan by swinging it from side to side. This old seal was hoisted on board whole so as not to delay the steamer. He was apparently quite dead. As, however, he came over the rail the strap broke and he fell back into the sea. The cold water must have revived him, for I saw him return to the same pan of ice distinguished by the blood stains left by the recent battle. The edge of the pan was almost six feet above water, but he leapt clear up over the edge and landed almost on the spot where his family had met its tragic fate. The men immediately ran back and killed him with bullets."

Until well into the nineteenth century, sealers took few hoods. The animals were too big and powerful to be held by nets and generally too tough to be killed in open water with the kind of firearms then available. Because they were so seldom taken, some biologists have concluded that they must have always been rare. They were, in fact, extremely abundant. Although never approaching the harp nation in terms of absolute numbers, the hood nation may not have been far inferior in terms of biomass—until the day when it became the companion in bloody misfortune to the harp.

Black days for the hoods began when Newfoundlanders started searching for whitecoat nurseries. Since these were usually embedded deep in the great ice-lobe that hung pendant off the southeast coast of Labrador and were protected by rugged barriers of old polar pack along the outer edges, wooden sealing vessels could only penetrate to the harp sanctuaries when wind and weather made the pack go slack. Consequently, they were often held at bay for days along the outer edge, and here they encountered the hood seal.

Hoods offered no small reward to killers with fortitude enough to tackle them. For one thing, their pups—called bluebacks—were clothed in lustrous blue-black fur above and silver-grey below, and unlike the whitecoat, whose fur would not remain "fast" when tanned by then-existing methods, that of the blueback would. The skin of a hood pup was therefore of considerable value. Furthermore, its sculp would produce twice as much oil as that of a whitecoat. And the parent hoods, both of whom could usually be killed along with their pup, together produced as much oil as several adult harps.

By as early as 1850, Newfoundland ship sealers were regularly and intensively hunting hoods to such effect that, during the later years of the nineteenth century, according to a study by Harold Horwood, as many as 30 per cent of all sculps landed were from this species.

Hoods whelped on the Gulf floes, too, where easier ice conditions made them still more vulnerable to sealers. In the spring of 1862, schooner sealers from the Magdalens slaughtered 15,000–20,000 in a five-day period. A few years later the crew of a Newfoundland barquentine "log-loaded" their vessel with hoods during a voyage to the Gulf.

Mass industrial slaughter was particularly disastrous to the hood nation. When sealers savaged a harp whelping patch, most males and a goodly proportion of the females escaped alive and so could at least help to make good the loss of that year's pups. But when sealers assaulted a hood whelping patch, almost none of its occupants escaped destruction. That patch was wiped out for all time.

Despite the fact that hood seals are referred to in the current scientific literature as being "a comparatively rare species"..."few and scattered" .. "much less numerous than harps, and have always been so," careful analysis of the history of sealing not only demonstrates that they were once exceedingly numerous, but also shows that their current rarity was brought about entirely by our slaughterous assault upon them.

The period between 1830 and 1860 is still nostalgically referred to in Newfoundland as the Great Days of Sealing. During those three decades, some 13 *million* seals were landed—out of perhaps twice that number killed. Indeed, they *were* great days for those who controlled the industry, and this monumental massacre provided the substance for many Newfoundland merchant dynasties that survive into our day.

Many changes in the nature of the hunt took place, none of them advantageous to the seals. For one, the previously ignored or, it may be, virtually unknown harp and hood whelping patches in the Gulf of St. Lawrence came under sustained attack from the ever-growing Newfoundland fleet.

For another, the skins of adult seals, particularly hoods, became extremely valuable as leather, a large part of which was used in the manufacture of industrial belting. The pelts of young hoods had always fetched a good price in the luxury clothing trade, but now a way was found to market some whitecoats, too, not by inventing a fur-fast tanning process but as a result of the gruesome discovery that the fur of just-born or unborn whitecoats, called cats by the sealers, would remain fast on its own. Early in the 1850s, some Newfoundland entrepreneur shipped a consignment of cats to England. When muffs, stoles, and other female adornments were made out of them, the soft, white fur proved well-nigh irresistible to wealthy women. Such was the origin of the fashion-fur demand for whitecoats that became a multimillion-dollar business in recent times. However, until the post–World War II discovery by a Norwegian company of how to fix the fur of *all* whitecoats, the market had to be satisfied for the most part with the fur of unborn pups. This, of course, led to a huge increase in the butchery of pregnant harps.

It is axiomatic that modern economic progress depends on a never-ending elaboration of ways and means to turn a profit from available raw resources. By the 1860s so much ingenuity had gone into "product development" of seals that the demand was outstripping the supply. Furs and skins were being sold for such diverse uses as ladies' jackets and blacksmiths' bellows; while seal fat was being used for a multitude of purposes ranging from locomotive lubricants to a substitute for olive oil. The industry was coining money and, although most of it stuck to the fingers of the merchant masters, some dribbled down to ordinary fishermen, a few of whom found themselves relatively wealthy, if briefly so. Dr. Grenfell tells of one liveyere who ran a net fishery in a remote bay on the Labrador at about this time.

"At one little settlement a trapper by the name of Jones became so rich through regular large catches of seals that he actually had a carriage and horses sent from Quebec, and a road made to drive them on; while he had a private musician hired from Canada for the whole winter to perform at his continuous feastings. I was called on awhile ago to help supply clothing to cover the nakedness of this man's grandchildren."

The destruction engulfing the ice seals was not confined to North America. Early in the 1700s, Scots and English whalers sailing west in European Arctic waters had discovered a gigantic population of whelping harps and hoods on the so-called West Ice of the Greenland Sea, in the vicinity of uninhabited Jan Mayen Island. So long as sufficient bowhead whales could be killed in these waters, the seals generally went unmolested; but, by the middle of the eighteenth century, the whale population to the east of Greenland had been so decimated that it was a lucky ship that could kill enough to make her voyage pay. It was at this juncture that the whalers began turning their attention to the hordes of hoods and harps on the West Ice and in Davis Strait.

As was the case with Newfoundlanders, they learned ice-sealing the hard way, but by the spring of 1768 a dozen British whaling ships each loaded about 2,000 hood and harp seals at the West Ice. They were soon joined on that living oil field by Germans, Danes, Hollanders, and the inevitable Norwegians, and amongst them they were landing a quarter of a million sculps a year before the nineteenth century was well begun.

The massive devastation that engulfed the harp and hood nations off Newfoundland as the nineteenth century aged was matched by a similar orgy of destruction at the West Ice. In 1850, about 400,000 seals were landed from there, and in the following year the figure for Newfoundland and the West Ice combined passed the million mark.

Greed took its toll of men as well as seals at the West Ice. During the spring of 1854, the skipper of the British sealer *Orion* dispatched a rally of his men to kill what appeared to be a patch of hoods amongst a torment of upthrust ice. The patch resolved itself into the frozen corpses of seventy shipwrecked Danish sealers, keeping company with hundreds of blueback carcasses with which the doomed men had tried to construct a barricade against the killing edge of a polar gale.

As at the Newfoundland Front, mounting competition for skins and fat forced the ever-diminishing West Ice seals deeper and deeper into the protective pack until they were all but inaccessible, even to the most foolhardy skippers. Losses of ships and men soared, and the catch began going down. For a time, it looked as if the halcyon days of sealing were coming to an end.

It was the English who found a way out of this impasse. In 1857, the Hull whaler *Diana*, newly equipped with auxiliary steam power, challenged the West Ice and was able to return home "log-loaded with fat." She also rescued eighty men from two sailing sealers that had been beset and had sunk in the ice when the wind failed them. The point was made. Crude and inefficient as it was, *Diana*'s forty-horsepower engine, driving an awkward iron screw, was the technological key to mastery of the ice fields, and a flood of steam-auxiliary sailing vessels followed on her heels.

The first of the steam-auxiliaries to try their luck in Newfoundland waters were the British whaler/sealers *Camperdown* and *Polynia*, which made a trial voyage to the Front in 1862. They took only a few seals because ice conditions were so appallingly bad that some fifty sailing vessels were crushed and sunk. But the steamers were at least able to extricate themselves, and the lesson was not lost on the St. John's sealing tycoons. Another bad season in 1864, which saw twenty-six more Newfoundland sailing sealers crushed, drove it home.

Thereafter the steam-auxiliaries quickly took the lead, and as quickly proved their terrible effectiveness. During the spring of 1871, eighteen of them unloaded a quarter of a million sculps on St. John's greasy wharves, bringing Newfoundland's total landings that year to well above the half-million mark for a value of about $12 million in today's currency. Seals were by then second only to cod in the Newfoundland economy.

It was not uncommon for a steam sealer, with her superior speed and ability in ice, to make several trips to the Front during one spring season; loading whitecoats and adult harps on her first trip; bluebacks and harp and hood adults on a second; and moulting harps on a third and even fourth. The *Erik* once landed 40,000 seals from three such ventures.

Although the advent of steam enormously increased the efficiency of the massacre, it did not change its nature, as the Reverend Philip Tocque, writing in 1877, confirms: "The seal-fishery is a constant scene of bloodshed and slaughter. Here you behold a heap of seals which have only received a slight dart from the gaff, writhing, and crimsoning the ice with their blood, rolling from side to side in dying agony. There you see another lot, while the last spark of life is not yet extinguished, being stripped of their skins and fat, their startlings and heavings making the unpractised hand shrink with horror to touch them."

While the steamers ravaged the seal sanctuaries deep within the ice tongue at the Front and on the ice plains in the Gulf, the remaining sailing vessels scoured the outer reaches of the pack. Meantime, landsmen went swatching in inshore waters and made rallies into any whelping patches they might find; and the net fisheries killed as many as 80,000 adult harps each year, mostly during the southbound migration when the females were carrying young.

The all-embracing nature of the slaughter was awesome tribute to the genius of modern man as mass destroyer. It also bore awesome testimony to the vitality of the western ice-seal nations, which between 1871 and 1881 suffered decimation in excess of a million individuals each year *yet still managed to endure*.

They endured—but both nations were fast wasting away. Average landings declined by almost half between 1881 and 1891 and continued to decline until after the turn of the century, when there was an improvement, from the point of view of the sealing industry, due to the determined application of that basic principle of exploitation whereby a diminution in supply is countered by ever more ruthless effort.

After 1900, the "catch-to-effort ratio" was much improved by the introduction of really large, full-powered, steel-hulled ice-breaking steamers on the one hand, and modern repeating rifles on the other. Assisted by wireless telegraphy, which enabled the sealing fleet to co-ordinate its assault, the Newfoundland fishery maintained landings averaging nearly 250,000 a year until World War I. By then, however, sealers had been living on capital for more than half a century. It could only have been a matter of a few more years before the industry collapsed, had not the war intervened.

By the time the Armistice was signed, most of the new steel sealers had been sunk by enemy action, and those auxiliary steamers that still remained afloat were so old as to hardly dare face the ice again. Furthermore, the price of seal oil, which had risen to outrageous heights during the war, now slumped below pre-war levels and soon, with the onset of the Great Depression, became only marginally profitable. Although sealing still continued, it was at a much lower level of intensity than it had known for a century. The eruption of World War II in 1939 virtually brought it to an end.

While that war raged in Europe and the North Atlantic, the seals had five whelping seasons in which to bear and rear their young in relative security. By 1945 females born at the war's beginning were themselves bearing pups, with the result that the western harp and hood nations were showing a modest increase for the first time in a hundred years.

War's end brought no revival of interest in commercial sealing in North America. By then all but two vessels of the Newfoundland sealing fleet were gone, and the island's capitalists preferred to concentrate their resources on rebuilding the Grand Banks fishing fleet.

Although the Great Sealing Game had rewarded with enormous wealth the handful of mercantile aristocrats who ruled the island, it had returned precious little to ordinary men, thousands of whom had perished along with the tens of millions of ice seals they had slain. Now, it seemed, the time had come for the dead to bury the dead; time for the great dying of men and seals to become no more than a memory of an earlier and darker time, when human rapacity had known no bounds.

19

Death on Ice (New Style)

Close on a thousand years after the Nordic adventurer Karlsefni sailed his *knorr* into New World waters seeking profits from their abounding wealth, he was followed by another of his lineage impelled by the same desires. This latecomer was a man we have already met in connection with his exploits as a whaler. Karl Karlsen was to succeed in his ambitions on a scale that would have been beyond the wildest dreams of his distant predecessor.

In devastated post-war Europe a dearth of animal fats had sent the value of marine oils soaring and those most efficient of all sea-ravagers, the Norwegians, had been quick to respond to this opportunity. Shortly after the end of hostilities at sea they began dispatching whatever makeshift vessels they could find into the nearby White Sea to kill harp seals. They proved so destructive here that the Soviets eventually had to bar them. But they were also, and urgently, building new ships—multi-purpose killer boats designed (as we have seen in the story of the whales) for hunting sea mammals in any seas, no matter how far afield.

As the new ships came into service, those intended primarily for sealing were directed westward. Their first target was the West Ice off eastern Greenland where, as far back as the 1860s, Norwegian sealers had established a hegemony of slaughter. However, they had so savaged both harps and hoods in those waters prior to 1939 that even the wartime lull had not allowed the herds to make any significant recovery. What remained of them now melted fast away in the furious fire of this renewed assault.

Having quickly bloodied the remnants of two of the three tribes of the harp nation, the modern Vikings turned their vessels' heads toward the stink of oil and money in the distant west. So it was that, in 1946, a new company was born in Nova Scotia. Innocuously christened the Karlsen Shipping Company, its advent went almost unnoticed. Few knew that it was a Norwegian entity whose real interests lay, not in shipping, but in killing whales and seals in Canadian waters. And few could have known that it was the herald of a maritime scourge as terrible as any that Western man had previously inflicted in the seas of the New World.

Incorporation as a Canadian company brought Karlsen many advantages, including access to federal and provincial subsidies, but the chief value was that it enabled a foreign interest to seal and whale without restraint inside Canadian territorial waters and, especially, in the enclosed waters of the Gulf of St. Lawrence.

The Karlsen organization was soon operating a fleet of Norwegian-built, Norwegian-officered whale-cum-seal killers out of Blandford, Nova Scotia, against the ice seals of the Gulf. Simultaneously, another fleet of home-based Norwegian sealing ships appeared at the Front off Newfoundland. Since the Front whelping and moulting patches normally formed in international waters, this fleet was subject to no national restraints or supervision.

Goaded by this alien presence on their traditional sealing grounds, and with their cupidity belatedly aroused by the increasing value of seal fat, Newfoundlanders now returned to the ice. By 1947, they were again manning a small handful of sealing ships. However, theirs was a nondescript fleet consisting mostly of small motor vessels normally employed in the cod fishery or the coastal trade. These were hopelessly outclassed by fourteen brand-new Norwegian sealers, which by 1950 were ravaging the Front while the Karlsen fleet did the same in the Gulf. Amongst them, the Norwegians landed better than 200,000 sculps that year. A year later they brought back twice as many—a slaughter the like of which had not been attained since 1881. The fire had flared up anew.

Not content with killing pups and adult females on the whelping ice and adults of both sexes at the moulting patches, the Norwegian offshore fleet took to pursuing the migrating herds northward, even as far as west Greenland waters, killing all the way. The seals they killed would normally have returned south to pup the following spring. Most were not given the chance. In a single year, the new Vikings landed 60,000 sculps out of probably 300,000 adults shot in water and on ice.

This was bloodletting on such a scale as to quickly wipe out whatever gains the harp and hood nations had made since 1919. By 1961, according to Dr. David Sergeant, the western harp nation had declined to an estimated 1,750,000 individuals, or about half of what it was thought to have numbered ten years earlier.

Now, under the prodding of an alarmed Sergeant and of a few others such as Newfoundlander Harold Horwood, whose magazine article, "Tragedy on the Whelping Ice," was one of the earliest public warnings of what was happening, the governments of Canada and Norway made their first gesture toward "protecting and conserving" the ice seals.[1] Having agreed to an opening date designed to ensure maximum production of whitecoats, they proclaimed that the hunt for adults must end by May 5. However, since this date came after the Norwegian pursuit of the northbound herd was usually abandoned anyway, it was meaningless. Moreover, adult seals were no longer the prime object of the sealers.

During the late 1950s, Norwegian chemists had finally discovered a way of treating whitecoat pelts so that the soft and silky hair would remain fast to the skin. The resultant fur delighted the fashion market in affluent Western countries. Although in 1952 a whitecoat sculp unloaded at the docks had only been worth about a dollar, and this mostly for the fat, by 1961 it was worth $5, four of which were for the fur alone. Since a single sealer loose in a whelping patch could kill and sculp as many as 100 whitecoats a day, truly enormous profits could now be made. In 1962 the price for whitecoats rose to $7.50 as a mindless passion for seal fur swept fashion salons and fired the acquisitive desires of civilized women in Europe and America. The result was a frantic rush to the ice that spring, one that turned the harp and hood nurseries of eastern Canada into bloody abattoirs as sealers sculped 330,000 hoods and harps, of which more than 200,000 were whitecoats.

In the light of what followed it is only fair to emphasize that, up to this point, Canadians had played a relatively small, and usually menial, part in the post-war history of the sealing industry. For the most part they served as low-paid butchers and draft animals, assisting a foreign nation to destroy a Canadian resource. Not that there was anything new about this. Canada has always been content to divest herself of natural resources in exchange for jobs for her citizenry as haulers of water and hewers of wood.

Canadian governments, federal and provincial, did everything in their power to assist the Norwegians. Aerial ice reconnaissance was provided to the sealing fleet. Canadian Coast Guard ice-breakers were made available to assist the sealers. Most helpful of all perhaps was the refusal of the federal government to implement conservation legislation that would have interfered with the uninhibited pursuit of profit at the ice.

In the 1960s, the so-called seal "hunt" became a veritable orgy of destruction as get-rich-quick entrepreneurs congregated like vultures over the ice floes. Nor is this simile far-fetched. In the spring of 1962 some ships began using helicopters to transport sealers to distant pans and to ferry sculps back to the vessels. The following year, with whitecoat pelts fetching $10 each, an

---

[1] Until 1949 Newfoundland was an independent state. In that year it became a province of Canada and the federal government thereafter bore responsibility for the seal hunt at the Front, as well as in the Gulf.

airborne assault was launched against the Gulf seals by dozens of light planes equipped with skis or balloon tires so they could operate on ice.

These planes were mostly owned by the pilots who flew them: aerial gypsies who knew little or nothing about sealing, but who were hot on the scent of a literal quick killing. The pilot-owners hired local men from the Magdalens or Prince Edward Island, flew them out to the whelping patches at dawn, then spent the rest of the day ferrying sculps to makeshift landing strips ashore.

The rivalry that developed amongst these airborne raiders, landsmen sealers, and the sealing fleet brought anarchy to the ice. Whatever rules of sense or sensibility might previously have been observed were now abandoned. Air sealers even hijacked panned sculps left on the ice by sealing ships, and not a few aircraft arrived back at their shore bases with bullet holes in their wings and fuselages. The whelping nurseries of the harp seal nation became a grisly shambles. One of the pilots who flew at the Gulf in 1963 gave me this graphic account of what transpired.

"We had to take what we could get in the way of sealers. The competition for anybody big enough to swing a club or use a knife was wild. I had to go into Charlottetown and round up a bunch of deadbeats out of the beer parlours. They didn't know from nothing, and couldn't have cared less so long as they made a few quick bucks.

"There was so many planes buzzing around out there it was like a war movie...flopping down anywhere there was a pan big enough to hold 'em. And I guess every seal bitch was drove right off the ice, whether she'd pupped or not. Nobody give a damn. It was only the pups we wanted and there was millions of the fat little buggers.

"I put my crowd out just about eight A.M. and waited for them to kill me my first load. But, Jesus, they was dumb! They could smash a pup on the head alright, but skin? Couldn't have skinned an orange right. I wasted half the morning showing them how, and at that they spoiled as many as they saved.

"Everybody had the fever. To beat the other guys. There was guys running around as never stopped to skin a pup at all—just banged 'em on the head and run on to bang the next one they could see before some other guy could get it first. You'd have to see it to believe it.

"One trip I landed on a soft patch and damn near lost the plane. Had to gun her out of there and make a landing some ways off where a different crowd was killing. They waved me off, but I landed anyhow. I never seen nothing like it. They weren't even *trying* to kill their seals. Guys was holding them down with one foot and ripping them up the belly, then trying to peel the skin off. What a mess! With the pup wriggling like crazy, they'd slice the skin in a dozen places and ruin it for sure. Not to worry. Stick the knife into the next pup and try again.

"I seen things I won't forget. *You* ever see a *skinned* pup trying to wiggle out of the water where some guy'd kicked it? Yeah, sure, I made a pile that season, but I never went back next year. It was too rough for me."

Most of the pilots did go back, however, and were joined by many more, since the rewards for two weeks of hard living and considerable risk-taking could exceed $10,000. In 1964, whitecoat sculps went up to $12.50 each, fuelling a carnage that was becoming wanton beyond belief. At least sixty-five light aircraft, together with several helicopters, "worked" the Gulf seals that spring, along with hundreds of landsmen and the sealing fleet. The competition was ruthless, and the sealers pitiless. Even the best of them became driven machines, wasting or abandoning many pups in their frenzied haste to forestall competitors.

Eighty-one thousand whitecoats were removed from the Gulf ice that spring. Although the actual number killed will never be known, there is agreement amongst those who were there that the year's "crop" was effectively wiped out. At the Front, where light aircraft could not operate, things were almost as grim. An estimated 85 per cent of the pups born were killed by the Norwegian fleet. The saving grace, if it could be called such, was that at the Front the butchers were at least professionals and there was comparatively little waste.

Meanwhile, seal products continued to diversify. Après-ski slippers for women and boots and sports jackets for men made of the silvery skins of adult seals led to a renewed slaughter of mature animals after the annual whitecoat and blueback massacre ended. Even the net fishery flourished anew, particularly along the south Labrador coast. Fishermen who had never previously bothered with seals began catching adults and bedlamers on huge, baited hooks. Worse still, crowds of men and youths started gunning for bedlamers and beaters from every sort of boat, using lightweight .22 calibre rifles. Only a lucky hit in the brain with a .22 was likely to kill even a beater. The accountant of a fish plant in northern Newfoundland who got seal fever and went swatching told me he estimated the ratio of hits to kills at about ten to one.

Not since the mid-nineteenth century had the ice seals endured such merciless persecution. In 1963, reported landings from the northwestern Atlantic totalled 352,000—"reported" because the Norwegians were believed to always land many more than were admitted. Assuming a most conservative loss ratio, the kill that year must have been close to 500,000. The following spring the death toll was almost as huge.

By the summer of 1964 it had become brutally obvious to everyone involved in the business that the ice seals were destined to commercial, if not actual, extinction. From as many as 10 million (the estimates vary) in its aboriginal state, the western herd of the harp nation had been reduced to little more than a million. As for those at the West Ice, not more than 200,000 survived. The Soviets had also joined in the outbreak of uncontrolled avarice by grossly over-killing whitecoats in the White Sea in order to profit from the Western world's mania for sealskin artifacts.

Those departments of the Norwegian, Canadian, and Soviet governments entrusted with the regulation and protection of fisheries were fully aware of what was happening. They had been briefed by their own scientists, most of whom, it must be said in all fairness, were predicting a devastating collapse of harp and hood populations unless the mayhem on the ice was quickly halted.

Norway and Canada ignored the warnings. However, in the autumn of 1964 the Soviet government prohibited further ship-borne sealing in the White Sea. When challenged to follow suit, a spokesman for Canada's Department of Fisheries asserted that, far from declining, harp seals were actually increasing in numbers. Furthermore, there could be no thought of interfering with the rights of free enterprise to continue making a legitimate profit from this "rational harvesting of a natural resource which was of great importance to the Canadian economy."

The Norwegian response was to point out that, since the Front and West Ice seals lived in international waters, it was nobody's business what their sealers did. Norway would accept no restraint on her freedom to "fish" on the high seas.

Up until this time, the world at large had remained in ignorance of what was happening. This condition might well have continued until the western Atlantic harp and hood nations had been totally destroyed had it not been for a singularly ironic twist of fate. In 1964 a small, Montreal-based company called Artek won a contract from Quebec's tourism department to make some television films extolling the attractions of La Belle Province. Having filmed the usual subjects, it occurred to the producer that something special would add spice to the series. One of his staff, a Magdalen Islander, mentioned a seal hunt that took place there every spring, and this sounded like the very thing. So, in March of 1964, the Artek crew went to the archipelago and filmed what was intended to show an archaic but exciting struggle between man and nature on the harsh world of the ice fields—a glimpse, as it were, of Old Quebec in pioneering days.

The resulting film was exciting enough—but excruciatingly gory. Not only did it show the stark vista of crimson slush on white ice, which is the hallmark of the seal hunt, it captured harrowing scenes of sealers with steel-hooked staves gaffing what may well be the most appealing young creature in the animal kingdom, together with stunning close-ups of one of these attractive little animals—being skinned alive.

When the French television network of the Canadian Broadcasting Corporation screened this film, the audience response was so overwhelming that the corporation decided to broadcast it on the national network, with English subtitles. The subtitles were hardly needed. The images were so devastatingly revolting that words were superfluous.

The reaction of many viewers, including a number of Americans who tune in to CBC, was a massive outpouring of revulsion and outrage. Local branches of the Humane Society and the Society for the Prevention of Cruelty to Animals obtained copies of the film and showed them across the country in church basements, community halls, and schools. Members of Parliament and the federal Department of Fisheries were inundated by a wave of indignation as thousands of ordinary people registered their protests and demanded that the massacre of baby seals be stopped forthwith. An appalled Quebec Bureau of Tourism did its best to squelch the film. It was far too late for that.

Copies had already gone overseas, there to be further copied and distributed. In West Germany, Dr. Bernard Grzimek of the Frankfurt Zoo not only showed it on television, Europe-wide, but launched a popular crusade to force the Canadian government to "halt this murderous atrocity." Bewildered Canadian embassy staffs soon found themselves beleaguered by picketers and showered with hate mail. As one unhappy spokesman for the sealing industry put it, with surely unconscious humour, "The fat was in the fire."

Indeed it was. Although the Canadian and Norwegian governments, supporting and supported by the sealing industry, did everything in their power to smother the uproar, they only succeeded in intensifying it. In the words of a federal employee, "The combination of that lovable little seal-pup image and the visible result, when what was really just a sack of blood and guts was spilled onto the ice, couldn't be handled rationally...facts and figures can't counter stuff like that. If we'd been killing baby squids we could've held our own maybe, but baby seals?"

Goaded and prodded into angry reactions, Canadian authorities counter-attacked by stigmatizing those who complained about the seal slaughter as deluded dupes, bleeding hearts, or self-serving publicists. The Department of Fisheries rallied its experts and set them to disseminate the "true facts." Having vehemently denied that any cruelty was involved in commercial seal-ing—"such accusations amount to an unwarranted slur on honest, working fishermen"—departmental spokesmen insisted that the sealing industry was a vital and sustaining element in the Canadian economy and was being rationally and humanely managed.

"The seal fishery is properly regulated," said the Honourable H.R. Robichaud, the federal Minister of Fisheries, as he hurriedly introduced the first regulations ever to be imposed on the sealers. As of the spring of 1965, he announced, access to the seal fishery would be reduced by the introduc-tion of a licensing system requiring the owner of each ship or aircraft to pay a fee of $25 for the right to "harvest" harp or hood seals. Furthermore, in order to protect the stock, a quota of 50,000 seals would be imposed on the Gulf sealers, and Fisheries officers would be assigned to supervise the oper-ation and ensure adherence to the laws. Finally, in order to give the lie to accusations of cruelty, representatives of animal welfare groups would be escorted to the Gulf ice fields so they could satisfy themselves, and the world, that the seals were being killed with all due consideration.

Licensing ships and aircraft was a mockery. Even had the fee imposed been realistic, it would have had little or no effect unless the *number* of licences issued was limited, and it was not. Supervision of the slaughter in 1965 by Fisheries officers consisted of counting the sculps delivered by planes and ships—a rather rough count, too, since the quota was exceeded by some 4,000 whitecoats. The visit of the observers to the ice that season was thoughtfully scheduled for the *second* week of the "harvest" and there-fore did not take place, because the quota, quite predictably, had been filled in the first four days by ten big ships and sixty or more aircraft that ravaged the Gulf whelping patches.

Finally, the quota of 50,000 whitecoats applied *only* to the Gulf, and *only* to big ships and aircraft. Landsmen, small vessel operators, gunners, and netters everywhere remained free to take all the seals, young or old, that they could kill. As for the slaughter at the Front, by mutual agreement between Canada and Norway, it continued without any supervision or restrictions, pretended or real.

Mr. Robichaud's smoke-and-mirrors trick might conceivably have worked had it not been for the intransigence of a single individual. He was Brian

Davies, a Welsh-born thirty-five-year-old immigrant to Canada who, in 1964, was supporting himself as a student teacher while working part-time for the New Brunswick Society for the Prevention of Cruelty to Animals.

Davies saw the Artek film and was deeply disturbed, but not entirely convinced that such horrors could be perpetrated in the land of his adoption. How to find out the truth? There was only one way. Davies went to the ice himself.

"Maybe it's pompous, but what I saw changed my life," he told me some years later. "You've been there. You've seen what goes on. Words don't work to describe that kind of barbarism. It couldn't be allowed to go on. Somebody had to stop it. I never had any doubt what I had to do."

During the years that followed, Davies was to find himself pilloried by government authorities, the sealing industry, and some of the media as a self-seeking, self-serving fanatic of dubious morality and questionable ethics. At the same time he was being elevated to the godhead by animal lovers everywhere, who saw him as a latter-day St. Francis of Assisi. Davies waged his war to save the seals mainly by manipulating the media, and he did this with such skill that, almost single-handedly, he transformed the image of the dark-eyed, soulful-seeming whitecoat into an international symbol of revolt against the old established, merciless, and selfish view of non-human life. Eschewing reason, he frankly played on emotions in the belief that this was the only way to defeat the forces arrayed against him. These forces responded not only by savage vilification of the man and his supporters, but by attempting to bury him, together with the truth about the seal slaughter, under an avalanche of persiflage.

The worthlessness of the $25 licence fee was demonstrated in 1966 when not less than a hundred fixed-wing aircraft and helicopters took part in the slaughter at the Gulf. Planes and ships harvested their 50,000 quota in jig time, and that spring Gulf whitecoat landings rose to 86,000, together with some 18,000 adult seals.

This time, the official observers reached the scene on opening day. The group included government officials led by Mr. Robichaud and representatives from the Ontario Humane Society. An independent biologist, Dr. Douglas Pimlott from the University of Toronto, also attended. Although Pimlott reported seeing three sealers club fifty-nine pups on one floe and then abandon them, the group issued this joint statement: "[We examined] the skulls of many hundreds of whitecoats...killed by men working from both ships and aircraft. Examination of the carcasses indicated that the majority had been struck on the head by some instrument with sufficient force to crush the skull. In our opinion, these animals have been rendered completely unconscious and unable to feel any pain."

However, members of the official group were not the only observers on the ice that spring. Brian Davies was there, too, and he also brought an expert, Dr. Elizabeth Simpson, a qualified veterinarian. She reported that as many as *half* the whitecoat corpses she examined could well have been alive when they were skinned.

Such was the beginning of a singularly unedifying battle between various humane and animal welfare agencies, with some vehemently supporting the official contention that the baby seals perished, if not happily, at least pain- lessly, while others insisted that many whitecoats died agonizing deaths.

While press and public concentrated their concern on this aspect of the carnage on the whelping ice of the Gulf, sealers elsewhere carried on as usual. During the spring of 1966, thirteen Norwegian and seven of Karlsen's vessels loaded 160,000 whitecoats at the Front. They also took at least 45,000 adult harps as well as 25,000 hood seals from a total local hood pop- ulation that probably no longer exceeded three times that number.

That autumn the Canadian government, acting to protect itself in antici- pation of the inevitable discovery by the public of the horrendous destruction at the Front, arranged for the nominal control of sealing there to be vested in the International Commission for the North Atlantic Fishery (ICNAF), a body including bureaucrats and scientists of the governments of Canada, Norway, and Denmark that was already notorious for taking little or no action directed at conservation if this might cause distress to the com- mercial fishing industry.

The Department of Fisheries also decreed some new conservation meas- ures for the Gulf, including a prohibition on hunting during the hours of darkness (when not even the most foolhardy sealer would risk being on the ice) and a ban on the killing of adult female seals on the whelping patches— except in self-defence, which meant except when sealers wanted them. The efficacy of the regulations was clearly demonstrated by the 1967 "hunt." Although the quota for whitecoats remained at 50,000 in the Gulf, actual landings there were above 100,000 seals, of which the great majority were harp pups. This year saw the largest single slaughter in the Gulf since World War II. And at the Front 232,000 harp and hood seals died. They, too, were mostly pups.

After the butchery of 1967 had ended, Mr. Robichaud addressed the media. He first remarked of the anti-seal hunt activists, who were becoming increasingly numerous and vocal: "One cannot but be awed at the intensity of the campaign being waged by a group of people led by Mr. Brian Davies, which is blackening the Canadian image both here and in other countries." He then went on to assure the reporters that "In 1967 the Canadian seal fishery was the most tightly regulated operation of its kind anywhere in the world. The regulations specified the type and specifications of the club which could be used in taking the young and the types of firearms and ammunition which could be used to kill older seals. It was clearly emphasized that the flensing operation was not to be started until the animal was, without doubt, dead. A system of licensing and identification of sealers was also brought in. Moreover special responsibilities were placed on sealing ship captains and aerial operators to have the regulations adhered to."

The Minister of Fisheries concluded by saying: "I hold firmly to the basic tenet that in the utilization of any creature for our welfare, the utmost attention must be given to handling them in the most humane way possible, and to their continuance as a species in perpetuity. This is the objective we have set ourselves and which we are achieving in the harvesting of our Atlantic seal resources."

In the spring of 1968, photographer John de Visser and I went to the Gulf to observe this "most tightly regulated operation of its kind anywhere in the world." It was a grim experience. On one occasion, de Visser watched an aircraft hunter club his way through a patch of about thirty pups, killing six and wounding a number of others before leaping to another pan and abandoning his victims. On two occasions, I saw pups returning to consciousness while being skinned alive. When I remonstrated with a ship sealer for clubbing to death a female that had elected to try to save her pup, he grinned at me and replied, "We got to protect ourselves, now don't we?"

I talked to members of the Brian Davies contingent and to the rival "official" observer group led by Mr. Tom Hughes of the Ontario Humane Society. Hughes was adamant in insisting that the hunt, as he persisted in calling it, was "just as humane as any other well-regulated abattoir operation." I talked with Fisheries officers, scientific experts, and ordinary sealers. I concluded that the massacre was just that—an almost uncontrolled orgy of destruction conducted by, and for, people who were prepared to commit or to countenance almost any degree of savagery in order to maintain a high rate of profitability. But, unquestionably, the aerial sealers were guilty of the worst atrocities.

When I asked a senior Fisheries official why his department did not ban the aircraft "hunt," which was the cause of so much of the public criticism, he replied, off the record, that it would be impolitic to do so. The aircraft owners, he pointed out, were independent Canadian businessmen and any attempt to keep them off the Gulf ice would provoke an unacceptable political backlash.

In any event, the Norwegians arranged to rid themselves of these interlopers. They did this by the simple expedient of dropping the price of whitecoat pelts, of which they were the sole buyers. In 1967 they reduced the price to $6, which was intended to be low enough to prevent aircraft sealers from making a worthwhile profit. This did have some effect, but not as much as had been hoped for; so the report was circulated that the top price next year would be a mere $2. At that price, all but a handful of the aircraft hunters quit. However, after the 1968 ship/aircraft quota had been filled (mostly by the ships), the buyers began paying landsmen as much as $6 a sculp. That was the end of aircraft "participation in the seal harvest," as a Charlottetown newspaper prettily put it.

My visit to the Gulf convinced me that, although the cruelty problem was real enough, the main issue was whether the ice seals could survive at all in the face of the enormous and virtually uncontrolled destruction they were suffering.

Robichaud had now given way to a new Fisheries Minister, the Honourable Jack Davis, a politician who was something of an anomaly since he was not wholly encapsulated within an impermeable membrane of preconvictions and prejudices. It seemed possible that he might be persuaded to reconsider the policies of his department toward the seals. I had some discussions about this with Robert Shaw, his Deputy Minister, who gave me grounds for hope. Early in 1969 I was told the Minister of Fisheries would take steps to halt the haemorrhage of the ice-seal nations, which had accounted for some 300,000 seals that spring.

Davis established an ad hoc seal advisory committee, and when this group confirmed to him that both harp and hood seal herds were in severe decline and urgently needed protection, he responded by proposing to prohibit the killing of any whitecoats at the Gulf in 1970 and by forging what he believed was a valid agreement with the Norwegian government to refrain from taking whitecoats at the Front.

Thereupon all hell broke loose.

Assailed by the sealing industry on the one hand and by politicians from the Atlantic Provinces on the other, Davis's position was undercut by his own senior civil servants and some of his scientific advisers. These sided with ICNAF (of which they were a part) in its refusal to countenance even a reduction, let alone a ban on whitecoat killing. The final blow came when Norway repudiated the agreement to prohibit its nationals from taking whitecoats at the Front. Backed into a corner, Davis withdrew his intended conservation measures and, as his Deputy Minister put it, "pulled back to lick his wounds."

The 1970 slaughter took place as usual. The Gulf quota of 50,000 for large vessels remained unchanged and, in the absence of the airborne killers, was now filled in the main by the Norwegian interests. There were no quotas at the Front, and no restraint was exercised by ICNAF. There was, however, such a notable decline in seal numbers that the Norwegian fleet (which was now alone in those icy waters) could only manage to load 257,000 sculps of all ages and both species.

By now Brian Davies and his supporters were having such an inflammatory effect internationally, as well as in Canada, that they were disowned by the conservative wing of the animal protection movement. Undaunted, Davies (who had formed his own organization, the International Fund for Animal Welfare) redoubled his efforts to enlist world opinion against the ongoing slaughter. By mid-1970 he was having such success that the "seal affair" was becoming a matter of real embarrassment to Ottawa. At this juncture, the Department of Fisheries, which was naturally the chief target, was merged into the newly created and innocently named Department of the Environment, from which camouflaged retreat it issued a new set of Seal Protection Regulations.

Henceforward, no unauthorized aircraft would be permitted to fly lower than 2,000 feet above harp or hood seal whelping ice or to land within half a nautical mile of a breeding patch. This decree was later amended to make it illegal to land within that distance of *any* seal of either species during the whelping season. Spokesmen from the department explained that this cabinet order (it was never debated in Parliament) was intended not only to stop aerial hunting but to protect the seals from being disturbed by aircraft while whelping or nursing their offspring.

Although the uninitiated in Canada and abroad regarded this new regulation as highly laudable, it constituted a cynical deception. Aerial hunting had been defunct since 1968 and enjoyed no prospects of revival; in consequence, the only aircraft to visit the whelping ice were either those carrying government scientists and officially endorsed observers and Fisheries officers, or anti-hunt protesters, the press, and independent scientists and investigators. Those in the first category were authorized to "disturb the seals" where, when, and as they desired. In general, those in the second category were to be denied access, not only to the whelping patches, but effectively to the entire region, since single seals were to be found almost anywhere in the Gulf and at the Front.

In short, this despotic stricture was not designed to protect the seals, it was intended to protect the sealers (who, presumably, did not disturb the whitecoats or their mothers when bashing in their skulls), as well as the sealing industry and the government of Canada, by preventing the truth of what was happening on the ice from reaching the general public.

Oddly enough, the Minister of the Environment, as Jack Davis had now become, was not yet resigned to an acceptance of the political realities as defined by his own mandarins. In the same year that the new Seal Protection Regulations were promulgated, he formally established a House of Commons Advisory Committee on Seals and Sealing (COSS). In January of 1971, this group, which included two respected independent scientists, recommended to Parliament that the entire ice-seal hunt be phased out by no later than 1974 and that both harps and hoods then be given at least six years free from sealers to allow them to at least partially recoup their numbers. Davis agreed to implement these recommendations.

Much of what ensued thereafter in the murky bowels of Ottawa remains opaque. However, the outcome was crystal clear. A somewhat subdued Minister announced that, after all, Canada did not feel she could take unilateral action in what was clearly a matter of international commercial concern, therefore she would place the future of *all* harp and hood seals that frequented her waters in the hands of ICNAF; which was about the same as shifting it from the right hand to the left.

ICNAF, which had done nothing to conserve or protect either the Front herds or the dwindling remnants off the east Greenland coast, rose to the occasion by sonorously proclaiming a Harp and Hood Seal Protocol, under which it would establish an overall quota for western Atlantic seals. The quota would be determined on the basis of impeccable biological data and used as a tool for "scientific management," not only to ensure that there would be no further depletion, but to restore the harps and hoods to something approaching their original abundance.

In 1971, ICNAF set its first Gulf/Front quota—200,000 harp seals for the ships and 45,000 for landsmen—a total just 18,000 short of the previous year's actual landings. By season's end in 1971, the sealers had landed 231,000, which was all they were able to get despite a massive effort to legitimize and sustain the quota by filling it. With their failure to do so, ICNAF had no alternative but to cut back. Thus the 1972 quota was reduced to

150,000. But all the sealers could kill and land that year was 136,000! They failed to fill it the next year, too.

Whitecoats were now in decreasing supply and increasing demand, so in 1974 the price went up to $12 a pelt. This incited the industry to add more ships and men and they managed to top the quota with 154,000. In 1975, whitecoat prices went wild, soaring to as high as $22; 180,000 ice seals were reportedly landed that year, including 15,400 hoods taken against a newly established hood quota of 15,000.

The year 1975 was also notable because of an aerial photographic survey that indicated the combined Gulf and Front adult harp seal populations now numbered no more than a million and, according to a paper by Dr. David Lavigne published by the Food and Agriculture Organization of the United Nations, no more than 800,000 animals one year of age and older. Concern about these figures generated by conservation and anti-sealing organizations forced ICNAF to respond by significantly lowering the quota for 1976 to 127,000.

The sealing industry responded by ignoring the quota. The big-ship fleet, consisting of eight vessels sailing direct from Norway and seven of Karlsen's, took advantage of a second "good ice season" and, together with the landsmen, exceeded the quota by over 40,000. Needless to add, no punitive action of any kind was taken against them.

By now it was apparent to even the dullest intellect that ICNAF was the patsy of the Norwegian and Canadian sealing industries. Its major role was simply to deflect public outrage away from the governments of Canada and Norway, upon whom responsibility for reining in the industry and protecting the remaining seals properly rested.

Public outrage continued to rise. While Canadian and Norwegian governments, and the sealing industry, together did their worst to conceal the magnitude of the biocide being committed against the ice seals, their opponents were doing their best to bring it to public knowledge. One observer of the anti-sealers in action was Silver Don Cameron, contributing editor of *Weekend Magazine*, who went to the Front in the spring of 1976. Along with other journalists, he was a guest of Brian Davies, who had decided to challenge the Seal Protection Regulations. Cameron's account of the affair appeared in May, 1976, under the title "The Seal Hunt: A Morality Play." I have condensed it.

"'The helicopter regulations', one of Davies' people told me, 'protect the seals by preventing those who would save them from landing within half a mile of seals which are being beaten to death.' Since no charter company would risk the seizure of a costly helicopter, the International Fund for Animal Welfare has had to buy one, and Davies has learned to fly it. His plan is to land [four other, chartered helicopters] safely distant from the hunt then ferry the passengers right into the killing ground in his Bell Jet Ranger. If he's impeded, he'll point out that he's a citizen of the United Kingdom as well as Canada, and that he's operating in international waters outside the twelve-mile limit—and thus outside the grasp of Canadian law.

"At 7.30 the golden light seeps westward over the frozen harbours and snowy woods. The choppers lift off and fly in formation north over the tiny fishing villages around this most northern finger of Newfoundland. Then we are over the ice, a stunning spectacle of rounded pans whirled in the tidal streams, pressure ridges where the ice has been raftered upon itself, ragged breaks and 'leads' of open water skimmed by ice as filmy as plastic wrap.

"The morning is superb: bright, windless and sunny, even warm in the greenhouse of the helicopter I am in and Davies is flying. North of Belle Isle he dips down to look at two ships in the ice, but we see no seals. We fly on, our four other helicopters hanging like gigantic mosquitoes in the vast clarity of icefields and sky.

"Finally a trio of ships lifts over the horizon, widely scattered, barely visible one from the other. They are 'in the fat', killing seals. The chartered helicopters set down, far from the nearest ship. Brian flies closer for a look at the hunt and we see down below the dark bodies of the mother seals, the squirming white forms of the pups, the streaks of red on the white ice near a ship.

"Brian sets us down perhaps 200 yards from the *Arctic Explorer* [one of Karlsen's ships] out of Halifax. The air is heavy with the cries of seals. Long red trails lead to the ship showing where loads of pelts have been winched aboard...And there's this mother seal 10 feet from me.

"She's rocking back and forth, all 300 lbs. of her, rhythmically lifting her mouth to the sky and keening. By her belly is a plum-coloured heap of meat, all that remains of her infant. As I watch her the crying ceases. She makes no further sound, though she seems to be trying. She rocks back and forth without pause.

"It's like a battlefield. As far as you can see the ice is splashed with blood. Whitecoats, still living, whose mothers have ducked into the water, cry aloud. On the horizon, in black silhouette, men are swinging clubs up and down in the white glare. Our party tramps over the ice, pausing to peer down a breathing-hole where a mother seal glides past with the elegance of a ballet dancer. The tiny carcasses of whitecoats, not much bigger than a good-sized roast once the fur and fat are taken, stare at us with bulging eyes protruding from heads smashed by sealers' clubs.

"Here and there a red flag flutters where a pile of sculps is being assembled. Four sealers are working this part of the patch. As they approach a whitecoat, the mother lunges at them once or twice, then slips into the water. The sealer raises a blood-soaked club about like a baseball bat. With a soft thump like a muffled drumbeat the bat crushes the seal's skull. Thick, crimson blood spouts from the whitecoat's eyes, mouth and nose. As the pup twitches and writhes to the dying jangle of its nervous system the sealer draws a long knife and a whetstone, and hones the steel.

"He makes a long cut from the chin down the belly to the hind flippers. The seal opens like an unzipped purse, its fat quivering like jelly, its inwards steaming in the cold.

"We walk toward a flag and happen on a truly horrible scene: a mother seal whose head has been smashed, whose snout has been driven sideways, and who is still alive, breathing shallowly through her battered face. The women with us scream; some burst into tears; others are enraged. They rush to nearby sealers.

"'Put her down!' cries Lisa. 'Put her out of her misery!'

"The sealers refuse. By law they are not permitted to kill adult seals this early in the hunt, though they may 'defend' themselves if a mother interferes with their work. 'Take the flagpole', one man tells Lisa. 'Do it yourself.'

"A Fisheries helicopter clatters down. Lisa rushes to it, waving her arms at the Protection officer. 'There's a mother seal...'

"'I can't do anything about it', says the officer. 'I have no weapons. I'm not a doctor.' He goes and looks, then flies away. Nothing can be done. We pursue the hunters, leaving the seal in her agony.

"What we're watching is comparable to killing kittens with claw hammers; it can't be called a 'hunt'. The day almost mocks the activity below, with the floes jammed solidly together and the sun bright and warm. As sheer spectacle, the seal herd is unforgettable: pups and mothers tucked in every nook and cranny of the ice as far as you can see. Black, sleek heads popping up in the leads and holes, inspecting the scene, then diving in unison. This endless wasteland teems with life."

When Cameron's group returned to the land that evening, the Royal Canadian Mounted Police seized Davies' helicopter and he was charged with violating the Seal Protection Regulations. Two other helicopters belonging to the Greenpeace protest movement were also impounded. Following publication of Cameron's article, a new Minister of Fisheries, Roméo LeBlanc, assured an interviewer that he was determined to uphold the law of the land and protect the seals. To ensure that these objectives were achieved, he planned to place the seal fishery completely out of bounds to any except legitimate sealers.

He was as good as his word. In June of 1977, a new Seal Protection Regulation was proclaimed making it an illegal act, subject to immediate arrest, for any person to interfere in any way with a seal hunter engaged in his proper business. It was also announced that Fisheries protection officers would henceforth be vested with the authority of peace officers and would be armed, to enable them to enforce the regulations.

In this same year, Canada proclaimed limited sovereignty over her surrounding seas to an offshore distance of 200 miles, which brought the entire western Atlantic ice-seal population, and of course the seal hunt, under her jurisdiction and made them subject to Canadian law.

Having reclaimed the seal "management" role, LeBlanc's department issued a statement explaining its intentions. "Canada's policy in seal management is consistent with its policies in the management of other living marine resources—the resources are harvested in a humane fashion, at levels which will permit a continuing sustained yield, based upon sound conservation principles which ensure the survival of the stocks, *and which take into account the relationships among species as competitors, predators and prey.*" I have italicized that final phrase because it contains the first public intimation of the real, but covert policy the Fisheries department was pursuing in regard to seals. A veiled reference to this policy had appeared in a departmental publication the previous year. Written by M.C. Mercer, a senior Fisheries civil servant, it included this intimation of things to come: "An argument can be advanced from the fishing industry to reduce the population [of harp seals] to a low level."

The covert policy, as opposed to the expressed intent, was in fact designed to reduce all species of seals inhabiting commercial fishing waters to relic levels.

We have already seen how it was and still is being applied to grey and harbour seals. In the case of harp and hood seals, the Department of Fisheries *deliberately* employed the sealing industry as the instrument with which to achieve its goal.

Not all the employees of the department were in support. One, who for obvious reasons does not wish to be identified, has this to say about it: "The Minister is usually just your average politician doing what his experts tell him, and whatever he thinks is expedient. It's the deputies and assistant deputies backed by subservient science that really produce the policy. Remember, this is *Fisheries*, and seals are nowhere as economic an asset to Canada compared to fish. You have to remember, too, that since the sixties, all the important western Atlantic fisheries have been commercially depleted at such a considerable rate that natural recruitment can't keep up, and all the main stocks are going down.

"Fish processors and provincial government people in the Maritimes have been yelling blue murder for quite a while, and blaming federal incompetence for the decline. They had to be cooled out, but there was no way we could reduce the Canadian catch level without getting into worse trouble. For a while, we blamed the Russians and the East Bloc fishing fleets, but after we put in the 200-mile limit, that wouldn't wash.

"That's where the seals came in. We'd been dumping on seals for so long, in connection with salmon and herring, that maybe some of us had begun to believe they really were major culprits. Anyhow, it wasn't hard to make them look that way. They were a good thing to go for because nobody much gave a damn about them until Brian Davies began to stir things up. For LeBlanc, it was kind of Hobson's choice. If he didn't convince the fish people he was doing all he could to protect the fish stocks, he and the Liberal Party were in big trouble down east, which is where he comes from. But if he *did* convince them a war on seals was going to make a difference, he was going to get it in the neck from the conservationists.

"I guess he chose what looked like the lesser of two evils, figuring he could ride out any storm the anti-sealing crowd blew up, by letting the sealers carry the ball in public. Some of us weren't too happy about it, but what was there to do? It was the Minister's game, and we had to play it his way."

I asked him whether the already grossly depleted seal population ever has been, or if it still remains, a factor in the decline of the fisheries.

"You can make a case for it if you juggle the data—cook the figures a bit. You can also make a case for putting birds on the hit list as a threat to civil aviation because they sometimes get sucked into jet engines. There's no solid proof seals ever were a major problem. In fact, there's good evidence that, as an integral part of the marine biota, their presence is important to the successful propagation of a number of commercial fish species. Look at it this way: in the nineteenth century, over twice as much cod was being landed, even with old-fashioned methods, as we can get now. And there were millions of seals out there then."

The expectation that a policy of extirpation would succeed was buoyed by departmental studies that showed pup production of western Atlantic harps to have sunk below 230,000. This meant that reproductively active females no longer numbered much more than 250,000. If reinforcement or replacement of this breeding pool could be prevented by the annual extermination of most pups and beaters, then, when the current adult female population ceased to be productive, the harp seal nation would collapse into virtual extinction. Some experts predicted that this "final solution" could be achieved as early as 1985—*providing* that the sealing industry continued to perform its exterminator role.

This could only be ensured if a profitable market for seal products could be maintained. And here was the rub, because the anti-sealing movement was campaigning internationally (and with increasing success) for a boycott of those very products, particularly whitecoat fur.

As we have seen, LeBlanc and his predecessors had sought to deal with the protest movement by imposing arbitrary regulations intended to quarantine and sanitize the slaughter. Now Fisheries engaged in a massive, publicly funded campaign to discredit the actions and debase the motives of the protesters, at the same time aiming to convince the world that the seal pup "harvest" was a humane, properly managed, and legitimate use of a "sustainable natural resource."

Under cover of this propaganda barrage, LeBlanc's department, making its first "management" decision since resuming direct jurisdiction over the seals, *raised* the quota from ICNAF's 127,000 of 1976—to 170,000 for 1977. (Remember, these are landings, not the actual number of seals destroyed.) This decision was made in defiance of the recommendation of Parliament's Advisory Committee on Seals and Sealing, which maintained that 140,000 was the absolute maximum the harp seal population could endure.

Although reported landings of 155,143 that year seemed to confirm the COSS judgement, LeBlanc nevertheless again raised the quota, to 180,000 for 1978, nor was he deterred when in both that and the following year the sealers failed to pass the 160,000 mark. In 1980 they did better, with 172,000. Most of these "harvests," be it noted, were composed of harp seal pups.

The size of this last catch did not indicate an increasing seal population, as Fisheries and Oceans and the newly formed North Atlantic Fisheries Organization (a reincarnation of the now thoroughly discredited ICNAF) maintained. It was due to increased hunting pressure brought to bear through LeBlanc's department (which had also undergone a sea-change and was now grandiloquently called Fisheries and Oceans). Through the use of federal subsidies it had encouraged construction of scores of multi-purpose fishing boats with sealing capabilities. These brought many more

Newfoundlanders, Madelinots, and northern Gulf coast fishermen into the offshore hunt, and so increased the kill. Government technical support of the sealing industry had also been much improved during the late seventies. New methods of ice-forecasting and reporting were being used, as well as aerial reconnaissance that pinpointed the location of every significant patch of ice seals and directed the sealers to them. And more Canadian Coast Guard and Fisheries patrol vessels were being assigned to assist the sealers.

Meantime, the Fisheries and Oceans contention that ice seals were becoming ever more numerous was being challenged. Early in 1979, two of the department's own senior research scientists, Dr. W.D. Bowen and Dr. D.E. Sergeant, complained that population estimates being used by NAFO (and by LeBlanc's mandarins) were unduly optimistic. In this same year, an independent study commissioned by the U.S. Marine Mammals Commission, employing Dr. John Beddington and H.A. Williams, experts in animal population dynamics at England's York University, was completed. The report concluded that ICNAF/NAFO scientists were consistently overestimating harp seal pup production by as much as a third!

The Fisheries and Oceans' response was to brazenly raise the quota yet again for 1980.

The extirpation program was proceeding on schedule, though not without furious opposition from the anti-sealing movement. While Brian Davies' organization remained at the forefront, the protest had by now been seconded by almost every major animal welfare group extant, but not, be it noted, by the Canadian Wildlife Federation, previously referred to in connection with the wolf. The CWF publicly supported the sealing industry. More and more concerned scientists, appalled at the liberties NAFO and Fisheries and Oceans were taking with scientific methods and principles, were adding their voices to what was fast becoming a thunder of dissent.

Toward the end of 1980, LeBlanc seems to have realized that the protest movement could neither be suppressed nor contained and that it might eventually succeed in bringing about an end to sealing in Canadian waters. Concrete evidence of its effectiveness was already at hand in the form of a sharp decline in the demand for sealskin products on European markets due to the adverse publicity sealing was receiving there. Even on the home front, informal polls showed that at least half of all Canadians were now opposed to the annual slaughter.

Considering these circumstances, LeBlanc and his bureaucrats determined to make the best use of what time remained. In 1981, Fisheries and Oceans unleashed what amounted to total war against the ice seals.

NAFO's and the department's creative statisticians (they were really one and the same) outdid themselves by producing figures suggesting that, despite the enormous destruction of recent years, harp seal pup production had almost doubled to nearly half a million whitecoats annually. Release of these statistics was accompanied by dire prophecies of a "seal emergency" that could inflict crushing economic damage on the entire northwestern Atlantic fishery unless the seal explosion was contained. Drastic action was needed to forestall such a calamity.

It was forthcoming.

Although the NAFO quota for 1981 was set at the extremely generous figure of 183,000 for the Front and Gulf regions, the sealers perfectly understood that it would not be enforced. They were deliberately encouraged to "go for broke." Norwegians and Canadians alike extended themselves to the limit to take advantage of this open-ended opportunity. As a result, they slaughtered well over a *quarter of a million* ice seals, most of which were pups. The official figure released by NAFO for catches by Norwegian and Canadian sealers in the Gulf of St. Lawrence and in Canadian-controlled waters off Newfoundland and Labrador was 201,162. However, Statistics Canada reported that, in 1981, Canada *alone* exported at least 224,000 seal pelts, the vast majority of which were from harp seals. Neither figure takes into account the number of seals killed and not recovered. The destruction was so massive that the Norwegian buyers were surfeited and subsequently had to dump at least 20,000 pelts. However, they suffered no financial loss thereby, having been "reimbursed" by the Canadian government. There is reason to believe that Fisheries and Oceans had, in fact, been subsidizing the industry in this way with taxpayers' money for several years, in effect guaranteeing payment for skins taken in excess of market needs.

This otherwise eminently successful "cull" was marred, from LeBlanc's point of view, when part of the Gulf whelping ice was gale-driven onto the beaches of a national park in Prince Edward Island. As the ice that bore the seal pups began to come ashore, Fisheries and Oceans officers hastily licensed about 200 local fishermen to go after them. Most of these men and youths had never killed or skinned a seal before, and the instructions given to them were rudimentary in the extreme. Before the guardians of law and order could cordon off the area and exclude media people and anti-sealing protesters, some of these were able to observe an effectively unregulated slaughter of whitecoats (including the skinning alive of pups) that amounted to outright massacre. When films of this atrocity appeared on television worldwide, the flames of protest mounted.

Brian Davies took full advantage of this gory publicity to spotlight a bold new campaign against commercial sealing. In collaboration with several other conservation groups, he had established a powerful lobby directed at persuading the ten-nation European Economic Community to prohibit the import into Europe of the skins of ice-seal pups. As 1981 drew to a close it began to look as if this remarkable initiative might come to something, and the Canadian governments, which at first had taken the matter lightly, became alarmed. The state of affairs early in 1982 is described in this contemporary column by Barry Kent MacKay in the *Toronto Star*:

"The parliament of the European Economic Community...will [soon] consider a motion for a ban on products from harp and hood seal pups...The Canadian government has tax-funded representatives there now, trying to convince members of the European parliament that the seal hunt is an institution supported by most Canadians and an important part of our economy and that a ban would be seen by us as some form of anti-Canadian bigotry.

"It's utter nonsense, of course. The seal hunt has generated more protest mail to Ottawa than any other issue, for all the good it has done. There has never been a national plebiscite on the seal hunt. The people I've met who support the hunt do so either for illogically emotional reasons or because they trustingly believe the pro-hunt propaganda of the federal government, not realizing most of it is misleading or false.

"To prepare the way for its lobbyists, the federal government recently increased the quota...This gives the impression seal stocks are increasing, but you can be sure the Canadian lobby won't think to mention...the independent Canadian and foreign scientists who are in disagreement with the federal government's figures and fear that seal stocks are in decline...

"The lobbyists will doubtless prattle on about seals eating too many fish at the expense of Canada's commercial fishing industry although, in truth, the decline in fish stocks was caused by the greed of the commercial fishing industry.

"The Canadian delegation will, I suspect, forget to mention that [ice] seals fast while whelping and, at other times, eat primarily non-commercial fish species far from the fishing banks of Newfoundland. If left alone the harp and hood seals would have no significant effect on commercial fish stocks.

"The Europeans won't hear that our government refuses to make public how much it costs us to regulate, monitor and promote the hunt.

"No one will be told that the gross value of the seal hunt to Canada is the economic equivalent of two McDonald's restaurants.

"The EEC won't hear about Canadian citizens and foreign visitors who have been assaulted and had their films of [the] hunt stolen by federal police, nor are they likely to be told of Canadian citizens jailed and heavily fined for trying to observe, photograph or protest the hunt.

"Europeans won't hear that the regulations governing the hunt are not passed by Parliament, but are achieved through orders-in-council and function primarily to keep observers from the hunt. Violations of the regulations by humanitarians are always vigorously prosecuted, but violations by sealers are always ignored.

"The Europeans may even be asked to believe the sort of nonsense spewed by the Canadian High Commissioner in London, who claimed: 'One blow kills a seal, and since exsanguination follows, it is a physical impossibility to skin a seal alive.'"

On March 11, 1982, even as the annual slaughter was beginning, the EEC parliament, meeting in Strasbourg, voted 160 to 10 in support of a resolution calling for a ban by member states on the import of the skins of both harp and hood seal pups. Since the parliament's role is mainly advisory, it was left to the EEC Commissioners and Council of Ministers to decide whether or not to act on the resolution. This they were in no hurry to do. Nevertheless, the resolution itself so infuriated Roméo LeBlanc that he forsook caution and announced that, should "commercial harvesting" of the ice seals be ended, government agencies would themselves take over the "cull" in the name of fisheries protection, even as they had done with grey and harbour seals.

The cat was finally out of the bag.

I do not know if this outburst had anything to do with it—perhaps LeBlanc was simply exhausted by the struggle—but shortly thereafter he was replaced as Minister of Fisheries and Oceans by the Honourable Pierre de Bané.

The 1982 spring slaughter, which even some protesters (having been insensibly seduced into using newspeak) were now calling a cull, took place as usual. And yet, the sealers were only able to find, kill, and land 69,000 whitecoats out of the half-million that NAFO and de Bané's scientists estimated had been born that year. The discrepancy was embarrassing, and so was the result of a Gallup Poll that confirmed that 60 per cent of Canadians now wanted the seal slaughter stopped.

Even more perturbing for the new Minister was the prospect that the EEC Commissioners might implement the recommended European ban. Not-so-genteel threats were made by high Canadian officials to the effect that such a move could lead to the restriction or even cancellation of quotas for European nations fishing in Canadian waters. Canada's Prime Minister, Pierre Trudeau, was quoted as saying that Canada would think about reprisals. This put the EEC Environment Commissioners in a pretty plight, for they had already received petitions carrying as many as 5,000,000 signatures from their own constituents, demanding that the ban be imposed. Under the leadership of Commissioner Karl-Heinz Narjes, they decided to postpone a decision, which was to have been made in July, until September of 1982. This was only the first of several such delays.

As 1983 began, the Commissioners were enduring increasing pressure from an international coalition that included the Europgroup for Animal Welfare, Friends of the Earth, Greenpeace, International Fund for Animal Welfare, People's Trust for Endangered Species, World Society for the Protection of Animals, and the Royal Society for the Prevention of Cruelty to Animals. On the other hand, they were being heavily pressured by Canada and Norway. To make things worse, some of the EEC nations, especially France and Britain, were beginning to side with the Canadian government.

Finally, on February 28, 1983, the EEC Environmental Council bit the bullet and directed the member states to prohibit the import of the skins of harp whitecoats and hood bluebacks into their territories. The ban was subject to two caveats negotiated by Norway and Canada. It would not come into effect until October, 1983; and it would remain in place for only two years.

Fisheries and Oceans had reason to be pleased if not contented by this outcome. The decision would have no effect on the 1983 "cull"; and it was not a permanent ban. Furthermore, as we shall see, it contained (and had been designed to contain) a loophole that rendered its restrictions all but meaningless.

Mr. de Bané's department was less pleased by the actions of some of its allies. The chief European purchaser and processor of sealskins, Christian Rieber of Bergen, announced that, due to the effect of the voluntary boycott on seal products throughout Europe and an enormous resultant backlog of unsold pelts from previous seasons, he would accept no whitecoats from the 1983 hunt and no more than 60,000 beater and adult skins. Rieber's suppliers in Canada, Karlsen and the pelt-buying company Carino, confirmed that they would buy no more than that number and, furthermore, would offer sealers only half the price paid the previous year.

Despite this setback, de Bané's department did everything it could to ensure the maximum destruction of ice seals that spring. Dangling a quota of 186,000 harps and 12,000 hoods in front of the sealers, it encouraged them to kill as many as possible in the expectation that the existing market would improve and that new ones would be found. Magdalen Island sealers were given to understand that the limits set by Karlsen and Carino were only a ploy; that every pelt brought ashore would find a market and a fair price, even if this had to be subsidized by Ottawa. Newfoundland's Minister of Fisheries, Jim Morgan, whipped the sealers of his province on with a rousing challenge to defend their "traditional way of life and culture." Furthermore, he told them, they *must* kill at least 100,000 seals in order to save the cod fishery from destruction. He also offered to provide $500,000 to "subsidize" the purchase of pelts by Carino.

As it had done every year since its inception, Davies' IFAW sent an observer team to the Gulf hunt. It included representatives from the Toronto Humane Society and the Animal Protection Institute of America. Based in Charlottetown, the capital of Prince Edward Island, the group made several visits to the whelping ice before the season opened. Although the trips were legal because the hunt had not yet started, the visitors were nonetheless harassed and warned away by Fisheries protection officers.

On the morning of March 8, members of the group were awakened by the ugly sound of a mob outside their motel. It consisted of sixty to a hundred P.E.I. fishermen supporting a group of Newfoundland sealers flown in for the occasion. The message of this belligerent crowd was chillingly direct: either the IFAW team (which included several women) would voluntarily leave Prince Edward Island before 5:00 P.M.—or face the prospect of being "shipped out in garbage bags." Whether or not those threats were seriously meant, a few days later when an IFAW crew attempted to launch a small boat at Savage Harbour, they were attacked by another mob and considerable damage was done to both their boat and truck.

There were other troubles. On March 22, the sealing vessels *Chester* and *Technoventure* entered the Gulf whelping ice and began killing pups. *Chester* belonged to the Karlsen Shipping Company, while *Technoventure* was killing for the Carino Company. The sealers had been "into the fat" for only two days when a third ship appeared on the scene. She was an antiquated ex-trawler called *Sea Shepherd II*, crewed by sixteen men and five women of the Sea Shepherd Conservation Society, a radical organization led by Paul Watson, who had already acquired a considerable reputation for taking direct action against pirate whalers. During the early hours of Friday, March 24, *Sea Shepherd* crunched through the floes toward *Chester*, whose sealers had already left their ship and were working the ice, leaving patches of ruby-red slush glowing in the light of the rising sun as they clubbed and sculped successive patches of pups.

Sea Shepherd's arrival was not unexpected. Some days earlier, Watson had warned that his organization was prepared to intervene directly in the hunt if he found sealers engaged in slaughtering pups. Shadowed by Canadian government ships and aircraft, *Sea Shepherd* had first blockaded St. John's harbour, then, when no sealing vessels emerged, had set course for the Gulf. During the night of March 23, *Chester* and *Technoventure* were warned of Watson's approach. *Technoventure* developed engine trouble that did not, however, prevent her from hurriedly steaming off for Halifax. *Chester* held her ground.

Watched with considerable apprehension by *Chester*'s sealers, many of whom were Newfoundlanders, Watson's old fishing boat bore steadily down upon them with siren blaring. When barely a ship's length separated the two vessels, Watson put his helm over and, stepping out on the wing of his rusty bridge, shouted an ultimatum. Either *Chester* would cease sealing immediately, or take the consequences of having the trawler rampaging through the ice where pup killing was taking place.

Chester's tough Norwegian Master decided not to call Watson's bluff. He sounded his own siren, bringing his sealers scrambling back on board. As radio messages crackled through the spring air, several small fishing vessels carrying seal hunters from the Magdalens discreetly returned to port. The morning sun blazed down on what had become a peaceful tableau. The two ships lay at rest within the pack. Around them the bleating of seal pups calling to their mothers was almost the only sound. Then the day was shattered by the hellish clatter of helicopter rotors.

During the next twenty-four hours, Fisheries and RCMP helicopters and Canadian Forces tracker aircraft roared and chattered over *Sea Shepherd*. Heaving huge on the horizon, the massive Canadian Coast Guard icebreaker *John A. Macdonald* came crashing through the pack to take up station a stone's throw from Watson's vessel. Radio, verbal, and visual signals ordering Watson to take his ship into the Magdalen port of Cap Aux Meules were ignored. So long as *Chester* remained in the patch, *Sea Shepherd* would remain as well. An RCMP helicopter attempted to land a posse on Watson's ship but sheered off when it was seen that her decks were barricaded with barbed wire.

On Sunday, March 26, this "rabid interference with the rights of ordinary Canadians to earn a living" came to an abrupt end. While the towering bulk of the 350-foot *Macdonald* lay across *Sea Shepherd*'s bows to prevent her from attempting to escape, a second icebreaker, *Sir William Alexander*, carrying an RCMP Emergency Response Team, moved in. What followed is described by one of *Sea Shepherd*'s volunteers.

"The *Sir William Alexander* rammed *Sea Shepherd* in the stern and slid along the starboard side. A weight hanging from a boom swung down and cleared off the barbed wire fence. Smoke cannisters were lobbed onto the deck, water hoses were trained on the bridge windows and engine exhaust stack. A gangplank was lowered and the SWAT squad, armed with handguns, commando knives and crow-bars, ran across. The bow of the *Sir John A. Macdonald* towering over us was lined with Mounties holding automatic rifles. A couple of helicopters hovered over the scene. The SWAT squad was fast. In 5 minutes we were all handcuffed and lined up on deck."

After being transported to Sydney, Nova Scotia, in the unheated hold of the icebreaker, the prisoners were then flown by military aircraft to Gaspé, where they were jailed and charged with violating the Seal Protection Regulations. On December 21, 1983, Quebec Provincial Judge Yvon Mercier convicted Watson and his crew of, amongst other heinous crimes, unlawfully coming within half a nautical mile of the site of a seal hunt. Watson was fined $5,000 and sentenced to fifteen months in jail. His chief engineer was fined $4,000 and three months. The other crew members were fined $3,000 each. *Sea Shepherd II*, valued at $250,000, was confiscated.

By way of contrast, during this same spring eight Nova Scotia lobster fishermen chased Fisheries protection officers off two patrol boats, which they then burned and sank. Charged with piracy, the eight were given suspended sentences and ordered to perform community service in lieu of paying fines or damages.

The results of the 1983 spring "cull" did not bode well for the "seal management" policies of Fisheries and Oceans. For the first time since 1946, none of the super-efficient vessels of Norwegian registry appeared on the scene. Only two Canadian vessels, one of which was under charter to Fisheries and Oceans, reached the Front whelping patches. No new markets opened up. It was obvious to anyone with half an eye that the repugnance generated by years of protest against the whitecoat slaughter was now so pervasive that neither new markets nor a revival of the old could be looked for in the foreseeable future. Their warehouses bulging with unsold pelts, the Norwegians understood this all too well and so made good on their warning that they would pay only half the 1982 prices for 1983 pelts. In fine, total landings of harp seals from Gulf and Front together amounted to little more than a third the number landed the previous year.[2]

Despite all this, Pierre de Bané professed to believe that all was well with the "industry." Stoutly asserting that not a single whitecoat had been taken in the spring of 1983, he expressed his confidence that the EEC would not ratify its import ban. Furthermore, now that the anti-sealers were deprived of the stereotype of the bloodied whitecoat pup with which to fuel public indignation and generate financial contributions, he expected the protest movement to dry up and blow away. Meanwhile the federal government was arranging to compensate Canadian sealers to the tune of a million dollars for the poor prices they had received in 1983. De Bané did not explain to Canadian taxpayers that this largesse was necessary because east-coast fishermen were losing interest in the sealing business and that, without them, Fisheries and Oceans' most telling justification for maintaining an annual slaughter—that many Maritimers were dependent on it for their livelihood—would lose what little validity it retained. I should note here that in 1982 the average return to Canadian sealers had amounted to less than $800 apiece.

Despite this display of optimism about the future of the sealing "industry," de Bané and his advisers were facing dark portents. On October 1, 1983, despite furious last-minute lobbying by Canada, the EEC directive banning imports of harp seal whitecoats and hood seal bluebacks took effect for a two-year period. Meantime, a potentially even more serious obstacle to Fisheries and Oceans' "final solution" to the seal problem was beginning to loom on the horizon.

As early as March of 1982, Brian Davies and the directors of the IFAW had reluctantly concluded that even an effective ban by the EEC might not be enough by itself to end the hunt. They therefore began preparing an action of such audacity and magnitude that many of their own supporters were convinced it would not work. What they had in mind was no less than a consumer boycott of all Canadian fish products imported into Britain.

"Britain is Canada's second most important customer for fish," an IFAW spokesman explained to me. "On average, gross sales to Britain amount to a hundred million dollars a year. We decided we could, and would if we had to, change all that. If Canada continued with the hunt, we would make her pay through the nose."

---

[2] Hood seals, which even most government scientists now admitted were near or at the endangered level, received a new lease on life. As a result of the collapse of sealing at the Front, only 129 hood sculps were taken during the 1982 hunt in Canadian waters.

There was never any secret about what was planned. In September, 1982, Davies had told Ottawa precisely what was intended if the seal hunt continued. Initially, it would appear, the Ottawa mandarins were simply contemptuous of what one referred to as "this bumbling attempt at blackmail." They remained unimpressed even when, in January of 1983, as many as 150,000 postcards were sent by IFAW supporters in Britain to the fisheries ministers of the Canadian Atlantic Provinces, pledging the signatories to support the boycott of Canadian fish if the spring hunt took place as scheduled. Ottawa dismissed this as mere bluff.

When the 1983 "cull" went ahead as advertised, the IFAW got down to business, working with an umbrella group in Britain, the Seal Protection Group, that consisted of eight major conservation and animal welfare organizations. The anti-sealers were particularly incensed because, regardless of de Bané's denials, the slaughter again included whitecoats.

"Despite the Seal Protection Regulations," I was told by an IFAW member, "our group, Greenpeace, and the Sea Shepherd people *all* had got evidence that whitecoats were being killed. We didn't know how many but we suspected plenty. So then it was full-speed ahead with the boycott. And we were determined to make it as brutally effective against the Canadian economy as a sealer's club against a seal pup's skull."

Initially budgeted at $1 million (U.S.), the operation was the best-organized boycott ever mounted by any animal welfare group. It got under way in September, 1983, with a write-in campaign directed at British wholesale firms importing Canadian fish. In October, the second phase opened with a torrent of letters and cards to major grocery chains. Both actions were backed by widespread advertising, street theatre, and masterful use of the media.

The campaign was deliberately designed to take effect in stages, any one of which might serve to persuade the Canadian government to end the commercial ice-seal hunt. As the months went by and de Bané not only showed no sign of acquiescence but became ever more bellicose, the pressure was increased. When, in December, the Newfoundland Minister of Fisheries announced that the 1984 "harvest" would take place as usual, the IFAW pulled out all the stops.

On February 7, 1984, Tesco, the largest grocery chain in Britain, controlling 465 retail stores, decided to comply with its customers' wishes as expressed through tens of thousands of protest cards. Tesco agreed to remove all stocks of Canadian fish products and to buy no more until the seal hunt ended. This was the breakthrough, and it was clear that several other major British firms would soon find it expedient to follow suit.

Alarmed at last by this very real threat to its fish trade with Britain, Canada counterattacked. While the Canadian High Commissioner in London categorically denied that baby seals were still being killed, de Bané accused the directors of the IFAW of knowing full well that the whitecoat hunt had been stopped but of deliberately "spreading the lie" that it had not.

Under increasingly heavy pressure to justify the ongoing "cull," Fisheries and Oceans unleashed a flood of press releases, most of which were dutifully echoed by the media. Typical of these was a feature in the *Globe and Mail* in late January headed "Seals Making Comeback, Scientists Believe." It began: "Today seals are blanketing beaches and ice floes of eastern Canada in huge numbers and the situation is prompting fishermen to call for annual seal kills to keep populations in check." The balance of the piece consisted of bald assertions by Fisheries' officials, bolstered by statements from an organization calling itself the Canadian Sealers Association. Funded by a $500,000 grant from the Newfoundland government and $50,000 from federal sources, the CSA's professed task was "to put pressure on the Government for a regular seal cull."

Fisheries spokesman Yvon Bureau was quoted to the effect that "Canadian seals eat about four million tonnes of fish a year, an amount equivalent to the annual commercial catch off Canada's shores." No scientific basis was given for this fearsome figure; the kinds of seals involved were not specified; nothing was said as to whether or not the fish supposedly consumed were commercially useful, or even whether they were eaten in the Atlantic, Pacific, or Arctic Oceans. Typically, and despite its headline, the article made no reference to the conclusions of seal scientists, including the government's own Dr. Sergeant, who denied the charge that harp seals had any significant adverse effect on Canadian fisheries.

As February began, de Bané's spokesmen announced that the 1984 spring "cull" would proceed as planned, and that Carino had again agreed to buy at least 60,000 skins, *none of which would be whitecoats.* There was reason to believe, although proof was lacking, that Carino was to be directly subsidized this time with government funds.

At the end of February, only a few weeks before the "cull" was due to begin, the IFAW dropped another blockbuster. Davies announced that, unless the hunt was halted, a second boycott of Canadian fish products would begin—this time in the enormous U.S. market. Five million direct-mail kits were ready to be sent to U.S. consumers, each of whom would be asked to return a protest card to major food companies currently using large amounts of Canadian fish. Prominent amongst these were the McDonald's and Burger King chains.

This time the threat was taken seriously, and it brought considerable dissension into the Canadian Cabinet, where both the Minister of External Affairs and the Minister of Trade counselled putting an end to the seal hunt once and for all. With fish sales of well over a billion dollars now at stake, de Bané began finding himself more and more isolated.

On March 5, Allan MacEachen, Minister of External Affairs and Deputy Prime Minister, publicly announced that Canada was considering putting an end to the east-coast commercial seal hunt. "We haven't reached any decision yet, but we are considering what we ought to do," he said. De Bané responded with a statement of his own in which he claimed that ending the hunt would mean "surrender to blackmailers and liars." A revealing afterword in the same news release reported that "other Government officials [read: Fisheries and Oceans bureaucrats] suggested that banning the hunt could make it harder for the Government to start an annual cull of the seal herd as their numbers swell."

The battle in Cabinet raged for several days, and it was only the knowledge that there would be a federal election in the latter part of 1984, and that the ruling Liberal Party would desperately need every seat it could get in the Atlantic region, that persuaded the majority of Cabinet ministers to let de Bané have his way.

He was now making increasingly inflammatory statements. "Those who resort to lies and blackmail," the press reported him as saying in reference to the protesters, "are the most despicable criminals I can think of, and seeing them trying to destroy the livelihood of our fishermen is another crime that they will have to bear." To buoy the sealers' flagging enthusiasm, he announced that a new market for sealskins was being sought in Japan, and strongly intimated that the price of seal pelts would again be subsidized by government agencies.

Perhaps his most intemperate statement was made on March 8, when he insisted that the EEC ban was redundant, because the killing of whitecoats was already at an end; then he concluded with the warning, "Let's not forget who we are dealing with [in the protest movement], we're dealing with blackmailers, with liars, with fanatics, so obviously no rational argument can convince fanatics, people I would call fascists!"

The following day, with the seal "cull" about to begin, he told the House of Commons he had assurances from all major fish buyers in the United States that they would not succumb to pressure for a boycott on Canadian fish products. Having once again denied that any whitecoats had been killed in 1983, or would be killed in 1984, he reiterated his charge that the protesters were liars. Oddly, neither the Minister nor any of his officials was able to name a single foreign company that had given an assurance it would continue to buy Canadian fish in spite of any boycott. On the contrary, two more major food chains in Britain were on the point of removing Canadian fish products from their shelves.

Even the Minister's closest allies were now beginning to desert him. The chairman of the British Columbia Fishing Association, which had been vociferously backing the sealers, telexed de Bané urgently asking him to prohibit the taking of *all* seal pups of whatever age, because the boycott in Britain was already affecting export sales of canned B.C. salmon. Even the Canadian Sealers Association, all too unhappily aware that the income of the majority of its members came mainly from the export trade in fish, now bit the hand that fed it and suggested that the Minister forbid the further killing of all seal pups. De Bané angrily rejected both requests.

On March 9, he was betrayed again. On that day, the IFAW helicopter made a sortie from Prince Edward Island almost to mid-Gulf to check reports that Magdalen Islanders were again killing whitecoats. It was a long flight for the Jet Ranger carrying three photographers in addition to its pilot. By the time the machine turned for home, it was low on fuel. A decision was made to refuel at the Magdalen Island airport.

The landing was uneventful, but the agent of the Esso station there refused to supply the aircraft. When five bystanders approached the helicopter, threatening it and its occupants with lengths of 2 x 4, the pilot hurriedly took off and flew to an ice floe offshore, from whence he radioed a report of the incident to the Department of Transport authorities, requesting that an escort be provided for the hundred-mile journey over ice and water back to Prince Edward Island.

Federal Transport officials replied that arrangements would be made with the Quebec Provincial Police on the Magdalens to ensure safe refuelling there and the pilot was told to proceed back to the Magdalen airport. Having no real alternative, he did so, to find two unsympathetic policemen making no attempt to control a mob of thirty or more Madelinots. Fuel was again refused, and when some of the local men began pounding the sides of the helicopter, the crew abandoned it to seek shelter in the terminal building. Here they were besieged for several hours. They were finally permitted to leave the island in a chartered local aircraft, but only after the film and tape they had taken that day had been surrendered to the crowd.

The Jet Ranger remained behind. Although nominally protected by eight provincial policemen and five RCMP constables, it was nevertheless severely damaged during the night. During the succeeding night, a crowd of at least a hundred men and youths swinging chains and wielding iron bars attacked it yet again, effectively destroying the $350,000 machine, together with some $25,000 worth of camera equipment.

Despite the fact that several of those who helped trash the helicopter freely admitted their involvement to the press, almost two months elapsed before the police laid any charges. Then, on June 9, fifteen men were accused of mischief, intimidation, and the theft of an emergency radio beacon from the aircraft. All pleaded not guilty and were ordered to appear for a preliminary hearing in September.

The reaction of Mr. de Bané to this incident was one of gentle forgiveness. "I understand very well the reactions of our fishermen who have seen their livelihood endangered by people who come and protest one week during the year ... and live the rest of the year in luxury hotels on the money they have collected from the general public."

The reaction of much of the rest of the Western world was, however, one of outrage. In Ottawa, more Cabinet ministers leagued themselves against Fisheries and Oceans, trying without success to persuade the intractable de Bané to call off the hunt. Supported by the Prime Minister, he would not be moved. According to an observer, even the usual arguments in support of the hunt, such as the need to reduce seal populations for the sake of the fishery, had been superseded. "The ministers were told that the protest *had* to be defeated because the government could not afford a precedent where the wishes of outsiders could override internal departmental decisions. To put it another way, we could not afford to admit that Fisheries was in the wrong so there was no way we were going to back down."

That Fisheries and Oceans was indeed deeply in the wrong became shockingly clear on March 16, when Dr. David Lavigne, who had conducted seal population and other studies for the federal Fisheries department, was interviewed by a newspaper reporter. Asked if whitecoats had been killed in 1983, Lavigne drew the reporter's attention to a report compiled by Fisheries and Oceans officers in Newfoundland that listed 5,609 whitecoats as having been sculped that year, together with about 35,000 beaters and 25,000 adults.

This revelation exposed the loophole in the EEC ban. Although the 5,609 were pups of an age that in any previous year would have been classified by both NAFO and Fisheries and Oceans as whitecoats, they had been reclassified as "overgangs," "tanners," or "raggedy-jackets." Unfortunately for Mr. de Bané, somebody had failed to instruct the St. John's officials of this cosmetic change.

The bleak truth was that, despite the new nomenclature, Canadian seal-ers were continuing to sculp baby seals under three weeks of age, most of them not even weaned and still in the process of moulting their all-white neo-natal coats. As for beaters—this is a generic term embracing all young harps between about three weeks and a year in age; many of the beaters killed in 1983 were little if any older than three weeks. And the seal-hunt protesters devised a bitter little riddle after this denouement. "When is a whitecoat not a whitecoat? When de Bané says it's not."

In response to another question, Dr. Lavigne gave it as his opinion that "The bulk of misinformation that has come out in the past two years [about the hunt] has not been from the protesters." Truly a masterpiece of under-statement.

De Bané's position continued to worsen. On March 20, Ron Bulmer, president of the powerful Fisheries Council of Canada, whose member com-panies account for more than 90 per cent of Canada's fish exports, renewed a request that Canada forbid the killing of all baby seals. "The times are changing," said Mr. Bulmer.

Indeed they were. A Department of Trade assessment of the probable effects of an IFAW-sponsored boycott in the United States was, to say the least of it, unsettling—particularly in view of the fact that the Canadian fish-ing industry was already experiencing severe marketing problems due to other factors. The destruction of the IFAW helicopter under the eyes of Canadian police, coupled with confirmation that it was Fisheries and Oceans, not the protesters, that had, to put it politely, prevaricated about the continued killing of infant seal pups, was doing nothing to soothe public opinion either at home or abroad.

Although the governing Liberal Party still found itself in a state of indeci-sion, the opposition Conservative Party had apparently seen the light. Its fisheries critic now asked Parliament to declare a total prohibition on the killing of all seals under a year of age. "It is time to admit," said he, "that the anti-seal hunt protest has too much momentum, the public relations battle has been lost and it is time to ban the killing of immature seals."

He was, of course, ignored by the government in power. On March 17, Fisheries officers under questioning by a *New York Times* reporter on Prince Edward Island admitted that indubitable whitecoats, only a few days old, were even then being killed at the Magdalen Islands. A spokesman for the department claimed these were being killed for food, and not for sale. Moreover, he pointed out defiantly, it was not illegal, nor had it ever been, for Canadian sealers to kill whitecoats if they so desired.

This was pouring oil on the fire. Nor was the sense of outrage assuaged when, on March 28, two Greenpeacers flew a light aircraft over the Gulf ice in an attempt to get photographic confirmation of what was happening. Although they claimed to have stayed above the 2,000-foot altitude demanded by Seal Protection Regulations, they were subsequently arrested and their aircraft seized.

Even nature seemed to be taking an active hand at frustrating the Fisheries and Oceans "seal management" program. A fleet of eleven fishing vessels going sealing from northern ports in Newfoundland was trapped within sight of shore when the pack closed in. For six weeks the fleet remained immobilized and helpless while a succession of northeasterly winds pinned the ice against the land. The pack was so heavy that not even a Coast Guard icebreaker could free the vessels; so they had to be maintained by helicopter, at government expense, until the ice finally released them in mid-May. Not a single ship managed to reach the Front whelping patches in the spring of 1984.

The upshot was that, by the effective end of the sealing season in late May, only about 23,000 sculps had been landed from a quota of almost 200,000. The majority of these were classed as beaters by Fisheries officers, but there is a strong presumption that many, if not most, were pups only a few weeks old.

The spring of 1984 will be remembered as the worst year for sealers in more than a century and a half—and the best year for the seals.

There can be no question as to where the credit belongs or, depending on the point of view, to whom the blame should go for this enormous reduction in the ice-seal slaughter. It belongs to those several committed conservation and animal welfare organizations that unleashed and directed a tidal wave of international public protest on the sealing industry and those government bodies that supported it. For the protest groups it was victory after long years of hard-fought action.

For Mr. de Bané and his officials and supporters, it was a humiliating defeat. Nevertheless, the war between those who would preserve the seals and those who would destroy them is by no means over. Canada's Department of Fisheries and Oceans believes it has merely lost a battle and is already planning new strategies. In order to obtain a breathing space, during which (so it is hoped) the tremendous momentum generated by the protest movement will wane and dissipate as a result of the conviction that the war is won, de Bané announced, in June 1984, the establishment of a

Royal Commission to study the sealing industry, its needs, and its problems. (Pierre de Bané has since resigned and has been rewarded for his services by an appointment to the Canadian Senate, as has Roméo LeBlanc.)

The Royal Commission is a time-honoured device, part delaying tactic and part diversion, frequently employed by Canadian governments who find themselves backed into a corner. Such commissions generally take many months or even years to carry out their investigations, the eventual results of which are often irrelevant or out of date. It can be confidently predicted that this commission, led by Mr. Justice Albert Malouf of the Quebec Court of Appeals and consisting of nine members, six of whom are to be "foreigners," will not break with precedent. While the Royal Commission conducts its deliberations, Fisheries and Oceans will be freed from the necessity of responding to pressures to change its seal policies. Furthermore, when the commission's findings and recommendations *are* eventually announced, the department will make its own decision as to whether or not to accept or implement all or any part of them.

There is no doubt whatsoever that Canada intends to continue the "cull," not only of harp seals (and hoods if they begin to recover their wasted numbers), but of harbour and grey seals as well. James Morgan, the Newfoundland Fisheries Minister, has, with Ottawa's blessing, shipped a sample lot of 250 seal pelts to "interested companies in the Far East to be assessed." Morgan states that he expects firm markets to be developed in the Far East (by which he mainly means Japan) before the spring sealing season begins in 1985, with final purchase agreements being signed this autumn.

The Department of Fisheries and Oceans will continue its campaign of vilification against the seals, charging that they are destroying the commercial fisheries. It will ignore the authoritative assessment of independent scientists such as Dr. Sydney Holt, eminent marine biologist and former director of the Fisheries Resource Division of the United Nations Food and Agricultural Organization. As Dr. Holt has pointedly stated: "There is not one single case, anywhere in the world, where scientific evidence, critically evaluated by independent experts, demonstrates that 'culling' of marine mammals would be beneficial for fisheries resources."

It is not really relevant whether the Liberal Party, which was still in power when this book went to press, is returned to office or not. The Department of Fisheries and Oceans will continue to follow its own course unless, and until, its policies become so disadvantageous to Canadian politicians that they are forced to dismantle this bureaucratic empire.

What *will* save the remnants of the seal nations of the northeastern seaboard of America—if they *are* to be saved—will be ongoing and unrelenting action by such organizations as the International Fund for Animal Welfare. This group is currently implementing its boycott directed at halting Canadian fish imports into the United States, and is determined to continue so to do until the Canadian government formally agrees to end the "cull" that has incarnadined the ice fields of the Sea of Slaughter for so long a time.

And here the bloody history of the ice seals rests.

❖ Hereafter 2003

I sit at the window of my home beside the Atlantic Ocean. My work is almost done. Having led me through so many dark and bloody chronicles, this book comes to an end. The question with which it began is answered.

The living world is dying in our time.

I look out over the unquiet waters of the bay, south to the convergence of sea and sky beyond which the North Atlantic heaves against the eastern seaboard of the continent. And in my mind's eye, I see it as it was.

Pod after spouting pod of whales, the great ones together with the lesser kinds, surge through waters everywhere aripple with living tides of fishes. Wheeling multitudes of gannets, kittiwakes, and other such becloud the sky. The stony finger marking the end of the long beach below me is clustered with resting seals. The beach itself flickers with a restless drift of shorebirds. In the bight of the bay, whose bottom is a metropolis of clams, mussels, and lobsters, a concourse of massive heads emerges amongst floating islands of eider ducks. Scimitar tusks gleam like a lambent flame . . . . The vision fails.

And I behold the world as it is now.

In all that vast expanse of sky and sea and fringing land, one gull soars in lonely flight—one drifting mote of life upon an enormous, almost empty stage.

When our forebears commenced their exploitation of this continent they believed the animate resources of the New World were infinite and inexhaustible. The vulnerability of that living fabric—the intricacy and fragility of its all too finite parts—was beyond their comprehension. It can at least be said in their defence that they were mostly ignorant of the inevitable consequences of their dreadful depredations.

We who are alive today can claim no such exculpation for our biocidal actions and their dire consequences. Modern man has increasing opportunity to be aware of the complexity and inter-relationship of the living world. If ignorance is to serve now as an excuse, then it can only be wilful, murderous ignorance.

Five centuries of death-dealing on this continent are not to be gainsaid; but there are at least some indications that we may finally be developing the will and the conscience to look beyond the gratification of our own immediate needs and desires. Belatedly we seem to be trying to rejoin the community of living beings from which we have, for so long, alienated ourselves—and of which we have, for so long, been the mortal enemy.

Evidence of such a return to sanity has yet to be found in the attitudes and actions of those who control and direct the human world, but indications of it are to be seen in the actions of individuals and groups who, revolted by the frightful destruction to which we have subjected animate creation, are beginning to reject the killer beast within us.

It is to this new desire to reassert our indivisibility with life, to recognize the obligations incumbent on us as the most powerful and deadly species ever to exist, and to begin making amends for the havoc we have wrought that my own hopes for a continuance of life on earth now rest.

If we persevere we may succeed in making the human race humane...at last. And then the Sea of Slaughter may again become a Sea of Life.

Twenty years have passed since I wrote the above. Now that the "Hereafter" has become the present, let us see how much has changed.

The Birds of Sea and Air

The clouds of shorebirds that once filled the coastal skies have continued to thin, as the numbers of individuals within them have declined—though perhaps not as precipitously as in the past. More than half the shorebird species are now at risk; many are threatened; and at least one—the piping plover—seems destined to follow the Eskimo curlew into extinction.

Most seabirds remain in decline. They are suffering from a continuing loss of breeding places; from massive oceanic pollution (especially oil spills, which despite official denials are increasing in frequency); from reduction by human fisheries of the mass of marine small fry upon which they feed; and from persecution by sport and commercial fishermen, fish farmers, and pot hunters.

Ospreys and bald eagles in remote areas are doing well enough, perhaps in part because they are such highly visible symbols of nature's majesty that we are prepared to admit them to our admiration and protection.

There has been a drastic slump in the numbers of many smaller birds, especially insectivores. This may be due in part to loss of habitat in their tropical and semitropical wintering grounds, which are being deforested at an appalling rate. However, the continuing use of insecticides and herbicides by the general public at home, but especially by agriculture and the forest industry, still plays a major part. Over a twenty-year period at least forty-three species of summer residents studied by the Mowat Environmental

Institute research centre on Cape Breton Island have declined in numbers, some by as much as 80 per cent.

Overall numbers of ducks, geese, and other game birds have generally fallen, some precipitously, although a few species may still be holding their own, if at much-diminished levels from those of the not-so-distant past.

MEAT, HIDES, AND FUR

All of the larger mammals prized by trophy and recreational hunters are afforded protection according to the best scientific protocol, in order to ensure a sufficiency of targets for those who enjoy blood sport. In consequence only a few large mammals are currently threatened with annihilation but, with some notable exceptions such as white-tailed deer, most maintain only vestigial numbers of what once was.

During the 1990s it seemed that fur-bearers were to be granted a new lease on life. The environmental movement came close to ending the truly abominable practice of slaughtering animals in order that their fur and skin could be used to advertise the human wearer's fashion sense, wealth, and prestige. Now, however, it would appear that the tide has been reversed. The environmental movement is increasingly being rejected by the body politic; increasingly ignored by governments and subjected to continuous denigration by industry and business. It is, in truth, itself threatened with becoming an endangered species.

The current resurrection of the fur trade makes the point. Only a few years ago animals such as the otter were considered to be hardly worth killing because their fur fetched so little on the market. Now, otters and most other fur-bearers are being killed with increasing avidity because, as a trapper recently exulted on television, "Now we can get rich!" Fur is back in fashion. Indeed a good many people in the fur garment business will doubtless grow rich—while many fur-bearers that were just beginning to recover from centuries of persecution will again be put at risk.

One break has appeared in the dark clouds gathering above the fur-bearers. As recently as the 1960s, the coyote, though a native of western Canada, found its way to the shores of the Atlantic and now inhabits all the maritime provinces, including Newfoundland. In some sense it has replaced the wolf, which was exterminated regionally long ago. Remarkably, the coyote has been able to find a niche for itself in "our" world. Unless a full-scale pogrom complete with bounties, poisons, and aerial hunting is mounted against it, the coyote may survive and even prosper in the Atlantic region. But already the alarm is being sounded. Deer hunters, some farmers, and those who seem innately unable to tolerate coexistence with other animals, have begun demanding that the coyote in the Atlantic provinces be exterminated.

FISH OUT OF WATER

In 1983 Canada's extension of her jurisdiction to the two-hundred-mile offshore limit made me hope that the mass slaughter of fishes would at least be slowed. I was wrong. The savaging of the fish stocks by foreign fleets was at once replaced by an even more effective savaging by domestic fishing corporations.

During the following decade Canada's entire Atlantic fishery collapsed— as most of the fishes being sought were killed.

Since 1983 almost every major commercial fish in Atlantic coastal and offshore waters, including cod, haddock, pollock, most of the flat fishes, hake, skates, halibut, redfish, tuna, salmon, even sharks, have become (as the fishing industry delicately puts it) "economically irrelevant."

There is no convincing evidence that they are likely to recover. According to Nova Scotia biologist Deborah MacKenzie, the destruction of "bait" fishes such as capelin and herring for their roe or for fertilizer seems to have inflicted chronic malnutrition (call it starvation) on the surviving stocks of many predacious fishes ranging from cod to salmon—a state which does not auger well for their chances of survival, let alone recovery.

Following on the destruction of the larger and most valuable kinds of fishes we are now fishing for whatever remains in unconscionable quantities. The spider crab, renamed snow crab for cosmetic reasons, is a prime example. First commercially fished in Atlantic waters only a decade ago, there are indications it may already be going the way of the cod. The spider crab may soon disappear and be forgotten, to be replaced in the profit columns of our ledgers by yet another doomed form of marine life.

It is apparent that nothing will be spared that can be processed into human food, cattle feed, fish meal for farmed fish, chemical feed stocks, or fertilizer. Anything and everything is up for grabs—including plankton, the foundation of all animate life in the seas and oceans.

Our attitude toward this ongoing holocaust can still best be summed up in the words of the dissident scientist I quoted in 1983, who quite reasonably insisted on anonymity.

"For those bastards there's no tomorrow.... No matter what anyone in the fishing industry or the Department [of Fisheries and Oceans] tells you, there's just one thing on everybody's mind: make money...make as much as you can before the whole damn bottom drops out of ocean fisheries."

Or, as he might as well have said: before the oceans die.

GIANTS OF THE SEA

Despite strenuous efforts on their behalf by a few resolute human beings, only residual numbers of great whales still exist. Many species are so reduced that their long-term survival is in grave doubt. For example, there may only be seven or eight hundred black right whales extant; and the Arctic right, or bowhead, probably numbers not many more than a thousand. Although nominally protected, both are still being killed: the black right by commercial fishing nets, and run down by ships (including high-speed warships); and the bowhead by natives in Alaska and northern Canada who hunt it with exploding harpoons and antitank rifles mainly for sport, but also to demonstrate political ownership of arctic resources.

Despite the tacit admission of the industry-dominated International Whaling Commission that all species of great whales are severely reduced, Japan and Norway continue commercial whaling on a major scale. They are aided and abetted by several smaller countries engaged in frequently illegal whaling on Japan's behalf. Japan will continue killing whales so long as whaling remains a profitable enterprise, although the official Japanese government position is that whale killing is all done for scientific reasons. In any case, for the most part science has always been, and presumably will remain, at the service of commerce.

So all whales, both great and small, continue to be at risk and to suffer heavy losses from pollution; from naval and commercial shipping, especially those that use explosives or high-powered sonar; and from the diminution of their food supplies caused by massive overfishing, which is presently turning *all* of the planet's oceans into one common Sea of Slaughter.

DEATH ON ICE—THE FINFEET

One of the few good-news stories from the western Atlantic region has to do with the return of the grey seal, which in the mid-1940s was thought to be extinct in Canadian waters. Unbeknownst to us a handful had managed to survive and, taking advantage of the respite afforded by World War II, when men were concentrating their destructive energies on one another, the grey seals staged a modest comeback. When, in the 1950s, their presence was discovered by industry and government, a concerted effort was made to eliminate them on the usual grounds that they were robbing us of fish that were rightly ours. However, despite a vigorous campaign waged against them by the federal Department of Fisheries using bounty payments and annual raids on the whelping grounds by Fisheries protection officers armed with guns and clubs, grey seals held on and now may number several thousand.

Their future might have been considered reasonably secure—except that the greys and the two species of ice seals, the harp and the hood, have been fingered by industry and government as major culprits in the collapse of the fisheries and as *the* most significant obstacle in the way of "rebuilding commercial fish stocks."

This is the mantra; one which by constant repetition has gained the semblance of truth and which is now so powerfully established in the public mind that those who rule us can safely orchestrate the massacre of the seals.

Although for a few years in the 1990s a temporarily aroused humanity on both sides of the Atlantic was able, through the use of economic boycotts, to force Canada to cease slaughtering the remaining ice seals, the Big Lie has now gained supremacy and the slaughter has begun anew—and with increased vigour. The largest massacre of any marine mammals—probably of any large mammals in the sea or on the land—is again taking place each spring in the Gulf of St. Lawrence and off the northern coast of Newfoundland. Between 1998 and 2002 the skins of about 1,400,000 harp and hood seals of all ages, including hundreds of thousands that had barely been weaned, were tallied by Fisheries protection officers. But this figure, horrendous as it is, takes no account of seals illegally landed, or killed or fatally wounded and not recovered during the gun hunt, which represents a major part of the slaughter. If these additional deaths are factored in, the total kill rises to at least 2,000,000 seals, and may considerably exceed that figure.

The Department of Fisheries and Oceans and its provincial counterparts assert that an "exploding" harp seal population currently exceeds five million animals (independent assessments put that figure at less than three million) and, simply in order to keep the explosion in check, we must "cull" (that sanitary euphemism for "kill") at least 350,000 a year *over and above* the toll taken by bad ice years and other natural causes. To this end, the federal government has given the seal "fishery" a TAC (total allowable catch) of 975,000 over the next three years. The TAC on seals is seldom enforced, however, and in recent years the actual kill has often exceeded it.

There is no question as to what is afoot. When natural losses, the untallied collateral kill, and at least 150,000 killed annually in Greenland and Canadian Arctic waters are factored in, it seems certain that the death toll will suffice to bring about the effective extermination of the ice seals.

Will that bring back the cod and the salmon and all the rest of the vanished multitudes that once abounded in and around the Sea of Slaughter? Or will it simply add one more ghastly act of biocide to our bloody history?

The proceeds from this book are committed to the support of the work of the Mowat Environmental Institute, a registered charitable organization for the study, protection, and enhancement of the natural environment and its inhabitants. Amongst the MEI's current projects are:

Oasis: Designed to encourage and enable individuals and organizations to protect, restore, and monitor habitats and ecosystems in order to ensure that these and their natural inhabitants survive and prosper. The emphasis is on developing privately owned land as plant and wildlife sanctuaries to serve as elements in a network of interacting oases linking major protected regions such as provincial and national parks and preserves.

Future Sea: An ongoing study of what is happening to life in the oceans, and of what can be done to prevent and to repair damage thereto. Special emphasis is on Canada's coastal seas.

Republication of *Sea of Slaughter* is a key part of the Future Sea project. The MEI hopes to ensure that at least one copy of this book will be available in every secondary and post-secondary school in Canada.

If you would like to support the MEI or any of its projects, or if you have any inquiries, please write to:

The Director
Mowat Environmental Institute
RR1, River Bourgeois
Nova Scotia B0E 2X0
Canada

Donations should be sent to the above address. Tax-deductible receipts will be issued promptly.

Please visit our web site at: www.mowatenvironmentalinstitute.ca

Select Bibliography

Because of space limitations, many of the scientific papers consulted have been omitted.

Adams, A.L. *Field Notes and Forest Rambles with Notes and Observations on the Natural History of Eastern Canada*. London: H.S. King, 1873.

Alexander, J. *Salmon Fishing in Canada, by a Resident*. London: Longman; Montreal: B. Davison and Son, 1860.

Allen, Elsa G. "Nicolas Denys, a Forgotten Observer of Birds." *The Auk* 36 (1919).

Allen, G.M. "Dogs of the American Aborigines." *Bulletin of the Museum of Comparative Zoology, Harvard* 63 (1920).

————. *Extinct and Vanishing Mammals of the Western Hemisphere with the Marine Mammals of All Oceans*. American Committee on International Wildlife Protection Special Publication 11 (1942).

Allen, J.A. "The Extinction of the Great Auk at the Funk Islands." *American Naturalist* 10 (1876): 48.

Allen, K.R. "A Note on Baleen Whale Stocks of the Northwest Atlantic." *International Whaling Commission Report* 20 (1970).

Allen, R.L. *A Life Table for Harp Seals* . . . International Council for the Exploration of the Seas (1974).

Allingham, E.G. *A Romance of the Rostrum*. London: H.F. and G. Witherby, 1924.

Anderson, R.M. "Catalogue of Canadian Recent Mammals." *Bulletin of the National Museum of Canada* 102 (1946).

Anspach, L.A. *A History of the Island of Newfoundland: Containing a Description of the Island, the Banks, the Fisheries, and Trade of Newfoundland, and the Coast of Labrador*. London: 1819.

Aubert de la Rue, E. "Le territoire de Saint-Pierre et Miquelon, étude de géographie physique et humaine." *Journal de la société d'américanistes* 29 (1937): 239–372.

Audubon, J.J. "The Eggers of Labrador."

————. *Ornithological Biography*. 6 vols. 1835.

Banfield, A.W.F. "The Distribution of Barren-ground Grizzly Bear in Northern Canada." *Bulletin of the National Museum of Canada* 166 (1961): 47–59.

———. *The Mammals of Canada*. Toronto: 1977.

Banfield, A.W.F., and N.S. Novakowski. "The Survival of the Wood Bison... in the Northwest Territories." *National Museum of Canada Natural History Papers* 1 (1960): 8.

Bangs, O., "List of Mammals of Labrador." Appendix IV of *Labrador, the Country and the People*, by W.T. Grenfell et al. New York: Macmillan, 1909.

Barbeau, Marius. *The Language of Canada in the Voyages of Jacques Cartier*. Ottawa: 1959.

Belanger, René. *Les basques dans l'estuaire du Saint-Laurent: 1535–1635*. Montreal: Les Press de l'université du Québec, 1971.

Benjaminsen, T. "On the Biology of the Bottlenose Whale." *Norwegian Journal of Zoology* 20 (1972).

Bent, Arthur Cleveland. *Life Histories of North American Birds of Prey*. Part 1. Smithsonian Institution, United States National Museum Bulletin 167. Washington: Government Printing Office, 1937.

———. *Life Histories of North American Birds of Prey.* Part 2. Smithsonian Institution, United States National Museum Bulletin 170. Washington: Government Printing Office, 1938.

———. *Life Histories of North American Diving Birds*. Smithsonian Institution, United States National Museum Bulletin 107, Washington: Government Printing Office, 1922.

———. *Life Histories of North American Marsh Birds*. Smithsonian Institution, United States National Museum Bulletin 135. Washington: Government Printing Office, 1926.

———. *Life Histories of North American Petrels and Pelicans and Their Allies*. Smithsonian Institution, United States National Museum Bulletin 121. Washington: Government Printing Office, 1922.

———. *Life Histories of North American Shore Birds*. Part 1. Smithsonian Institution, United States National Museum Bulletin 130. Washington: Government Printing Office, 1925.

———. *Life Histories of North American Shore Birds*. Part 2. Smithsonian Institution, United States National Museum Bulletin 146. Washington: Government Printing Office, 1929.

————. *Life Histories of North American Wildfowl*. Smithsonian Institution, United States National Museum Bulletin 126. Washington: Government Printing Office, 1923.

————. "Notes from Labrador." *Bird Lore* 15 (1913): 11–15.

Biggar, H.P. *The Early Trading Companies of New France*. Toronto: University of Toronto, 1901.

Bishop, Morris. *White Men Came to the St. Lawrence*.

Bollan, W. *The Importance and Advantage of Cape Breton*. 1746.

Bonner, W. Nigel. "Man's Impact on Seals." *Mammal Review* 8 (1978).

Bourne, A.G. "Exploitation of Small Whales of the North Atlantic." *Oryx* 8 (1965).

Brodie, Paul F. *The Growth of the White Whale*. Government of the Northwest Territories, Department of Information: 1972.

Cabot, W.B. *Labrador*. Boston: Small, Maynard, 1920.

Cahalane, V.H. *Mammals of North America*. New York: Macmillan, 1947.

————. *A Preliminary Study of Distribution and Numbers of Cougar, Grizzly and Wolf in North America*. New York Zoological Society, 1964.

Cameron, Austin W. *A Guide to Eastern Canadian Mammals*. Ottawa: National Museum of Canada, 1956.

————. "Mammals of the Islands in the Gulf of St. Lawrence." *Bulletin of the National Museum of Canada* 154 (1958).

Cartwright, G. *A Journal of Transactions and Events, During a Residence of Nearly Sixteen Years on the Coast of Labrador: Containing Many Interesting Particulars, Both of the Country and Its Inhabitants, Not Hitherto Known*. 3 vols. London: Allen and Ridge, 1792.

Chafe, L.J. *Chafe's Sealing Book: A History of the Newfoundland Seal Fishery from the Earliest Available Records down to and Including the Voyage of 1923*. St. John's: Mosdell, 1923. Reprint, Newfoundland Fisheries Board, 1940.

Champlain, Samuel de. *Works*. 6 vols. Edited by Biggar.

Chappel, E. *Narrative of a Voyage to Hudson's Bay*. London: 1817. Reprint, Coles Canadian Collection.

————. *Voyage of His Majesty's Ship Rosamond to Newfoundland and the Southern Coast of Labrador*. London: Mawman, 1818.

Charlevoix, Pierre de. *Journal of a Voyage to North America*. 1761. Reprint, Readex Microprint, 1966.

Chartraine, P., and J.Y. Cousteau. "Cousteau: 'Plus de capelan, plus de baleines...'" *L'actualité*, mars 1981.

Christensen, G. "The Stocks of Blue Whales in the Northern Atlantic." *Norsk Hvalfangsttid* 44 (1955): 307–15.

Clermont, Norman. "Le contrat avec les animaux bestiaire sélectif des Indiens nomades du Québec au moment du contact." *Recherches amérindiennes au Québec* 10, no. 1–2 (1980): 91–109.

Collard, Edgar Andrew. "Of Many Things...Buffalo Robes." *Montreal Gazette*, 10 May 1980, 2.

Collins, J.W. "Notes on the Habits and Methods of Capture of Various Species of Sea Birds that Occur on the Fishing Banks off the Eastern Coast of North America, and Which Are Used as Bait for Catching Codfish by New England Fishermen." *Smithsonian Miscellaneous Collection* 46, no. 22, 13 (1882): 311–38.

Comeau, Napoleon. *Life and Sport on the North Shore of the Lower St. Lawrence and Gulf*...Quebec: 1909, 1954.

Cormack, W.E. "Narrative of a Journey across the Island of Newfoundland in 1822." *Edinburgh Philosophic Journal* 10 (1823). In Bruton, 1928.

Cowan, Ian McTaggart. "Threatened Species of Mammals in North America." In *Proceedings of the 16th International Congress of Zoology*, edited by J.A. Moore. Vol. 8. Washington: 1964.

Crespel, M. *Travels in North America*...London: Sampson Low, 1797; Québec: A. Côté, 1884.

Dagg, Anne Innis. *Canadian Wildlife and Man*. Toronto: McClelland and Stewart, 1974.

Davis, R.A., K.J. Finley, and W.J. Richardson. "The Present Status and Future Management of Arctic Marine Mammals in Canada." Science Advisory Board of the N.W.T. *Report* 3 (1980).

Dawson, S.E. *The Saint Lawrence*. New York: Frederick A. Stokes, 1905.

Deane, R. "Audubon's Labrador Trip of 1833." *The Auk* 27 (1910): 42–52.

De Loture, R. *Histoire de la grande pêche de Terre-Neuve*. Paris: Gallimard, 1949. English translation: U.S. Fish and Wildlife Services, *Fisheries Special Scientific Report* 213 (1949).

Denys, Nicolas. *Description géographique et historique des côtes d'Amérique septrionale avec l'histoire naturelle du pais* (Paris: 1672). Edited by W.F. Ganong. Toronto: Champlain Society, 1908.

Dey, Wendy. "The Great White Bear." *Imperial Oil Review* 2 (1976).

Diereville, Sieur de. *Relation of the Voyage to Port Royal in Acadia or New France*. Edited by Mr. and Mrs. C. Webster. Toronto: Champlain Society, 1933.

Du Creux, Father François. *The History of Canada or New France*.

Dudley, P. "An Essay upon the Natural History of Whales with a Particular Account of the Ambergris Found in the Sperma Ceti Whale." *Philosophical Transactions of the Royal Society*, ser. B, 33 (1725).

Dunbar, M.J., et al. *The Biogeographic Structure of the Gulf of St. Lawrence*.

Durant, Mary, and Michael Harwood. *On the Road with John James Audubon*. New York: Dodd, Mead, 1980.

Duro, Cesareo Fernandez. *La pesca de los vascongados y el descumbrimiento de Terranova. Arca de Noe*. Vol. 6 of *Disquisiciones Nauticas*. Madrid: 1881.

Elson, Paul, and H.H.V. Hord. *Fisheries Fact Sheet: The Atlantic Salmon*. Ottawa: Fisheries and Environment Canada.

Elton, Charles S. "Further Evidence about the Barren-Ground Grizzly Bear in Northeast Labrador and Quebec." *Journal of Mammalogy* 35 (1954): 345–57.

———. "Labrador Barren-Ground Grizzly Bear: State of the Evidence in 1976."

Erskine, J.S. "The Archeology of Some Nova Scotian Indian Campsites." Part 1. *Proceedings of the Nova Scotian Institute of Science* 27 (1970–71): 1–9.

Fisher, H.D. *Seals of the Canadian East Coast*. Fisheries Resource Board of Canada, 1950.

Fisher, J., and H.D. Vevers, "The Breeding, Distribution, History and Population of the North American Gannet." *Journal of Animal Ecology* 12 (1943): 173–213.

Fitzhugh, Bill. "Labrador Grizzly Bear." *Kinatuinamot Illengajuk* (Nain) 1, 9 September 1976, 37.

Fowle, David C. *A Preliminary Report on the Effects of Phosphamidon on Bird Populations in Central New Brunswick*. Canadian Wildlife Service Report Series 16. Ottawa: Information Canada, 1972.

Gabarra, Abbé J.-B. *Anciens marins de Cap Breton*. 1922.

Gagnon, François-Marc. "'Gens du pays' ou 'suiviages': Note sur les désignations de l'indines chez Jacques Cartier." *Recherches amérindiennes au Québec* 10, no. 1–2 (1980).

Ganong, W.F. "The Identity of the Animals and Plants Mentioned by the Early Voyagers to Eastern Canada and Newfoundland." *Transactions of the Royal Society of Canada* 3 (1909): 107–242.

———. "The Walrus in New Brunswick." *Bulletin of the Natural History Society of New Brunswick* 5, no. 22, part 2 (1904).

Gilbertson, Michael, and Lincoln Reynolds. *A Summary of DDT and PCB in Canadian Birds, 1969–1972*. Canadian Wildlife Service Occasional Paper 19. Ottawa: Environment Canada, 1974.

Gilpin, J. Bernard. "On the Seals of Nova Scotia." *Proceedings and Transactions of the Nova Scotian Institute of Natural Science for 1871–1874*. Vol. 2, part 4: 377–84.

———. "The Walrus." *Proceedings and Transactions of the Nova Scotian Institute of Natural Science for 1867–1870*. Vol. 2: 8–10.

Godfrey, W.E. "Birds of Canada." *Bulletin of the National Museum of Canada* 203 (1966).

———. "Rare or Endangered Canadian Birds." *Canadian Field Naturalist* (January–February 1970).

Gosling, W.G. *Labrador, Its Discovery, Exploration and Development*. Toronto: Musson, 1910.

Greene, J. Orne. "September among the Game Birds of Miscou Island." *Bulletin of the Natural History Society of New Brunswick* 5, no. 24, part 4 (1906): 553–58.

Greene, W.H. *The Wooden Walls among the Ice floes: Telling the Romance of the Newfoundland Seal Fishery*. London: Hutchinson, 1933.

Greenway, J.C. *Extinct and Vanishing Birds of the World*. New York: Peter Smith, 1967.

Grenfell, W.T., et al. *Labrador, the Country and the People*. New York: Macmillan, 1909; 1922.

Grieve, S. *The Great Auk or Garefowl*. London: T.C. Jack, 1885.

Haig-Brown, Roderick. *The Salmon*. Ottawa: Environment Canada, 1974.

Hakluyt, Richard. *The Principal Navigations, Voyages, Traffiques and Discoveries of the English Nation*. London: 1599–1600.

Harper, F. "Land and Freshwater Mammals of the Ungava Peninsula." *Miscellaneous Publications of the Museum of Natural History, University of Kansas* 27 (1961).

Harrington, C. Richard. *Denning Habits of the Polar Bear* (Ursus maritimus, Phipps). Canadian Wildlife Service Report Series 5. Ottawa: Queen's Printer, 1968.

————. "The Life and Status of the Polar Bear." *Oryx* 8 (1965): 3.

Harrington, Lyn. "Penguins of the North Atlantic." *North/Nord* 25 (November–December 1978): 6

Harrisse, Henry. *Jean et Sebastien Cabot, leur origine et leurs voyages*. Paris: Ernest Leroux, 1882.

Herbert, H.W. [Frank Forester, pseud.]. *Frank Forester's Field Sports of the United States, and British Provinces, of North America*. New York: Stringer and Townsend, 1849.

Hoffman, B.G. *Cabot to Cartier*. Toronto: 1961.

Howley, James P. *The Beothuks or Red Indians: The Original Inhabitants of Newfoundland*. Cambridge: University Press, 1915.

Innis, Harold A. *The Cod Fisheries: The History of an International Economy*. Toronto: University of Toronto Press, 1940.

————. *The Fur Trade in Canada*. Toronto: 1930.

Jangaard, P.M. *The Capelin* (Mallotus villosus). Fisheries Bulletin 186. Ottawa: Department of the Environment, 1974.

Jenkins, J.T. *A History of the Whale Fisheries: From the Basque Fisheries of the Tenth Century to the Hunting of the Finner Whales at the Present Date*. London: Kennikat Press, 1971.

Jomard, E.F. *Les monuments de la géographie*. Paris: 1854–62.

Josselyn, John. *The Voyages to New England*.

Jukes, J.B. *Excursions in and about Newfoundland During the years 1839 and 1840*. London: Murray, 1842.

King, Maj. W. Ross. *The Sportsman and Naturalist in Canada*. London: Hurst and Blackette, 1866. Reprint, Toronto: Coles, 1974.

Laborde, J. "La pêche à la baleine par les harponneurs basques." *Gurre Herria* (1951).

Lahontan, Baron de. *New Voyages to North America*. 2 vols. (London: 1703). Edited by Reuben Gold Thwaites. Chicago: 1905. Reprint, New York: Burt Franklin, 1970.

Laird, Marshall. *Bibliography of the Natural History of Newfoundland and Labrador*. London: Academic Press, 1980.

Lavigne, D.M., and W.W. Barchard. "Notes, Interpretation and Evaluation of Harp Seal Census Data." *Polar Record* 19, no. 121 (January 1979): 381–85.

LeClercq, Father Chrestien. *New Relations of Gaspesia.*

Lescarbot, Marc. *Histoire de la Nouvelle France* (Paris: 1609–11). Edited by W.L. Grant. Toronto: Champlain Society, 1907.

Levett, Christopher. *Voyage into New England, Begun in 1623 and Ended in 1624.*

Lindroth, C.H. *The Faunal Connections between Europe and North America.* New York: Wiley, 1957.

Lloyd, F.E.J. *Two Years in the Region of Icebergs and What I Saw There.* London: 1886.

Low, A.P. "List of Mammalia in the Labrador Peninsula, with Short Notes on Their Distribution, etc." *Reports of the Geological Survey of Canada*, n.s., 8 (1896).

———. "Report on Explorations in the Labrador Peninsula, along the East Main, etc. etc." *Reports of the Geological Survey of Canada*, n.s., 8 (1896).

Lysaght, A.M. *Joseph Banks in Newfoundland and Labrador, 1766.* London: Faber, 1971.

Mann, K.H. "The Impact of Man on Environmental Systems in the Maritimes." In *Environmental Change in the Maritimes*, edited by J.C. Ogden II and M.J. Harvey. Halifax: Nova Scotian Institute of Science, 1975.

Mansfield, A.W. "The Atlantic Walrus (*Odobenus rosmarus*) in Canada and Greenland." *IUCN Publications*, n.s., supplementary paper 39 (1973): 69–79.

———. "Occurrence of the Bowhead or Greenland Right Whale (*Balaena mysticetus*) in Canadian Arctic Waters."

———. *Seals of Arctic and Eastern Canada.* Fisheries Research Board of Canada Bulletin 137. 2d ed., revised. Ottawa: 1967.

———. "The Walrus in Canada's Arctic." *Canadian Geographic Journal* 72 (1966): 88–95.

Mansfield, A.W., and B. Beck. *The Gray Seal in Eastern Canada.* Fisheries and Marine Services Technical Report 704. Ottawa: Department of Fisheries, 1977.

Marsden, Joshua. *The Narrative of a Mission to Nova Scotia, New Brunswick and the Somers Islands.* 1816.

Mason, John. *A Brief Discourse of the New-Found-Land.* Edinburgh: 1620.

Mathiesson, Peter. *Wildlife in America.* New York: 1959.

Mercer, M.C. "Records of the Atlantic Walrus, *Odobenus rosmarus rosmarus*, from Newfoundland." *Journal of the Fisheries Resource Board of Canada* 24 (1967).

Millais, J.C. *Newfoundland and Its Untrodden Ways*. London: Longmans Green, 1907.

Milne, L. and M. *The Cougar Doesn't Live Here Anymore*. Englewood Heights, N.J.: Prentice-Hall, 1971.

Montizambert, Edward Louis. *Canada in the Seventeenth Century* (Translation of Pierre Boucher, *True and Genuine Description of New France, Commonly called Canada, and the Manners and Customs and Productions of That Country*. Paris: Florentin Lambert, 1664.) Montreal: George E. Desbarats, 1883.

Moreau, Jean-François. "Réflexions sur les chasseurs-cueilleurs: les montagnais, décrits par Le Jeune en 1634." *Recherches amérindiennes au Québec* 10, no. 1–2 (1980): 48–49.

Nero, Robert W. *The Great White Bears*. Winnipeg: Manitoba Department of Renewable Resources and Transportation Services, 1976.

Nettleship, D.N. "Breeding Success of the Common Puffin...on Different Habitats at Great Island, Newfoundland." *Ecological Monographs* 42 (1972).

Northcott, Tom H. *The Land Mammals of Insular Newfoundland*. St. John's: Newfoundland Department of Tourism (Wildlife Division).

Novakowski, N.S. "Rare or Endangered Canadian Mammals." *Canadian Field Naturalist* (January–March 1970).

Olaus Magnus. *Histoire des lays septentrionaux*. Translated by Plantin, 1560.

Patterson, Rev. George. "The Magdalene Islands." *Proceedings and Transactions of the Nova Scotian Institute of Science for 1890–94*. 2d ser. Vol. 8, part 1: 31–57.

———. "The Portuguese on the North-East coast of America, and the First European Attempt at Colonization There: A Lost Chapter in American History." *Transactions and Proceedings of the Royal Society of Canada* 8 (1890): 127–73.

———. "Sable Island: Its History and Phenomena." *Transactions and Proceedings of the Royal Society of Canada* 12 (1894): 3–49.

Pearson, Arthur M. *The Northern Interior Grizzly Bear,* Ursus arctos l. Canadian Wildlife Service Report Series 34. Ottawa: Information Canada, 1975.

Pelletier, Gaby. "From Animal Skins to Polyester: Four Hundred Years of Micmac and Maliseet Clothing Styles and Ornamentation." *Papers of the Tenth Algonquin Conference,* 1978.

Peterson, Randolf L. *The Mammals of Canada.* Toronto: Oxford University Press, 1966.

Pichon. *Lettres et mémoires pour servir à l'histoire naturelle, civile et politique du Cap Breton, depuis son établissement jusqu'à la reprise de cette île par les anglais en 1758.*

Pinhorn, A.T. *Living Marine Resources of Newfoundland-Labrador: Status and Potential.* Bulletin 194. Ottawa: Department of the Environment, 1976.

Prance, G.T., and Thomas S. Elias. *Extinction Is Forever.*

Privy Council (G.B.). *In the Matter of the Boundary between the Dominion of Canada and the Colony of Newfoundland in the Labrador Peninsula.* Vol. 3. [Courtemanche's memoir and the 1715 anonymous memoir are included.]

Prowse, D.W. *A History of Newfoundland from the English, Colonial and Foreign Records.* London: Macmillan, 1895.

Purchas, S. *Hakluytus Posthumus, or Purchas His Pilgrimes: Contayning a History of the World in Sea Voyages and Lande Travells by Englishmen and Others.* London: 1625. Reprint, Glasgow: Maclehose, 1905–7.

Reade, John. "The Basques in North America." *Transactions and Proceedings of the Royal Society of Canada,* 1st ser., 6 (1888): 21–39.

Reeves, R. "White Whales of the St. Lawrence." *Canadian Geographic Journal* 92, no. 2 (March–April 1976).

Reid, John. "The Beginnings of the Maritimes: A Reappraisal." *American Review of Canadian Studies.*

Rostlund, Erhard. "Freshwater Fish and Fishing in Native North America." *University of California Publications in Geography* 9 (1952).

Rowan, John J. *The Emigrant and Sportsman in Canada: Some Experiences of an Old Country Settler with Sketches of Canadian Life, Sporting Adventures and Observations on the Forests and Fauna.* London: Edward Stanford, 1876. Reprint, Toronto: Coles, 1972.

Sagard, Father Gabriel. *The Long Journey to the Country of the Hurons.*

Saint-Cyr, D.N. "The Pinniped Mammalia of the River and Gulf of St. Lawrence." *Quebec Legislature Sessional Papers* 3 (1886): 39–65.

Schmidt, John L., and Douglas L. Gilbert. *Big Game of North America.* Harrisburg, Pa.: Stackpole Books, 1978.

Schorger, A.W. *The Passenger Pigeon.* University of Oklahoma Press, 1977.

Scisco, L.D. "Lescarbot's Baron de Lery." *Transactions of the Royal Society of Canada* (1911).

Scoresby, William. *An Account of the Arctic Regions with a History and Description of the Northern Whale-Fishery.* Vol. 2.

Scott, W.B., and E.J. Crossman. *Freshwater Fishes of Canada.* Fisheries Bulletin 184. Ottawa: Fisheries Research Board of Canada, 1973.

Sergeant, D.E., and P.F. Brodie. *Identity, Abundance, and Present Status of Populations of White Whales,* Delphinapterus leucas, *in North America.* Ottawa: Fisheries Research Board of Canada, 1975.

————. "Current Status of Seals in the Northern Hemisphere." *Seals: Proceedings of a Working Meeting of Seal Specialists on Threatened and Depleted Seals of the World, Held under the Auspices of the Survival Service of IUCN*: 113–24.

Seton, Ernest Thompson. *Life Histories of Northern Mammals.* New York: 1909.

Slattery, Brian. "French Claims in North America, 1500–59."

Spiess, Arthur. "Labrador Grizzly (*Ursus arctos l.*): First Skeletal Evidence." *Journal of Mammalogy* 57, no. 4 (November 1976).

Spiess, Arthur, and Steven Cox. "Discovery of the Skull of a Grizzly Bear in Labrador." *Arctic* 29, no. 4 (December 1976): 194–200.

Stewart, Darryl. *Canadian Endangered Species.* New York: Gage, 1974.

————. *From the Edge of Extinction.* Toronto: McClelland and Stewart, 1978.

Stirling, E. "The Grizzly Bear in Labrador." *Forest and Stream* 22 (1884).

Swenk, Myron H. "The Eskimo Curlew and Its Disappearance." Smithsonian Institution *Annual Report* (1915).

Tanner, V. *Outlines of the Geography, Life and Customs of Newfoundland-Labrador.* 2 vols. Cambridge: Cambridge University Press, 1947.

Thevet, André. *Les sinlaritez de la France antarctique, autrement nommé Amérique & de plusieurs terres & îles découvertes de nostre temps.* Paris: 1557.

————. *La cosmographie universelle.* Paris: 1575.

Thwaites, Reuben G. *The Jesuit Relations and Allied Documents*. Vol. 2. Cleveland: Burrow Brothers, 1896.

Tocque, P. *Newfoundland As It Was and As It Is in 1877*. London and Toronto: 1878.

Tuck, J.A. "Basque Whalers in Southern Labrador, Canada." *Proceedings of the International Symposium on Early European Exploitation of the Northern Atlantic*: 800–1700.

Tuck, L.M. *The Murres: Their Distribution, Populations and Biology. A Study of Genus* Uria. Canadian Wildlife Service Monograph Series 1 (1960).

United Nations Working Party on Marine Mammals. *Mammals in the Sea*. Vol. 1. Report of the FAO Advisory Committee on Marine Resources Research. FAO Fisheries Series 5. Rome: Food and Agricultural Organization of the UN, 1978.

Warburton, A.B. "The Sea-Cow Fishery." *Acadiensis* 3 (1902): 116–19.

Waters, J.H., and C.E. Ray. "The Former Range of the Sea Mink." *Journal of Mammalogy* 42: 380–83.

Whitbourne, Richard. *A Discourse and Discovery of New-Found-Land . . .* London: 1620.

Williamson, G.R. *The Bluefin Tuna in Newfoundland Waters*. St. John's: Newfoundland Tourist Office, 1962.

Wood, Thomas, and Stanley A. Munroe. *Dynamics of Snowshoe Hare Populations in the Maritime Provinces of Canada*. Canadian Wildlife Service Occasional Papers 30. Ottawa: Supply and Services Canada, 1977.

Index

411

FARLEY MOWAT is the author of thirty-eight books, including *People of the Deer, Never Cry Wolf, The Farfarers, Walking on the Land,* and *High Latitudes.* Combined, they have sold more than 14 million copies in twenty-four languages throughout the world. Farley Mowat and his wife, writer Claire Mowat, divide their time between Ontario and Nova Scotia.